# Young Rupert

# Young Rupert

## THE MAKING OF THE MURDOCH EMPIRE

### WALTER MARSH

SCRIBE

*Melbourne · London*

Scribe Publications
18–20 Edward St, Brunswick, Victoria 3056, Australia
2 John St, Clerkenwell, London, WC1N 2ES, United Kingdom
3754 Pleasant Ave, Suite 100, Minneapolis, Minnesota 55409, USA

Published by Scribe 2023
Copyright © Walter Marsh 2023

Excerpts from *Time Without Clocks*, copyright Joan Lindsay estate 1962,
have been reproduced by permission of Text Publishing.

Typeset in 11.5/15pt Garamond Pro by the publishers

Printed and bound in Australia by Griffin Press

Scribe is committed to the sustainable use of natural resources and the
use of paper products made responsibly from those resources.

Scribe acknowledges Australia's First Nations peoples as the traditional
owners and custodians of this country, and we pay our respects to their
elders, past and present.

978 1 761380 04 4 (Australian edition)
978 1 915590 50 3 (UK edition)
978 1 957363 51 6 (US edition)
978 1 761385 25 4 (ebook)

Catalogue records for this book are available from the
National Library of Australia and the British Library.

scribepublications.com.au
scribepublications.co.uk
scribepublications.com

# Contents

'There is no attempt to create an empire or anything like that—it would not interest me.'

– Keith Rupert Murdoch, 29 July 1958

# PROLOGUE

# One-paper town

'BEFORE WE GO any further, I'd like to acknowledge that we're meeting on the traditional home of …' said the emcee at the microphone, pausing for comic effect before delivering the punchline: '… the Murdoch family.'

A wave of laughter and a handful of gasps spread over the rooftop terrace of Keith Murdoch House, where a crowd had gathered for the launch of a glossy food magazine. Across 21st-century Australia, an acknowledgement of Country has become standard protocol at official events and many public gatherings, a gesture of respect towards the First Nations whose lands the modern Australian state is built over. But this joke, with its tongue-in-cheek fealty to the building's owners, was something else.

In Adelaide, South Australia, Keith Murdoch House sits in the heart of the central business district, five open-plan floors of glass and concrete, blue-and-beige carpet, and grey office cubicles. It's a self-styled temple of modern news reporting, its glass façade frosted with letters spelling out a jumble of sans-serif nouns and verbs. Some allude to the day-to-day mechanics of newsgathering: 'photography', 'interview', 'leader', 'report', 'word'. Others amount to little more than corporate buzzwords: 'negotiate', 'invest', 'innovate', 'achieve'. At its

1

centre is a vast atrium, where each floor looks out onto a staircase running from the ground to the rooftop.

It's the home of *The Advertiser*, the 164-year-old masthead that in March 1992 became Adelaide's last surviving daily newspaper, and the loudest voice in a one-paper town. The building was opened in 2005 by Keith Rupert Murdoch, universally known by his middle name, Rupert. He named it in tribute to his late father, and with an initial price tag in the tens of millions, it now sits among a peculiar class of Australian architecture. You can find them all around the country, these modern office complexes and production facilities whose foundations were being poured just as the august legacy companies that built them began to crack. Some lie empty, some have been sold off, and others have been taken over by the very tech giants that ate up their former occupants' business models.

For now, at least, Murdoch's name is still on the building, and it's an old black-and-white photo of Sir Keith Murdoch's long-departed face — the stony jaw, the dark-brown eyes — that stares down every single person who passes through the revolving door. It was his son, now a far older man than his father ever lived to be, who would make a show of bounding up that central staircase upon every visit, in full view of all his employees. News Corporation, the publicly listed but family-controlled company that owns *The Advertiser* and Keith Murdoch House, remains inseparable from the Murdoch name 70 years after Sir Keith's death. After seven decades of extraordinary growth, audacious gambles, and outrageous scandals, the biggest news company in the world remains, to many, the 'Murdoch press'.

Adelaide has been a one-paper town for nearly my entire life. I can remember visiting *The Advertiser*'s old headquarters as a child, accompanied by my grandfather after winning a colouring-in competition in the 'Possum Pages'. Later, on a primary school excursion I marvelled at the automated machinery and mammoth paper rolls at its printing plant in Mile End, west of the city. A high school work-experience placement introduced me to the terrifying art of shorthand — the secret journalists' language that seemed like hieroglyphs from some bygone age. But as I grew older, and more aware of the world beyond this sleepy southern capital, it became clear that the paper I knew was part of a much bigger picture. It was one small link in a global chain that spanned hemispheres and transformed industries, that shaped politics and popular culture, from Fox Mulder to Fox News, from Lisa Simpson to the Leveson Inquiry. And Adelaide wasn't just part of that story—it was ground zero. The emcee's joke on the rooftop might have been in questionable taste, but it did hold a kernel of truth. The company hasn't officially called the city home since 2004, when it uprooted itself to the corporate haven of Delaware after 80 years, but Adelaide remains, in many ways, a Murdoch town.[1]

In 1999, decades after people first began speculating about his legacy and succession plans, Rupert Murdoch told *Vanity Fair* that he wasn't worried about the history books. 'If they go back and read everything that's been written about me and use tall stories as source material, I'll be seen as a pretty terrible person,' he said.[2] Murdoch himself rarely gives interviews, abandoned an attempted autobiography after just a few months, and, as numerous official inquiries have discovered, isn't always the most reliable narrator of his own life story.[3] But in archives around Australia and the United Kingdom, in letters, court transcripts, unpublished manuscripts and interviews, and a mountain of newspaper clippings lies a paper trail of how this all came to be. They tell the story of a young man who waged public battles against press monopolies and the old dinosaurs who ran them, argued passionately for socialism and the power of the union, and bristled at a political and media class captured in a feedback loop of power and patronage. Adelaide wasn't always a Murdoch town, and Rupert Murdoch wasn't always a hardened tycoon with a global media empire. There was a time when News Limited and its all-powerful patriarch were treated like enemies of the state.

AT 2.45 PM on the afternoon of 4 January 1960, two plainclothes police officers walked westward down North Terrace. A wide boulevard spanning the length of the city, North Terrace hems in the square mile of metropolitan Adelaide—an orderly grid of streets and parks whose layout had barely changed in 130 years. The street was lined on either side by some of South Australia's most weighty institutions, sandstone-and-granite strongholds of cultural and political power from the Museum to Parliament House. But a little further down the road, towards the rougher west end, sat a complex of two solid but un-flashy brown buildings, one bearing a string of painted letters running vertically down its side: NEWSPAPER HOUSE. This was the headquarters of a company called News Limited, and its daily afternoon paper *The News*.

At 39 years of age, Edwin Calder was relatively young for an inspector; having graduated top of his class from the police academy, winning a trophy sponsored by *The Advertiser* for his efforts, he had cut his teeth tracking local crime rings in a unit nicknamed 'the breaking squad'.[4] The detective beside him, John Giles, had won a medal for outstanding courage a few years earlier after talking down a gunman who had opened fire on a cricket match — *The News* had even splashed a photograph of him and the shooter on its front page.[5] The pair had little reason to expect anything quite so heated on this assignment, but it was a high-stakes job all the same. There was still a buzz about the building as they made their way upstairs; the day's second edition of *The News* had just hit the streets, its pages dominated by reports of an oppressive summer heat wave that had claimed seven lives across the state.[6] But there were still two more editions to put to bed before its staff could step outside and breathe in the cool change that had broken over the city.

The two men were ushered into the first-floor office of Rohan Rivett — six-foot tall, in his early forties, and with a strong chin and a shock of strawberry-blond hair. It was a big office, lined with panelled wood, world maps, and shelves stuffed with books. The stale smell of burnt tobacco hung in the air — cigar smoke, judging by the ashtray that sat between inkwells and in-trays on his vast wooden desk.

Calder spoke first. 'We wish to have a talk with you and ask you certain questions about a certain matter we are investigating,' he said opaquely.[7]

'I take it that it is a personal matter?' Rivett replied. 'Is it anything to do with the paper?'

'Well, actually,' Calder said, 'both'.

They had come to gather intelligence on a string of articles that had appeared in *The News*, and, based on all the evidence present in the paper-strewn office around them, Rivett was its editor-in-chief. Rivett demurred, telling the officers that when it came to the newspaper, he had been advised not to say a word without a lawyer present. Calder told him they didn't mind waiting, and Rivett picked up the telephone. Half an hour later, the trio reconvened three city blocks away, at the Grenfell Street offices of the legal firm Alderman, Brazel, Clark and Ligertwood. At 3.30 pm, Robert Clark, the lawyer who had been on the other end of the telephone, got straight to the point.

'Are you going to take notes?' Clark asked the officers. 'If so, I will have a stenographer present.'

This sentence carried more weight than it might have 12 months earlier. Recently, the reliability of police record-keeping during interviews with suspects and witnesses had become a matter of life and death, and all four men knew it.

'I understand that you are the editor-in-chief of *The News*?' Calder asked.

'Yes,' Rivett replied.

'And, as editor-in-chief, you would be responsible for what was published in the newspaper?'

Clark interjected. 'I advise you not to answer,' he told Rivett.

Calder pressed on: 'Would you be responsible for what was published in relation to the newspaper posters or hoarding?'

More of the same advice came from Clark, and there was yet more silence from Rivett. As a journalist, Rivett was used to asking difficult questions, and had the roles been reversed he might have found his own intransigence deeply frustrating. But he had tasted imprisonment before, in a faraway jungle surrounded by disease, death, and an often-senseless disregard for notions of justice. That was fifteen years ago, when he was a much younger man. Now he was a father of three with a reputation to uphold and a newspaper to run, and was in no rush to return to captivity—whether the cage was made of bamboo or South Australian iron.

From a briefcase, Calder produced two pages from *The News*, one dated Friday 21 August 1959, and another from Thursday 3 September. He asked if either page had been printed by *The News*, but was met by silence.

'Am I to take it your attitude is a general refusal to answer?' Calder asked. There was a hint of frustration in the inspector's voice.

'We are quite prepared to listen to what you have to say,' Clark replied. 'I can't say at this moment what my advice would be.'

Calder asked a dozen more questions, and received a dozen empty responses, before giving up. 'There are a number of other questions I could ask, but I see very little point in it. This matter will be reported—and it is quite possible some other action will be taken,' he cautioned Clark and Rivett. The interview was over within 15 minutes.

TEN DAYS LATER, the heatwave had returned. The night of 15 January had been Adelaide's hottest in eight years, and all across town shirtless construction workers cooked in the sun, stoic businessmen slung suit jackets over sweat-soaked shoulders, and youths cooled off in the waters of the Karrawirra Parri river that runs through the city.[8] Calder and Giles, meanwhile, were back at the lawyers' chambers bright and early at 8.00 am. This time, they were joined not by Rohan Rivett, but a young man named Keith Rupert Murdoch, the publisher and managing director of News Limited. A few months shy of his 29th birthday, Rupert still carried a hint of puppy fat about his cheeks—or perhaps it was the sign of an executive's lifestyle of liquid lunches and late-night restaurant sessions that he also bore around his waist and neck. At any rate, he looked softer, rounder, more like his mother, Lady Elisabeth Murdoch, than his late father, Sir Keith. For much of his twenties, Rupert had cut a boisterous figure through his Adelaide newsrooms and social circles, but on this morning he adopted a tone of sobriety—to an outside observer, it might have seemed like the most humble day of his life so far.

Calder began, as he had days earlier, with the basics: 'First of all, are you a director of *The News*?'[9]

Rupert replied in the affirmative—he had been in the role for seven years, give or take. He confirmed that Rohan Rivett was editor-in-chief, but as for the pair's working relationship at *The News*, whether Rupert played an active role in its publication, or who Rohan answered to, all questions were met with the same advice by Clark.

'I advise you not to answer,' the lawyer repeated.

In truth, there barely a soul in Adelaide whom Murdoch had known longer, or worked more closely with, than Rohan Deakin Rivett. Rivett had been there in his father's old newsroom in Melbourne, then on the family holiday in Rome when Rupert was still a teenager. He had been a co-conspirator, egging him on as he flirted with Oxford's uptight political left, and an ally and confidant as they each sought to stake a place in the shadow of the great Sir Keith Murdoch. But today, all Rupert would concede was that, yes, he did keep an office in News Limited's North Terrace building, one floor below Rohan's.

'Perhaps at this juncture I might say that you are not obliged to answer any further questions unless you wish,' Calder noted, sensing where the morning was heading, 'as what you do say may be used in evidence.'

Calder produced two large posters, the kind that might be unfurled by a curbside news vendor. These relics of the daily news-churn were by their very nature loud and attention-grabbing; unlike their morning counterparts, which were tossed onto readers' lawns, an afternoon newspaper lived or died by how well its posters caught the eyes of passers-by. They were usually discarded and forgotten faster than the papers they advertised, but for the past four months these two had been carefully stored as evidence, waiting for this exact moment.

'I would like you to have a look at these two posters,' Calder said, drawing Murdoch and Clark's attention to the thick crimson text splashed across the paper. 'Have you seen these posters before?'

'Yes,' Murdoch said, looking at the five-inch-tall letters.

'Were they published by *The News*?'

The answer was obvious, of course. In front of them, above the red text, was a fat masthead with the paper's name — 'THE NEWS' — printed in pitch-black ink.

'You can answer,' Clark told his client, who conceded the undeniable.

Calder then pulled out the two pages he had showed Rivett a week earlier, and repeated the questions. 'Were you a director of *The News* at the time of the Stuart royal commission?' he asked.

'Yes,' Murdoch said.

Now they were getting somewhere.

'In that case,' Calder said, 'you would have been a director of *The News* at the time these two papers were printed?'

'Yes,' Murdoch said.

That was something, at least. Calder decided to cut his losses; he had asked 27 questions that morning, and for all but a handful, Murdoch had responded with the same non-committal silence as Rivett. Something had transpired on North Terrace in August and September 1959; somewhere between Rivett's office, the deafening presses in the ink-caked bowels of the building, and the small army of footpath newsagents and street-corner newsboys, words had been chosen, trimmed to fit, printed *en masse*, and distributed all around the city. *The News* pumped out thousands upon thousands of words each week, but, after a week's investigation, Calder and Giles had barely scraped together enough to fill a one-inch column. By any reckoning, Rupert Murdoch and Rohan Rivett were the two men who should have known better than anyone how the paper was put together, but based on their testimonies alone, it was as if those scarlet letters had materialised out of thin air.

When Calder and Giles arrived at 116 North Terrace on that January afternoon, they did so not just as two police officers — they had the backing of the entire South Australian government, judicial system, and half the state's readers. All of them were baying for one answer: who ran News Limited? Or, more accurately, who could be hauled to account for what it had done?

For the moment, Calder had no further questions, but before he left, he added ominously, 'you may hear more about it later'. It took another ten days before Calder's promise came good: the newspaper and its editor-in-chief were each charged with having committed nine offences, comprising six counts of libel with knowledge of its falsity, and three counts of a rarely invoked, practically archaic common-law offence, seditious libel. Those sheets of paper that Calder had waved in front of Rupert and Rohan were supposed to contain, somewhere in their red and black ink, evidence of 'seditious intention', of seeking to inspire hatred or contempt for the state itself. Someone powerful had decided to send the company a message: they would not only have the book thrown at them, but their own incriminating words, too. Rupert Murdoch and Rohan Rivett were about to be taught an important lesson in how things really worked in this town.

# CHAPTER ONE

# Absolute control

IN THE FINAL years of his life, Sir Keith Arthur Murdoch acted like a man who knew he was running out of time. He had spent the previous 30 years building Australia's biggest newspaper chain, zealously guarding his position at its head, and wielding the status and influence that came with it. To his admirers, he was one of his country's great 20th-century patriots: a truth-teller, a philanthropist, and nothing less than the father of modern journalism in Australia. To his critics, he was little more than a home-grown 'pocket-Hearst', and an 'undeviating, insatiable seeker' who had seized control of the Herald and Weekly Times empire like 'a cuckoo in the nest in which he still lays golden eggs for his own enrichment'.[1]

The truth lay somewhere in between, but by 1950 it was all up in the air. He still towered over most people he met, but his hair had grown silvery-white, his forehead lined in a semi-permanent furrow, and the heart problems that had first surfaced in 1933 were making a comeback, joined by new troubles in his bowel and prostate. The past two years had seen him spend more and more time in hospitals and doctors' offices — sometimes kept secret from his colleagues and even his wife, Lady Elisabeth.[2] The doctors were scrambling to buy him more time, but every new diagnosis and intervention meant sacrificing another precious handful of months to recovery. He promised Elisabeth that someday soon he would finally wind down, step back, and make the most of what years they had left at Cruden Farm, the country retreat on Melbourne's outskirts he bought as a wedding present in 1928. Healthy or not, it was no longer a question of if, but when the 25-year age gap—that had set Melbourne society alight with gossip and judgement when a 42-year-old Keith spotted the 18-year-old debutante's photograph in the social pages—would catch up with them.[3] But, for now, he had unfinished business.

He knew that his rivals and protégés alike could smell blood. Just before Christmas in 1949, he had reluctantly ceded the day-to-day management of the Melbourne *Herald*, but he continued to hang around, clinging to the chairmanship and undermining the men who were meant to succeed him. The longer he refused to retire completely, the more likely it seemed that others would move against him—and this time he might not come out on top.

'I am getting old and moved a little slowly at the beginning,' he wrote to a former rival, whose newspaper had fallen on hard times and was now ripe for acquisition.[4] But he had missed the boat, and now its new owners ('salvaging jews', he called them) would strip and sell the company for parts. *Smith's Weekly* was not a great paper, or even a good one—in fact, it was a newspaper that Murdoch had once openly despised. A decade earlier, he'd bombarded the same editor with letters complaining of the 'vindictive defamation' it had published about him.[5] But these days Sir Keith had to choose his battles and his enemies with care; every move, every manoeuvre he could make, mattered, because there might not be many more left. 'I confess that being somewhat ailing, I am not anxious to extend difficult operations,' he told the editor of *Smith's*, 'but this one I would have undertaken. I had so much on my mind.'[6]

Sir Keith had been staring down challengers since the moment he had accepted the role of managing editor at *The Herald* three decades earlier. Back in 1922, he had secured an early triumph over its long-time business manager, whose contempt for the new editor had soon exploded into open conflict.[7] Murdoch had hit back hard, lobbying the board of directors one by one to disregard his rival's 'jealousy' and 'grotesque lies' until they backed him unanimously.[8] 'The enemy was routed,' Murdoch wrote to his mentor, Lord Northcliffe. 'He tried to make it up but I refused and told them to choose.'[9] In the end, Murdoch won out, with his rival exiled to the advertising department before leaving town altogether.

A decade later, he fended off a bid by *The Herald*'s long-serving chairman and part-owner Theodore Fink to turn the firm into a family business. With his white moustache, round face, and twinkling eyes, Fink seemed to some a kindly koala of a man.[10] But the lawyer and politician had claws; during the land-boom crash of the late-19th century, he managed to cover up his own near-ruin through some legal sleight of hand, and pivoted to newspaper publishing to launder his reputation.[11] It was Fink who had first installed Murdoch as editor, and along with his main partner and fellow speculator turned parliamentarian, William Lawrence Baillieu, had stuck by Murdoch in the 1922 showdown. But Fink had been grooming his youngest son, Thorold, to take his place as chairman, and could now see that Murdoch's years-long pursuit of a place on the board was another step in an ambitious long game to succeed him. Such a move would hand Murdoch a degree of authority enjoyed by no other editor in Australian newspapers—the cuckoo at work. When Murdoch had his first heart attack in 1933, keeling over on a tennis court and then being forced to spend a year out of the office, Fink struck. A 'tooth and nail' struggle ensued, but Murdoch somehow managed to flip the casting vote from the Finks' column to his, and survived.[12]

Both Fink and his son were long dead by 1950, but now Sir Keith faced a different problem: John 'Jack' Williams, his successor as managing editor of the Melbourne *Herald*, clearly had designs on his position. A former editor at *The Barrier Miner* in Broken Hill, Williams could be prickly, curt, and mercurial, but he was also a dedicated newspaperman with little regard for the influence or material comforts that came with the role—things that Sir Keith clearly enjoyed. ('I know you despise me for my love of money,' he once told an employee as they surveyed his vast collection of antique glassware, 'but how else do you think you could acquire such beautiful things as these?').[13] And there were deeper incompatibilities: Williams was a Catholic and a drinker, while Murdoch was the moralising son and grandson of Presbyterian ministers. Author and journalist Keith Dunstan recalled one occasion in 1948 when his father, Bill Dunstan, *The Herald*'s chief secretary and a rusted-on Murdoch loyalist, received a late-night call: Williams was in police custody, having been picked up in an alley near *The Herald* offices following an after-hours drinking session.[14]

But to Williams and others in the *Herald*'s upper echelons, Murdoch's own recent behaviour made the prospect of a coup increasingly justified—even Bill Dunstan found some of his actions 'outrageous'.[15] For years, the old man had been making moves of his own, reshuffling the small interests he owned in companies inside and outside *The Herald* fold to string together a set of newspaper and magazine interests that increasingly resembled his own private fiefdom. From Brisbane to Adelaide, newspapers that were once considered part of the Herald and Weekly Times family now represented a small but significant rival chain quietly owned and run by its own chairman. Few had the clout or audacity to push back on these machinations—after all, most senior staff owed their positions to Sir Keith. But to anyone who was paying attention, he had been cannibalising the empire from within. As Williams confided to one of his Fleet Street counterparts, it was nothing less than 'skulduggery, absolute unblushing theft'.[16]

Murdoch's endgame became clear in his Last Will and Testament, first signed in January 1948, less than a month after another health scare:

> I desire that my said son Keith Rupert Murdoch should have the great opportunity of spending a useful altruistic and full life in newspaper and broadcasting activities and of ultimately occupying a position of high responsibility in that field with the support of my trustees if they consider him worthy of that support.[17]

His only son, Rupert was still a teenager, sent away to board with the other children of Melbourne's elite at Geelong Grammar—the colony's answer to Eton. All the same, Sir Keith was spending what limited time and energy he had left in dogged pursuit of the very thing he had denied Fink all those years earlier: creating a legacy. One night in his study in the family's city mansion at Toorak, he confided his fears and ambitions to a young family friend. 'I can't afford to die,' he said, 'I've got to see my son established, not leave him like a lamb to be destroyed by these people.'[18]

A QUARTER OF a century earlier, a young Keith Murdoch's fortunes had been transformed by the outbreak of war. His first attempt to crack Fleet Street as a 22-year-old had been a miserable failure; he had retreated to Melbourne with hardly a friend or by-line to show for the 18 months he had spent in London. 'The newspapers don't want my stuff,' he conceded to his father in 1909, having barely seen the inside of a British newspaper office or begun to cure the nervous stammer that reduced his speech to pangs of chaotic breathing when faced with unfamiliar or strange company ('and all society here is strange,' he added).[19] It was the stammer that derailed his one big break, when a letter of introduction from journalist-turned-prime minister and family friend Alfred Deakin finally scored him an interview at *The Pall Mall Gazette*. He sailed through the preliminary tests, but his luck ran out when he opened his mouth: 'When it got to the final effort, the few minutes talking with the editor, my speaking collapsed, and of course we both realised that I would not do.'[20]

Six years later, things would be different. With the help of Australian speech therapist Lionel Logue, he had wrested some control over his tongue, and worked his way up from a bottom-rung, penny-a-line freelancer at the Melbourne *Age*. His prolific output earned him a staff job, which led to a role in the parliamentary press gallery for rival newspaper *The Sun*. By 1915, his second crack at London had arrived, this time as a correspondent for a cable service jointly owned by *The Sun* and *The Herald*. When his younger brothers, Ivon and Alan, enlisted to join the war in Europe, Keith was torn between following them or remaining a reporter. Passed over by his fellow journalists in the vote to become Australia's official war correspondent, Murdoch's ticket to the frontline eventually came from Labor prime minister Andrew Fisher—another old Presbyterian Scot like Deakin. At Fisher's request,

Murdoch's journey to his new London job would include a stopover in Egypt, ostensibly to investigate bottlenecks in mail deliveries to the frontline. But Fisher's endorsement also convinced Sir Ian Hamilton, the British general in charge of the campaign in the Dardanelles, to allow Murdoch to visit Australian troops — provided he observed all censorship rules. It was a decision that Hamilton would come to regret.

By mid-1915, Australia's attention was fixed on a narrow strait of water between Europe and Asia that Britain's leadership hoped would open a second front and knock the Ottoman Empire out of the war. But the attempt to invade the Ottoman-held Gallipoli peninsula had been a mess, with thousands of soldiers from the newly minted Australian and New Zealand Army Corps dying in a failed attempt to seize the steep, unforgiving terrain from its Turkish defenders. Murdoch's brief visit to Anzac Cove and Suvla Bay was the young journalist's first exposure to the realities of war, and his startled observations were further galvanised by the influence of Ellis Ashmead-Bartlett. A correspondent for the London *Daily Telegraph* and an avowed critic of the campaign's leadership, Ashmead-Bartlett conspired with Murdoch to smuggle a damning letter to the British prime minister, HH Asquith. When the memo was seized by army censors in Marseille, Murdoch decided to write his own 8,000-word account, cribbed together from his fleeting impressions, second-hand reports, and the half-remembered material laid out by Bartlett.

This 'Gallipoli letter' valorised the doomed gallantry of Murdoch's countrymen, and condemned British officers in terms that often bordered on caricature. He wrote admiringly of the 'determined and dauntless' sons of squatters and farmers, whose 'ingenuity and endurance' was betrayed by the 'conceit and complacency of the red feather men' who 'have never worked seriously' prior to the war, and had now 'bungled' the operation.[21] While Australian men were dying due to the 'gross selfishness and complacency' of the British staff, some of its leaders were living on a 'luxurious yacht in Mudros'. It was akin to murder, Murdoch wrote, but his finger was not pointed at the enemy. Hamilton would later struggle to reconcile the 'sensible, well-spoken man with dark eyes' who gave an 'elaborate explanation of why his duty to Australia could be better done with a pen than with a rifle', with this document calling for the general's removal—which happened soon after.[22]

The letter was a stirring but flawed polemic, riddled with inaccuracies and exaggerations, even as its basic premise of military failure at Gallipoli rang true. Murdoch was later forced to concede that many claims in his 'highly coloured' account—from rampant sedition to a baseless anecdote that officers were ordered to 'shoot without mercy any soldier who lagged behind or loitered in an advance'—could not be verified. It was 'an irresponsible statement by an ignorant man', Hamilton later remarked, while wondering: 'Murdoch must be mad. Or, is there some method in his madness?'[23]

Murdoch justified the breach of censorship by claiming it was a private letter in which he had addressed the prime minister as a friend ('I shall talk to you as if you were by my side, as in the good days,' reads its opening page).[24] Inevitably, Fisher saw that it was leaked to ever-wider circles, first to Asquith and the British cabinet, and then to the newspaper editor at *The Times*, whose Fleet Street building housed Murdoch's new offices at the United Cable Service. Such a sensational rebuke of the leadership of Asquith, Hamilton, and the first lord of the Admiralty, Winston Churchill, was seized upon by their domestic rivals—and opened doors for its author. After the failure of his first London trip, Murdoch was not going to let a single opportunity or powerful friendship go to waste, and there was no friend more important than Alfred Charles William Harmsworth, the owner of *The Times*, who by 1915 was better known by his title: the 1st Viscount Northcliffe.

With a thumb-shaped head and a mop of brown hair parted crisply to one side, the 50-year-old Irish-born press baron had charted the very path Murdoch hoped to emulate: a jobbing journalist and Fleet Street freelancer who took a handful of ailing London newspapers and transformed them into a populist publishing empire that ranged from high-circulation rags such as *The Daily Mail* and *The Evening News* to venerable papers of record like *The Times*. Northcliffe rode the twin waves of a growing, literate British middle class and a booming advertising market to sell papers that were cheap, slick, and entertaining, and targeted both men and women with an eclectic mix of news, serials, features, and gossip. Parliamentary coverage was cut down and buried, while circulation-building crusades—from social causes to jingoistic nationalism—played to readers' emotions and morality.[25] By the time Murdoch arrived on the scene, Lord Northcliffe and his papers had become a fearsome and influential player in British public life.

Murdoch had caught a glimpse of Northcliffe back in 1909, when his well-thumbed Deakin letter and a £10 top hat and coat helped him blag his way into a conference attended by many of the world's leading newspaper editors and proprietors.[26] Northcliffe had impressed the young Fleet Street wannabe, and just a few years later the man known as 'the Chief' had reached out to share how 'haunted' he was by Murdoch's Gallipoli letter.[27] Murdoch seized this opening, telling Northcliffe of his embarrassment that a supposedly private letter to Fisher, 'of so intimate a character, and expos[ing] a friendship which I hold sacred' had spread so widely, before coyly adding, 'any information I ever collect is at your disposal and that of the *Times* staff, for whom I have already formed a high regard'. [28]

A direct line to Northcliffe could transform a young journalist's career, and Murdoch wasted no time using his new connection to get ahead, taking up Northcliffe's offer of *Daily Mail* material to one-up his cable rivals at Reuters and *The Daily Chronicle*.[29] With no legitimate children of his own, Northcliffe's mentorship of this Australian interloper took on an almost paternal quality, while his patronage gave Murdoch a golden ticket into the highest levels of power and influence in London. Within the month, he was helping Murdoch navigate the well-connected networks that ran London from behind closed doors at a cluster of gentlemen's clubs around the city—private, male-only dens of food, alcohol, and power. 'You could easily join one of the Imperial clubs, but then you would not meet anyone,' Northcliffe pondered in December 1915. 'At luncheon at the Automobile Club you will find Cabinet Ministers of both parties, returned officers and all sorts of people—and excellent foods.'[30]

When Fisher resigned the prime ministership due to ill health, Murdoch became an unofficial back-channel promoter of his successor, William 'Billy' Hughes—while still technically working as a journalist. Northcliffe played a role there, too, with Murdoch thanking the 'newspaper king' for the 'personal attentions' and 'thoughtful arrangements' shown during Hughes' visits to London.[31] Although Murdoch had lobbied to save Australian troops from slaughter in the Dardanelles, he later helped dial up Australia's role in what had become a devastating and seemingly endless war. Blurring the line between journalism and propaganda, Murdoch's cables relayed breathless accounts of Australian heroism, victory, and sacrifice that served to boost morale and recruitment back home—and, like his 1915 letter, laid the groundwork for a patriotic narrative of Anzac exceptionalism that would achieve quasi-mythological status in 20th-century Australia. He even tried to help Hughes sway public opinion in support of two failed conscription referendums by burying evidence of its deep unpopularity among serving troops.

By the end of the war, Murdoch had achieved things his 22-year-old self could scarcely have imagined. His new contacts across British politics and the media helped fill his cables with gripping wartime coverage, which he unabashedly leveraged for his own gain. Reporters' by-lines were not typically included in most British and Australian papers, and certainly not in cabled news, in the early 20th century, but he lobbied to make sure readers back home knew the name Keith Murdoch. 'I rather understand that what you really want is "publicity" in a personal sense, so as to get the "kudos" attached to the authorship,' wrote a slightly baffled Hugh Denison, proprietor of *The Sun*, in April 1918 after another request for prominent billing.[32]

After the armistice, Murdoch found himself at a crossroads; he was living his Fleet Street dream, but longed to return to Australia for fear of becoming 'completely anglicised, probably marry[ing] an English woman'.[33] In 1920, he sailed home in triumph as part of the press pack shadowing a royal visit by the Prince of Wales, and gossip about his homecoming plans soon spread among the upper levels of Australian newspapers. Before he left, Murdoch wrote a gushing letter to Northcliffe, full of gratitude for the 'many kindnesses' over the past four years. 'I will not say more than that you have been the biggest influence and the biggest force for me over here,' he wrote, 'I am certainly coming back, but if I never met you again I would retain this influence to the end of my life.'[34]

NORTHCLIFFE FINALLY OFFERED Murdoch a job when he returned to England, but his mind was made up. The Chief's fondness for his Australian acolyte was now well established, but if Murdoch sought to keep some distance from his mentor, he had good reason. By the end of the decade, the ageing tycoon's behaviour was becoming a source of dread for those in his orbit; already notorious for inspiring fear in his employees, the evidence of Northcliffe's mental and physical deterioration was now undeniable. He had grown paranoid and erratic, wracked by insomnia and a complicated set of maladies ranging from his heart to his appendix. (Years later, his nephew claimed that the official family story, ulcerative endocarditis, was a cover-up for tertiary syphilis.)[35] By August 1922, his doctors had relocated him to a makeshift, open-air hut on the rooftop of a friend's city manor—just within view of the Automobile Club he had recommended to Murdoch in 1915.[36] He spent his final days on the roof plied with morphine, issuing strange orders, and madly waving a revolver. How much of this unravelling Murdoch was privy to is debatable, but when he returned to Melbourne in 1920, he was in a position to venture beyond Northcliffe's reach. When Fink and Baillieu offered him the recently vacated *Herald* editorship, he accepted—he felt his wartime cables and by-line requests had been best received in Melbourne, and he looked forward to 'start[ing] there at least with a good following and a good name'.[37]

Even as he returned to Australia for good, he continued to lean on Northcliffe for advice and guidance. Reverentially addressing Northcliffe as 'Chief of All Journalists / of all ages', in April 1921, Murdoch made a request: would Northcliffe allow him to consult copies of the memos the Chief circulated to his staff at *The Evening News*, *The Times*, and *The Daily Mail*?[38] It was a big ask; Northcliffe had grown immensely successful, but his domination of Fleet Street was not without controversy. His papers' pursuit of sensational, circulation-building stories, and the political influence of its owner, had tarred them with the label of 'yellow journalism' originally associated with the North American press barons that Northcliffe happily emulated, such as Randolph Hearst and Joseph Pulitzer. In the wrong hands, these private documents, showing just how Northcliffe's sausages were made, could prove embarrassing or ruinous.[39] Under condition of secrecy, the memos were sent, and Murdoch pored over them as he sought to make *The Herald* a more readable, attention-grabbing, circulation-building product. They also laid out how Northcliffe ran his empire, with an army of 'ferrets' and 'spotters' inside the organisation and beyond who quietly fed him on-the-ground reports from the newsroom to the newsstand. 'My three books of 'communiques' remain my bible—daily consulted,' Murdoch wrote in March 1922.[40] 'All the *Herald* success is due to them.' Northcliffe himself summarised the model while visiting Australia in October 1921:

> Throughout the English-speaking world there has been great development in evening journalism. The change for brighter, lighter, pithier and briefer evening newspapers began before the war, and throughout Great Britain, Canada and the United States the tendency to take an evening paper home is increasing rapidly … the news is so arranged that it leaps to the eye at once.[41]

Keith Murdoch, he added, had closely studied London's evening journals, soaking up methods that 'have evolved out of the fierce competition that exists in our little island with its 50 million inhabitants and splendidly organised press'.[42]

Northcliffe also contributed in more active ways, taking a bundle of *Herald* editions with him on the return voyage to England. Among the marked-up pages he sent back to Murdoch were private notes that offered technical feedback and advice on appealing to readers' more basic instincts.[43] He also told Murdoch to never waste a page-turning scandal, and when one arrived on the last day of 1921, Murdoch could barely contain his excitement. 'You remarked "When a sensation comes you will get all the new readers you want",' Murdoch wrote in March 1922. 'Perfectly true. I had only put on about 8,000 [in circulation] when we got a mystery murder—an unprecedented one, leading to such scenes as mounted police having to be called out to check the grounds about the residence of the supposed murderer.'[44]

In the early hours of 31 December 1921, the body of 12-year-old Alma Tirtschke was found raped and murdered in an alley off Little Collins Street, Melbourne, and the 'Gun Alley Murder' soon dominated the city's papers. Before long, a 28-year-old publican named Colin Ross, whose wine saloon backed onto the laneway where Tirstchke was found, was arrested, with police claiming that strands of hair found in the saloon matched the girl. Ross maintained his innocence, while his lawyer argued that the public had been 'so inflamed by sensational *ex parte* statements published in certain newspapers, as to make a fair trial impossible'.[45] But their appeals failed, and, after a five-day trial, Ross was found guilty and hanged in April—less than four months after Tirstchke was killed. Murdoch was thrilled: Ross's downfall boosted *The Herald*'s circulation from 105,000 copies upon Murdoch's arrival to an average of 125,000, peaking at 230,000 during the trial, and continued to hover at 144,000—even on 'no murder news' days, he added.[46] Ross was exonerated by DNA testing 75 years later, but in the decades after his execution, the Herald and Weekly Times' imposing new headquarters on Flinders Street earned a grim nickname among workers and enemies alike: the 'Colin Ross memorial'.[47]

Imposing the Northcliffe model on the Australian paper wasn't always easy. Keith dismissed his Melbourne colleagues as 'well-meaning but hopelessly stodgy people', and felt choked by a place 'so smug and conservative that reforms do not come quickly'.[48] His impact was also being noticed beyond the *Herald* offices. 'Of course I am attacked in Roman Catholic papers and elsewhere for being a "yellow journalist"', he wrote in March 1922, 'and *The Bulletin* makes the charge that I have brought *Daily Mail* journalism to Australia. I wish I had!'[49] His efforts to make himself a household name had been a roaring success: within a decade, many of the qualities attributed to 'yellow' papers would gain a new label in Australia: 'the Murdoch press'. As the scale and influence of his papers grew, his surname would be spat with disdain in union meetings, speakers' corners, and rival papers, even as he stockpiled respectability and cultural capital in the business and art worlds.

Many assumed that Murdoch owned the company that was now synonymous with his name, but in reality there was one lesson from Northcliffe, spelt out in a December 1921 telegram, that Murdoch was finding harder to execute:

FACT YOU HAVE COMPLETE CONTROL / ONE MAN
CONTROL / ESSENTIAL / NEWSPAPER BUSINESS /
CHIEF [50]

The transcribed syntax was stilted, but the message was clear: if you want to make it in the newspaper business, you must have complete, unchallenged personal power. As soon as his return to Australia was confirmed, he began moving to ensure he wasn't simply gaining employment, but authority. Murdoch knew that his predecessor at *The Herald*, JE Davidson, had resigned in frustration in 1918 after butting heads with Fink, so negotiated to secure the right to retire with a £3,000 payout 'if [he] found any interference irksome or could not get on with the company'.[51] Murdoch had kept Northcliffe apprised of the trouble that awaited him at *The Herald* before he'd even accepted the job, and it was Northcliffe who advised Murdoch to force an ultimatum upon the board during his face-off with the general manager in 1922.[52]

'Whenever I think of you, Chief, which is constantly, I think of big questions and big movements,' he wrote to Northcliffe in December 1921.[53] Establishing personal control over what was technically a public company became crucial, and by the end of the year he had successfully talked his directors out of a merger proposed by his old boss, Hugh Denison. Denison was in the process of launching his own Melbourne paper in competition with *The Herald*, and while Fink and Baillieu entertained the offer, Murdoch resisted for one specific reason: it would dilute the power he was working so hard to achieve. 'It would not suit me—I would get some shares but would be overweighted, with the Sydney influence always against me.'[54]

By March 1922, Murdoch had established 'practical control' over *The Herald*, but was already looking further afield; he was hungry to expand, and used Northcliffe's name—and money—to help rally support.[55] He had set his sights on *The Evening News* in Sydney, 'a dull, unenterprising and badly managed paper' that nonetheless seemed a 'wonderful proposition' once it had been 'toned up'.[56] It would also serve an important secondary purpose of undermining Denison's designs on Melbourne, and he telegrammed Northcliffe with excitement: 'Feeling this [is] my big chance, am willing [to] put ten thousand pounds into scheme.'[57] He lobbied Northcliffe to invest £5,000, hoping the Chief's backing might help drum up further investment, and encountered zero resistance. At this stage of his life, Northcliffe didn't seem to care about the details or even about getting a return on his money. ('Lose it if you like,' he wrote in a letter sent the next month, adding, 'PS. I don't frankly understand project but I trust you'.)

The £5,000 from Northcliffe helped Murdoch gather £50,000 of 'Melbourne money', half of which came from his *Herald* associates, and a further £75,000 of his own savings. (Precisely how the £10,000 he had proposed in December turned into £75,000 is unclear.) This parcel, along with a substantial stake owned by a family who had agreed to vote with Murdoch for at least five years, gave him a working majority. However, a 'group of big Sydney traders' convinced the *Evening News* board to issue them 100,000 new shares, watering down the 107,000 that Murdoch controlled. 'Unless I can buy another 18,000—that is, secure an absolute majority—my position after five years may be difficult. I expect to get these and have absolute control,' he wrote to Northcliffe.[58]

After this 'flaw in the scheme', Murdoch and *The Herald* eventually abandoned the Sydney venture, but the episode set a template for the expansion that Murdoch would oversee across the coming years, from Perth's *West Australian* in 1926 to *The Register*, *The Advertiser*, and *The News* in Adelaide. Murdoch would front a syndicate in the takeover of a paper, providing the public face and editing nous needed to overhaul the new acquisition into shape, while an opaque group of backers, often including Baillieu and his associates, provided the capital.

For his efforts, Murdoch would often be rewarded with the promise of 'practical control' via shares controlled by the *Herald* and his fellow-schemers, but rarely did he control a company outright.

Not only did Murdoch provide an acceptable front for patrons such as Baillieu and Fink, whose connections to private industry had already caused consternation in some quarters, but he also went into business with shadier figures such as John Wren, the Melbourne boxing and gambling tsar turned political powerbroker upon whom Frank Hardy sensationally based his 1950 novel, *Power Without Glory*. Wren had bought out the majority owner of Brisbane's *Daily Mail* in 1915; but by the late 1920s, Murdoch had also acquired an interest in the paper. When the owner of *The Courier* sold out to Murdoch in the early 1930s, he and Wren became unlikely bedfellows in the creation of a new company, Queensland Newspapers, that would publish the newly merged *Courier-Mail*—with the controversial Wren primarily a silent partner.

By the 1940s, Murdoch had earnt a nickname inspired by his late mentor: Lord Southcliffe.[59] He had helped establish a national newspaper empire that spanned the continent, used its influence to become a self-styled kingmaker in the ascendancy of prime minister Joe Lyons, and during World War II he had even exercised almost-unrivalled power over the rest of Australia's media as director-general of information. But without majority ownership, it all came with a firm use-by date. As he put it plainly to one employee in 1945: 'I told you in my cable that if I died the control would pass into other hands. This, of course, is obvious. But I wanted you to weigh up that fact. It is, I trust, unlikely that I will shuffle off, but my shares are controlling shares only as long as I live.'

AS HIS HEALTH failed and his son approached adulthood, Murdoch became fixated on untangling his web of overlapping interests. Elisabeth would see him scribbling endless notes and figures in little notebooks, indecipherable to his wife and anyone else reading them, but to their author it was the delicate arithmetic of his legacy.[60] Using borrowed money and no small amount of boardroom manoeuvring, he now had controlling stakes in Queensland Newspapers; News Limited, the Adelaide-based publisher of *The News*, *The Sunday Mail*, and Broken Hill's *Barrier Miner*; and a stake in Southdown Press, publisher of women's magazine *New Idea*. It was a delicate game, which often saw him use his influence at the Herald and Weekly Times for his own personal gain.

Few people were privy to more of Murdoch's moves than Colin Blore Bednall, a journalist who had started as a copy boy at *The News*, spent World War II flying in Allied bombing raids and filing reports for *The Daily Mail*, and since 1945 had been Murdoch's man at Queensland Newspapers. Even in his late thirties, Bednall had an impish look, with his hair flicked back and usually wearing thick-rimmed statement spectacles. His loyalty to Murdoch was unquestioned, but even he had begun to feel that Murdoch was 'constantly making a monkey out of [him]'.[61] In an unpublished memoir, Bednall recounts how his boss exploited the findings of a British royal commission into the hazards of newspaper monopolies:

> I wrote to Murdoch and he immediately telephoned me, saying my reactions were of the utmost importance and asking me for a detailed report. I went about my document with the warmest of feelings towards my mentor, only to discover weeks later that he had wanted it purely for use in persuading the board of the Herald and Weekly Times Ltd that they should off-load Adelaide's News Limited and sell it to him.[62]

To his colleagues, Sir Keith maintained that disentangling the companies' interests was 'more natural, wholesome and free', but it was little wonder that Williams had begun to grow suspicious.[63] In March 1950, Murdoch added a codicil to his 1948 will, directing his trustees to sell Booroomba, a pastoral property outside Canberra, and any other assets, before resorting to selling any newspaper holdings, and to 'provide the fullest opportunity to my son' to take charge of Queensland Newspapers and News Limited. He even cut out small bequests to his children's schools and other favoured causes mentioned in the previous will—nothing could be spared. Another update in September saw the 55,000 A Preference shares in Queensland Newspapers previously earmarked as Rupert's inheritance folded into the family's holding company, Cruden Investments, of which Rupert was allotted 70,000 shares. It would be 'the only legacy to which he shall be entitled'.

He had also begun buying up additional shares in News Limited, hopeful that holding joint ownership of Brisbane's *Courier-Mail* and the Adelaide interests would give Rupert enough of a base to make something of himself. But, for now, as he entered a new decade that he was unlikely to see the end of, Murdoch was overdrawn, overstretched, and uncertain that things would fall into place in time. There were looming tax bills, mounting newsprint costs, and a need for capital across his little empire. To make sure there was anything left, he'd need to boost his papers' cashflow and bring down the debt—and fast.

'We have no hope, Colin, of holding News Limited shares and I think, from every point of view including that of my own capacities, we should clear up our financial position and get out on to a reasonable cash basis as soon as possible,' Murdoch told Bednall in August 1950. 'The world is dark in our quarters, and we are not justified, on any score, to keep our company stretched as it is today.'[64]

He couldn't be everywhere at once, and neither could Bednall. He needed an extra set of hands, someone who knew the newspaper business but was, above all else, a Murdoch man.

# CHAPTER TWO

# Comrade Murdoch

'GOOD MORNING, GENTLEMEN,' said Sir Keith Murdoch, sweeping into the reporters' room at 44–74 Flinders Street, Melbourne, one morning in 1947.[1] The two journalists looked up, attentive but not alarmed by the sudden appearance of the chairman and managing director of the Herald and Weekly Times. Almost daily, he would venture over from the executive suites—'mahogany row', they called it—and parade through the bullpen. The younger of the two, a man named Stewart Cockburn, had first met Sir Keith on one of these office tours years earlier as a teenage copy boy at *The Advertiser* in Adelaide. One day in 1938, this giant man appeared before him, and said matter-of-factly, 'Morning, my name's Murdoch, what's yours?'[2] Sir Keith's long-dead mentor, Lord Northcliffe, might have ruled his Fleet Street kingdom through fear and paranoia, but it was here, from the bottom rung up, that Murdoch cultivated an almost paternal soft power.

Every cadet that came through *The Herald* had been interviewed by Sir Keith, which meant virtually every *Herald* journalist owed him some loyalty from the moment they entered the building. To many, Murdoch was like 'Caesar', and on his daily loop he would push through the awkward conversation, just as he had learnt to push through his stammer.[3] He made a point of knowing names, not just of staff but their families, too, always picking up the thread of his last run-in with a cadet, subeditor, or secretary. He often made promises, too, of a heart-to-heart talk, or some future opportunity—dangled carrots that might or might not ever materialise. It was how he subtly shaped *The Herald* to his own liking, his own image, right down to how a Melbourne reporter should dress: light-grey suit, white shirt, light-blue tie, brown pork-pie hat, and *never* wearing a beard.[4]

The other reporter was in his early thirties, lean and gangly with ginger hair, pointed cheekbones, and a sharper chin. His name was Rohan Deakin Rivett, and, unlike Cockburn, whose bad lungs had made him one of the few young men left in an Australian newspaper office during the war, his journey to Flinders Street had taken a more circuitous, calamitous route. Rivett had been a 22-year-old student at Oxford when the outbreak of war sent him racing home, and after a fleeting six-month cadetship at the Melbourne *Argus*, he joined the crush of young men enlisting in the Australian Infantry Forces. Before long, he found himself in Singapore volunteering with the Malaya Broadcasting Corporation, where, on the morning of 9 February 1942, he stepped up to the microphone and announced to the world that Japanese troops had landed on the island. A day later, he was forced to abandon the post and begin a harrowing 21-day journey through jungle and across water, before finally being captured in Java.

He spent the rest of the war as a prisoner at Changi, along the deadly Burma-Siam railway, and in Thailand; but even in captivity, Rivett practised journalism where he could. When the guards weren't watching, he circulated what scraps of outside information could be compiled from rare letters from home or surreptitiously transcribed from improvised radios built and carefully hidden by other prisoners. 'Only one copy of the *Aungganaung News* ever saw the light of day,' he recalled of a makeshift newspaper produced in the camp, 'but I am not sure that it did not arouse more interest among those who heard its contents than anything I am ever likely to write subsequently.'[5] He didn't know it at the time, but Sir Keith's next words would set Rivett on a path that would alter the course of his life almost as dramatically as the words he broadcast on that fateful day in Singapore.

'I wonder if you gentlemen would do me a favour,' Sir Keith asked the reporters. 'Young Rupert is coming into the office from Geelong Grammar for a few weeks ... I was wondering if you gentlemen would be good enough to show him the ropes?'[6] The boy wasn't an uncommon sight at the Colin Ross memorial, a five-storey, neo-classical monolith of concrete and steel that housed the Herald and Weekly Times' operations. On weekends, he would occasionally accompany his father into work, barely 11 years old but already watching the Sunday *Herald* being put together.[7] Sometimes he could even be seen sitting quietly in the corner of board meetings as his father held court. The two men said they would be delighted—what else could they say?—and in no time at all, there he was.

There were plenty of teenage boys in a typical newspaper office, but it was plain to see that Rupert had a different path ahead of him to the average copy boy's. At first, the 16-year-old didn't draw too much attention to himself, just the occasional polite question about how this or that worked. 'He was a nice young fellow,' recalled Cockburn.[8] 'I think we all liked him—even the communists.' The *Herald* office was at the time home to several members of the party who, in a few years' time, would be purged by the emphatically anti-Red Sir Keith.

Rivett was no communist, but he and the young Murdoch got along so well that, before long, he and his wife, Nancy—called Nan by everyone—were summoned to visit Rupert at Geelong Grammar. By the time their paths crossed on Flinders Street, Rivett had become a well-known author and a minor war celebrity. As soon as he touched down in Australia in 1945, he began pouring his experience of captivity into a memoir, *Behind Bamboo*; when the book became a bestseller, Rivett also made a name for himself as a foreign correspondent, spending three months representing *The Herald* on a press delegation through China on the cusp of revolution. On a Friday in August 1948, he told the boys at Geelong Grammar about his trip; how the government of Chiang Kai-shek was fighting a losing battle against the communists, whose popular support was grounded not in ideology, but in the simple fact that anything seemed better than the 'rotten from the bottom up' current regime.[9] It was the duty of every responsible Australian, he told Murdoch and his classmates, to pay attention to what was happening in the north.

Rivett might not have been a communist, but he was undoubtedly progressive—radical even. At Oxford, he had caught a glimpse of the British Labour movement while volunteering in a camp for unemployed Welsh miners, and his years in Japanese-run camps had steeled his political radar. He came back dreaming of a fairer, less insular Australia, and after all those ugly, wasted years in the jungle, was in an awful hurry to get there.

Depending on how long he lingered that Friday in 1948, he might have heard that at Geelong Grammar, the young Rupert Murdoch cut a more polarising figure than he did on Flinders Street—not as the likeable, deferential son of the boss, but as a loud, if not entirely convincing, radical, whose left-wing politics and rough, shambolic manner invited mockery from the other sons of millionaires and scions at the school. On Flinders Street, he might have been Caesar's son, but at Geelong Grammar they were calling Rupert by a different name: 'Comrade Murdoch'.[10]


AT THE STROKE of midnight on 11 March 1931, Elisabeth Murdoch gave birth to her second child at Avonhurst private hospital, a boy who would bear the two names of his father and grandfather. Rupert Greene, Elisabeth's father, was a pastoralist and prominent Melbourne racing personality with a love of gambling that Sir Keith dearly hoped his son would not inherit along with the name. In the end, Keith Rupert Murdoch would come to split the difference between his two namesakes.

For Sir Keith, the day of his son's birth was an auspicious moment in more ways than one. The same edition of *The Herald* that ran the birth notice led with a triumphant front-page story announcing that 'man of the hour' Joseph Aloysius Lyons would form a new ministry after splitting from the Australian Labor Party.[11] The Labor government, led by prime minister James Scullin, had taken office just days before the Wall Street crash of 1929, and the Great Depression that followed had wrought chaos across the party and the country. Lyons had already served as premier of Tasmania when he was elected to federal parliament in Labor's 1929 landslide, but the crisis had opened a deep fault line between him and his caucus colleagues.

In print, Murdoch and *The Herald* welcomed Lyons' ascendance, and behind the scenes Keith worked to firm up support for him among the Victorian business community. *The Herald*'s announcement that the Scullin government had crumbled when confronted by this 'idealist' and 'clear thinker' would ultimately prove premature—on 13 March, the remaining Labor caucus weathered a no-confidence motion by four votes.[12] Despite the setback, Lyons would go on to form a coalition with the Nationalist Party as the United Australia Party, and, with the support of Murdoch's papers, the UAP won a resounding victory at the December election, making Lyons Australia's tenth prime minister—an office he retained until the moment he died of a heart attack in 1939. On Rupert's birthday, however, it seemed that Murdoch had gained both a male heir and a prime minister in the space of 24 hours.

The Great Depression had inflicted misery and political upheaval all around Australia, but the Murdoch family were insulated from its worst austerities. Despite the impact of a collapsing advertising market on the broader newspaper industry, Keith and Elisabeth were comfortable enough to make use of the droves of unemployed men who roamed Melbourne in search of work. Their labour turned Elisabeth's wedding present, Cruden Farm at Langwarrin, into a handsome country seat; its main house, an Australian facsimile of an American plantation house, and grounds filled with stables, gardens, tennis courts, and white eucalypts made a rich backdrop for the next generation of Murdochs to enjoy an idyllic country childhood. For Rupert and his siblings—he and Helen were later joined by Anne and Janet—their days at Cruden were often filled with pony-riding and rabbit hunting. By turns shy and mischievous, Rupert was also the most enterprising of the Murdoch children, selling the furs they caught together and pocketing the money.[13] To their neighbour at Langwarrin, the author Joan Lindsay, the Murdochs made for an 'unforgettable spectacle' when out riding on Sunday mornings, 'a sort of medieval cavalcade of children, servants, outriders, horses and dogs':

> At the head of the gay motley procession rides Keith, mounted on a massive charger, an upright rather heavily built figure

immaculate in English tweed and riding boots, proud and happy.[14]

Trotting along at the back of the party was 'little tow-headed Rupert bouncing up and down on Joy Boy the miniature Shetland' (a present from Rupert's godfather, Lindsay's artist husband, Daryl).[15] After a long day of play, Rupert would crawl into a semi-enclosed hut away from the main house; a lone boy among three girls, only Rupert was encouraged to sleep outdoors, a detail seized upon by consecutive biographers as evidence of a stern, unforgiving childhood. Late in life, his mother insisted that this angle, appealing as it was, had been overplayed: she had loved sleeping outdoors as a child, but admitted she 'thought it would be very good for him to have a little bit of hardship' in an otherwise comfortable country life.[16] The knowledge that the only son of Sir Keith might one day be forced to sink or swim manifested itself more literally: Rupert himself recalled being taught to swim on a voyage to England, when his mother threw him in the ship's pool and refused to let anyone help the blond-haired little boy flailing and screaming in the deep end.[17]

Elisabeth described her parenting style as one of 'loving discipline', but neither she nor Keith were particularly hands-on parents. In a hangover from Edwardian and Victorian styles of aristocratic child-rearing, the Murdoch children were primarily raised by their nanny and governess, and usually ate separately from their parents. Rupert was a toddler when Sir Keith's heart troubles in 1933 forced him to spend months at home, watching from a deckchair as the children played, but for much of their childhood he would spend long hours at the office, save for what Lindsay observed as the 'few glorious sun-drenched hours' when he became a family man.[18] Sometimes Rupert would accompany his father to the office on weekends, or watch him pore over the weekend papers at home—always with a pen at the ready to make corrections and notes for his subordinates.[19]

At the age of ten, Rupert was bundled off to Geelong Grammar, 110 kilometres away from Cruden on the opposite side of Port Phillip Bay. Looking out over Corio Bay, the campus consisted of a cluster of stately, ivy-covered brick buildings and manicured sporting fields,

centred on an imposing quadrangle and surrounded on all sides by
tree-lined paddocks. As an adult, Rupert claimed to have hated the
school, the 'fascist' prefects, the regimented schedule and military
school affectations, and gave his mother the firm impression that he
had a miserable time.[20] Neither he nor his father wanted him to go,
but it was Elisabeth who insisted — another exercise in toughening
the boy up. Some classmates thought Rupert shy and reserved, while
others found him brash and insensitive; in later years, he claimed to
have been a loner, and the target of bullies — thanks in part to his
famous father.[21]

But to those he did grow close to, he didn't *seem* all that miserable
or lonesome. To some in his small circle, he could be warm and fun to
be around, and always seemed to have a girlfriend from Melbourne.
(He kept a motorised bicycle to occasionally sneak away and place bets
at the races.)[22] 'The fact that Rupert had a well-known tycoon father
would not have made him extra special,' recalled his schoolfriend
Daniel Thomas, later a famous art historian.[23] 'Most of the students at
Geelong Grammar had famous or wealthy parents — that *was* Geelong
Grammar. He would have been just one of several sons of famous,
wealthy, influential Australians.'

Despite his outdoorsy childhood at Cruden, Rupert shunned the
many sporting codes that dominated Australian school life, instead
becoming active in the Public Affairs Society, the Political Society,
and the Historical and Philosophical Society. And if he was bullied,
he certainly made little effort to become a small target. Another
classmate, Donn Casey, whose father was a minister in the Lyons and
Menzies governments, found him a 'wild, gaily rebellious bloke, full of
high spirits'.[24] 'As a boy he was rough as guts — he wasn't very subtle
or gentle,' Casey recalled years later. 'He was known alternatively as
"Bullo Murdoch", being a bullshit artist or something, and "Commo
Murdoch", because he pretended to be a communist. He was rebelling
against a capitalist father, I suppose.'

Murdoch was a regular participant in the Areopagus Society — a
loftily named debating club — where he exhibited a messy kind of
radical streak.[25] Just where these views came from was a mystery. Was
it the influence of his older sister, Helen, who had already taken a keen

interest in issues of inequality?[26] Was it the impact of the grown-ups around him, such as Geelong Grammar teacher Stephen Murray-Smith (at the time a member of the Communist Party of Australia, and later the founder of left-wing literary journal *Overland*), who would walk Murdoch through the basics of socialism on laps of the grounds?[27] Or was it perhaps a simple act of adolescent rebellion, the postured rejection of privilege and wealth favoured by so many children of the rich, only to be discarded in adulthood?

Wherever it came from, few of his classmates seemed take Murdoch or his politics seriously, and when a debating opponent referred to him as 'Comrade Murdoch' in May 1948, they were almost certainly taking the piss. In the school newspaper, *The Corian*, his contributions to Areopagus debates refer to a young man who spoke with an 'inimitable, racy style', occasionally 'rambling all over the place' or accusing his opponents of hiding his notes.[28] The society explored a range of subjects, but Murdoch's arguments typically drew from the political left. Around the time of Rivett's visit to Geelong Grammar in August 1948, the debating club also welcomed Harold Holt MHR, the former Menzies government minister who was at the time stuck in opposition. As the guest speaker in a lively debate on socialism, Holt told the boys it was capitalism that built Australia, while the state represented 'the worst monopoly of all'.[29] In a performance that brought 'a quite unmerited reception on his head', Murdoch called out the 'whitewashing' of the Menzies government's record, which he dismissed as a 'failure'.[30] Such comments were typical of his pot-stirring contributions — on one occasion, he even caused 'considerable uproar, particularly when he made a jibe at the reporting by the press'.[31] A lengthy digression into the merits of communism was so impassioned that he had to qualify it with the 'emphatic' declaration that he was 'not a Commo!'[32] In December 1948, he criticised the 'racial intolerance' in America, and a political system that 'had fallen into the hands of capitalists', while the first meeting of a newly formed Political Club in December 1949 saw Murdoch give a short talk on the Socialists' plan for 'the provision of a better life for every man'.[33]

Rupert was still a student when he took on the title of editor for the first and perhaps only time in his life. In September 1949, he was the driving force of *If Revived*, the reincarnation of a short-lived literary journal founded by an earlier generation of Geelong Grammar students in 1929. *The Corian*'s reportage of Rupert's debating career often bears a hint of mocking disdain for the antics of Comrade Murdoch rarely applied to the other boys — despite him having briefly served as one of its subeditors — and perhaps this played some role in his foundation of a new journal. In its first editorial, *If Revived* promised to act as a counter to the 'purely factual' *Corian*, canvassing a broad range of opinion with no fixed editorial policy. But it also included a pointed, pre-emptive attack on its critics: '[T]here is no editorial policy. That is to say, if any accusations are made to the effect that *If Revived* is "red", "pink," [sic] or "blue" they are absolutely baseless.'

Its content ranged from a lengthy rebuke of the White Australia policy that his father's papers supported ('an attempt to remain static while the world is changing'), to a pithy piece about smoking on campus (and avoiding detection).[34] Only one article in *If Revived* bears the KR Murdoch by-line — an essay on the Bauhaus movement, bearing the influence of German émigré Ludwig Hirschfeld Mack, who taught painting and sculpture upstairs from the school's printing press. But the second and final issue also features a two-part article arguing the cases for and against socialism. While the case against carries Casey's by-line, the second lists no author — and if it wasn't written by Murdoch, it was certainly edited by him:

> What seems to be well established is that not only do Australian conditions lend themselves to monopolies, on account of the small population, but also that private monopolies are detrimental to the interests of any community ... it is likewise often pointed out that socialism would merely mean government monopoly instead of private monopoly. This is quite true — but what a difference between the two![35]

Perhaps most presciently, the piece also concludes that capitalism was clearly less democratic than socialism, made evident by the 'power and influence which goes with the possession of wealth'.[36]

By 1949, Sir Keith Murdoch's will had already set out his hopes for Rupert's journalistic future, and his influence on his son's early forays into publishing are evident. *If Revived* was printed on a press donated to the school by Murdoch senior, and its editorials recognised the 'very material assistance' given by the Herald and Weekly Times, and the help given by Clem Christesen, an ex-*Courier-Mail* journalist who by the 1940s had become the founding editor of the literary journal *Meanjin*. His friend Daniel Thomas, who contributed a piece on Gertrude Stein in the first issue of *If Revived* and became assistant editor for its second, once accompanied Rupert to visit Sir Keith on Flinders Street. 'It was my first sight of a real tycoon in his habitat,' Thomas recalled years later, along with his amazement at the collection of paintings that not only hung around Sir Keith's office, but also lay on the floor, leaning against the walls — apparently an attempt to hide his purchases from his wife. 'One of them was a painting by Russell Drysdale from the mid-1940s,' Thomas said. In the acknowledgements of *If Revived*'s second issue, a thank-you is addressed to the National Gallery of Australia, of which Sir Keith was a leading patron and trustee, for lending the plates for a Drysdale print that illustrated one article.

In one of his debating scraps back in 1948, Rupert declared that he could 'not see why the chance of birth into a rich family should enable some boys to enjoy an education most of them did not deserve'.[37] But when it came to the world of journalism, the advantages of birth were already coming to bear for young Rupert. And there would be much more to come, provided that his father, stretched as he was, could pull it all off.

## CHAPTER THREE

# Bright young men

'HOW WOULD YOU like to edit a newspaper?' Sir Keith Murdoch, half-dressed and on his way to the shower, called out through the ajar bedroom door.[1] It was the kind of offer most journalists would leap at, but in the next room of Murdoch's suite at the five-star Claridge's Hotel in Mayfair, Rohan Rivett was caught off guard. Since ten o'clock that morning he'd been little more than a glorified valet, chauffeuring Sir Keith around Surrey as he visited a church, an art dealer, and a string of English acquaintances. By the time they'd arrived back at the hotel seven-and-a-half hours later, he'd begun to wonder why he was there at all. 'Get me a whisky, and pour yourself one,' Murdoch had said as he went into the next room, and now Rivett's unusual day took a more surreal turn: sipping Scotch in an opulent establishment frequented by British aristocrats and exiled European royalty, as this giant of Australian newspapers casually offered up the keys to a kingdom—with a shirt pulled halfway over his head.[2] Rivett paused, took a few deep breaths, and called back to Murdoch: 'Can I ring Nan?'

By July 1951, Murdoch's long game of building Rupert's inheritance was falling into place. Despite the bleak forecast of 1950, he had managed to keep both Queensland Newspapers and News Limited in his column. The possibility of landing another big acquisition, whether it was *The Canberra Times* or *The Argus* in Melbourne, had so far eluded him, but he had at least managed to outpace death or ruin—whichever came first. But in the three years since he began to carve News Limited out from the Herald and Weekly Times, the company had entered a slow decline. Its profits were sliding year on year—from £31,076 in 1949 to £24,877 in 1951—and something had to give before the rot set in.[3] He needed someone on the ground, someone he knew and trusted, who might also light a long-overdue fire under the place.

In Rivett he saw the raw material of a great editor; he was, as Murdoch wrote in a glowing letter of introduction, an 'Oxford scholar, war veteran, author of one of the best war books, and to boot, a fine redhead and good journalist'.[4] There was their shared Scottish heritage and their career-making experiences as wartime reporters, but, perhaps most importantly, he knew his family. Rivett's mother, Stella, was the daughter of the late Alfred Deakin—the same person who had written the young, London-bound Murdoch a letter of introduction all those years ago. Rivett's father, Sir David, a respected and knighted CSIRO scientist, was already a friend of Sir Keith, and Murdoch's uncle, Professor Walter Murdoch—who wrote a biography of Deakin back in 1923—had helped Rohan navigate the publishing world when he came back from the war with a book to write.

Sir Keith took a shine to Rivett during his time on Flinders Street, and, when he was posted to *The Herald*'s London cable service in late 1948, began grooming and shaping the young reporter much as Lord Northcliffe had done for him decades earlier. From afar, Murdoch's letters schooled Rivett on everything from adjective use to Fleet Street networking, and in return Rivett moonlighted as Murdoch's travel agent, stringer, and taxi driver whenever he visited the northern hemisphere.[5] 'I have great hopes for you, Rohan,' Murdoch wrote in April 1949.[6] 'I want you to become the type of newspaper man who has ink in his blood, or—to put it more mildly—really sniffs when he smells the ink of the printing press and becomes happy. In other words, I want to equip yourself as an editor.' [7]

Of course, Rivett wasn't the only young journalist granted an inside track with Sir Keith—or the first to receive such lofty promises. Of all the relationships he cultivated on the office floor, there were always a handful of men who were handpicked for greater glory. 'There was a small camp, almost a club, of young men chosen by Keith Murdoch,' recalled Keith Dunstan, himself a favoured protégé and son of a friend. (His father, Bill, had even named him after Murdoch.)[8] According to another journalist, being one of Murdoch's 'bright young men'—*Murdoch* men—was like having a 'foothold on Olympus'.[9] 'Murdoch collected houses, paintings, crates full of old English glass, Poll Hereford stud cattle, great flocks of merino sheep, forests of trees, and journalists,' recalled Colin Bednall, whose loyalty to Murdoch had elevated him from his start as a teenage reporter in Adelaide to one of Sir Keith's most trusted confidants.[10] But according to Bednall, being collected by Sir Keith could also be fraught with internecine rivalry: 'Murdoch always protected his own position by keeping his lieutenants fearful and even loathing of one another.'[11] With Murdoch's health deteriorating and influence waning, such a foothold looked increasingly slippery. Inside Flinders Street, being a Murdoch man meant running the risk of being shunned by Williams' camp, while outside the office, you could be chased out of the Trades Hall or have the door slammed in your face. ('I won't speak to any Murdoch cunt,' said one member of the public to Keith Dunstan.)[12]

Just as Sir Keith feared his son would be eaten alive after his death, this breakaway venture could prove a lifeboat for a someone like Rivett, whose fortunes had grown irrevocably tied to the Murdoch name.[13] Their relationship defied the evident differences in their politics ('Are you really very Left, Rohan?' Sir Keith wrote with surprise in 1949), but Rivett seemed like the kind of person who wasn't afraid of driving change.[14] 'I expect to have a fine job for you to come back to,' Murdoch wrote in September 1949, but as the months went by it remained only a vague proposition.[15] In 1950, when Murdoch was mulling over his doomed *Smith's Weekly* bid, he considered Rivett for the task of reinventing it as a 'truly critical, informative, pungent, clear-headed [and] uproariously funny' paper.[16] Then, in February 1951, Murdoch floated the idea of Rivett helming a new weekly through the recently acquired Southdown Press.[17] As each opportunity stalled, Rivett began to feel stuck; he had spent six years with the Herald and Weekly Times, and craved the kind of responsibility he had tasted while in Singapore. ('[T]his situation is that one you strike only once in your life when you really are at the centre of all things,' read one diary entry written in the final days before Singapore fell. 'This is the time when you're weighed in the scales.')

'I like the whole business of organising and believe I can handle it,' he told Murdoch, hopeful that the coming year might bring a chance to prove it.[18]

Back in Australia, Bednall had been sent on a week-long mission in March 1951 to get to the bottom of the Adelaide problem (a 'vivisection inquest, a deep probe,' as Rivett later called it).[19] Bednall had started his career at *The News*, but was clear-eyed about how his old stomping ground needed to change. ('Since my days as a copy boy in the office I have always thought '*The News*' the dullest of titles,' he once told Murdoch.) [20] Although slightly baffled that Sir Keith didn't simply fold it all back into the safe embrace of the Herald and Weekly Times, Bednall made another recommendation: News Limited needed a 'high level editorial mind' with a 'sense of vocation' to lead the whole organisation and give it 'a strong missionary editorial outlook'.[21] Bednall himself had no desire to play 'seat-warmer for the schoolboy Rupert Murdoch', and none of the other candidates he suggested could be spared from the power struggle brewing on Flinders Street.[22] Fortunately, Murdoch had another name waiting in the wings in London. But News Limited was not the first family legacy Rohan Rivett had been entrusted with — there was also the matter of Rupert, for whom all these efforts were being made.


BY OCTOBER 1950, Rupert had finally escaped Corio Bay and Geelong Grammar, and while he had matriculated with only middling results, he was about to live out another unfulfilled dream of his father's: higher education. He was granted a place studying Politics, Philosophy and Economics at Oxford's Worcester College, a 230-year-old bastion of privilege, enlightenment, and influence more deeply ingrained than any colonial institution back home. At Oxford, Murdoch cast a similar impression to his Geelong days: well liked among a small coterie of friends and amused mentors; dismissed as gauche, spoilt, and crass by some; and regarded as quiet and dull by others. 'He was mainly known to be richer than the rest of us in the sense that where everyone else went on foot or on a clapped-out bicycle, he was the only person one knew who had a car,' said one contemporary.[23] Even the modest, beige number was an uncommon luxury, akin to a 'private aeroplane or a Rolls Royce in terms of being noticed and envied'.

To some, Murdoch's brashness could be chalked up to a culture clash between English and Australian sensibilities. A small article titled 'Australians at Worcester' in the student magazine *Cherwell* hints at his antipodean otherness, as Murdoch is photographed beside the college's other two prominent Australians—a pair of wallabies purchased for the grounds as a novelty.[24] But if he felt out of place among Worcester's elegant archways and arcades, medieval cottages, and neat lawns, at least the days of cold showers at Geelong were behind him as he settled in the well-appointed De Quincey room, named for a Worcester alumnus who had found fame as an opium-addicted writer.

Now half a world away from Cruden Farm, the Rivetts became the closest thing to home or family. Rohan and Nan had met up with the newly graduated 19-year-old Rupert in Rome in April 1950, when they joined the Murdoch family on a tour across Europe. Rivett had grown close to Sir Keith, but the invitation was born of necessity: after all, somebody needed to run in the new Land Rover that would be the family's chief mode of transport throughout their trip.[25] Setting out from Calais, the Rivetts spent six-and-a-half days on the road, inching along well below the speed limit for the first 1,600 kilometres to preserve the new car's engine, before their eventual rendezvous with the Murdochs in Italy. (Sir Keith, meanwhile, had wrangled an audience for his wife and son with Pope Pius XII.)[26]

Rivett's letters to Sir Keith soon included regular reports on Rupert's progress, and he was generous with praise for his young friend: 'He is already obviously more mature and self-reliant than when I met you all in Rome ten months ago,' Rivett wrote, while predicting that Rupert would 'make his first million with fantastic ease'.[27] By the end of the year, he reported that Rupert was 'looking very fit, full of enthusiasm and obviously getting the maximum out of his first time at Oxford'.[28] These dispatches bear an almost familial intimacy; he fretted over Rupert's acquisition of a two-stroke motorcycle, poked fun at his mediocre French and German, and marvelled at his financial shrewdness — or nose for a grift. ('He will probably prove the greatest income-maker from an expense account in *Herald* history when he comes back on payroll,' Rivett wrote, not yet realising Sir Keith's plans for Rupert lay outside the Herald and Weekly Times.)[29]

While Sir Keith was preparing to make Rivett an indispensable cog in the family business, Rupert was becoming a treasured part of the Rivett family in Sunbury-on-Thames. His visits would see the house filled with calls of 'Rooooopeee' as he raced the children up and down the street in an old go-cart.[30] The Rivetts' young son, David, shadowed Rupert 'like Man Friday', eagerly rousing him each morning, and upon his return to Oxford the children took to calling the attic of the family home 'Rupert's room'.[31] In April 1951, he joined Rohan and Nan on a 3,000-kilometre trip through Austria and Switzerland, taking in Salzburg, the ski fields of Hintertux and Mayrhofen, and visiting Hitler's eyrie on the Berchtesgaden mountainside ('all debris amid the snowdrift,' Rivett recounted).[32] In a pair of photographs taken on the trip, Rupert still looks every bit the teenage schoolboy — fair-haired, slightly scrawny, and sharing a conspiratorial grin with Nan and Rohan. Upon their return, Rivett told Sir Keith that Rupert 'came back bronzed and very fit — none of the gastric trouble he had last year on the continent':[33]

His development in 12 months has been amazing. His resource and ability to work things out and get things done are first-rate. I can't say the same of his French, but I gather he means to work much harder at Oxford this year and after all, he has had a great deal on his plate for a boy not yet 21 in his first year at Oxford. Nan and I found him a grand travelling companion in every way and from the first moment until the return he was picking up information, asking questions and absorbing new impressions and enthusiasms.[34]

Most importantly, Rivett reassured Sir Keith that Rupert remained very much on the path his father envisioned. 'Your letters are—quite literally—his Bible,' he wrote, echoing Sir Keith's words to Northcliffe years earlier.[35] 'He reads us bits of two of them and has been chewing over your advice all the time before he takes any major step.'[36]

While Rupert seemed indifferent to academia, a patchwork apprenticeship for a future in newspapers was also being prepared for him. Before leaving Australia, he had undertaken another whirlwind cadetship with *The Herald* between January and March 1950, and then accompanied his father to the Imperial Press Conference in Canada, where he became friendly with the youngest member of the British delegation, John Grigg of *The National and English Review*. The future Lord Altrincham thought it obvious that Rupert came from 'a home where newspaper talk was the air he breathed'.[37] 'He was all agog with excitement about newspapers, the clash of personalities,' Grigg later recalled. 'He was absolutely fascinated by the game.'

During his first English summer, Rupert spent two months working at the Birmingham *Gazette*, where he struck the paper's deputy editor as lacking any reporting experience.[38] Meanwhile, the *Gazette* photographer who he briefly lodged with found him to be a hungry, opinionated loner: 'He seemed to have a mission in life and that was to know as much as possible in the shortest possible time.'[39] In December, he took up Rivett's recommendation to seek work at *The Chronicle* on Fleet Street, and was soon 'copy-tasting' and building up 'an amazing string of contacts'.[40] In October 1951, he travelled to London to meet with the 1st Baron Beaverbrook, the Canadian-British newspaper publisher Max Aitken, who owned the high-circulation working-class paper *The Daily Express*. Dropping in on Rivett before the meeting, Rupert seemed more energised and alert than Rohan had ever seen him.[41]

When Sir Keith met up with Rupert for a European tour in June 1951, Rivett primed him to expect a 'pleasant revelation'.[42] Murdoch had just offered Rivett *The News* editorship, and when Sir Keith told Rupert the news he was thrilled, immediately sending his 'mate' a 'quick and pretty chatty' note of congratulations—and the promise of a drink when he returned.[43] The plan was for Sir Keith and Rupert to pick up a brand-new Ford Zephyr, drive it through Europe, and then have it shipped back to Australia from Port Said in Egypt. The car was a write-off by the time it reached Australia, but for the moment, Sir Keith was thrilled to see his son 'blooming', just as Rivett had promised—even if his rash driving on the 'dangerous hairpin bends' of Greece troubled him.[44]

But by October, Sir Keith was growing concerned; while Rupert had initially stayed in regular contact, the 'cordial family letters full of interest in his life' he had once sent had all but dried up.[45] Neither Rivett or Murdoch heard from him for almost a month after he left Athens, where he was due to meet up with a schoolmate and a pair of his Oxford tutors. By the time a cable confirmed his arrival in Istanbul, Sir Keith had spent anxious weeks ruminating on Rupert's driving in the Greek mountains and the bumpy roads he would now be speeding along. Another October update from Rivett also brought more cause for concern: Rupert had fallen behind on his university work, and might not make it back to Australia for Christmas. 'The lad is worried,' Rivett wrote. 'He wants very much to come home to see you all but hasn't done any work this vac and wonders if he shouldn't work through the winter.'[46] Sir Keith responded coolly:

> I am very worried about Rupert in that he does not write home enough. When he gets going he writes well, and win marks; but he must learn that all human relationships even those with his family have always to be kept in repair, and are infinitely worth a lot of trouble and study.[47]

He continued to stew, reflecting on the months of glowing reports that Rivett had been sending him. A few days later, he sent a stern request:

> A private word, Rohan. Do be careful not to inflate Rupert. You have talked once or twice in your letters of his "brilliant prospects". His prospects depend entirely on himself. I can assure him of a fine opportunity in the newspaper world, but it will be useless unless he has the right qualities and these are not easy

to attain. By the time the Taxation Commissioner has finished with anybody these days, and he doesn't until you have been dead quite a time, there is not much money for anybody to inherit and I hope Rupert will earn whatever he gets. He is inclined to look forward with gusto to his opportunities. The real opportunity is that he makes himself a good man. I feel confident he will do so.[48]

Sir Keith wasn't shy about his concerns, telling Hugh Cudlipp, editorial director of *The Daily Mirror*, that Rupert was developing 'most alarming Left-wing views' at Oxford.[49] In May 1949, he told prime minister Ben Chifley that his 18-year-old son was 'at present a zealous Laborite, but will I think (probably) eventually travel the same course of his father'.[50] But Rupert had not outgrown his schoolyard fascination with socialism, and news that he had installed a bust of Lenin—who he called 'the Great Teacher'—in his plush lodgings at Worcester did little to allay his father's concerns.[51] Rupert, meanwhile, continued a correspondence with Chifley, who recommended that the young man read up on John Maynard Keynes while they swapped notes on the British left, socialism, and the coverage of the 'Murdoch press' back home.[52]

Rupert's contemporaries at Oxford treated his radical posture about as seriously as his Geelong classmates did, but at Worcester he grew more intrigued by the Labour movement. Perhaps some of this came from his main tutor—a small, energetic, bespectacled academic named Asa Briggs. Barely a decade older than Rupert, Briggs had been recruited straight out of Cambridge to work as a codebreaker at Bletchley Park during the war, and as a fellow at Worcester was developing a career as one of England's foremost social and economic historians of the 20th century. Despite Briggs' Labour ties—his area of specialty was the history of Britain's urban working class—Sir Keith had asked him to give Rupert additional instruction, and the two grew close enough that Murdoch addressed him by the nickname 'Isa'.[53] Briggs was one of the young Oxford dons who joined Rupert on the second leg of his grand tour, travelling from Turkey to Egypt, via Syria, Lebanon, and Palestine in Sir Keith's increasingly battered Zephyr. The party often camped in sleeping bags in the open air, drawing suspicion from the local police as they went. As the Zephyr swerved and shuddered along rough and crumbling roads, Murdoch launched into long, broad tirades from behind the wheel at the elitist 'pommies' back in Oxford.[54]

Rivett hadn't helped either; he had encouraged Rupert to take part in debates in the university union as a way of networking, and perhaps seeking office. In a place surrounded by 'the lads who will be the top political, civil and academic leaders of the sixties, seventies and eighties', Rivett reasoned, such a position could open 'many doors to him'.[55] Rupert took his advice, and soon launched a contentious campaign for treasurer of the university Labour Club — complete with the campaign slogan 'Rooting for Rupert' — but was ultimately struck out of the race after throwing a party to encourage members to vote for him.[56] Such a faux pas stood in direct violation of one of the club's rules against openly canvassing for votes — this was a place that was that was used to more respectable, quiet displays of influence. (Sir Keith was thrilled by this development, dashing off a handwritten note to Rivett, exclaiming: 'Rupert has been expelled from the OU Labour Club!!')[57]

On the charge of 'inflating' Rupert, Rivett sought to allay Sir Keith's fears, writing that 'if anything I do exactly the reverse to his face … I hope has no idea how very far I believe he will go or how much I admire his qualities'.[58] At the beginning of 1952, when Sir Keith was tempted to cut Rupert's studies short and drag him back to Australia, Rivett helped talk him down. ('If unable to finish his course there will always be a personal feeling of some dissatisfaction,' he pleaded.)[59] But Murdoch's concerns that the matey rapport between his son and protégé might affect the accuracy of the reports he was receiving weren't so unfounded; the friendship between the two young men stood quite apart from the reverential tone that characterised Rivett and the elder Murdoch's relationship. From a passing allusion to Rupert once winning £88 in an evening of roulette, to affectionate jibes like 'Ruperto, my old dear and occasionally drunken mate', their correspondence hints at a life of gambling, drinking, fast cars, and other youthful misadventures that would have horrified Sir Keith. [60] Rivett declined to relay much of this to his mentor back in Australia.

In Rupert's gleeful retelling, his intercontinental road trip turned into a colourful and chaotic joyride. First, Rupert had to swing by the Australian embassy to collect a new passport and Israeli visa. He was already cutting it fine—they were due to leave the city in half an hour—when he was informed that the 'bloody fool Holt protégés' at the immigration department had invalidated his visa to Yugoslavia. He was forced to invoke the 'godly' influence of the Murdoch name, scrambling to call in whatever favours or connections he could muster by phone to confirm his bona fides.[61]

He was perturbed by the 'fat old woman' who retched beside him for the entire plane ride, and on arrival slummed it on camp beds in a 'filthy, out of the way' French village. In Belgrade, he was arrested—for taking photos in the wrong place, he claimed. One morning, Rupert misplaced his set of car keys, and the next day went to get a new set cut. As he reached for his wallet to pay for the new keys, he found the originals—they had been in his pocket the whole time. Such hijinks were evidently not uncommon to Rupert or Rivett—it was, simply, 'real Murdoch style'.[62] In Greece, he complained about the locals ('the most awful people I've come across'), and having to contend with a 'mass of shouting dagos' at the airport.[63] Outside Belgrade, he observed a collectivised farm and socialised factory, and was 'quite stunned' by the happiness and energy of its workers compared to the 'dirt and sordidness' of the city itself.[64] By the time he had met up with his father, he complained that Sir Keith was 'bellyaching' him about the 'compression of words'.[65] Unbeknownst to any of them, the trip would be the last time Rupert saw his father.

RIVETT DIDN'T KNOW a soul in Adelaide when he arrived in December 1952. They called it a capital city, but, after four years in London, it felt to him an awful lot like a country town.[66] Since Nan had granted her blessing over the phone at Claridge's Hotel in July, the family had uprooted their London lives, sold their car and furniture, and flown back to Australia. But until the company settled on permanent accommodation for them, Nan and the children would stay in Melbourne while Rohan lived out of a suitcase in a hotel overlooking the Botanic Gardens, on the north-east tip of the square mile. It was just a short walk in a straight line down North Terrace to reach the News Limited office, where he had orders to ease himself into the existing hierarchy.

'You will need to go quietly of course for some time, Rohan,' Sir Keith had warned ahead of his arrival.[67] But there was nothing quiet about 116 North Terrace. The editorial floor rumbled with the percussive click-clack of typewriters, the ripping of paper, the yells of 'copy!', and rushed footsteps of the copy boys spiriting the white scraps to the subeditors. Half the staff were prone to disappearing into clouds of cigarette smoke, while up from below came the smell of hot metal and ink, and the roar of heaving machinery that grew louder and louder as the first editions rolled off the presses. In the background, the churn from the teletype machines announced chits of cable news arriving from around the country, which unfurled into coils of paper on the floor.

David Bowman was a 21-year-old cadet when Rivett first arrived, sporting a wide-set face, big eyes, broad smile, and sloping, expressive eyebrows. Bowman was impressed with how the incoming editor 'swept through the corridors as if he owned them, [and] spoke to people in an aura of youthful energy and purpose'.[68] Others resented the new presence, earning him the nickname 'Big Red', or, in a reference to his height and corner office, 'that big bastard in the corner'.[69] One morning, Bowman heard a senior subeditor unleash 'one great long Celtic curse upon that bastard and all his works, while the room put its collective head down and pretended it wasn't happening.'[70] Some of Bowman's fellow cadets sniggered at Rivett's more idiosyncratic habits: who or where did this newly parachuted blow-in think he was, carrying a small wireless into the office lavatory just in case some news broke over the radio? But compared to his predecessor, Don Stevens, who struck Bowman as a 'remote being', Rivett had 'an eager note in his voice' and 'natural air of command'.[71] Before long, he'd won over most of the staff—even the cadets.

Rivett was to take on the role of editor-in-chief, above Stevens, who edited *The News*, and *The Mail*'s Ron Boland, while learning the topography of Adelaide's media landscape.[72] Although physically distant, for close to a year Murdoch would guide Rivett from Melbourne, sending issue-by-issue feedback, rewriting leaders and correcting subediting errors. He even gave notes on the etiquette of cartooning. ('Never caricature a woman unless it is splendidly clever and slightly flattering,' he said after *The News* ran an illustration of Lady Jean Bonython, matriarch of the old Adelaide family that had surrendered *The Advertiser* to Sir Keith 20 years earlier.)[73]

Rivett later described himself as 'the greenest editor who has ever stepped into the job in South Australia', and was the first to admit he knew little about the day-to-day mechanics of newspaper production.[74] But he did his best to execute Murdoch's instructions and to revive the look, feel, and presence of the paper; if Sir Keith wanted a paper that was 'more truthful, briefer, more direct, more liberal and brighter', Rivett would do all he could to deliver.[75] He searched for efficiencies, like getting *The News* out on the street closer to midday by going to print a fraction earlier. 'It wasn't half as difficult as many people expected,' he reported to Murdoch — all it took was getting half the day's copy to the linotype operators the previous evening.[76] 'Like a lot of things here that I've been told at first were "impossible" or "bound to cause endless trouble", it seems, in fact that it makes for much better performance in many ways.'[77]

One pressing matter was the paper's use of pictures; advances in printing and camera technology had been reshaping the modern newspaper since the 19th century, but in Adelaide there was still some catching up to do. 'They were ill-chosen and, in the main, ill-used,' Murdoch complained of *The News*' picture selection prior to Rivett's appointment, 'there was little sizing of pictures and frequently the subjects were just completely dull.'[78] Just as Sir Keith had ruffled feathers when he crashed through at *The Herald*, the new approach was met with 'looks of shocked bewilderment merging into incredulous joy'.[79] Murdoch didn't always approve of Rivett's choices, with a January 1952 memo raising concerns about the excessive use of images he felt weren't 'newsy' enough. ('It is so important to get the news into this paper,' Murdoch said bluntly.)[80] Lighter, locally skewing fare ran against Rivett's own instincts, too, but in parochial Adelaide that seemed to be a recipe for success:

Again and again I find that the local episode, however flat the picture, is the thing that Adelaide people talk about, demand and remember weeks later. When I came here in December I had a violent bias against over-use of flat local pictures. But in eating the pudding I find that the local picture is what your reader wants. The overseas picture—even a dramatic earthquake, fire or arrest seldom excites as much interest as something involving South Australians.[81]

Rivett tapped the cadet Bowman to pen captions to accompany the paper's photography, who soon found it to be 'enormous fun' ('[T]he only sin was to be dull,' he later recalled).[82]

It wasn't just the quality of photojournalism that begged to be modernised; like all city newspaper offices, and many workplaces around mid-century Australia, the News Limited floor could be a rigid, homogenous place. It was a 'stuffy male enclave' that counted over a dozen father-and-son pairs and nearly as many sets of brothers among its 600 employees.[83] So abundant was the supply of men called John or Don that it became a regular source of confusion and humour in the office. ('Whenever anyone calls "John" they are practically killed in the rush,' joked a 1954 issue of *House News*.)[84]

The women who worked at the paper were largely found in secretarial roles, typing pools and answering telephones, and those who did break into journalism were often confined to the 'Women's Bureau' and social columns. (There were some exceptions; Bettyanne Sullivan became the first woman to write captions for *The News* in July 1954—albeit relegated to the unpopular Saturday-evening shift.)[85] One of Rivett's earliest hires was Rita Dunstan, a veteran reporter and editor with experience at *The Sunday Telegraph*, *Woman's Day*, and the Singapore Free Press, who had been the first Australian woman to become an accredited war correspondent during World War II. Rivett soon rocked the boat a little too hard when he appointed Dunstan to the subeditors' desk, and within ten minutes the chief subeditor, a serious, thickly moustached man named Arch Bell, was at Rivett's door 'prophesysing mutiny and mayhem'.[86] Rivett went ahead anyway, but three days later the rest of the subs demanded a group meeting: 'The sin I had committed, they tacitly made clear, was to breach the sacred portals of that all male club—an Australian daily's subs room,' he later recalled.[87] 'How could one relieve one's tension or frustration at some clottish reporter's snafu if you couldn't swear?' Rivett tried to argue that, after 12 years in newspapers she was unlikely to be surprised or offended, but the subs won out: Dunstan would head up the Women's Bureau, while the subeditors' room's 'sacrosanct masculinity' endured for a few more years.

Rivett also tried to harness the growing diversity of South Australia's population; the post-war period had seen the White Australia policy soften slightly to accommodate an influx of European migrants, particularly in South Australia. But many of these 'New Australians' encountered prejudice and suspicion in their new home. 'I have issued a memo cutting the term "New Australians" out of country reports and other derogatory references to migrants, unless the term is essential for understanding of the story,' Rivett told Murdoch in February 1952.[88] 'There is no doubt that the majority of law-abiding new citizens are suffering severely from public prejudice aroused by the actions of the law-breaking minority among them. Anything that fosters the present prejudice can only be damaging.' With the state's growing migrant community, extending such an olive branch also had an important commercial undercurrent—if other newspapers weren't making an effort to court this bloc of potential readers, *The News* stood to boost its own circulation. While Murdoch was initially sceptical, Rivett was encouraged by the response: '[W]e certainly have become known in South Australia as the paper which does take an interest in the New Australian.'[89]

Rivett also had the paper's circulation department to appease, which insisted that photographs on the front and back page could increase city sales in their hundreds.[90] But such rewards sometimes meant challenging the sensibilities of the local community. In February 1952, a few months into Rivett's tenure, word reached the News Limited offices that a gunman had fired six shots at a cricket carnival just outside the city, killing one player—a 31-year-old army captain—and injuring another. The shooting occurred at 10.00 am, perfectly timed for *The News'* afternoon edition, which ran with a headline proclaiming 'Murder on Cricket Field: Adelaide Sensation When Man Fires Rifle at Players', and issued similarly eye-catching newsstand posters around the city.[91] Beneath the headline, and spanning nearly the entire breadth of the front-page, was a photograph of the panicked scene, and of the dead man lying prostrate and alone in his cricket whites.

This was far more graphic than Adelaide readers were used to, and the response was bracing. 'As might have been expected we are under fire here for publishing the picture with the body in the foreground,' Rivett told Murdoch.[92] Rivett insisted that the photograph had nothing on the 'ugly or revolting' excesses seen in American magazines and newspapers ('[which] so frequently publish of bullet-ridden gangsters'), and that the story was met with similar coverage in Sydney, Melbourne, Brisbane, and Perth papers. 'I feel that any editor having such a picture and such a story of an event barely a mile from his office should have been fired if he didn't publish it front page,' he wrote.[93] 'I thought over the matter carefully at the time—and time was very short—and I feel that if the same sort of thing happens tomorrow and we are lucky enough to get an equally graphic picture I would do the same thing again.' Murdoch agreed, and in commercial terms, at least, Rivett's gamble paid off; despite the controversy *The News* recorded a 15,000-unit increase in city sales on the day of the shooting—or, as Rivett put it, the numbers 'shot up'.[94] He would later meet the policeman, Detective John Giles, who helped apprehend the shooter, in the News Limited offices eight years later—albeit in very different circumstances.

It didn't take long for the changes to take effect; in July, the paper was reporting a daily net circulation of over 100,000 copies—a 5 per cent increase from April 1952.[95] Rivett also seized upon anecdotal signs that *The News* was making ground:

At an ABC party for their commissioners the other night no fewer than five people made remarks about it to Boland or myself. Occasionally it is accompanied with a gibe about never having previously found anything serious minded in *The News*, but it is genuine and it is widespread. Ernest [Bridges, News Limited's general manager] finds the same thing among the business community.[96]

Most importantly, Rivett seemed to be energising the paper's culture — just as Bednall had hoped eighteen months earlier. Max Fatchen, a 33-year-old poet, humourist, and feature writer who had become one of *The News* and *The Mail*'s marquee contributors, vividly recalled Rivett's impact on the newsroom:

> He was tall, handsome, he had flaming hair, and he was an idealist. And he would address us in the morning, like a young general addressing his people ... he was so inspiring that, you know, I would have gone out and covered the last days of Pompeii if I'd had a chance.[97]

BUT THERE WERE factors beyond the newsroom that troubled Rivett. Time and again, he saw how News Limited's relationships with local advertisers, public institutions, and interstate publications were undercut by their cross-town rivals: *The Advertiser* and its chairman, Sir Lloyd Dumas. 'We still seem to move towards Rundle Street like a despised second cousin,' Rivett complained of the city's main retail strip, dominated by department stores such as the Myer Emporium and John Martins, whose owner, Bill Hayward, made little effort to hide his contempt for *The News* or his close ties to *The Advertiser*.[98] Hayward's own advertising department confirmed to Rivett that there was no logic behind their boycott of *The News*: 'He simply dislikes our liberal policy, has always done so, and would gladly see us on the rocks.'[99]

But the problem was bigger than one department store. 'Sir Lloyd, with great shrewdness and ability, has pursued a most damaging whispering and denigrating campaign against News Limited for many years — this has been particularly effective in Rundle Street, or rather with Rundle Street executives in the Adelaide Club,' Rivett wrote three months after arriving.[100] Set in a redbrick-and-sandstone Victorian-era manse on North Terrace, with a view of Government House's front yard and barely a 30-second walk from Parliament House, the Adelaide Club was an exclusive institution that had existed as an unofficial point of intersection between private interests and political power in South Australia for generations.

Established just after the colony's 25th birthday, the gentlemen's club became the forum for pastoralists, capitalists, and professional men to cement the networks of influence and power that would establish in the colony a new kind of ruling class and aristocracy—an Adelaide establishment, or 'Old Adelaide', whose membership featured surnames that would mark many of Adelaide's colonial institutions and halls of power: Elder, Mayo, Angas, Barr Smith, Waite, Hughes, Morphett, and Downer. By the 1950s, its rooms remained a hotbed for dealmaking and gossip among the state's elite. Murdoch would attend the club on visits to Adelaide, having learned the importance of Melbourne and London's clublands long before, but it bought little influence for Rivett in a circle dominated by their rivals. 'This is a funny town, where family counts a great deal in some quarters, and those quarters control most of Rundle Street,' he wrote despairingly.[101]

Then there was the premier. Sir Thomas Playford was a giant in every sense: a lumbering, dominating figure, equally at home in his family's cherry orchards in the steep hills and valleys east of the city and in the halls of parliament. He inherited both from his grandfather and namesake, 'Honest' Tom Playford, who had entered state parliament in 1868, served as premier twice, then joined the new federal parliament in 1901. Despite this powerful pedigree, opinion varied about Playford's bona fides in the Adelaide establishment: there was long-running enmity between his family and South Australia's other great Liberal dynasty, the Downers; he was not a member of the Adelaide Club, nor had he passed through many of the institutions favoured by children of the local elite—describing himself self-effacingly as a 'simple cherry grower'.[102] But he soon became an establishment of his own, entering parliament as part of the Liberal and Country League Party in 1933, and ascending to the premiership in 1938. He had initially been a compromise candidate, but grew to dominate his cabinet, the parliament, and the state, thanks in no small part to a gerrymander, an electoral distribution that granted twice the electoral weight to voters in country areas—a hangover from the previous century's idea of democracy, where the colony's strength and political power lay with landholders and pastoralists, not the urban masses.

Playford was socially conservative, but often pursued interventionist economic policies that earned him the compliment—or slur—of being 'the best Labor premier South Australia ever had'.[103] As premier, influenced by a Keynesian auditor-general, he pursued a policy of industrialisation, transforming the state from a wool, wheat, and mining economy by luring private and federal investment during and after the war, pumping out munitions, ships, textiles, and automobiles. To better harness this growth, Playford wasn't afraid of flying in the face of his own party's ideology and base—from the creation of entire suburbs' worth of new public housing to accommodate workers, to nationalising the state's electricity grid (previously run by a privately owned monopoly) with the support of Labor prime minister Ben Chifley. His unpolished, anti-intellectual style and forceful personality was both disarming and domineering, and helped him railroad his allies and opponents—Chifley once remarked that Playford's tactics had achieved things 'no socialist government could have'.[104] He was backed in hard by *The Advertiser*, whose unofficial policy was to support the government of the day, as Playford dictated news stories and opinions directly to journalists, and regularly conferred with Dumas. One former *Advertiser* editor recalled one of his first jobs as a political roundsman was to walk over to the steps of the Treasury building in Victoria Square at 5.00 pm daily, with a copy of the latest *News* in hand for a very low-key doorstop interview. 'He'd flick through, and I'd say: "Have you got anything to report, Sir Thomas?"'[105]

As Playford's rule entered its second decade, the injustice of his 'Playmander' had been thrown into a harsher light as the metropolitan areas became home to masses of disenfranchised Labor voters. Meanwhile, a young, educated generation of progressives grew tired of the unabashed provincialism with which the state was governed, and of the apparent submission of the Labor leader, Mick O'Halloran. When Rivett arrived in South Australia, he quickly grew familiar with the criticisms of Playford, but admitted to Sir Keith that, despite an 'extraordinarily mediocre' ministry of 'backslapping ciphers', South Australia might have been the 'best governed state in the Commonwealth'.[106]

To date, News Limited had done little to rock the boat; only Murdoch had the clout to resist Dumas's interventions, but he was too far removed, too wary of upsetting his long-time colleagues. 'It would be the worst to do anything threatening, it would put us in their hands,' Murdoch wrote after Rivett suggested he meet with Hayward and threaten to retaliate 'with all weapons' if John Martins' advertising blackout continued. 'We cannot attempt any blackmail of that sort,' Murdoch cautioned.[107]

The deep ties between the city's political and commercial establishment, and a morning paper that seemed happy to exploit its influence with zero accountability, infuriated Rivett. He had waded into a cosy, highly concentrated media landscape that had been entrenched for 20 years. But if Sir Keith was reluctant to push back against the system, there was a good reason: he had helped make it that way. And Sir Lloyd Dumas, the bane of Rivett's life in Adelaide? He was once one of Murdoch's bright young men.

# CHAPTER FOUR

# A pernicious and corrupting monopoly

TECHNICALLY SPEAKING, THE newspaper business in South Australia has been around longer than the colony itself. When copies of its first newspaper, *The South Australian Gazette and Colonial Register*, appeared in the London summer of 1836, even its publishers admitted that their ambition of swiftly publishing a second issue 'in a city of the wilderness of which the site is yet unknown' required an optimism that bordered on 'chimerical'.[1] In the end, it took a whole year for its editor, a London journalist named George Stevenson, to put a second edition to bed. First, after dropping anchor in November 1836, the crew tasked with unloading the settler ship, the *Africaine*, decided to leave Stevenson's specially procured Stanhope press—a heaving apparatus of cast iron and wood—until last.[2] It took ten men to lug it ashore, and by the time Stevenson and his business partner, a Welsh bookseller named Robert Thomas, realised that the precious metal letters needed to typeset the paper were still below deck, it had already set sail to lutruwita (Van Diemen's Land, or Tasmania) on a desperately needed supply run. Scurvy, after all, seemed a slightly more pressing concern than a broadsheet.

Even after the *Africaine* reappeared on the horizon with half a tonne of type rattling among its ballast, it was a bumpy ride. Stevenson and Thomas had brought a printing assistant over from England, but the young man died almost immediately after stepping off the boat, sick and lost in the scrub of Karta Pintingga (known as Kangaroo Island by whalers and settlers).[3] It left *The Register* hopelessly short-staffed, and when printing finally resumed in June 1837, new issues limped out once a month at best. Back in England, the colony's supporters were baffled:

> People ask, where is the much promised newspaper? News, News, News, regular and plentiful, this is the one thing needful to make yours a great colony very soon, believe me.[4]

The note's author, Edward Gibbon Wakefield, spoke from experience: the printed word had been essential to the idea of a South Australian colony since it had first appeared as ink on a page. Curly-haired and mutton-chopped, Wakefield had witnessed its birth in newsletters, essays, and pamphlets that flew out of printing presses and circulated through 19th-century British society, thrust into the hand of the moneyed and the powerful by the cheerleaders and stakeholders who tried to will 'South Australia' into existence. But from the outset, it was a vision that often looked better on paper. At the start (but not the *beginning*; in the deep time of the Australian continent, British colonisation is a turbulent latter chapter in a very long book), South Australia was meant to be a brave new experiment for the empire. Half a century had passed since the First Fleet had arrived in the bays and coves of the Dharawal and Gadigal nations on the east coast, and their story so far had been a bloody and chaotic one, as Christianity and the Crown, gunpowder and grog, Shakespeare, and smallpox all took root in this 'new' land. But in the free colony of South Australia, its supporters promised, things would be different: a clean slate, unmarred by transportation, slavery, massacre, sectarian conflict, and state-sanctioned plunder—all the things that had won Britain its wealth and global influence. The neighbouring colonies might have tied their fortunes to the forced labour of a criminalised underclass, but the people who dreamt up South Australia had a different model.

And Wakefield was one of its chief architects. An enterprising social climber, he had big dreams of land ownership, influence, and perhaps, one day, even political office. His plan to attain them, however, mainly consisted of marrying vulnerable teenage heiresses. When the inheritance from his first wife (Eliza, married at 16 and dead by 21) proved too modest for his ambitions, he lured another well-connected adolescent away from boarding school and tricked her into eloping to Gretna Green. The honeymoon—that is, the *kidnapping*—ended with the marriage annulled by special act of parliament, and the groom thrown into prison. It was from behind bars at Newgate Prison that Wakefield looked towards the colonies, poring over every scrap of reading material he could find. He grew fixated on the overlapping problems of crime, poverty, politics, and colonisation, and in 1829 published a series of anonymous writings collectively known as the 'Letter from Sydney'. Purporting to be written by a frustrated settler in New South Wales, it was published in 11 parts by the London *Morning Chronicle* before being syndicated across the emerging colonial press from Sydney to Hobart. One Tasmanian newspaper labelled its mysterious author 'the best political writer in these colonies', while others wrote it off as 'scraps of political economy, of Jesuitical sophistry, of libel and misrepresentation'.[5] Fake news, in other words.

Wakefield painted an unflattering picture, but he also offered a solution that was part real estate development, part globe-crossing labour-hire scheme, and part back-of-napkin social engineering. Private capital would purchase 'waste' lands from the Crown sight unseen, which in turn would bankroll the new colonial government. The release and pricing of real estate would be carefully controlled to ensure that land ownership—and all corresponding political rights—would remain out of reach of workers or an emerging bourgeoisie. The money paid would fund surveyors, like the Malaya-born Colonel William Light, who would use paper, pencil, rope, and peg to perform the old colonial magic trick of turning unceded lands—in this case, of the Kaurna, Ngarrindjeri, and Peramangk peoples and their neighbours—into sellable parcels of Crown land.

It would also fund the passage of working-class migrants to work the properties these capitalists bought, clean the houses they planned to build, and protect their investments from the Indigenous peoples whose stolen lands they now claimed. By keeping those workers locked out of the market, the colony had a ready-made, self-renewing labour supply.

The plan showed promise: with the British parliament's passage of the Slavery Abolition Act in 1833, private coffers around the empire were flush with government compensation for their now-emancipated slaveholdings. However novel Wakefield's proposition seemed, if you had cash to spare in the mid-1830s there were worse places to invest it—or launder it. Along with a handful of other would-be colonists whose names now appear as streets and towns around South Australia, Wakefield used his pen and words to write the colony into reality. Eventually, it found favour with parliament and the colonial office, and in 1834 Gibbon was responsible for the passage of another act of parliament: the Act to Create the Province of South Australia.

WHEN THE STANHOPE press finally began cranking out copies of *The Register* from its new premises in Colonel Light's freshly mapped city of Adelaide, it only took three issues to stir up trouble. A power struggle had been brewing between governor John Hindmarsh and other colonial officials since they had landed, and *The Register* made perfect kindling. Stevenson wasn't just a newspaperman—he performed his editorial duties while moonlighting from his primary roles as Hindmarsh's private secretary and clerk of the Executive Council. *The Register* printed fierce criticism of the governor's rivals, much of which was written by Stevenson's own wife, Margaret. (Back in England, she had been a music critic for the London *Globe*, which her father edited.) Under the *nomme de plume* of 'A Colonist', she accused the resident commissioner of underhanded tactics in the selling of Crown land, and in return the paper was branded a 'circulating poison through the colony'.[6] Word soon spread to other colonies that the smugly superior South Australian experiment was losing its sheen. 'South Australia has not a free press—it has a tyrant press', reported *The Launceston Advertiser*.[7]

Clearly, Adelaide's days as a one-paper town were numbered. Its second paper, *The Southern Australian*, was born in this storm of outrage, volleying accusations, and the colony's first cases of sedition and libel. Backed by Hindmarsh and Stevenson's opponents, its first issue in June 1838 used fighting words for 'that one Journal' it refused to name: 'It is needless to show that up to this time we have had no Free Press in the Colony', it proclaimed, condemning a 'pernicious and corrupting monopoly' that 'makes a despotic use of its as yet exclusive powers'.[8] *The Southern Australian* was soon joined by a proliferation of new titles—the *Egotist*, *Guardian*, and *Chronicle*—and as the colony snaked up and out from Adelaide, regional titles such as *The Port Lincoln Herald* began to appear. Over the coming decades, dozens upon dozens of titles would emerge and fold, in sync with the ups and downs of the colony's fortunes—or a brush with a particularly damaging libel suit.

In the meantime, the acrimony between Hindmarsh and virtually everyone else in the colony saw the governor recalled and replaced, and Stevenson, now sitting outside the governor's tent, turned critic. He had plenty of material; delays in the surveying process slowed land sales and thus bottlenecked the entire Wakefieldian system. The new governor, George Gawler, responded with public works to occupy the idle workers who continued to arrive by the boatload. Far from a self-sufficient enterprise, the three-year-old colony soon faced financial collapse. Gawler had other problems; in June 1840, a ship carrying 25 passengers was wrecked on a reef off the south-east coast. Those who made it to shore were initially helped by a group of Ngarrindjeri observers, but something went awry on the journey to Adelaide, and the passengers were all killed. Gawler authorised a martial expedition, culminating in the summary hanging of two Ngarrindjeri men, violating the legal rights that had been enshrined in South Australia's founding documents. (By the 1830s, even the British parliament had grown unsettled by reports of violent frontier wars, and insisted that the new colony set a better example.) The snowballing crises saw Gawler recalled to England, but he left Stevenson a parting gift: *The Register* lost its government printing contracts, and a new *Government Gazette* was established, to be printed by his rivals. The paper, now simply titled *The South Australian Register*, was soon bankrupted, and was taken over by a Baptist preacher.

Eventually, *The Register*'s greatest competitor emerged from inside the paper. The Reverend John Henry Barrow was a teacher, preacher, and journalist who juggled pastoral duties with a job as principal leader writer at *The Register*. In July 1858, he abruptly broke away from the paper and his church to embark on two new projects: he would be running for the seat of East Torrens in the upcoming election, and starting his own daily newspaper, *The Advertiser*. When Barrow wound up dead in 1874 — two decades of politics and newspapers had left the now-wizened elder statesman crippled by exhaustion and reliant on opiates to find even a moment's rest — his successor was already getting into position. John Langdon Bonython joined *The Advertiser* as a 16-year-old reporter in 1864, but this son of a Cornish carpenter had ambitions to not only edit the paper, but to own it as well. When Barrow died, Bonython began working his way up from subeditor to junior partner and chief of staff by 1880, before finally seizing the editorship in 1884. Within a decade, he'd paid out Barrow's stepson, and would enjoy absolute control of the paper for nearly 40 years.

Under Bonython's watch, *The Advertiser* became the city's most successful newspaper — by 1886 it had double the circulation of *The Register*, and was soaking up an advertising market pumped by a decade of economic growth.[9] Bonython grew fabulously rich, even if *The Advertiser*'s columns were often filled by freelancers whose work was insecure and poorly compensated, or by overworked staff whom Bonython expected to be on call at all hours of the day, seven days a week.[10]

Nevertheless, for all the miserly instincts he showed towards his employees, Bonython could be a generous philanthropist; by the end of his life, he had used his newspaper fortune to fund a string of major public works, from a £100,000 donation towards the completion of Parliament House, to the construction of the Gothic-inspired Bonython Hall at the University of Adelaide. (One urban legend holds that the Bonython family, dedicated Methodists, insisted that the hall be built with a sloping floor to prevent it being used for dancing.) With his signature walrus-like moustache now long, white, and droopy, Bonython gained a knighthood in 1898, then followed Barrow's lead and entered politics to join 'Honest' Tom Playford in the brand-new federal parliament.

For years, *The Advertiser*'s reign was virtually unchallenged, until a journalist and editor named JE Davidson blew into South Australia, fresh from a feud with Theodore Fink that had ended his seven-year run as editor and general manager of the Melbourne *Herald*. The son of a miner and station worker, Davidson had built a respectable career in journalism with a five-year stint at *The West Australian*, then nine years at the Melbourne *Argus*, before joining the Herald and Weekly Times.[11] Over seven years, Davidson made great strides in modernising the paper, laying the groundwork for Keith Murdoch's later success, before his relationship with Fink soured beyond repair in 1918.

Davidson resurfaced a year later in South Australia, where he had taken over the 22-year-old *Port Pirie Recorder* and 31-year-old *Barrier Miner*, just over the New South Wales border in Broken Hill. Then, in July 1922, Davidson's papers announced the formation of a new company that would absorb both *The Recorder* and *Barrier Miner*, and introduce a new afternoon daily, *The News*.[12] The new company would be called News Limited, and in March 1923 it bought the Sunday paper, *The Mail*, and the goodwill to the city's two existing afternoon papers, *The Advertiser*-aligned *Express* (founded in 1863) and *The Register*-aligned *Journal* (founded in 1869). They both printed their final editions on 23 July 1923, the day before the first edition of *The News* rolled off the press with the promise of an 'independent attitude' and a 'powerful voice in the three centres most essential to the prosperity and wellbeing of South Australia'.[13]

Like Bonython, and later Keith Murdoch, just how a working journalist such as Davidson came to possess the capital for these ventures is something of a mystery—it's unlikely that his payout from *The Herald* would have covered his 1919 acquisition spree, let alone the two afternoon titles he shuttered to make way for *The News*. The company's official line recounts a folksy origin story of Davidson hatching the idea of News Limited on the train with an acquaintance named Gerald Mussen. A journalist, one-time gold miner, and public relations expert, Mussen had been hired as a 'consulting industrialist' by Broken Hill Associated Smelters (a subsidiary of the Broken Hill Proprietary Company—BHP) to improve conditions and mollify growing unrest among workers at Port Pirie and Broken Hill in the post-war period.[14] Historian Sally Young poses an interesting origin theory; her analysis of what limited paper trail remains suggests that Davidson may have been quietly backed, via proxies, by his old *Herald* colleague William Baillieu and his associates at Collins House—the Melbourne address that served as a base for a cluster of overlapping corporate and mining enterprises, including Broken Hill Associated Smelters.[15] Both Port Pirie and Broken Hill were home to a growing workers' movement bolstered by a strong labour press, and building up alternative outlets that were supportive of, or even neutral about, mine managers' interests would have made a sound investment.[16]

Whatever the true nature of Davidson's backers, News Limited's tendency to appear uncomfortably in step with corporate and mining interests raised eyebrows at the time; in October 1924, *Smith's Weekly* claimed that 'Adelaide's evening paper, *The News*, seems to be filling ably the role of official or unofficial apologist for the BHP.'[17] Workers at the Port Pirie smelters had been advocating for a wage increase, and Mussen was once again representing their employers in the Arbitration Court. *The News*, which still counted its co-founder Mussen as a major shareholder and director, had reported Mussen's dire warning that higher wages would cause the 'extinction of the lead smelting industry' as locally mined raw materials were sent offshore for processing instead.[18] When Mussen cited *The News'* reporting, which in turn parroted his own claims, the deputy president of the Arbitration Court was unimpressed. He thundered that if the articles 'were written with the intention of influencing the Court, then it was an abuse of the privilege of the press ... it would not be done by any paper with a pretence to be an organ of public opinion'.[19]

THEN, IN 1928, Keith Murdoch arrived in Adelaide, fronting a syndicate that openly included Baillieu, Fink, and the Herald and Weekly Times. They had set their sights on Bonython's cash cow, and when Sir John baulked at their opening £1.5 million offer, they instead approached the Thomases—the descendants of *The Register*'s co-founder, who had reclaimed proprietorship in the 1870s. The syndicate bought and overhauled the 93-year-old paper, and quickly boosted its circulation—though not enough to turn a profit, or to significantly impact *The Advertiser*'s circulation. Murdoch explicitly wanted to avoid 'material damage' to *The Advertiser*—the point was to simply spook the ageing Bonython enough to sell it to him.[20]

*The Register* had been the more conservative of the city's papers, but under its new owners became a tabloid. 'This really shocked Adelaide,' recalled Harry Plumridge, a journalist recruited by Murdoch's syndicate to work on the retitled *Register News-Pictorial*.[21] Bonython rose to the bait and finally sold his stake to the Melbourne syndicate, but, having spent decades in control, had trouble letting go. To oversee the peaceful transition of power after 36 years of Bonython rule, Murdoch sent a 37-year-old named Lloyd Dumas.

A stout man with thick-rimmed glasses and pale skin that was often flushed red around the cheeks, Dumas was the son of yet another South Australian publisher-slash-politician. (His father founded and edited *The Mount Barker Courier* in 1880, and represented the state seat of Mount Barker from 1898 to 1902.) During the war, he moved to *The Argus* in Melbourne, where he became friendly with newly installed and publicity-hungry prime minister Billy Hughes. When Hughes began his two failed conscription campaigns, Dumas joined him as a press secretary and stenographer, travelling around Australia and the United Kingdom. (Dumas was by Hughes' side when an anti-conscriptionist pelted the prime minister with an egg—the closest thing Australia had seen to a prime ministerial assassination attempt.)[22] Like Murdoch, his relationship with the irritable and demanding Hughes eventually broke down, and Dumas found work back in Australia with Murdoch's old employer Hugh Denison as he launched *The Sun-Pictorial*—a new competitor to *The Herald*. When Denison eventually agreed to sell it to the Herald and Weekly Times, Dumas spent long nights at Murdoch's bachelor pad as the pair worked out the details of the merger before it went public.[23] He then moved to London in 1927, accepting an offer from Murdoch to take up his old job running *The Herald*'s cable service, before being lured back to

Adelaide and his original stomping ground, *The Advertiser*.

Murdoch told Dumas to be 'extremely tactful'; despite agreeing to sell, Bonython had no plans to relinquish control, and he ignored Murdoch's hints that someone else might be brought in to assist the handover.[24] Bonython assumed he would be appointed editor for a further two years, even as Murdoch was orchestrating Dumas's arrival. In July 1929, he warned Dumas:

> [Bonython] is now in a peculiar position in the organization. He was such an autocrat that his position as Chairman became intolerable. It would be a pity for the newspaper if his influence were hostile or semi hostile, and moreover, he has a great fund of wisdom and knowledge … sentimentally I could not bring myself to the point of being unsympathetic or unkind to him. He would probably die if he were removed from the paper.[25]

It didn't help that the pair had a history: Dumas had got his start as a 16-year-old *Advertiser* cadet, thanks to a deal between his father and Bonython. 'When I resigned [in 1915], Sir Langdon was extremely bitter,' Dumas told Murdoch in May 1929.[26] 'He also probably remembers me as a boy reporter, and cannot imagine that I have grown up and matured in the intervening years.' Murdoch asked Dumas to 'humour and use the old man and bend to his will when such bending is doing no injury to the journal'.[27] When Dumas and his family sailed into Outer Harbor, *The Mail* reported that he had come to assume control of the paper — which was apparently news to an incensed Bonython.

It didn't take long for Bonython to be finally shown the door, retiring from newspapers at the ripe old age of 83. A year later, on 1 June 1930, Davidson died, alone and surrounded by empty bottles in a London hotel room — he had fallen on hard times, with a hidden drinking problem and a string of recent bereavements. (His brother and son had died in quick succession.)[28] Murdoch swooped in, scooping up shares in News Limited from Davidson's family on behalf of the Herald and Weekly Times and Advertiser Newspapers (the public company he had founded in the takeover from Bonython), and by November 1931 he was on News Limited's board of directors.[29]

The onset of the Great Depression in 1929 eventually killed *The Register News-Pictorial*, which cited 'economic conditions' as it announced its own demise on 20 February 1931.[30] On the front page of the final edition ran a photograph of the old Stanhope press hauled off the *Africaine* all those years earlier—its hulking iron frame was now literally a museum piece, held in one of the sandstone institutions that had sprung up along North Terrace in the intervening century.[31] Murdoch's syndicate had used the city's first and oldest newspaper as a pawn in their attempt to invade South Australia, but now that its purpose was achieved, the paper was quietly amalgamated into *The Advertiser* just a few years shy of its centenary.

Keith Murdoch's Melbourne syndicate had achieved a rare thing: they now owned Adelaide's major morning and afternoon newspapers, and the high-circulation Sunday paper *The Mail*. It was a level of press concentration unseen since those early days when George Stevenson was savaged in letters complaining of 'partial and garbled articles' and a poisonous monopoly.[32] With Bonython deposed and Dumas installed at its head, *The Advertiser*, News Limited, and the Herald and Weekly Times were poised to entrench their influence on South Australian public life over the next two decades. *The Register* was dead, but for the first time in almost a century, Adelaide was once again a one-paper town—in practice, at least. Just a few weeks later, across the Victorian border, Keith Rupert Murdoch was born.

## CHAPTER FIVE

# Palace revolution

TODAY, IT'S HARD to form a full picture of just what happened on the morning of 3 October 1952, when the five members of the Herald and Weekly Times board converged upon Flinders Street. In 1970, Rohan Rivett wrote that 'when Sir John Williams tells the full story of the last weeks of his relationship with his old chief and mentor, it will open many eyes'. 'It may prove a better story than the rise and fall of most Prime Ministers,' he predicted.[1] Williams never did; like everyone else in the room that day, he is long dead, and the official records that survive only tell half the story. For the best part of 30 years, Sir Keith had the run of the old Colin Ross memorial from the ground floor to mahogany row. But since he had begun to hand over power in the final weeks of 1949, there had been a realignment, and one way or another this Friday-morning meeting would be the ultimate test of where he stood. Williams didn't have a vote on the board, but as the man who, for all intents and purposes, ran the company, his presence was usually uncontroversial — essential, even. But as the meeting got underway, Williams was left cooling his heels in his office, pointedly snubbed.[2]

Despite never committing his story to paper, Williams would on occasion tell colleagues what happened next. When he was finally summoned into the boardroom, it was Sir Keith, the man who was supposed to have entered semi-retirement two years before, who had somehow survived two cancer scares and a heart attack, who had spent months away from the office, and whose self-interested scheming had become an open secret among the company's upper echelons, who told Williams that *his* time was up.[3] Williams took it all in, then spoke with barely concealed fury: 'Alright, I'll go, but it's going to cost you plenty.'[4] Murdoch suspected it would not be the last he heard of Williams; but for now, he had completed another difficult, delicate boardroom purge—his third since he had joined *The Herald*. And, just like in 1921, and then in 1933, he was once again the last man standing. He would not, like Lord Northcliffe, Theodore Fink, or Sir John Langdon Bonython, be gradually forced out of his own company—even if the company wasn't his, technically speaking. After the meeting, he drove out to Cruden Farm to spend the weekend with Elisabeth, read through the latest correspondence from his children, and breathe in all that spring air.

LESS THAN FOUR months earlier, in the winter of 1952, Sir Keith had been basking in sunshine. In May, he had gone under the knife again—for his prostate this time—but by all accounts, the operation was a success. After leaving hospital, he and Lady Elisabeth retreated north to Surfer's Paradise, a sun-kissed resort town on Queensland's fast-developing Gold Coast, and for a few fleeting weeks in June the Murdochs seemed to be living in a blissful bubble. Ocean views greeted them at every window, and clean, white sand came right up to the door.[5] He was, as a rule, a difficult patient who rarely followed doctor's orders, but on this trip he had actually made an effort to neither work nor worry.[6] The beach reminded him of California, all beauty, sunshine, and friendliness, as he spent his days reading, sleeping, swimming, and eating. His mood was further lifted by an influx of correspondence from Oxford—even if it had taken a broken ankle for Rupert to finally sit down and write home.[7]

Of course, going cold turkey on a decades-long newspaper habit was out of the question; Sir Keith carefully studied the local paper, his own *Courier-Mail*, had the Adelaide office send him copies of

*The News*, *The Advertiser*, and *The Mail*, and pored over the latest circulation numbers. 'I am really on top of things,' Murdoch wrote to his secretary, Eileen Demello, on 8 June, after a morning spent wading in the surf.[8] For the unrepentant workaholic, even a few days' inactivity felt strange, but after years of wringing all he could out of every waking moment, even he had to admit that slowing down had its benefits—he was feeling better than he had in four years. Elisabeth declared it the 'best holiday' she had ever had.[9]

But while Sir Keith was swimming in sub-tropical waters off Queensland, a tide had been turning—and now the Caesar nickname seemed worryingly prophetic. Murdoch's physical presence at Flinders Street had been key to his control of the company, and even after he stepped down from the chairmanship, there was rarely a day when he wasn't in the office. But that kind of soft power can dissipate with absence, and the weeks and months he'd spent in convalescence or overseas had a cumulative effect. When he was there, he seemed increasingly distant. Once, when asking a *Herald* staffer about her mother, the answer—that she had died two years earlier—simply didn't seem to register with Sir Keith. 'Tell her to give Miss Demello a ring,' he said, inviting the dead woman to afternoon tea anyway.[10]

A vacuum was being created on the third floor at Flinders Street, and Jack Williams had slowly but surely filled the void. His closest associates began to coalesce around him in an exclusive clique, vanishing behind closed doors or in drinking sessions away from the office.[11] Meanwhile, executives who appeared to be Murdoch men, such as Bill Dunstan, found themselves increasingly frozen out. In early July, shortly after returning to the office, Sir Keith confronted Williams, and over two long discussions told the editor about the 'good deal of unhappiness that [Murdoch] and other directors felt stemmed from him'.[12] He waved extracts from a letter by another senior executive that noted a troubling 'drift' in the *Herald* office, one that bordered on 'disintegration'. The situation had grown so dire, he said, that several of Williams' colleagues were on the cusp of resigning.[13]

In a private memorandum sent to his fellow company directors on 10 July, Sir Keith replayed the encounter with Williams. He didn't mention Williams' drinking, but was otherwise unsparing: 'The great difficulty is that he is so hasty in decisions and statements, is brusquely dictatorial, and has not got a good editorial touch.'[14] Without a hint of irony, he complained that Williams' 'dictatorial' tendencies made it 'impossible to influence the Editorial side to any marked extent'.[15] Others, he said, found Williams 'tough and rough', and Murdoch himself felt the paper was suffering as a result.[16] In an additional note sent to one of his closest board members, Murdoch recounted telling Williams that he 'personally would no longer be associated with the papers whilst their meretricious aspects were being so patently supported by him'.[17] Williams seemed surprised by the charges laid against him, which he claimed were 'unfounded and inaccurate', but told Murdoch that his position seemed untenable in light of his colleagues' comments.[18] Murdoch seemed unconvinced that Williams would walk, but grew increasingly resolute: he had to go. 'I'm afraid I can see no way in which Mr Williams can be kept here with final success for the company,' he confided to one colleague in July.[19]

Williams, of course, hadn't been totally unjustified in freezing Murdoch out. Sir Keith was supposed to be in a kind of semi-retirement, even if his constant presence in the office said otherwise. According to one colleague, Williams had also stumbled upon a document spelling out all the numbers and strategic moves for one of Murdoch's side projects—one that ran directly counter to *The Herald*'s interests.[20] Beyond the Queensland and Adelaide papers, Murdoch had explored the possibility of acquiring the Melbourne *Argus*, which had recently been bought by Northcliffe's nephew Cecil Harmsworth King. But King was now looking to sell, and for Murdoch the paper not only presented a strong, established foothold in the Melbourne market, but also held a generous allocation of newsprint in what was still a tightly rationed supply chain.[21] It would have proved a tempting third column for this new, independent Murdoch chain, with a base in three states and space to grow. But, like the mooted *Smith's Weekly* bid, the idea stalled. Both King and Murdoch probably realised that a deal hinging on the personal knowledge and skills of an ageing newspaperman, who was about to have a tumour removed, was not wise for either party. With the previously unthinkable prospect of Murdoch leaving *The Herald* for a crosstown rival once again relegated to a hypothetical scenario, retaining his control over Flinders Street remained essential.

One way or another, there was a showdown looming on Flinders Street, and whatever the outcome, Murdoch needed every ally he had on the board—especially Sir Lloyd Dumas. It was Dumas who sent the June letter that Murdoch showed to Williams in their fiery confrontation. It was Dumas who gave legitimacy to Murdoch's charges of 'drift' and 'disintegration'. It was Dumas who backed Murdoch decisively. ('I am sure not one member of the board would hear of your retirement,' he wrote in the June letter. '… we all realise the final responsibility must come back on you'.)[22] And it was Dumas whose vote Murdoch would need in the Herald and Weekly Times boardroom if it all came to a head. After 25 years, Dumas was not the kind of ally that Murdoch could afford to alienate—even if it meant undermining the frustrated young editor-in-chief he had left behind in Adelaide.

WHILE THE MURDOCHS basked in sunshine, Rohan Rivett was cold and depressed as he suffered through his first Adelaide winter. 'For the third day it is as cold as charity here,' he noted on 23 May 1952, as a perfect storm of torrential rains, cancelled flights, and a ban on overtime by union workers at a local power station caused circulation to go backwards. One particularly bad day saw circulation fall by 1,300, when Rivett needed it to rise by 500.[23] Industrial action at the power station didn't only cut sales of *The News* at the factory gate—it ensured that everyone was feeling the chill. 'All radiators are forbidden everywhere because of this confounded overtime ban and everybody is miserable with cold,' Rivett complained.[24]

Six months had passed since his arrival, and he was now an official member of the News Limited board, had left the hotel and reunited with his family, and was gradually chipping away at the company's papers and culture. But he remained frustrated by the deep-set inertia around him, from the subeditors' room to the company's lawyer, who, Rivett complained, was 'notorious for his constant attacks on the press'.[25]

But nothing pained him more than the behaviour of Sir Lloyd Dumas and *The Advertiser*. The strange relationship between *The News*' owner and the Melbourne chain that owned his rivals continued to surface in new and infuriating ways. Shortly after arriving, Rivett had tried to recruit a 'first-rate layout man and headline expert' to compensate for his own technical limitations, but there was a problem: the man in question, James Wilson, was already working at *The Herald*, and Williams seemed reluctant to let him go. Rivett was insistent—he needed the help badly, and even threatened Murdoch with an ultimatum of his own if he couldn't make it happen. Williams claimed ignorance when approached by Sir Keith, and said that if *The News* began taking *Herald* men, they would begin poaching theirs.[26] Sir Keith insisted 'that *The Herald* had already taken *News* men with [his] consent and that there could be a free two-way traffic as far as *The News* is concerned'.[27] Williams eventually relented, but the tension of the exchange reflected the uneasy limbo that Rivett and *The News* existed in. Rivett had been tasked with making *The News* competitive again, but every effort to actually compete against *The Advertiser* was trumped or discouraged. And it only got worse.

At the end of August, Rivett wrote a long letter to Sir Keith after a syndication deal with *The Herald* was upturned at the eleventh hour by Dumas's intervention:

> At this stage, *The Advertiser* having been beaten to the punch in the whole business by a clear six weeks, Sir Lloyd appeals to the *Herald* hierarchy to unglue the whole arrangement with us disregarding their firm contract. This sort of thing has happened before and will happen again. It is ethically wrong and makes nonsense of any contract into which the *Herald* enters with us.
>
> Believe me, I do understand how desperately awkward it is for you with the *Herald* chairmanship of the *Herald-Advertiser* link. But the present position whereby Sir Lloyd can always go to the *Herald* hierarchy and break *Herald-News* agreements is totally unfair to us here.[28]

Rivett floated another bold move, suggesting that *The News* cut virtually all ties with *The Herald*. Even as he was writing the letter, Rivett must have known what the answer would be:

A fundamental point with *The News*. *The Herald* gives us an infinite amount of good things. We would be sorely tried indeed without it. We get the run of our teeth over all its Australian news services. We draw everything except South Australian news from it! Our teleprinter from The *Herald* office carries an immensity of matter for us. Where else could we get it?[29]

The South Australian material that *The News* sent to Melbourne was, on the other hand, 'not one tenth of the importance of our matter to us from them'. It was the kind of argument that, if seen by Williams and other members of the Flinders Street hierarchy, might raise eyebrows—why indeed was *The Herald* still party to such a one-sided deal with a paper in competition with its own South Australian interests?

Instead, Murdoch continued to encourage Rivett to look inside News Limited to make changes. The paper, as he saw it, still needed a lot of work. When Rivett was away for a handful of days, Murdoch said the issues produced in his absence were 'amongst the worst I have read'.[30] 'Frankly, Rohan, we can't stand that sort of work and I am afraid your staff needs some changes. The contrast between *The News* of those dates and *The Advertiser* is so serious it could not go on.' While Murdoch would occasionally pass on a watered-down version of Rivett's latest gripe, the fact that Murdoch and Dumas were in competition with each other in Adelaide barely registered in their correspondence. In the June letter about Williams, Murdoch added a postscript casually mentioning that '*The News* is doing well but is incredibly handicapped by inadequate revenues.'[31]

As the elder Murdoch reined Rivett in, the editor continued to exchange letters with his son, Rupert, back in England. 'Your father looks very well—vastly better since the operation and the Queensland convalescence, but, of course, he still overdoes things,' Rivett wrote in September 1952.[32] 'His mind is like an ice-pick, delving straight to the heart of every problem immediately and as you know sometimes into 16 problems in a quarter of an hour.' Sir Keith had just completed a rare in-person tour of his News Limited holdings, briefly visiting *The Barrier Miner* in Broken Hill and then pressing on to Rivett in

Adelaide. It was a somewhat historic event; in the years since he'd taken ownership, Murdoch had been a fleeting presence on North Terrace, preferring to send emissaries such as Colin Bednall, and now his man on the ground, Rivett. Upon Murdoch's arrival, a grand dinner was held with several dozen of the company's subeditors and staffers, and it had been a 'howling success'.[33]

Rivett told Rupert that Sir Keith had been in 'magnificent form' as he regaled the staff with stories from the annals of newspaper history. He reminisced about the early days of News Limited, when JE Davidson first came over to Broken Hill and Port Pirie, and, as the night wore on, reached further back into his memory, revisiting many of his own greatest hits that had, over three decades, taken on the status of a personal legendarium. There was the story of Gallipoli, the dispatches Sir Keith sent back to Fisher, the subsequent evacuation at Gallipoli, and a clean-out at the highest levels of British government and command. He even shed light on some of his formative battles in the Australian newspaper world, from his early days on *The Age* to how he 'frustrated the attempt by Fink to throw him out of *The Herald* (one time when the Jews met their master),' Rivett repeated, echoing the sectarian prejudices that coloured many of Sir Keith's rivalries, much like Northcliffe before him.[34]

'It would be very difficult to exaggerate how much I've learnt from him in these past pretty hectic 10 months,' Rivett reflected of his 'teacher and guide, friend and philosopher':

> He has been extraordinarily patient with my many obvious ignorances and stupidities and very tolerant when I get perhaps unduly excited about minor triumphs. He always says he owes a lot to Northcliffe. I can't imagine that Northcliffe was one-tenth as good to him or as wise and helpful in guidance as he has been to much less promising material.[35]

At the end of the visit, Rohan found himself, as he had in July 1951, driving Sir Keith back to another high-end hotel—this time it was the South Australian, a North Terrace establishment that had hosted the likes of HG Wells, Marlene Dietrich, and Anna Pavlova.

In the car, Sir Keith promised him a pay-rise, and then offered a backhanded compliment. 'Don't think it is because you are not still making all the mistakes about the place,' he said, 'but because I would rather have somebody making mistakes in trying to do things than somebody sitting on his backside hoping that people would carry the show for him.'[36] It was a conversation that stayed with Rivett for years.

Just as he had in London, Rivett continued to encourage Rupert's journalistic ambitions. From 16,000 kilometres away, he prodded Rupert to write articles for *The News* about the various travels and misadventures that had distracted him from his studies. 'If you do a really good one on this I will be very happy to increase your bank account,' he said after pitching a story on the 'lighter side of undergraduate life'.[37] 'To a man who has won £88 in a sitting at roulette this may sound a small inducement, but think of the fame of a by-line on *The News* centre pages,' Rivett said, with perhaps a hint of sarcasm.

In late September, Rupert finally caved, and headed to Morecambe, a resort town on the Lancashire coast that was hosting the annual conference of the British Labour Party. It was a good excuse for a seaside holiday and perhaps a bit of networking, but Rupert also planned to put on his reporter's hat. 'By all means,' Rivett replied, 'if there is a really hot story which will stand up to the basic tenet that 95 per cent of News Limited readers won't know and won't care that there's a Labor Party conference on in Great Britain.'[38] In the end, Rupert's cabled notes from the trip informed an article, published under Rivett's by-line, that announced the party's 'lunge to the left' under the 'man of the moment'—an up-and-coming Welsh politician named Aneurin Bevan, who Rupert had previously described to Ben Chifley as 'the most prominent, brilliant and able of the Left wing'.[39] On 2 October 1952, the day before the fateful boardroom showdown between Sir Keith and Jack Williams, Rohan also forwarded Rupert's original report to the Murdoch family home, where it sat among a bundle of letters for Sir Keith to read over the weekend at Cruden Farm.[40]

UP IN QUEENSLAND, Colin Bednall was insulated from the worst of the Melbourne intrigue. He would later claim naive ignorance as to his own place in the Flinders Street rumblings, but to some observers it seemed that if the situation with Williams continued towards its explosive endpoint, Bednall was in pole position to succeed Sir Keith at *The Herald*.[41] Instead, the reality was sheeted home to him during a visit to the Canberra in the first week of October 1952. He had been invited to a dinner at the Prime Minister's Lodge, and the next day made his way to Parliament House to check in with some elected members he was on friendly terms with. Arthur Calwell was certainly not one of them; the deputy leader of the Labor opposition was no friend to Bednall, or indeed anyone associated with Sir Keith Murdoch. For years, Calwell had been one of Murdoch's loudest and bitterest critics in parliament and the labour movement—to him, Sir Keith was a 'megalomaniac' who he despised and resented for seducing Joe Lyons, destroying the Scullin Labor government, and building an empire on the 'exploitation of human misery'.[42] When prime minister Robert Menzies appointed Murdoch as director-general of information during World War II, Calwell complained that Murdoch was now dictating government policy and stacking the department with employees of his papers. In April 1941, he told parliament that the Murdoch press was 'public enemy no. 1 of the liberties of the Australian people'.[43]

Calwell sent a message that he would like to meet with Bednall, and while Bednall expected a cool reception, the level of animosity astonished him. Behind closed doors in the private office of Labor leader Dr HV Evatt, Calwell delivered a startling threat: 'Within a year we will be back in power. One of our first actions will be to have you shipped off for frontline duty in Korea.'[44] It was an outlandish threat, but as he walked over to unlock the door, Calwell said something else that floored Bednall even more:

Perhaps I shouldn't be too hard on you. I know you and Jack Williams are plotting to get rid of old Murdoch and I expect things will be better for the Labor party when you do so.[45]

Bednall didn't know quite what to make of the comment—certainly, he had not been conspiring *with* Williams, but whatever the source of Calwell's claim, perhaps it had assumed he was as keen to unseat his long-term mentor as Williams was. It was certainly possible that Calwell had an ear to the gossip of Melbourne's newspaper industry—he'd also considered making a bid for *The Argus*, and reinventing it as a Labor Party mouthpiece with none other than Jack Williams as editor.[46] It's equally plausible that Calwell was simply stirring the pot, opportunistically sowing chaos in the backyard of an old nemesis. In his own autobiography, Calwell claims to have seen Murdoch around the time of his run-in with Bednall; despite everything, the pair had maintained a cordial relationship since the war years, but it exploded again when Murdoch wrote a column accusing Calwell of 'mak[ing] a goat of himself'.[47] Murdoch dismissed Calwell's demand for a retraction, and when they next crossed paths in 1952, Calwell called out across the hallway of federal parliament, 'You bloody old scoundrel!'[48] A few hours later, he walked out the doors of the Labor wing of parliament and saw Murdoch again, gazing up at the painted portrait of Lyons—the onetime kingmaker surveying his fallen king. When Murdoch looked up and saw Calwell, he fixed him with 'eyes of hate'.[49]

After his scrap with Calwell, Bednall abandoned plans to travel to Sydney and instead flew immediately to Melbourne, where he quietly met Sir Keith at the family's Toorak manor and filled him in. 'I said I found it offensive that Calwell could say I was a party to some sordid palace revolution and I wanted to return to the relative purity of a Fleet Street life,' he later wrote.[50] Piecing together the exact timeline of these exchanges is murky; Calwell places his and Murdoch's parliamentary staring competition in early October 1952, on the same day that Murdoch was in Melbourne sacking Williams. Bednall, on the other hand, offers a far more detailed breakdown, but puts his brush with Calwell a day earlier, on Thursday 2 October. It seems likely, however, that Calwell's comment to Bednall, swiftly relayed to Murdoch the day before the board meeting, was the factor that made Murdoch pull the trigger on 3 October—or at the very least, steadied his hand.

After lunch at Toorak, Murdoch invited Bednall to drive down to

Langwarrin to spend the weekend at Cruden Farm, perhaps to discuss the redrawn playing field on Flinders Street. He politely declined; some artist friends were throwing a party in his honour in Sydney on Saturday night, and, after a few tense days, he knew whose company he preferred. The party was wild, and when he woke up on Sunday morning he could feel himself paying the price. 'I feel so terrible this morning,' he said, turning to his wife, 'that if anything important were to happen I could not cope with it'.[51] Then the phone rang.

FOR LADY ELISABETH, as much as for Sir Keith, September 1952 had been filled with stress and worry—about money, about his health, about the situation at *The Herald*. They had hoped to travel to London the following June to attend the coronation of the 25-year-old Queen Elizabeth II—if Keith's health and work allowed it. They still had a 'whale' of debt to deal with, but for the moment there was some stability.[52] Williams was gone, Sir Keith's power at *The Herald* was once again unquestioned, and he still had the Adelaide and Brisbane shows. Before the operation in May, when the *Argus* deal was dead in the water, he sent Demello a to-do list that included the purchase of a further 20,000 A Preference shares in Queensland Newspapers to be held on behalf of News Limited, and a further 5,818 in his own name.[53] It meant shouldering another £16,300 of debt, but bolstered his controlling stake in the *Courier-Mail* even in the event of a new share issue. 'That will enable me to complete this business!' he told her.[54] If Rivett could just avoid inflaming the situation in Adelaide, perhaps *The News* could help pay down the debt.

Murdoch had even been to see his doctor on Thursday, who had given him an optimistic prognosis—the doctor seemed positively delighted. After a day spent enjoying the peace and quiet of the garden that Elisabeth had been nurturing at Cruden, Murdoch turned his attention to his children. He wrote a warm letter to his daughter Anne, now at boarding school herself. He thought about Helen, and her newborn baby boy—another generation of Murdochs already taking shape. Most excitingly, there was more word from Rupert. They hadn't heard from him for three weeks, and the house staff had become familiar with Murdoch' hopeful, daily refrain—'nothing in from Rupert?'—and the disappointment that usually followed. Elisabeth never forgot the letter, which buoyed her husband's spirits.[55] Rupert had written about his visit to Morecambe on Rivett's commission, and while his parents couldn't agree with all of his political observations, he finally seemed to be showing the promise his father had spent the last four years preparing for. 'It was heaven-sent,' Elisabeth said of the letter, which, in Sir Keith's eyes, 'spelt out this wonderful news to him that Rupert really had it, and that he was going to develop into the useful sort of person he hoped he would be. He told me that he could see daylight.'[56]

That night, he followed his usual routine, methodically taking off his watch and placing it on the bedside table. Shortly after, he let out a groan, and breathed his last breath. He had run out of time. Now it would all be up to Rupert—if there was anything left to inherit by the time he got back to Australia.

# CHAPTER SIX

# Cunning old bastards

BARELY SIX MONTHS had passed since his father's death, and Rupert Murdoch was under siege. He had missed the funeral, held out little hope of passing his final exams at Oxford, and, back in Australia, his father's colleagues and rivals were descending on his inheritance like seagulls on a bag of chips. And he had just turned 22. For the funeral, at least, he could once again rely on the support of Rohan Rivett—who now found himself reporting to just one Keith Murdoch instead of two. Hundreds of mourners had gathered beneath the towering sandstone of the Toorak Presbyterian Church for the afternoon service, and many hundreds more spilled silently into the breezy October air outside. Navigating the crush of black-clad bodies and cedar pews, Rohan slid into position just behind the four Murdoch women: Rupert's mother, Lady Elisabeth, and sisters Janet, Anne, and Helen. Helen was now Mrs Geoffrey Handbury, and it was in this same church, two years earlier, that Sir Keith had been a proud father of the bride walking his eldest daughter down the aisle on a crisp autumn day.[1] It was a happier time; a day of broad smiles, white satin and tulle, top hats, and morning suits. Now, it was just mourning.

The ground outside the church was carpeted with enough tributes to fill six carloads, but it was all little consolation. Lady Elisabeth was still in a state of stunned bereavement, and behind the brave face of sweetness and generosity, Rivett could sense a 'steel-like quality'.[2] She would later regret not standing firm and delaying the funeral until Rupert could make it, but it had spiralled out of her hands — the company that Sir Keith had never owned in life was now determined to take ownership of his death.[3] Within days, the powers at Flinders Street had orchestrated a state funeral in everything but name. Her own contribution was a simpler one: as the flowers and wreathes piled up outside, she insisted that the only tributes inside the church be a single vase of white lilac, her husband's favourite, and her own hand-made wreath of lilac, lily of the valley, and red and white roses picked from their garden at home.[4] As Rivett looked over at the surviving Murdoch family, now missing both its patriarch and only son and brother, he felt a lump in his throat that seemed to grow bigger with every glance in their direction.[5] Soon, he couldn't look bear to look at all.

All around them, delegations from federal, state, and international governments jostled for space alongside representatives from every metropolitan broadsheet and newspaper union. Packer, Baillieu, Syme, Henderson, Campbell — all the big names — were present. This was a day on which the hot-blooded rivalries of the newspaper world were briefly set aside.[6] As the final hymns were sung, Sir Keith's Union Jack-draped coffin was hoisted aloft and spirited away by a collection of high-profile pallbearers. Leading the procession was senator John Spicer, attorney-general in the Menzies government, and a string of Sir Keith's Herald and Weekly Times colleagues. Long-time allies such as Sir Lloyd Dumas and Harry Giddy — chairman of the National Bank of Australia, a Herald and Weekly Times director, and now the executor of Sir Keith's estate — were obvious inclusions, but among the other newspaperman shouldering a share of the casket was none other than Jack Williams.

Less than a week had passed since Sir Keith had convinced the board to sack his onetime successor, but now it was as if that final board meeting had never happened. As soon as he'd heard the news, Williams had workmen break open the safe in Murdoch's office, seizing the paperwork that made plain Sir Keith's extra-curricular activities.[7] Faced with a leadership vacuum, and an awkward situation to boot, Williams had been quietly reinstated in a hastily convened board meeting, and any mention of his firing was scrubbed from the previous minutes.[8] It's hard to imagine any circumstances in which Sir Keith would have approved of this chain of events, but as Williams helped carry him from the church, he was in no position to object.

Such ironies did not make *The News'* front-page report, filed just in time for the afternoon edition. Instead, it spoke reverentially of the carloads of floral tributes, and the three-kilometre-long motorcade that tailed the hearse and its cargo to a crematorium several suburbs over—its route passing by the Murdoch family's Toorak home along the way.[9] 'They were all absolutely stoic,' Rivett told Rupert, who would touch down in Melbourne the following Saturday—four days after the funeral. 'It was a tremendous family triumph, they would have made your father very happy'.[10]

Sir Keith might have been less pleased, however, with what came next. In March 1953, the matter of the family's Queensland holdings—and what needed to be sold off to cover death duties and Sir Keith's outstanding debts—was still being settled. The task of liquidating the vast sweep of property he had amassed over decades had taken months. In February, the Toorak house—a 20-room Georgian manor that Murdoch had bought from the Baillieu family—raised £35,000 at auction, and in March his collection of antiques went under the hammer.[11] Like a magpie, Sir Keith had feathered the family nest with hundreds upon hundreds of glimmering antique pieces collected on his travels; crateloads of rare Chinese pottery from the Han, Tang, and Song dynasties that were as old as 206 BC sat alongside first-century Roman glass and the largest collection of Chippendale and Hepplewhite furniture in the southern hemisphere.[12] Most of it had to go. Eventually, the 13,000-acre Booroomba estate would raise another £122,500, but the sale wouldn't be finalised until November. Despite Sir Keith's final efforts, the Murdoch estate remained stretched.

As the family followed Sir Keith's final instructions to sacrifice the furniture to save the newspapers, Sir Lloyd Dumas reached out to the widowed Lady Elisabeth.[13] In his capacity as Advertiser Newspapers' chairman, a position he owed to her late husband, Dumas frankly informed her that *The Advertiser* would soon be officially re-entering Adelaide's Sunday market. It was a move that posed a direct challenge to News Limited's *The Mail*, then South Australia's highest-circulation newspaper, and risked snuffing out the legacy that Sir Keith had been so intent on building. Such a contest, Dumas warned, would almost certainly break *The Mail* financially, but also posed a more existential risk: *The Mail*'s hitherto unopposed reign over Sunday morning had allowed News Limited to tie its advertising contracts to *The News*, making Sunday an essential piece of News Limited's balance sheet across the entire week. To lose the weekend could mean losing everything.

But he also proposed an alternative: the family could spare themselves the ordeal, and leave behind the stress and endless, daily grind of newspaper production that had consumed Sir Keith's final years, if not his entire life. They could unburden themselves of *The Mail*, or the whole of News Limited, into the safe hands of her husband's former colleagues, and walk away from the news business entirely.[14] Dumas tried to allay the predatory air of his approach, coming so soon after the death of a beloved friend and colleague. He would maintain publicly that the decision had been 'under consideration' by the board for some time, and that it was improved economic conditions and newsprint availability, rather than naked opportunism, that had set this purportedly long-held plan in motion.[15] This part, at least, was grounded in truth. Newsprint shortages had plagued Australian newspapers since the war, cutting *The News* down to just four pages in 1949 and forcing *The Advertiser* to scrap its previous weekend publication, *Express*, in 1951.[16] Less plausible, however, was Dumas's claim that Sir Keith himself had approved of Dumas's Sunday plans—after all, why would he have spent years fighting to establish an independent Murdoch press, while at the same time planning its eventual takeover by the very company he carved it out from?

*The News* might have publicly declared that 'genius cannot be handed on' in one of many hagiographic tributes printed in the days after Sir Keith's death, but it was of paramount importance that the company he was building would be passed on—and not handed back.[17]

RUPERT WAS PREDICTABLY enraged by Dumas's secret overture and his increasingly jeopardised inheritance. He wrote to Rivett, bitterly describing how Dumas—disdainfully referred to as 'old Lloydie D' and the 'cunning old bastard'—had 'turned on the sob stuff' to Lady Elisabeth.[18] Just two months earlier, Rupert had still been bullishly optimistic—or perhaps in denial—of his chances of clinging onto the family's Queensland holdings. He was even prepared to water down their controlling stake in News Limited to do so, and risk shedding the Adelaide operation to retain its foothold on Australia's more populous east coast. When Rupert finally arrived in Australia after the funeral, Lady Elisabeth gathered the family at Cruden Farm, and as they sat around the table in the room that was once the children's schoolroom, they looked to their future without Keith.[19] It was clear that with him gone, the family's long association with the Herald and Weekly Times was at an end, and that Rupert's future in journalism would depend on Queensland and South Australia. But Elisabeth was adamant that the family should become debt-free as soon as possible, and if that meant selling off some of the newspaper holdings, then so be it—despite Rupert's protests. As she and Giddy worked to balance the books, Murdoch had a nagging sense that in the eyes of the Herald and Weekly Times leadership, *The Courier-Mail* was already theirs ('Not if I have anything to do with it!' he wrote defiantly).[20]

Even before Dumas made his Sunday-paper proposal, tensions in Adelaide had begun to peak, and now that Sir Keith was gone, so were the limits he had imposed on the editor. Rivett and Rupert met in Melbourne after the funeral, and over the coming months he laid out the situation: 'It will take some years before we can teach the reactionary clique who control so many things in Adelaide that *The News* can neither be flouted nor ignored and that the age-old system here of giving preference to the '*Tiser* and of deferring to all requests from *The Advertiser*—however unfair—is unprofitable,' Rohan wrote in November 1952.[21] 'The fact that injustices are done couldn't matter less to these thick-skinned gentry. The trouble begins in the Adelaide Club where Dumas is constantly wining and dining the directors of a number of big local companies.'[22] For all Rivett's experience, pedigree, and Melbourne connections, in Adelaide he remained an outsider, with well-founded concerns that his own position and contribution would be erased in the event of a takeover after Sir Keith's death: 'I still feel there is some danger that Dumas and a syndicate of local tycoons might try to convert this into another reactionary paper like *The Advertiser*,' he warned.[23]

By March 1953, around the time of Dumas's pitch to Lady Elisabeth, Rohan and Rupert were discussing his latest underhanded tactics towards News Limited. 'It seems that Dumas has his two famous techniques of the lie-by-innuendo and the Big Lie working well,' Rivett complained, relaying a third-hand rumour that *The News* was giving away advertising space to the Myer Emporium.[24] 'This is a typical *Advertiser* lie to explain away the preponderance of Myer advertising in *The News* and *Mail*. It is meant to cause trouble in Rundle Street and elsewhere and to discredit us with the wider Australian fraternity.' Doubly frustrating was the fact that these reports had come to Rivett via Harry Giddy. 'It has worried me very much that the chief trustee of the Murdoch estate should make a statement about *The News*, obviously believing it,' Rivett wrote to Rupert. By April, he was speaking of a 'terrific advertising battle going on now with prominent city people acting as spies for both parties, and '*Tiser* ideas appear in *The News* the day before *The Advertiser* has announced the launching of them—and in one case vice versa.'[25] A cold war was well under way in Adelaide, but it wouldn't be long before it was all in the open.

Over in Brisbane, Sir Keith's other editor was feeling tortured and unsettled. Since the funeral, Colin Bednall had been having a rough couple of weeks full of troubling developments. First, there was the *Courier-Mail* advertising executive who reported, helpfully, that 'the agencies are saying, Mr Bednall, that now Sir Keith is dead you will never be heard of again'.[26] Then he had a strange run-in with Frank Packer in Sydney. A thick-set man with the nose of a former boxer, the 47-year-old son of the late Clyde Packer helmed the second generation of the Packer dynasty with pugilistic drive. Packer knew the Murdoch estate was encountering probate issues, and floated the idea of a merger between his Australian Consolidated Press—the publisher of *The Daily Telegraph* and *The Australian Women's Weekly*—and Queensland

Newspapers. Packer even tried his luck with the spectacular claim that Sir Keith had recently discussed the opportunity with him, a story that Bednall dismissed out of hand. It seemed that Dumas was not the only cunning old bastard using Sir Keith's name for his own ends. Sir Keith had several brushes with Packer over the years—back in 1938, he even floated an £800,000 bid by the Herald and Weekly Times to take over Consolidated Press. But by 1950, Murdoch had grown wary of Packer's unscrupulous dealings:

> Packer will keep no agreement that does not suit himself; no agreement is a bond to him if it cannot be enforced. I have seen this unhappy trait in him several times and finally and completely to my mind, it discounts all his qualities and makes him simply a rogue.[27]

But then again, Murdoch was known to make promises he had no intention of keeping. Who really knew what he might have said in those final, desperate years? Who else might he have misled, or played off against one another?

The full shape of Murdoch's final plans remained a mystery, either hidden in his Flinders Street safe and the illegible scribbles in his notebooks, or taken to the grave. At least the Packer proposal could be easily discredited; Bednall had heard he was in a 'very bad way financially', sweating under a balance sheet with a million-pound bank overdraft, and liable to say anything to pull off a merger that might help him wriggle out of ruin.[28] Even Rupert had come to regard Packer as perhaps 'the biggest crook in Australian newspapers'—but also one of the 'cleverest'.[29] All Bednall knew for certain, as he had known since he first arrived in Brisbane, was that it was of paramount importance that the company 'make every effort and meet every call necessary to cement the Murdoch position'. Sir Keith's death had done nothing to change that fact, and in the meantime Bednall did everything he could to steady the ship—even contemplating an employee-led buyout to spoil any takeover attempt and 'preserve the Murdoch tradition here'.[30] 'There are people here who not only work for *The Courier-Mail*, but live *The Courier-Mail*,' he pleaded to Giddy on 3 November.

By the end of November, Bednall caught wind from a 'certain well-known gentleman in the Melbourne *Herald* office' that the Herald and Weekly Times had already bought the 20,000 Queensland Newspapers shares held by News Limited. He told Rupert immediately, who took it as a 'pretty bad shock' to learn that his mother, and Giddy, had left the Herald and Weekly Times 'perilously close to holding the balance'.[31]

For a short time, Rupert remained undaunted, encouraged by the latest figures to believe that the family might be able to maintain control of both papers, even if it meant diluting its stake in News Limited.[32] Rivett was optimistic, too, and reassured Rupert that both the Queensland and South Australia shows would, in the long run, remain under family control. 'Don't for the love of mike worry your head too much,' he wrote. '... Anyhow, this paper won't let any Murdochs down in any way while I have anything to do with it.'[33] In the end, both men's confidences were misplaced. Sir Keith's estate had left Rupert and his mother in a 'mess', and by March one thing had become clear: it was Adelaide or nothing.

Rupert was bitterly disappointed to lose his foothold in Queensland, but there were other details about Sir Keith's dealmaking coming to light that suggested losing *The Courier-Mail* might have been a blessing in disguise. One day, in the brief window between the funeral and the Herald and Weekly Times takeover, Bednall was approached by a local boxing promoter. The man frankly informed Bednall that the editor was now 'one of the team — John Wren's team', with a membership list that apparently included 'a cabinet minister, a police commissioner, a turf club chairman, sundry lawyers' and the promoter himself.[34] 'I had heard vague stories about John Wren and his underworld associations, but I was too engrossed in my job to worry much about them,' Bednall later recalled.[35]

The promoter brought him up to speed: according to Wren, part of Murdoch's financial arrangements in setting up Queensland Newspapers included an undertaking that Wren and his heirs would gain control when Sir Keith died.[36] Such a deal flatly contradicted a written agreement between Murdoch and his Herald and Weekly Times colleagues giving them first option to acquire his family's Queensland holdings if he ever decided to sell. But then again, little of Queensland Newspapers company's true ownership was ever committed to paper. Even Lady Elisabeth had been perturbed by her husband's dealings with Wren—who she viewed as 'rather sinister'.[37] 'Wren's name did not appear on any of the Company records because he operated through nominees,' Bednall later wrote, 'but the boxing promoter, hungry for free plugs for the stadium he managed, had lost no time in explaining that his boss might one day be my boss.'[38]

If Bednall had previously chosen to remain blissfully ignorant of Wren's connection to his employer, he couldn't now: the 1950 publication of Frank Hardy's *Power Without Glory*, and its portrayal of a fictional gangster turned political heavyweight named 'John West' had cast a scandalising light on Wren's ascent. It gained further publicity when Hardy was unsuccessfully tried for criminal libel over the book's depiction of Wren's wife—inadvertently solidifying the connection between Wren and West in the public mind. When Wren's name came up again, Bednall was stunned. For a week, he kept away from the office, and might have stayed away if there weren't pay checks to sign.[39] Shortly after he returned, he encountered Wren himself:

> Walking through the general office, I saw sitting on a hard bench reserved for petty debtors, a short bandy-legged old man. Passing the bench again thirty minutes later, I saw he was still there. His legs did not reach the floor so he could swing them, and in this way he made it appear that he was happy. However, I walked over to him and asked if he was being attended to. 'I am hoping to see Mr Bednall,' said John Wren, 'But they tell me is a very busy man'.[40]

Wren politely explained that his deal with Murdoch gave him the right to appoint three new directors—a board majority—but, as a gesture of goodwill, would forfeit this claim. There was a good chance he was telling the truth: when Murdoch first invited Bednall to join *The Courier-Mail* in 1945, he hinted that 'his shares are controlling shares only as long as I live,' and that 'if [he] died, there would be new people brought in and I suspect the board would be stronger'.[41] But, as Rupert and his allies were finding out, the same could very well be said for most of the newspapers he ran.

Wren's magnanimous gesture regarding the board was tempered by other requests. Bednall agreed to help promote an upcoming boxing match, but drew the line at giving free coverage to a beauty aid being marketed by Wren's son. Wren never asked another uncomfortable favour of Bednall, but to the editor's embarrassment would repeatedly make a point of offering *his* services.[42] Later, when the Herald and Weekly Times had completed its takeover, Jack Williams heard of the arrangement, and on Bednall's next visit to Melbourne he was told to take up Wren's offer:

> I was so astonished to be asked a favour by Jack that I steeled myself and walked down Flinders Lane and put the request to Mr Wren. He unhesitatingly agreed to have his creatures block the Bill before it left the party room. To do so, he simply picked up a telephone, called Parliament house, and asked that a prominent member of the party be brought to the phone. 'Is it true you're thinking of setting up a government board to run the newsagents?' he asked, as I sat on the other side of his desk in the office of Stadiums Ltd. 'It is? Well, I don't care for that… please have it stopped'.[43]

When Bednall returned to Brisbane, he telegrammed Williams to confirm that Wren had done the deed, and immediately received an urgent reply claiming total ignorance. 'He was at a loss to know what my telegram was about, as he would never dream of asking any favours of the likes of John Wren,' Bednall recalled. Wren's death in 1953—of a heart attack while watching his beloved Collingwood Football Club win a premiership at the Melbourne Cricket Ground—saved Bednall from any more awkward entanglements, but he was so disillusioned by the whole episode, and his own naivety, that he soon abandoned *The Courier-Mail*. Within a few years, Bednall had left newspapers altogether for the new and hopefully less-corrupted medium of television.

HAVING RETURNED TO Oxford later in 1952, Rupert met up with his mother in Rome the following March around the time of his 22nd birthday. In the same city they had visited on holiday with Sir Keith and the Rivetts three years earlier, mother and son now convened to discuss Dumas's new proposal. They resolved to meet the challenge head-on — the quickest decision that Rupert had ever made.[44] With their minds made up, Rupert first sought to delay Dumas's plans. For a month and a half, he tried to string Dumas along with feigned indecision, until it was revealed he was too late: *The Advertiser* had already sent its new Sunday editor, Harry Plumridge, the same editor who Sir Keith had brought in to overhaul *The Register* in the 1920s, on a fact-finding mission to the United States. The wheels were already in motion, Dumas explained, but whether Plumridge would edit a brand-new Sunday paper or a bought-out *Mail* was up to the Murdochs. 'It is going to be a great fight,' Rupert told Rivett once news of the deal had spread, still bullishly optimistic, even with the knowledge that Dumas was prepared to lose a substantial sum of money to crush him.[45] 'Don't think that I am panicking, but this is a real challenge.'

Of course, competition between the publishers was nothing new; before Sir Keith's death it had been a 'fast and furious' rivalry that only grew in intensity in the lead-up to Rupert's arrival in Adelaide.[46] Not even Rivett was above invoking Sir Keith's name to nudge things along, telling Rupert in November that 'your father was very keen on fighting both the Adelaide Club, and we are now reintroducing the suggestion he made which was temporarily abandoned in deference to the advertising department that we should exclude all mention of John Martins from the paper.'[47] This, of course, was quite the opposite of Sir Keith's position — but what did any of that matter now?

Rivett also sent Rupert copies of *Mary's Own Paper*, a 'local gossip sheet' that published a colourful running commentary of the mounting battle. The typewritten newsletter was ostensibly published by local bookseller Mary Martin; but, like the bookstore bearing her name, the paper was primarily the work of her business partner, Max Harris. Harris was already a figure of local notoriety; once a precocious teenage poet and enfant terrible of Australian modernism, a decade earlier he had found himself at the centre of one of Australia's most infamous literary hoaxes. In 1944, Harris was the young publisher and editor of *Angry Penguins*, a literary journal closely linked to Melbourne's Heide Circle of artists and poets. It all made him a target, ripe for a tall-poppy-snipping prank by two frustrated poets who were sceptical of the movement's artistic credibility. In one afternoon, the pair cooked up a suite of wilfully obtuse poems and a fake backstory for the late, and entirely fictional, Ernest Lalor Malley, an undiscovered visionary of working-class Australia whose body of work had been discovered by his equally made-up sister, Ethel, after his death at the age of 25. The 22-year-old Harris fell hard for both the poems and the story that 'Ethel' spun, and in June 1944 he published Ern Malley's entire oeuvre in a special issue of *Angry Penguins*, complete with a cover painting by Harris's Heide comrade Sidney Nolan. For his efforts, Harris was not only subjected to the humiliating revelation of the hoax, but criminal prosecution in South Australia for publishing certain passages of Malley's work that were claimed to be immoral and obscene.

Nine years after this bruising episode had ended in a guilty verdict, a £5 fine, and the eventual collapse of *Angry Penguins*, Harris had largely refocussed his energies from publishing to bookselling. But he continued to needle South Australian institutions and to stimulate public debate using *Mary's Own Paper* as his mouthpiece, and in August 1953 ran an irreverent but pointed analysis on the 'War of the Newspapers' still raging:

> The Ant Men of the News are locked in mortal combat with the Robot Gangsters of the Advertiser. Will Lantern-jawed rivet-fisted Rohan conquer Superham, the Pressman of Yesterday? We puny mortals silently watch the interplanetary conflict between our morning star and our evening asteroid. On which side shall we throw the weight of our daily four pence?[48]

*The Advertiser*, it wrote, was 'composed so as not to disturb that state of morning befuddledness, [having] the great advantage of being a ritual and habit of Homo South Australiensis'.[49] 'The good conservative newspapers like *The Times*, *The Sydney Morning Herald*, *The Age*, achieve a certain objectivity, a dignity, an intellectuality, if you like, which permit of a certain amount of respect. *The Advertiser* has the sins and trappings of conservative journalism without the corresponding virtues.' *The News*, by contrast, exhibited 'as progressive a line on world affairs as any newspaper in Australia' that spoke to the more liberal-minded demographic of *Mary's Own Paper*. Nonetheless, it noted that *The News* often suffered from trying a little too hard. 'This circulation battle with the '*Tiser* brings out a wearisome amount of journalistic adolescence,' it bemoaned. '*The News* is in high danger, like an overzealous boy scout, of boring us to tears with its efforts to win our fourpenny affections.'

In many ways, these two weekday papers represented two competing halves of 1950s' Adelaide: the provincial paternalism of the Playford era supported by *The Advertiser*, and an emerging, progressive alternative that *The News* under Rivett had increasingly appealed to. Somewhere between the two lay a middle ground that both organisations would go to extraordinary lengths to capture: Sunday morning.

# CHAPTER SEVEN

# The weekend battle

THE FIRST EDITION of *The Sunday Advertiser* hit the lawns of Adelaide with a resounding thwack on the morning of 24 October 1953, and it didn't take long before *The Mail* returned fire. Running the length of the entire front page, its 21 November issue published a 700-word call to arms where no reader could miss it. If Rivett's first year in Adelaide was undercut by Sir Keith's cautious approach to *The Advertiser*, it seemed Rupert Murdoch took little convincing to rip off the Band-Aid. Titled 'The Newspapers of South Australia', the special column did what would have been unthinkable when Sir Keith was still alive: it lifted the lid on the months of subterfuge and behind-the-scenes machinations that had been going on between North Terrace and Waymouth Street, and told the public in no uncertain terms that the two camps were now in 'avowed competition'.[1]

Part manifesto, part exposé, it aired details of Sir Lloyd Dumas's back-channel overture to Lady Elisabeth, framed in bold block letters as a 'Bid for Press Monopoly'.[2] In *The Mail's* indignant telling, it all sounded practically extortionate—Dumas had even pressured her not to seek advice from anyone connected to News Limited. *The Mail* claimed that Dumas viewed the Sunday paper as a threat to *The Advertiser* that must be bought out or crushed, and in the face of such tactics, News Limited's continued independence meant more than safeguarding one 22-year-old's inheritance—it was practically a public service. Anything else would have created a monopoly, with South Australia's morning, afternoon, and weekend papers 'all in the hands of the one group of businessmen'.[3] The article welcomed the challenge of its new competitor—even publishing its circulation statistics and daring *The Advertiser* to do the same. But it also added a final missive in all-caps, declaring its belief that the public would reject any bid to 'CORNER THE COMMUNITY'S PRESS IN THE INTERESTS OF ANY ONE PARTICULAR GROUP, SECTION, PARTY, COMPANY OR CLIQUE'.[4]

Drawing a clear distinction between the two companies, *The Mail* also highlighted *The Advertiser*'s links to the Herald and Weekly Times—and the fact that two of its board members were based in Melbourne. Of course, in its attempt to stoke fears of a 'blanket press monopoly' controlled by an interstate chain, *The Mail* buried the lede in one important way: such a scenario was virtually identical to Adelaide's pre-1949 status quo, which Murdoch's own father had been instrumental in building. It was a sly appeal to its readers' parochial streak, but one that quickly backfired. A week later, *The Sunday Advertiser* and Dumas vigorously asserted their South Australian credentials, while pointing out the obvious: News Limited's two young leaders might live in Adelaide for now, but Rivett had arrived less than a year before, and Murdoch had only been in town a few weeks. But, Dumas added in a patronising tone, *The Advertiser* hoped that 'these two estimable young men' would 'become good South Australians'.[5] The awkward detente of Sir Keith's era was well and truly over: this would be an all-out circulation war.

NOVEMBER'S DUELLING HEADLINES signalled the beginning of the conflict, but both papers had been on a war footing for months. Dumas's approach to Lady Elisabeth in March gave *The Mail* a long lead over *The Sunday Advertiser*'s October debut, but there was a problem: Dumas's attempts to spook Rupert and his mother into secrecy had been largely successful. Clearly worried, Murdoch tried to drop hints to Rivett about the oncoming storm; in April, he wrote that *The News* was improving in 'leaps and bounds' under Rivett's watch, but warned against being lulled into complacency by *The Advertiser*'s 'apparent dullness and inactivity'.[6] Dumas was a 'very tough and clever old man', and he prayed that Rivett was paying close attention to any movements on Flinders Street. 'For God's sake tear this letter up after reading it,' he added, scrawling 'BURN!' for emphasis in the margins of the letter (which, incidentally, is un-charred and preserved for posterity among Rivett's papers held by the National Library of Australia).

Over on Flinders Street, Dumas was also trying to keep a lid on *The Advertiser*'s plans. In a confidential memo sent in July to Harry Plumridge, *The Advertiser*'s directors, and Jack Williams, Dumas resolved to keep their Sunday plans secret from the 'father of the Chapel'—the industry term for a paper's printing department and its head—and the Printing Industry Employees' Union.[7] *The News* also had representatives on the union's Adelaide committee, who Dumas worried would catch on if any approach was made.[8] Meanwhile, Dumas kept an eye from afar on News Limited's preparations, anxiously inquiring about the printing capacity of its North Terrace plant in the event of a circulation battle.[9]

It wasn't until July that Murdoch finally revealed to Rivett the full story behind the Dumas bid, and he was shocked to hear the editor agree, matter-of-factly, that a Sunday *Advertiser* had been 'in the wind' all year.[10] Despite Dumas's best efforts, News Limited's head printer had learned back in January 1953 that *The Advertiser* was recruiting extra printing staff for a new weekly paper, and by February it seemed they were also hiring compositors and editors.[11] Rohan brought his concerns to News Limited's general manager, Ernest Bridges, who 'pooh poohed' the idea, insisting that Dumas's loyalty to Sir Keith would prevent him from ever betraying the Murdoch family.[12]

There was also the matter of money; a deal with the union meant *The Advertiser* had to pay its workers double time on Saturdays, but this offered little comfort to Rivett. He'd seen enough of Dumas to know he wouldn't hold back, even if it meant strong-arming Sir Keith's family or risking significant losses. From February, he treated a Sunday paper as a foregone conclusion and sought to prepare as best he could. 'Why didn't you tell me—or my mother?' wrote an incredulous Murdoch from Oxford after Rivett admitted he knew about *The Advertiser*'s plans—they had, after all, been 'sweating and worrying' for months.[13] Everything was now out in the open: Advertiser Newspapers were prepared to lose up to £100,000 in the first year to establish a solid readership and eat into *The Mail*'s numbers. With Plumridge installed as editor, the competition had already hired 11 extra journalists, 16 compositor and linotype operators, and recruited a subeditor from the Melbourne *Herald*.

With October fast approaching, Murdoch pressed the need to 'clear the decks … and pretty fast', and from Oxford floated a series of drastic measures—even suggesting that *The Mail* take out advertising in *The Advertiser*.[14] Most of his ideas fizzled out, but Rivett welcomed this new fighting spirit. 'This will at least serve the purpose of clearing the air and enabling us to have the all-out fight with *The Advertiser* which is essential to secure our position,' he told Murdoch in June.[15] He'd spent month after month passing newsagents plastered with signs that proclaimed '*The Advertiser*. Circulation Unapproached' or 'Read *The Advertiser*, The Premier Daily', but had been held back by both Sir Keith and the risk-averse Bridges.[16] With this latest challenge, Rivett laid out a detailed roadmap that included 'more thoughtful and weightier' editorial pieces, more 'serious and light' feature pieces, and the inclusion of a 'permanent, full-scale' serial section.[17] He also suggested an overhaul of the paper's layout, bringing *The Mail* on a par with many of its Sunday contemporaries around the world. Everything was made more urgent by the news that Plumridge had returned from his overseas fact-finding mission, ready to begin crafting the new paper.

In June, Plumridge wrote Dumas a long letter bursting with ideas from the Sunday papers of America and Britain, whose formulae he felt could be easily applied to Adelaide. 'We can draw ideas from both the American and English papers … from the Americans we can get ideas for the bread and butter side,' he wrote. 'The London papers provide an object lesson in the crisp, pointed handling of human interest stories and well-written special articles'.[18] Women's pages were important, but had to be 'feminine, not feminist', and should appeal to children as well (who would 'carry it through teenage and thus make sure of your adults'). They would aim to 'colour the news', but not 'harp on the sensational and the morbid'.[19] But Plumridge also looked closer to home, writing a six-page memo that broke down *The Mail* page by page and section by section, analysing each of its existing offerings—from women's pages and the children's section to theatre gossip and serialised features—and gauging how well *The Advertiser* was poised to match or outdo it.[20]

While Plumridge prepared for the October launch, *The Mail* already showed signs of change. The edition of 15 August 1953 unveiled a new masthead that leant into *The Mail*'s 40-year history, reviving the illustrated train motif that had been a staple since May 1912, but was now reinvented as a modern locomotive speeding across the page. There were also more strategic, structural moves; in a front-page bulletin entitled 'Your New Mail', the paper announced 'big changes' developed after 'months of research and testing of public readership'.[21] A new emphasis on lift-outs that could be 'easily distributed among members of the family' reflected a new marketing strategy: the family newspaper.[22] By specifically targeting the interests of each member of the family unit, the paper inserted itself into the Sunday-morning rituals of households all around the state. This strategy could be seen across News Limited's promotional material, such as a 1955 pamphlet for advertisers featuring a picturesque one-child family, all reading their respective sections of *The Sunday Mail* over breakfast in bed.[23]

By August 1953, Rivett was upbeat about their chances. 'We are confident that News Limited will still be functioning successfully when their attempt to crush us out of existence is only a memory,' he wrote to Stewart Cockburn—his old *Herald* colleague, who was now press secretary to prime minister Robert Menzies.[24] To Murdoch, he reported that 'we have turned the paper completely upside down and in the opinion of three interstate journalists, this is the certainly the best *Mail* yet'.[25] There was still more to be done, he said, but 'given the technical limitations we have here, of which naturally you cannot take account until you come here and see them, you will understand that it is a remarkable effort to turn out this paper with our small staff and mechanical limitations'.[26] Rupert would see for himself soon enough.

RUPERT MURDOCH FINALLY arrived in his new home on a 6.30 am
flight from Perth on 8 September 1953, and made a beeline for the
News Limited offices on North Terrace. He had scraped through
his final exams, had bidden farewell to Oxford weeks earlier, and
had narrowly avoided getting 'married off' on one last weekend
in Cornwall.[27] Once it became clear that retaining Queensland
Newspapers was a lost cause, he had resigned himself to moving to
Adelaide to work under Rivett, for a year at first ('I do not want to
be a cadet at the *Herald* for a day!!!' he underlined in May 1953).[28]
He initially sought no executive title, preferring to 'ease [him]self
in sideways' while reassuring Rivett that he had no intention of
acting like 'a cocky bastard'.[29] Instead, he hoped to first spend time
observing the workings of the company, while contributing whatever
'useful ideas and manpower' he could muster along the way.[30] But
before he arrived he made a curiously urgent editorial intervention:
on 21 August, he implored Rivett not to print a single word regarding
the recent publication of Alfred Kinsey's *Sexual Behaviour in the
Human Female*. By telegram, Murdoch dismissed Kinsey's book as
'ballyhoo', and insisted that 'FORNICATION MASTURBATION
FRUSTRATION UNSIUTABLE (sic) FOR ADELAIDE FAMILY
FIRESIDE'.[31] He also sent a handwritten note—he had already sold
his typewriter ahead of the move—that underlined the point: 'Cunt
is not our line'.[32] *The News* had run a full-page feature on the book
in July, but in the weeks after Murdoch's intervention only one small
notice appeared in *The Mail*.[33]

Rupert had spent his last weeks in England getting a final taste
of Fleet Street, with a three-week posting at *The Express*. He had
planned to do a glorified tour of several offices, but after ten fruitful
days 'poking [his] nose' into *The Express*, he was invited to join its
subediting staff. He found it invaluable, his hands kept full with a
surprising amount of work and responsibility.[34] On eight-hour night
shifts that finished at 2.00 am, he handled a wide variety of stories and
learnt about all parts of the process, from writing and typesetting to
layout. It was a 'tremendous experience', which he was eager to put to
use when he eventually returned to Australia.

In Adelaide, he wasted little time making his presence felt, penning memos to critique the odd 'flagrant piece of bad subbing' and the lack of 'flair or imagination' in the layout, and sought to 'limit the social muck—all immensely important, I know'.[35] As he floated around the office, he also took on less glamourous tasks; in one memo issued shortly after his arrival, he mentioned 'five painful minutes' spent dealing with a minor complaint from the Red Cross, who were upset that one of its 'maidens' had been photographed by a *News* photographer while off duty. ('I told the good lady that we would not say whether we would publish it or not.')[36]

To Max Fatchen, the new arrival seemed 'enthusiastic' and 'hands-on'.[37] 'He'd see the paper to bed, he'd take an interest in every part of it,' he later recalled.[38] One occasion that particularly impressed him came in January 1954, when *The Mail* was set to run a story about St Peter's Cathedral—perhaps the most prominent church in a city full of them—being lit up at night to celebrate the upcoming royal visit from the recently crowned Queen Elizabeth. Upon seeing the layout, Murdoch intervened to blow up the accompanying photograph from two columns to three. 'It had a galvanic effect on the page,' Fatchen recalled. 'I thought even then, in my inexperience, that somebody here's got an eye on something, and that enthusiasm pervaded the newspaper. And from then he never stopped, he was dynamic.'[39] Of course, not all staff were so appreciative of Murdoch's hazily defined role in the paper's chain of command—some complained to Rivett, dubbing these interventions 'Rupertorial interruptions'.[40]

WHEN THE FIRST edition of *The Sunday Advertiser* arrived after weeks of promotion, it wasted no time in trying to outdo *The Mail*. Matching its rival's sixpence price point, it boasted new serialised writing by the 'cream of current literature', including Winston Churchill's latest volume on worldwide democracies, and Agatha Christie's latest Miss Marple novel.[41] The paper also included five pages of colour cartoons, 'wide and varied' women's pages, exclusive highlights from *Time* magazine, and the 'biggest line up of distinguished sports writers in South Australia'. In the weeks following its debut, the weekday *Advertiser* and its country counterpart, *The Chronicle*, beat the drum for the new paper, with predictably glowing reports of the 'intense interest' from readers and 'congratulatory messages' from around Australia and abroad. ('I am naturally envious of this lavish and bountiful issue', *The Chronicle* quoted Lord Kemsley, chairman of London's *Sunday Times*, on 12 November.)[42]

Meanwhile, *The Mail* continued its quest to modernise. In April 1954, Boland set out on a transatlantic mission to soak up the latest newspaper production methods, with four days in San Francisco, the city that gave the world Randolph Hearst, six days in Washington for the conference of the American Society of Newspaper Editors, and then onto New York for the convention of the American Newspaper Publishers Association.[43] While in New York, the home of legendary papers such as *The New York Post* and *The Wall Street Journal*, he visited every newspaper office in the city, then did the same in London, with a sweep of all the Fleet Street papers that culminated in a day spent observing all the processes at *The Evening News*—part of Lord Northcliffe's old empire, and now run by his nephew, the 2nd Viscount Rothermere. In London, he met up with Rivett, who had also spent six weeks on a 'whirlwind' trip across South-East Asia, the United States, and Europe, before attending an editors' conference in Vienna, where he swapped notes with his counterparts from around the world.[44]

Back on North Terrace, the building's usual soundtrack of typewriters, telephones, and teletype machines was joined by the sound of hammering, nailing, and the grating singing of 'manly choristers', as a stream of painters, carpenters, electricians, and wreckers gave the place a contemporary facelift. The new works promised 'working conditions equal to and even better than those in many of the larger interstate papers', with a lighter, more open atmosphere, finished in trendy pastel shades and 'smooth, modern panelling'.[45] At its centre, a new stairway was constructed to allow easy access between all three floors of the building. Many staff welcomed the changes, but, after months of renovations, most were happy to be rid of the 'war of nerves' that came with the disruption—they did, after all, have another war to win.

As in any conflict, there were defections and betrayals. Back in

June 1953, Plumridge stressed the need for 'punchy comments by well-known names' in the new paper, and before long Dumas set his sights on one of *The Mail*'s biggest draws: Max Fatchen.[46] Six months after *The Sunday Advertiser*'s launch, Fatchen received a letter from Dumas himself, promising 'security for life' if he jumped ship.[47] He rejected the first offer, but when Dumas returned six months later with an even better deal, he took it.[48] Rivett felt the betrayal keenly. 'He couldn't understand why I did it,' Fatchen later said, adding that, despite any misgivings, he was still thrown a farewell dinner at the Rivett family home in Wattle Park.[49] Murdoch was less gracious, insisting that Fatchen's by-line be scrubbed from *The Mail* for his final three months on North Terrace—after all, why should News Limited help promote *The Sunday Advertiser*'s newest feature writer?[50]

Fatchen was the biggest, but certainly not the only, name to 'cross the town'.[51] The sieve-like quality of both papers' staff was sent up in the 1954 edition of *Fudge*, the once-yearly organ of the local branch of the Australian Journalists' Association, which satirised the heightening 'cold war' between the two local papers. 'A third Sunday paper is to be published in Adelaide, it was learnt tonight,' the mock news story read, beside a doctored photo of Murdoch and Dumas shaking hands in a 'secret rendezvous'.[52] The new paper, it joked, would be called *The Sunday Miser*, and contain the worst material that the existing Sunday papers were 'unable to flog to each other'. It would also be published in the neutral territory between Waymouth Street and North Terrace—to 'save journalists who wish to cross the town having to go all the way'.[53] In just over a year's time, *Fudge*'s joke would seem prophetic.

SOMEWHAT INEVITABLY, THE relentless brinkmanship of two papers chasing an identical audience ended in stalemate. By January 1955 both papers almost mirrored one another, while their numbers refused to budge. *The Mail* had shed only 3 per cent of its 1953 circulation rate by June 1955, while *The Sunday Advertiser* plateaued at 108,000 net sales—less than the 120,000 projected in its first issue.[54] There were still some differences between the two. *Mary's Own Paper* highlighted

*The Sunday Advertiser*'s stronger coverage of arts and 'intellectual' content, and across both general news sections and featured supplements the paper could draw on the networks and foreign bureaus of the Herald and Weekly Times.[55] *The Mail*'s international news section, meanwhile, was ridiculed as a 'scissor-and-paste' job of material from overseas papers 'disingenuously labelled' as the 'Mail London Office' and 'Mail New York Office'.[56] Differences between *The Mail* and *The News* also hinted at a burgeoning gap between Rivett's model and what the embattled *Mail* was evolving into. *Mary's Own Paper* offered this summary in November 1953:

> Why should the conservative *Sunday Advertiser* win the weekend battle so easily? *The News* and *The Mail* are one and the same thing, and *The News* has been winning slowly but surely in the weekly battle. *The News* has been winning because in the weekdays it has been using intelligent journalists (Walter Lippman, Clive Turnbull, Rohan Rivett himself) and wining over the intelligent, liberal section of the community... a section which is vocal, articulate, will propagandise the journalism it likes, and is far larger a section of the community than newsmen realise.
>
> But for some reason *The Mail* devotes every inch to the most pedestrian twaddle imaginable, and won't concede the reader a gram of elementary intellectuality. Its weekend magazine section for instance, never lets up for a moment on the tabloid idiocies of a human interest slant which bored even mum years ago ... reluctantly, fretfully, but inevitably, I shall have to inform my newsagent that this week I am shifting papers.[57]

Two years later, with *The Sunday Advertiser* approaching its second birthday, the battle of attrition had grown uneconomical. The rationing of newsprint and mounting production costs were unsustainable on Waymouth Street and North Terrace, but neither company seemed willing to admit defeat. Finally, the board of Advertiser Newspapers broached a compromise: the two companies would pool their resources and merge the Sunday papers, with a rebadged *Sunday Mail* to be published by a new company, Advertiser-News Weekend Publishing

Co. Its shareholding would be evenly split between the two parties, and while Dumas would be its first chairman and Boland its editor, both camps would have equal representation on the board. The merger was announced on 19 December 1955, before the new *Sunday Mail* debuted just in time for Christmas.[58]

On the surface, it seemed like a victory for News Limited, but the fine grain of the merger was more complicated, and was carefully worded to avoid either party sounding like a clear winner or loser. News Limited would be paid an annual sum of £4,000 to print and produce the paper, but the new *Sunday Mail* was barred from any 'expression of editorial policy [or] editorial campaign' without the approval of the joint board.[59] One caveat even spelled out how the first issue would be credited: in no less than 10-point type, as a 'joint product of Advertiser Newspapers Limited and News Limited', while the second would feature the names in the reverse sequence. This would alternate—week in, week out—for the foreseeable future.[60]

The deal locked both companies into a set of conditions that reached beyond Sunday; for the next decade, neither *The News* or *The Advertiser* could lower their advertising rates to undercut the other, and nor could either marry advertising space in *The Mail* to contracts with their other titles—the practice that had previously given *The News* an advantage. It also barred either paper from entering any partnership or ownership arrangement with any other party, a failsafe that would help close Adelaide's newspaper industry to outside interests, but that also prevented Murdoch from joining any new syndicate against *The Advertiser*. But, perhaps most importantly, the agreement made official each paper's territory across the rest of the week—*The Advertiser* owned 10.00 pm until 10.00 am, *The News* owned 10.00 am until 10.00 pm, and neither could use its name or resources to publish a daily paper in South Australia on the other's turf. Even as the truce was being hammered out, its wording suggested that 18 months after *The Mail*'s polemic against Dumas's 'Bid for Press Monopoly', there were still elements of distrust between the two companies. There were only ten days between the date of the agreement and its public announcement, but the deal included a clause barring an 'earlier announcement of any kind' or any details of the project—it would be a policy of 'strict silence'.

News Limited had salvaged enough small wins—from the *Mail* name to its editorship and lucrative printing contract—for Murdoch to frame it as a victory, but it was also partially a success for Dumas. He might not have wiped out the threat posed by the young Murdoch, but the deal put a ceiling on News Limited's newspaper ambitions in Adelaide. On the day of the merger announcement, Dumas wrote a consolatory letter to Plumridge insisting 'we did not fail', and reassuring Plumridge that he could look back on his brief editorship with pride. 'Not even your wife could be more appreciative of your disappointment than I am,' he wrote.[61]

The weekend battle had ended in a truce, but its terms would have a much wider reach. For News Limited, the Sunday race created a crucible in which *The Mail* quickly modernised, importing the latest developments in style and content being rolled out in the United States and England, and rapidly road-testing them in an Australian setting. But *The Mail*'s weaknesses also made it clear that Murdoch needed far greater resources and networks to resist or challenge his father's old firm. He had survived the first battle, but he needed to expand—and do it soon.

Importantly, the heightened competition also shook South Australia's previously well-established and largely unchallenged orthodoxy. After Sir Keith's death, and Labor's loss of the 1953 state election, despite outpolling the government by 51,000 votes, Rivett and Rupert grew restless while waiting for the end of the Playford era. 'I intend to follow your Dad's policy of supporting Playford generally at the moment while vigorously agitating for electoral reform,' he wrote to Rupert in February 1953. 'It is fantastic that 40 per cent of the electorate should impose their will on the majority ... while it continues with the present restricted franchise no Labor government has any chance.'

But it was Waymouth Street that drew the attention of the premier. After years of virtually unflagging support from *The Advertiser*, Playford was incensed by a story that criticised the government's slow progress on a hospital-building project. Not used to such scrutiny, he assumed that his government was being 'dragged into a newspaper war', and demanded to know 'who is concocting this policy and who *The Advertiser* supports'.[62] Adelaide hadn't seen this kind of competition between newspapers in decades, but it didn't take long for News Limited's new regime to expose fresh cracks in a previously unchallenged system. And they were just getting started.

# CHAPTER EIGHT

# Boy publisher

MAIN NORTH ROAD is not South Australia's most imaginatively named thoroughfare, but it has long been one of its most important. The 350-kilometre-long strip of bitumen funnelled traffic in and out of growing sprawl of metropolitan Adelaide, up past the then-brand-new housing commission blocks at Elizabeth and Salisbury, and onwards to the shipping hubs of Port Pirie and Port Augusta on the west coast and the wheat belt of the mid north. Just after midday on 23 February 1956, a police van was driving down Main North Road when another car—a big, flash American model—suddenly overtook it, travelling well above the 35-mile-per-hour speed limit. The officer put his foot down, the van's engine whirring as it climbed up towards 60 and then 70 miles per hour. But they still couldn't catch it, let alone overtake it. Eventually, the pursuing van caught the driver's attention, who finally slowed down and pulled over. The 24-year-old behind the wheel didn't try to deny that he was speeding, explaining to the officer that he was driving back from Port Augusta, just past the farthest limits of Main North Road. It was a familiar kind of excuse to any traffic cop, particularly on a road such as this; it was a notorious route—too narrow, too straight, too easy for drivers to plough through without noticing that the fields and paddocks had disappeared and what was country highway was now a suburban main road.

They took down the young man's details, and let him drive on to the city. But when he pulled out, they followed, and after another kilometre or so he reached a primary school. The driver stopped at a pedestrian crossing, letting three schoolchildren pass safely, before tearing off through the crossing without noticing that the limit had halved around the school. The officers saw it all and intercepted him a second time. A week later, a gossip-column item in *Truth*—a rag of a Sydney tabloid whose weekly Adelaide edition outmatched all its South Australian competitors for sensationalism and innuendo—gleefully alluded to the incident:

> Hear about the well-known newspaper executive who, after being cautioned for doing over 60 mph in Adelaide suburb the other day, was later booked for doing 32 mph past a suburban school?[1]

Anyone paying attention to the local newspaper scene needed little help in guessing the executive's identity. When the case reached a suburban courthouse two months later, Rupert Murdoch spoke only through his lawyer, Jim Brazel QC, who accepted the charges but pointed out there was nothing to suggest that anyone had been endangered by his client's driving.[2] Nevertheless, the magistrate said, his behaviour 'was well beyond the limits allowed', and fined him a combined £22, plus costs, and disqualified him from driving for 21 days for each offence, to be served concurrently. This time, *The Advertiser* devoted 11 paragraphs to the story in its law columns. Its afternoon competitor, however, made zero reference to the case—ironic, given the full-throated road-safety campaigns previously featured in its pages. ('Speed cribbing is senseless', read a November *News* editorial. 'Motorists now have only themselves to blame if the police get tough'.)[3] It seemed that the death of Sir Keith and the responsibility of steering his family's fortunes had done little to change the young man whose driving in the Greek mountains had filled his father with dread. But Rupert's lead-foot wasn't confined to the road; as one confidant later recalled, 'he was clearly a young man in a great hurry'.[4]

In a small item announcing his appointment to News Limited's board of directors, the company's staff newsletter, *House News*, printed a photograph of the fresh-faced 'son of the late Sir Keith', and praised his 'terrific zest for work and a breezy personality' that had slotted neatly into every 'phase of activity'.[5] He took a bachelor flat on the beachside Esplanade in Glenelg, dabbled in surfing, beach running, and sailing, and regularly dined out in the city. Murdoch could be boisterous, untidy, impetuous, and curious, but there was something disarming about the socially awkward, carelessly dressed young man that many in his orbit couldn't help but be charmed by—even if the responsibilities of a highly placed newspaper executive, like the uniform of suits and shirtsleeves they tended to wear, seemed like an odd fit on the young Murdoch. *Mary's Own Paper* soon took to calling him 'Rupert the Chick'.[6]

The older members of the board had been positively startled when he blew into Adelaide, but were initially content to humour him.[7] As the Sunday battle raged on, however, it became clear that he would not be satisfied with his unofficial role. A clash seemed inevitable if Murdoch tried to assert himself at the executive level; the risk-averse general manager, Ernest Bridges, was unlikely to retire any time soon, and the board was of no mind to sack him to make way for an unproven 23-year-old. In the end, fate intervened: on 26 July 1954, Bridges died suddenly of a heart attack, struck down in his office at the age of 50. The path now clear, Murdoch claimed the new title on 17 September of publisher, a figurehead position common in American newspaper publishing, but less frequently found in Australia. Its ambiguity was part of the appeal; as publisher, Murdoch would effectively wield all the authority of a managing director, while also pre-empting any critics who might scoff at a recently graduated 23-year-old being promoted straight to the top.[8] It also gave rise to another new nickname, uttered with a mix of scepticism and amazement at the chutzpah of it all: the Boy Publisher.

AWAY FROM THE office, Murdoch remained close with the Rivett family. At the start of 1953, Rohan and Nan had made him godfather to their third child, named after Sir Keith, and on visits to their home in the

Adelaide foothills, the old go-kart of the London days received an upgrade; now Rupert drove a Chrysler, which to the Rivett children seemed to take up half the road 'We used to think it was great fun, but it was very dangerous, actually,' their daughter Rhyll Rivett recalled fondly.[9] 'He used to put us in the back and then he'd go a million miles around the block, then put on the airbrakes and we'd land in the front seat—we thought it was hilarious, it was some kind of joke.'

The Rivett house on Rosedale Street, Wattle Park, became a loud and colourful outlier among the buttoned-down suburbs of 1950s Adelaide. The company-owned property was surrounded on every side by quiet, conventional households on dull quarter-acre blocks, where men set off to work each day while their wives stayed at home cooking, sewing, and making jams and preserves from the fruit trees that seemed to sprout up in every front yard. By contrast, the Rivett house became a venue for twice-weekly dinner parties, and on the weekend hosted big, boozy parties and tennis tournaments for *The News* staff. 'The whole place was jumping,' Rhyll said. 'They drank an enormous quantity of beer—how they played tennis I have no idea'.[10] Adelaide might have felt small to Rohan and Nan after three years in London, but to their new acquaintances, the Rivetts were a welcome dose of worldly cosmopolitanism. Children from surrounding neighbourhood would flock to the house to play, too, while the spare rooms were filled with an unusually diverse string of house guests for 1950s' Adelaide, as Rohan hosted journalists and editors he had met on his travels.

Between News Limited-backed research trips and overseas conferences for the International Press Institute, the Rivetts remained great travellers, leaving the kids at home for months at a time. In mid-1955, they spent two months travelling from Delhi to Washington and half a dozen countries in between, Rohan filing news reports as they went while Nan took notes for a planned travelogue, never published. In Greece, they visited Rohan's old *Argus* colleague George Johnston and his wife, Charmian Clift, on the island of Hydra, and in America he interviewed Eleanor Roosevelt, visited the United Nations in New York, and drove across 15 states in four weeks.[11] When they returned, the family hosted Suryanarayan 'Sharm' Sharma, a reporter from Delhi's *Hindustan Times*, as he completed a historic 10-month posting at *The News*—the first Indian journalist to be employed full-time by a major Australian newspaper.[12]

And Rupert was a part of it all, bounding around with a Great Dane called Webster and exhibiting a clumsy puppy-like energy himself. Something always seemed to end up broken after his visits, and he loved playing rough with the kids—as if living out a kind of extended childhood. 'He was good fun, he always tried to play with us,' Rhyll recalled, likening him to a bull in a China shop and a St Bernard dog.[13] Sometimes, when the Rivetts were still entertaining past the children's bedtime, more hijinks would ensure—even if sometimes the age gap disappeared a little too readily. 'We used to have these pillow fights; he would hit me quite hard, and I'd hit him right back,' she said. 'One day he got stuck into David, my brother, and David started to really attack him; Rupert realised that David was serious, although he was just a child, and he just belted and belted him until he cried. I watched it and I just thought, that's *so unfair*. Otherwise he was very friendly to us—but he didn't like anyone winning or competing on that level.'[14]

MURDOCH'S COMPETITIVE DRIVE quickly began to lead him away from Adelaide. He familiarised himself with the farthest reaches of the News Limited stable, flying across the New South Wales border to inspect the eastern end of JE Davidson's original chain of papers, Broken Hill's *Barrier Miner*. These trips also allowed him to indulge his love of gambling; since returning to Australia, he had bought into a handful of racehorses, and at Broken Hill he could indulge in poker machines—they weren't legal on the South Australian side of the border—and the time-honoured Australian coin-tossing game of two-up. (A photograph from the period shows him in a bowtie and shirt sleeves in the midst of an animated game).[15] But he was also becoming hooked on a bigger kind of game, with much higher stakes. If the hard-fought Sunday battle had shown News Limited's strengths, it had also made its disadvantages clear; cut off from the cosy, if questionable, connections it once had with the Herald and Weekly Times empire, Murdoch needed to expand the company's horizons to improve its coverage and to achieve economies of scale.

The first opportunity arose in September 1954, when News Limited acquired a 68 per cent interest in a Perth-based publisher named Western Press.[16] Its chief trade was a familiar one: the city's only Sunday paper, *The Sunday Times*, along with a network of 24 regional titles scattered up and down the west coast. The deal would let both companies pool its news, pictures, and features, while also giving News Limited's advertisers 'two-State coverage … embracing more than half [of] Australia'.[17] The board took some convincing, but eventually agreed that it might be a good test of the young publisher's mettle.[18] When the deal was initially announced, Western Press's managing director and chairman, Victor Courtney, an ageing journalist who had bought the paper 20 years earlier, claimed it 'would still be under the control of himself' and his colleagues, with Murdoch and Adelaide banker and News Limited board member Reg Wiltshire joining the board to 'strengthen' it.[19] By Christmas 1954, however, Courtney, his assistant manager, and a third director had resigned from the board and 'all other positions', effective from New Year's Eve. (In a small announcement in *The Sunday Times*, the break was attributed to 'differences on policy'.)[20]

Having asserted control over the paper, Murdoch began regularly flying over to Perth, staying with his great uncle Sir Walter Murdoch and putting the lessons he was learning in Adelaide to use to boost the paper's circulation.[21] Once Adelaide's *The Sunday Advertiser* capitulated, he sent over Ron Boland to take over as managing director of Western Press in April 1956, joining a subeditor and two journalists previously drafted from the *Barrier Miner* and *The Mail*.

He might have been able to talk the board and his mother into backing his western venture, and successfully turfed Courtney, but he didn't yet have the unquestioned control he later enjoyed. Peter Harries, a former clerk at *The Sunday Times*, recalled the weekend when Lady Elisabeth accompanied her son on the trip. Harries was just a few years younger than Rupert, and it became his job to make sure that Murdoch's apartment was stocked with supplies each weekend, and fetching tea and coffee for the board meetings. It was in the boardroom of Western Press that he watched as Lady Murdoch struggled to get her son's attention. 'Yes Mother,' he said finally, before turning to Western Press's new chairman, Ernest Shacklock. 'This paper we have on a Saturday ... we're going to cease publication of it,' he said.

*The Mirror*, the paper in question, was a thin and tawdry Saturday sheet driven by sporting results and titillating scandal, founded by Courtney himself a decade before his syndicate took over *The Sunday Times*. When asked why, Murdoch explained, with deference to his mother, that their family was not interested in any of that kind of rubbish. The next week, the paper was unceremoniously shuttered after 35 years, with a dozen staff laid off at once. Its final issue appeared on 11 August 1956, bearing the simple message, 'From today publication of *The Mirror* will be suspended', above its lead story about a local sporting personality's divorce following the infidelity of his 'pretty young wife'.[22] Years later, Harries would remember Lady Murdoch's intervention as her son's interests grew to include titles that more than matched *The Mirror*'s taste for sex and sensationalism.

MURDOCH'S LOVE OF gambling and speed weren't the only habits that followed him to Adelaide. One of his regular dinner partners in the city was Clyde Cameron, a federal Labor MP who had already heard whispers about Sir Keith Murdoch's leftist son. Years earlier, prime minister Ben Chifley had showed him one of Sir Keith's letters announcing with horror that Rupert had fallen in with the socialists in England.[23] As they sat across the table at the trendy city restaurant that became their regular haunt, Cameron was amused to find that Sir Keith's fears were realised: the young man seemed even further to the left than Cameron was.[24] He invited Murdoch to attend a meeting of the Fabian Society, the British socialist movement whose South Australian chapter Cameron had been trying to jump-start since 1947.[25] By 1953, the group were meeting in the redbrick library of the university's Zoology Department—a far less exotic location than it sounded, and an awkwardly large space for the one or two dozen people that attended meetings.[26] Along with progressively minded university types, such as a young history lecturer named Ken

Inglis, Cameron was joined by many of his parliamentary colleagues, including Norman Makin, Sid O'Flaherty, Jim Toohey, and a weedy, bespectacled young lawyer named Donald Allan Dunstan.

Born to South Australian expats in Fiji, Dunstan had spent his life bouncing between the Pacific and Adelaide, where he rubbed shoulders with the sons of the Adelaide elite at St Peter's College and lived with his Liberal and Country League-supporting extended family. Speaking with a plummy accent and exuding a worldly air that reflected the two halves of his early life, Dunstan was only a few years older than Murdoch when elected as the precocious young member for Norwood at the 1953 state election. Like Murdoch and Rivett, the establishment credentials of his upbringing didn't stop him from having a healthy scepticism of the status quo, or an appetite for its destruction. Among the Fabian Society's talking points was the problem of Playford's gerrymander and long-time Labor leader Mick O'Halloran's apparent embrace of endless opposition—once telling a friend that 'Tom Playford can do more for my voters than I could if I were in his shoes'.[27]

There was also the White Australia policy, which had long been a key tenet of the Australian Labor Party, leaning into racially charged fears that an influx of cheap migrant labour might undercut wages for white workers. For the cosmopolitan, university-educated members of the Fabian Society, however, it was a backward and prejudiced policy well overdue for abolition. To Dunstan and his peers, the direction of *The News* under Rivett and Murdoch gave 'hope to the side', and an outlet to quietly challenge the orthodoxy that the state's other daily newspaper seemed content to uphold.[28]

According to Cameron, the meetings were also attended by a woman—known to Cameron as 'Mrs Glen'—who he claimed had later been exposed as a plant of the Australian Security Intelligence Organisation.[29] Cameron often held suspicions of ASIO interference in Labor operations, but he was probably correct in this instance; the establishment of the Long Range Weapons Establishment at Salisbury, and the rocket range at Woomera, had made Adelaide the focus of intense scrutiny from ASIO, who feared that the Soviet Union's KGB and GRU might establish a spy ring to extract military secrets.[30]

ASIO's inaugural director-general was a South Australian Supreme Court justice named Geoffrey Reed, an Adelaide detective named Ray Whitrod was one of its early recruits, and the city became the site of a range of covert operations, most of which remain secret.

Throughout the 1950s, ASIO's spies—dubbed 'sparrows' by the agency—penetrated a range of left-wing groups suspected of communist influence. The most famous, by virtue of being one of the few to go public, was a white-haired, middle-aged widow named Anne Neill, who spent seven years infiltrating the Adelaide branch of the Communist Party of Australia, and even travelled behind the Iron Curtain. When she finally went public in *The Sunday Mail* in December 1961, Neill claimed to have attended 'a score of groups' while passing on intelligence about the party's 'trojan horse tactic' of creating front organisations and infiltrating legitimate ones—including an international film society, a theatre group, and a children's art exhibition run by the Union of Australian Women.[31]

In the early 1950s, the Fabians were regularly vilified as a 'fifth column' that, thanks to their 'aura of respectability and acceptability' posed greater danger than the Communist Party—after all, their membership held collective sway over the state executive of the Labor Party.[32] And, coming soon after the defection of British diplomat and Soviet spy Donald Maclean, left-wing university groups were subject to renewed scrutiny. One founding member of the South Australian Fabians—the physicist, former prisoner of war, and future University of Adelaide chancellor, Harry Medlin—had also been a target of sustained and fruitless ASIO attention for years. His work as a scientist often drew the attention of security services, and in 1953 they mounted a fresh probe, even asking Dunstan to make an official statement to ASIO officials. (Dunstan insisted that Medlin was an anti-communist and had helped purge the university's Socialist Club of communist elements years earlier.)[33]

Murdoch was ambivalent about the society; at Oxford in 1951, he had attended meetings of the 'Cole Group', likely a reference to the Fabians and their most high-profile proponent, the socialist historian and anti-fascist GDH Cole.[34] In Adelaide, Murdoch told Cameron that the Fabians seemed 'wishy washy', but agreed to give a speech about the international monetary system and the shadowy manoeuvres of Swiss bankers—a favourite target of scorn among British Labour circles in the 1950s.[35] But he continued to stay in touch with Cameron and Dunstan, who invited Murdoch and Rivett to his home in Norwood, where he and his wife hosted monthly social gatherings for like-minded reformists.[36] In turn, they gave Dunstan a recurring column in *The News* to air his views and commentary, an invaluable platform that helped the ambitious and media-savvy politician build his public profile.[37]

One day in 1956, Dunstan was summoned to the News Limited offices, where Murdoch and Rivett were waiting with a proposal. The Australian Labor Party was in the middle of its historic 'Split', and if Dunstan agreed to bring the division home to South Australia and join the new, breakaway Democratic Labor Party, he could count on *The News* for positive coverage.[38] It was an extraordinary offer, and in his political memoirs 25 years later, Dunstan recalled his 'bemused horror' at receiving it.[39] Dunstan knew that for all the pent-up frustrations that existed among him and his colleagues in South Australian Labor, the conditions in Victoria and New South Wales were fundamentally different. Despite South Australia's famous religious plurality, the state simply lacked the Catholic population that had underscored the divisions on the east coast between the federal executive, led by opposition leader Dr HV Evatt, and the Catholic, anti-communist breakaway movement that had formed under the leadership of BA Santamaria. Dunstan recognised that such a split could only prove destructive, and as a delegate to Labor's 1956 federal conference he had previously moved a motion to allow the national executive to abolish the New South Wales executive, which had fallen into the control of 'the Movement'.[40]

Faced with a choice between the status quo—a long, frustrating stint in opposition under O'Halloran—and mounting an insurgence against his party that would likely consign him to a lifetime of obscurity, he rebuffed their offer. But he left disturbed by what it said about Murdoch, Rivett, and their handle on South Australia and its politics. He had also spent enough time with Murdoch to be less convinced than Cameron about his progressive credentials, and thought the way he 'boasted' about his dealings with the unions 'augur[ed] an attitude to employees which boded ill'.[41]

THE NEED FOR a hardening stance towards unionism wasn't the only lesson in business that Murdoch had picked up since leaving Oxford; after seeing control of Queensland Newspapers slip out of the family's grip, despite all his father's efforts, it was essential that he consolidate family control as he looked to the future. Even before Murdoch had arrived in Adelaide, the family's controlling stake in News Limited was unquestioned; although notionally a public company, the input of independent shareholders had rarely been valued or needed. In September 1952, Rivett recounted the last annual general meeting of the Sir Keith Murdoch era to Rupert: when the doors were thrown open at the agreed 12.30 pm starting time, there was no throng of angry inquisitive investors, just a single shareholder (described as 'a deaf mute with a hearing aid') who seemed satisfied to move or second a handful of motions, before sitting back down.[42] It was all over in five minutes—they hadn't even bothered to go through the chairman's speech, which was taken as read. 'This is a perfect annual meeting and should serve as a classic example to less fortunate companies,' Rivett reflected.

On 18 September 1954, the same day that Murdoch's appointment as publisher was announced, the company reported a 'record' net profit of £37,363. Despite the challenges of *The Sunday Advertiser*, News Limited's chairman, Sir Stanley Murray, told shareholders that the company had enjoyed a year of unparalleled growth in the history of the company'.[43] It was a small improvement on the previous year's £31,420, but that wouldn't be enough to fund any big acquisitions. Rather than seeking new capital through a share issue, which risked diluting Cruden Investments' controlling stake, Murdoch sought to fund the Western Press acquisition with borrowed money. On 11 December 1954, News Limited announced the issue of £200,000 in registered unsecured notes, to be redeemed within three years at 6 per cent interest.[44] The company's 1955 annual report also revealed that a further £207,304 had been mortgaged against the company's freehold properties.[45]

When new share issues did occur, they were arranged to raise capital without upsetting the existing balance of voting shareholders, such as a 1954 share issue that was limited to existing ordinary shareholders, maintaining the ownership ratio dominated by the Murdoch family through Cruden Investments.[46] Between 1954 and 1960, these ordinary shares increased substantially from 105,109 shares (with a value of £105,109) in 1953 to 3,063,600 (with a value of £765,900) in 1960.[47] The largest release of non-ordinary shares came in 1960, following another big acquisition, with £500,000 worth of cumulative preferential shares released to further increase capital.[48] While increasing the shareholder base of News Limited, these cumulative preferential shares contained limited voting rights for ten years before being converted to ordinary shares, ensuring the continued control of the board and the prevention of any outside takeovers.[49]

But in the mid-1950s, the £400,000 debt acquired over the previous two years underscored the need to make an acquisition such as Western Press turn a profit and keep *The News*'s own numbers climbing. Years later, Murdoch described this pattern as a 'treadmill'; he was forced to expand to be able to compete with rivals such as *The Advertiser*, but the expansion, driven by borrowed capital, forced him to push his paper's profitability ever further.[50] It was a precarious, risky strategy that Murdoch would continue to pursue for decades, driving the company's growth while retaining Murdoch-family control. 'You bet on a run,' Murdoch once told his biographer, William Shawcross, when describing the games of two-up in his youth, before adding: 'The real game is the gamble on knowing when to stop.'[51]

OF COURSE, BUILDING a Murdoch dynasty was about more than merger deals and circulation numbers, and on 2 March 1956, barely a week after his run-in with the police on Main North Road, Rupert was waiting at the old Scots Church on North Terrace for his future to arrive. He had avoided any last-minute shotgun weddings before leaving England, and upon first arriving in Adelaide, marriage seemed far from his mind. Shortly after he landed, he took a call in the presence of Joy Saunders, Rivett's secretary, who had been assigned to dictate Murdoch's letters until his own secretary could be hired.[52] When he slammed the phone back down, she heard him exclaim: 'These Adelaide matrons—all after me for their daughters!'[53]

Patricia Dianna Booker was no daughter of an Adelaide matron; her mother had already passed away; and, like Murdoch, she was a transplant from Victoria, having grown up on the Mornington Peninsula just half an hour away from Cruden Farm. She moved to Adelaide in 1950, and it was while working in the menswear department at the Myer Emporium that she met the mutual friend who later introduced her to an awkward, slightly overweight 24-year-old who struck her as 'terribly young, terribly shy, and terribly nervous'.[54] 'I didn't know who Rupert Murdoch was, and I didn't really like him very much at all,' she recalled in a rare press interview given in her later years, when she lived alone in a modest flat in Adelaide. She was 28 when they met, blonde, and a perhaps a little more glamourous than the women Murdoch was used to encountering in Adelaide.

She rebuffed his first attempt to ask her out, but, as the world was beginning to learn, the young Murdoch was nothing if not persistent. By 8 February 1956, the pair were engaged, and Booker, now working as a secretary, was flown over to Melbourne for an audience with Lady Murdoch at Cruden Farm.[55] He might have found a prospective wife, but his priorities were unchanged: 'Circulation was everything to Rupert,' she later said.[56] When the pair went out and saw a street vendor whose presentation of *The News*' posters seemed lacking, Rupert would leap into action, enlisting her help in tidying up the display, or picking up any placards that had fallen over.

In a move that would have satisfied Murdoch's Presbyterian minister forebears, the wedding venue was set for one of Adelaide's oldest churches, originally erected as the Free Church of Scotland in 1850—the year that his grandfather, the Reverend Patrick Murdoch, was born in Aberdeenshire. None of the bride's surviving family came over for the wedding, so when Patricia walked down the aisle in off-white dress of lace and silk organza, her face covered in a billowing veil, and pearls around her neck, she did so on the arm of Norman Young, an accountant and the chairman of a local radio station in which News Limited had invested.[57] In a reflection, perhaps, of the extent of Rupert's social circle in Adelaide, Young and his wife, Jean, had been the first to hear the news of the engagement, when the freshly betrothed couple rocked up at their Victor Harbor holiday home asking to use their phone to call Rupert's mother.[58] After the ceremony, a reception was held, not at a restaurant or hotel, but at the Youngs' home in Erindale, where the Murdochs' old neighbour Daryl Lindsay raised a toast to the couple.[59]

Like his run-in with the police van a week earlier, there would be no reference to the wedding in the pages of *The News*, but a photographer from *The Advertiser* caught a shot of the newlyweds peering through the rear window of the car as they left the church — Patricia flashing a toothy grin, and her plump-cheeked husband wearing a look of assured satisfaction.[60] It was a big day, but the photograph is significant for another reason: it was a rare occasion when Rupert Murdoch could be seen looking back.[61]

# CHAPTER NINE

# The quality of mercy

'I ADHERE TO every word I wrote,' Rupert Murdoch dictated down the telephone line from Darwin. 'If the Western Australian Parliament summons me to justify what I have written I shall welcome the opportunity.'[1] He was defiant as one can be while bedridden, struck down by a mysterious stomach bug contracted along the many hundreds of kilometres he had travelled in the previous few days.[2] When he had set out from an airfield in Adelaide less than a week earlier, he had seemed confident of getting to the bottom of an issue that had broiled into a national political storm. That seemed like hubris now; as he put down the phone, it was becoming apparent that Murdoch hadn't only inflamed the situation—he'd brought the storm upon himself. But if he was breaking a sweat, at least he could blame it on the heat and humidity of a top-end summer. Or the gastro.

As he bisected the continent in January and February 1957, Murdoch joined a long line of young white men who had journeyed into the desert in search of adventure and revelation. The man who was threatening to haul Murdoch out west—a 36-year-old member of the Western Australian Legislative Assembly named Bill Grayden—was one, too. A veteran of the Kokoda trail during the war, Grayden became the youngest member of the Western Australian parliament when he won the seat of Middle Swan in 1947, and, like Murdoch, soon earned a reputation as something of an outsider. Although technically a member of the ruling Liberal Party, Grayden relished playing the rebel, frequently crossing the floor on government legislation; and when he wasn't voting against his own party, the young politician was also making a name for himself with publicity-courting stunts. In 1950, shortly after defecting from state parliament to take up a federal seat in the 1949 election, he tried to 'break down some of the prejudices against whalemeat' as an alternative to beef and mutton in Australian households.[3] The backbencher arranged for 40 pounds of cetacean to be flown from a whaling station in Carnarvon, north of Perth, to the parliamentary kitchens of Canberra for his colleagues to sample.[4] The stunt produced some entertaining newspaper headlines, but failed to win over the parliament's tastebuds, and within a few decades commercial whaling was banned outright.

Grayden made more headlines three years later, when in 1953 he set out on a six-week expedition into the desert with an audacious goal: to finally determine the fate of Ludwig Leichhardt. Leichhardt was a 19th-century Prussian explorer and naturalist who ventured out from Queensland's eastern edge in February 1848 with a plan to trek the breadth of continent from east to west. Leichhardt and his party expected their journey to last two-and-a-half years, but never emerged out the other side of the country's interior, and for a century their fate had stoked the imaginations of explorers, historians, and artists alike. (In 1957, Australian novelist Patrick White would take inspiration from the doomed expedition to write his celebrated fifth novel, *Voss*.) The mix of courage, hubris, and adventure also appealed to Bill Grayden, and 105 years after Leichhardt vanished, he set out on a desert quest of his own, fuelled by a 20-year-old rumour that artefacts from Leichhardt's party had been uncovered among the mountain ranges and sandy plains of central Australia. Some observers suspected that Grayden might also have been drawn to the mystery of Lasseter's Reef—a dazzling deposit of gold in central Australia that a strange and mercurial prospector named Lewis Harold Bell Lasseter claimed to have discovered, and then lost, as a young man. Lasseter went public with his claims in 1929, and, like Leichhardt, perished in the desert on a doomed attempt two years later to find it again—if it ever existed at all.

Grayden's party left Perth on 22 July in two jeeps loaned by the army, but the trip was marked by disappointment and harrowing near-misses; both vehicles caught fire among the sand and Spinifex grass, and Ludwig, the party's dog and mascot, met the same fate as his 19th-century namesake after consuming a poisoned dingo carcass.[5] On 25 August, Grayden admitted defeat. Four weeks of searching across an 800-kilometre radius had unearthed neither Lasseter's gold, Leichhardt's remains, nor a mythical metal chest thought to have been carried by the German explorer's party—and possibly carrying 200 gold sovereigns.

Buried treasure aside, for Grayden, the trip wasn't a total waste of time. For one, it demonstrated his growing savvy as a media operator; before his departure he wrote newspaper columns to pique the public's interest, and took a camera with him to make sure newspapers were splashed with images of the trip upon his return. (Perth's *Western Mail* published a four-page photo essay recounting their journey.)[6] But it also revealed something about life in the interior that would become one of the defining notes of his political career; the trip had given Grayden his first glimpse of how the Ngaanyatjarra people of the Warburton and Rawlinson Ranges lived, and he was troubled by what he saw. The federal government had incorporated their lands into a central Aboriginal reserve, and to Grayden, life in the desert seemed one of extraordinary deprivation.[7] Between the cold weather, limited food, and vast distances travelled, he was surprised that anyone could survive the conditions, and when he returned to Perth made it a personal crusade to document and campaign for the welfare of Yarnangu (the Ngaanyatjarra word for their people).

In October, he publicly lobbied prime minister Robert Menzies to fund the establishment of a pastoral industry through the sinking of wells and the purchase of sheep for Aboriginal families.[8] Later that month, Grayden launched a public debate with native welfare commissioner Stanley Middleton over the provision of clothing for Aboriginal groups in the area. Drawing on his wartime memories of starving locals in India and Egypt, Grayden also made a broader argument about the welfare of those he had visited months earlier: the current state of affairs, he said, showed 'an incredible indifference to large-scale human suffering'.[9]

Grayden lost his seat at the 1954 election, but in 1956 returned to state parliament as an independent — unseating the officially endorsed Liberal member in the process. His focus soon returned to the Ngaanyatjarra lands, which had recently been thrust back into the spotlight. By 1956, the British government had begun nuclear weapons testing at Maralinga, 1,150 kilometres north-west of Adelaide. It was the latest instalment in the long-running saga of British military activities in South Australia, the same tests that had made Adelaide a focus of ASIO surveillance and suspected Soviet espionage. Since 1946, the tests had also drawn the attention of activists concerned that firing rockets over the Central Aborigines Reserve, and the infrastructure built to support their observation, would negatively impact Aboriginal communities living in the area. A series of protests had occurred throughout 1946, and one of the more vocal advocates was Dr Charles Duguid, a Scottish-born doctor and Presbyterian lay preacher who had fought for Aboriginal welfare since the 1930s. Duguid had helped establish a mission at Ernabella in the Musgrave Ranges in 1937, and in 1946 began leading letter-writing campaigns and public meetings, demanding greater protections and criticising the British encroachment as the 'final token of Australia's disregard of her minority race'.[10]

The initial wave of protest eventually died down, their concerns dismissed by officials as the work of communist agitators, but a decade later the scaling-up of British programs triggered renewed protests on both sides of the Western Australian border. In 1956, the construction of the Giles Weather Station in the Purli Yurliya mountain range (named the Rawlinson Ranges by a white explorer) brought roads and airstrips into the heart of Ngaanyatjarra Country, and an important water source known as Warupuyu.[11] The meteorological data collected by the station was integral to British weapons tests, but its arrival during one of the worst droughts in living memory soon drew camps of Yarnangu to the area — to the dismay of authorities, who sought to limit contact between locals and station workers.

With the encouragement of Duguid, Grayden began pushing for
a fresh inquiry into the impact of Maralinga, the weather station,
and other government policies on Yarnangu lives, and in November
1956 he led a select committee comprising members from Labor,
the Liberal and Country League, and the Democratic and Country
League on a week-long trip into the desert. At the Warburton Mission
they encountered a group of 40 Yarnangu from Purli Yurliya who had
recently completed a 100-kilometre journey. Having arrived during
a time of extreme drought, many of them looked malnourished,
some suffered from a range of illnesses, and all of them left a grave
impression on Grayden's committee.

The committee's scathing report drew a muted press response
when it was unanimously passed by the Western Australian parliament
in late December 1956—a familiar story in an east coast-centric
national conversation. Then, in January, the communist newspaper
*Tribune* printed a horrified summary of the paper's more shocking
claims, and soon word spread to the mainstream press. Now having
interests on both sides of the Western Australia–South Australia border,
News Limited soon ran with the story, with a front-page report in the
11 January edition of *The News*, followed by an editorial bemoaning
the 'inhumanity, prejudice and apathy' in Australia's treatment of
Indigenous peoples.[12] Another entitled 'Inequality of Man' sought to
place the Grayden report's findings into a broader context, comparing
the plight of central Australian groups to the systemic disadvantage
seen closer to home, such as the recent story of 'Tiger', an Aboriginal
man hired as a full-time tracker by the South Australian Police but
paid a fraction of a standard police wage.[13] The story grew more
complicated when Middleton, Grayden's old sparring partner, rejected
the committee's findings and its call for the Commonwealth to commit
£50,000 to assist Western Australian authorities.[14]

After a fortnight of heated public debate, *The News* and its young
proprietor decided to weigh in decisively. On Australia Day in 1957,
Murdoch and two companions piled into a Czech-built Super Aero
light plane—the 'most suitable' aircraft the company could find
in South Australia—and flew out from a small private airfield in
Adelaide's north and into the continent's heart. It was unusual for

Murdoch to write under his own by-line, and it wouldn't be cheap, but the knowledge that any shock revelations could be syndicated across both Western Press and News Limited's papers justified the expense. The two men beside him in the plane were John Fisher, a *News* staffer, and Geoff Handbury, Murdoch's pastoralist brother-in-law—none of whom were particularly familiar with the history of the continent's interior, or with the people who lived there. On 30 January 1957, the paper publicly announced the 'fact-finding expedition' that had departed days earlier, and planned to mount a 'full investigation' across central, northern, and western Australia.[15] By that point, the men had already flown into Ernabella (known today as Pukatja) in the far-northern reaches of South Australia.[16] They then flew over the Western Australian border to a mining camp in the Blackstone Ranges, spent 24 hours at the Warburton Mission, and then Giles Weather Station, before touching down in Darwin to file Murdoch's 'exclusive, on the spot' report.

One photograph from the trip shows Murdoch in a corrugated-iron building, his Adelaide corporate attire swapped for a short-sleeved patterned shirt with several buttons undone, his hair frizzing out in every direction, and a hint of perspiration on his cheeks. He has both hands down on a table, and a look of uncertainty as he talks to two smartly dressed Aboriginal men with at least a decade on the young blow-in. Both men are leaning in, with knees up on the table and quizzical, discerning expressions on their faces.[17] From *The News'* sympathetic coverage of the select committee's report, and the eagerness with which he flew out of Adelaide, it seemed Murdoch had been expecting to encounter harrowing scenes, and to produce shocking, sensational revelations for his Perth and Adelaide papers. But when he arrived in Darwin, and began writing up his findings, it seems he found something quite unexpected.

MURDOCH'S FIRST AND only dispatch was published on 1 February, in a full-page story that declared decisively that 'Aborigines are not sick, starving'.[18] The article went on to label Grayden's findings a 'scare' report, argued that the bulk of the select committee's claims were 'hopelessly exaggerated', and that the nation-wide concern that his own papers had helped stoke had been unnecessary.[19] Having travelled for 'several days and many hundreds of miles' and spoken to geologists, missionaries, weather men, and some of the 150 Aboriginal people he claimed to have had encountered, he had met 'not one really sick' Aboriginal person, and decided they were 'a happy lot' who were 'oblivious of the nation-wide concern for their reputed misery'.[20]

The exposé was accompanied by an unsigned editorial further speculating that this group of 40 appeared to have been accepted by the select committee as 'typical of the majority'.[21] Despite Murdoch's findings, the leader reminded readers of the 'debt of conscience' that non-Indigenous Australia owed.[22] Both articles stressed a need for greater attention to Aboriginal welfare, irrespective of the flaws of Grayden's claims, warning against a return to the 'happy sleep of ignorance' that preceded the outcry.[23] Speaking to the journalist Simon Regan in the 1970s, one of Murdoch's travelling companions described the expedition as a 'hell of a trip'.[24] But, years later, they remained unsure whether Rupert had actually been interested in the wellbeing of Yarnangu, or 'just wanted a bloody good jaunt around Australia'.[25] Despite the seriousness of its subject, his report for *The News* included some passages that read more like a travelogue, from visiting 'some of the most picturesque mountains and gorges' to his account of 'a swim to remember':

> Combined with the fierce heat the freshwater was irresistible, and I soon found myself swimming about in the glorious coolness of Mr Grayden's 'Pathetically small dried-up waterhole'.[26]

Before long, however, Murdoch seemed increasingly out of his depth. The initial response to his story had been one of relief; on 2 February, *The News* published comments from the Reverend Gordon Rowe, secretary of the Aborigines' Friends Association, who thanked Murdoch and the paper, and said 'this scare will do good if it results in the ferreting out of the 6,000 primitive aborigines estimated to be in Western Australia outside the confines of civilisation'.[27] He also added, with an extra note of paternalism, 'these people should not be allowed to wander around northern Australia with no one to look after them'.[28] But on 4 February, Grayden issued a rebuke in *The West Australian*, accusing Murdoch of seeking to 'ridicule a careful and studied report' after just a few days' flying over the area, and warning of the 'great harm' he might cause by 'minimis[ing] their plight'.[29] He was also bemused to see that the 'recent picture' of healthy-looking Yarnangu that accompanied *The News*' report had been taken by Grayden himself back in 1953, submitted to *The West Australian*, and apparently kept on file by *The News*.[30] By the next day, Grayden's critique had escalated into a threat: when parliament resumed, he would move for Murdoch to be arraigned before the Legislative Assembly to either substantiate his claims or be charged with contempt of parliament.[31] 'Practically every point raised by him is either false or calculated to mislead,' Grayden told *The West Australian*.[32]

A follow-up report in that afternoon's *News* summarised Grayden's criticisms, alongside exclusive, newly arrived photographs that seemed to support Murdoch's claims, including the 'glorious' waterhole and a group of Yarnangu at the Warburton Mission. ('Rupert Murdoch says the natives camped at the mission are a happy lot,' read one caption. 'They look it.')[33] A small note signed 'Ed, News' also claimed that Murdoch's claims had been 'checked and rechecked' wherever possible.[34]

While Grayden sought out legal advice, Murdoch was unmoved, phoning *The News* from his bed in Darwin to call Grayden's bluff. He further goaded Grayden in comments to *The Advertiser*, saying he would be 'delighted' to be summoned to Western Australia, and that it would be a 'wonderful opportunity' to prove the 'misleading' nature of earlier reports.[35] When his stomach had settled enough to travel, Murdoch and his companions set off from Darwin, flying to the Kimberley before making their way down the west coast to the more familiar surrounds of Perth and the Western Press office.[36] When the next edition of *The Sunday Times* hit the newsstands two days later, it reported that Grayden was now demanding an apology and damages while his solicitors prepared to issue a writ for libel against the publisher.[37] Murdoch had initially seemed ebullient, but this latest threat seemed more real. It wasn't the first time that News Limited

had faced accusations of contempt and libel since he had arrived in
Adelaide—the company had finally closed a costly and drawn-out
courtroom saga just a few months before he flew off into the desert.


ON 7 JUNE 1955, a 22-year-old woman named Kaliopy walked out of
the Myer Emporium on Rundle Street, one of the biggest department
stores on Adelaide's busiest retail strip. She had her arms full that day,
between the six-month-old baby in her arms, the pram she pushed
along in front of her, and the 12-year-old stepson who tagged along
beside her.[38] Kaliopy hadn't been in Adelaide long and spoke little
English; she was just another new migrant from a far-off corner of the
Mediterranean, one of a cohort who were dubbed 'New Australians'
by politicians and the press. It was a label that often invited a level of
stigma and suspicion quite distinct from the treatment given to the
streams of British immigrants who arrived at the same time—they
were called 'Ten Pound Poms', nicknamed after the government-
subsidised fares that sought to entice them over. So when a store
detective suddenly appeared at her side, beckoning her back inside to
answer some questions, she was probably not surprised.[39] But, then
again, she did have two pairs of briefs stuffed under her overcoat.[40]
She tried to tell the detective that she had run out of money, but
when he searched her stepson, he found two more pairs under his
coat. When Kaliopy reached the Adelaide Police Court one month
later, she pleaded guilty to three counts of larceny, and admitted to
enlisting her stepson to help her. She had no legal representation, but
through an interpreter begged for leniency:

> I ask you not to send me to prison. I have a child. I am breast
> feeding. I swear I will not do it again.[41]

The next day, 8 July, *The News* reported an 'out-of-court
storm of criticism' among the legal profession following Kaliopy's
sentencing—despite her pleas, the magistrate had sentenced her
to six weeks' jail with hard labour.[42] But Kaliopy's case, the article
suggested, was not an isolated incident. Concerns had also been raised

about another man, a baker at the Royal Adelaide Hospital, who was imprisoned for three months for stealing a 'tin of spaghetti, one tin of tomatoes, and two tins of sardines' from his workplace.[43] The same magistrate ignored his previously clean record and a hard-luck story about his wife abandoning him to a £600 debt, forcing him to steal to feed his four children. Meanwhile, a co-worker accused of an even larger theft was let off with a fine by a different judge. Like Kaliopy, the baker had appeared without counsel, and, according to *The News'* sources, several lawyers had begun refusing briefs the moment they learned which magistrate was set to hear the case. 'He came up through Crown law,' said one 'prominent lawyer' who spoke to *The News*, 'and I don't think he has a real understanding of the defence point of view'.[44] Further into the paper, an editorial headlined 'The Quality of Mercy' asked how a community that 'venerates' the mother–child relationship could allow a child to be 'plucked from the mother's arms and deprived of her affection', especially when probation was an option.[45] 'We must have justice,' the editorial concluded, 'but should it not always be tempered with mercy?' The story as reported was not out of the ordinary for *The News*; ever since Rohan Rivett had arrived in Adelaide, he had tried to destigmatise New Australians and to draw attention to institutional injustice in South Australia. When Kaliopy's story came up in the newsroom, it must have seemed fair game.

A fortnight after the story was published, the magistrate in question, Derek Wilson, launched a libel writ against News Limited, and a week later the matter escalated further when the Crown filed two notices of intention in the Supreme Court, charging News Limited and its editor, Rohan Rivett, with contempt.[46] The notice was moved by crown solicitor Reginald Roderic Chamberlain, a veteran prosecutor with a quietly formidable courtroom manner. Chamberlain had grown up in Quorn in the state's mid-north, a farmer's son who left the country for the city after winning a series of prizes, scholarships, and bursaries that took him out of the state school system and into the rarefied halls of St Peter's College and the University of Adelaide.[47] At university, he became secretary of the law club and subeditor of the student newspaper, and after passing the bar in 1922, immediately took up a judge's associateship. After a few short years bouncing between private and public practice, he joined the Crown Law Department in 1926, and just two years later was appointed crown prosecutor at the young age of 27. Having worked his way from the farm to the heart of Adelaide's legal establishment, he stayed there for the next 21 years, and in 1952 the now-seasoned prosecutor was elevated again by Playford's Executive Council to the office of crown solicitor. By 1955, the 54-year-old had seen and heard much in his three decades with the Crown, and had garnered a reputation among the state's top silks for methodically demolishing his opponents, often by throwing their own words back at them.

When the case reached the Full Court on 10 August, Chamberlain laid out the charges, accusing Rivett and News Limited of bringing 'calculated' and 'very considerable public odium' upon Wilson, and damaging the administration of justice.[48] Given that Kaliopy and the baker were both in the process of appealing their sentences on 8 July, the same day that the article and the editorial were published, the pieces were also in contempt of the Supreme Court, and the Crown's submission recommended that Rivett be committed to prison and that News Limited be fined.[49] The court heard additional details about both cases not mentioned in *The News*; after Kaliopy's confrontation with the Myer store detective, police had searched her home to find over £86 worth of goods she had stolen between May and June.[50] The baker, on the other hand, had also pleaded guilty to stealing 'three tins of tomatoes and three pieces of cake', and had previous convictions for attempted suicide, income tax violations, and hindering police.[51] Chamberlain claimed that Wilson now faced the difficult task of trying defendants who had read in the newspaper that he was distrusted by the legal profession and 'outrageous in his sphere'.[52] He then took aim at News Limited and Rivett, who had refused to answer questions on legal advice. 'I should say, at once, that there has been a stony silence from *The News* and editor-in-chief in this matter,' Chamberlain said.[53]

Chamberlain argued that the author of the article wilfully distorted the facts, and that even if *The News*'s unnamed source had provided incorrect information, to publish without further inquiry was reckless.[54] As the hearing progressed, News Limited's lawyer Harry Alderman QC did his best to argue that the case was a matter of press freedom ('a newspaper has a right, even if an appeal is pending, to express its opinion to the public, or publish opinion of the result of the penalty'), but admitted that *The News* was not aware of either appeal at the time of publication. Chief Justice Sir Mellis Napier took him to task, insisting that the leading article was a 'threat to this court'.[55]

After initially reserving its judgment, the Full Court found Rivett and News Limited guilty of contempt on 26 August 1955, fining the company £200 and the editor £20. The judgment noted the continued silence from *The News*, the lack of apology, and the general impression that the paper seemed to think it had done nothing wrong:

> If the Press is at liberty to comment in this way and in effect tell the court how any particular case ought to be decided, the next step is likely to be still more unseemly controversy in the form of correspondence published in the paper.[56]

It was the duty of the court, therefore, to step in decisively — lest another 'unseemly' controversy arise. Rivett had avoided jail, but the case would continue to hang over News Limited for over a year, when it finally settled Wilson's private libel claim on 13 November 1956. News Limited agreed to pay unspecified reparations to Wilson as part of the settlement, while also publishing a statement from its other lawyer, Jim Brazel QC:[57]

> *The News* regrets that Mr Wilson SM was caused any embarrassment by the publication of which he complains. It withdraws the implication that in the discharge of his duty he was lacking in the quality of mercy.[58]

Rivett and the paper were in the clear, but there was more trouble on the horizon: just one month after the settlement, Grayden presented the select committee's report to the Western Australian parliament.

IN THE WEEKS and months that followed Murdoch's fact-finding trip, no less than three additional parties set out to test the select committee's findings. In March, University of Western Australia anthropologists Ronald and Catherine Berndt delivered a report that questioned the severity of Grayden's claims after spending five weeks in and around the Warburton area.[59] In February, a delegation of journalists, doctors, and officials, led by the Western Australian minister for native affairs, John Brady, left Perth, with the official ministerial pack shadowed by another group led by Grayden. A few nights before his departure, Grayden reached out to Pastor Doug Nicholls, a renowned Yorta Yorta community leader, activist, and former footballer, who had been a key voice in the 1946 campaign against the Woomera rocket range and had already begun raising money for a 'Warburton Ranges Welfare Fund'. The Brady and Grayden convoys both converged on Warburton on 23 February 1957, Grayden bringing with him a colour film camera to capture what he hoped would be incontrovertible proof of his earlier claims.

Before long, they encountered a group that included some of the 40 Yarnangu that the select committee had encountered at Warburton in 1956, who appeared to be in a similar state to Grayden's last visit. Grayden's camera lens lingered over their bodies and faces, and at an encampment outside Blackstone mining camp, he filmed as Nicholls distributed food to a large and eager group. When an older man who had lost his foot some years earlier appeared, Grayden convinced him to remove his bandage for the camera, despite the man's obvious reluctance to draw attention to his disability.[60] Near the end of the trip, Grayden's party were told that a man's body had been found near a water soak; no one was certain whether he was a local or had come from further afield, but Grayden filmed as the body was hastily buried in the sand. Grayden knew the footage was powerful, and wasted no time editing it into a short film dubbed *Their Darkest Hour*. The grainy but vivid footage was paired with a scripted narration that Grayden had written himself, and concluded with a shot of the body and a scathing indictment:

The body is buried. No cairn marks the spot. Human life has little value on the Warburton Reserve.[61]

Audiences in Perth and Melbourne were shocked when Grayden and Nicholls began screening the film in church halls and community meetings, from the shots of children with rounded stomachs and fly-blown eyes to the footage of the crowd clambering for Nicholls' gift of food. In Melbourne, the response was so stirring that a new organisation, the Aborigines Advancement League, was formed on the spot after a screening.[62] Within three months, the footage had spread far and wide, and in late March, Grayden flew back to Adelaide at the invitation of the league and Dr Duguid. In front of a packed house at the Public Library on North Terrace, he screened the film, critiqued Murdoch's report, and afterwards privately debated one of Murdoch's travel companions.[63] More prints were circulated and screened by church and advocacy groups around the country, and in May it was broadcast into peoples' homes via newly established television stations in Sydney and Melbourne.[64] Broadcast under a stark new title, *Manslaughter*, it became one of the first representations of Aboriginal people seen on Australian television screens, and viewers who might have had little to no contact with Aboriginal people in their day-to-day lives were now confronted by Grayden's images.

Stills from the film also appeared in a pamphlet published by the league debunking Murdoch's 1 February article. Across six pages, it picked apart Murdoch's investigation, which it claimed 'bristled with loose and false statements' and 'slip-shod reasoning'.[65] It framed Murdoch's expedition as shallow and inaccurate, from his estimate of the Yarnangu population to the prevalence of trachoma in the Warburton area — by any count, far more common than the 'only two cases' Murdoch claimed to have seen. It also pointed to official weather bureau data that showed that in the week before Murdoch left Adelaide, the Warburton region was hit by above-average rainfall and a thunderstorm — far more than the 'little rain' mentioned in his 'swim to remember'.[66] It concluded:

No one having any regard for truth would dare to make a definite assertion that there are no people dying of thirst or starvation or disease in an area covering many thousands of square miles, merely because he had not located any.[67]

Grayden had intended to shock viewers into action, and on this front, he achieved remarkable success. The work of the league and other activist groups over the next decade helped create a groundswell of domestic and international concern over the inequalities faced by First Nations peoples around Australia, and in May 1967, 90.8 per cent of the country voted 'Yes' in a historic referendum to amend the constitution to allow the Commonwealth to legislate for Aboriginal peoples.

But even as their images became part of history, the film made little impact on the lives of Yarnangu, and in subsequent years Grayden's footage became a source of discomfort and pain for many who saw their family members and younger selves portrayed as objects of pity and horror, filmed in a way that maximised shock value. As one patrol officer noted at the time, Grayden seemed to seek out 'any subject which might be used to support his published statements', and ignored those that didn't.[68] He had arrived at a particularly difficult moment, in the midst of drought, but it was by no means representative of life for Yarnangu, and some scenes Grayden clearly thought shocking landed differently for those with an intimate knowledge of how Yarnangu lived and survived. 'Life was hard, yes, but he came at the wrong time,' one man recalled in an interview with anthropologist Pamela McGrath decades later.[69] In the intervening half-century, the widespread dissemination of Grayden's images became another difficult legacy for Yarnangu to contend with. In 2006, the Australian Broadcasting Corporation was asked to cease distributing the archival footage without permission from the Ngaanyatjarra Council, who argued that the film was reductive, dehumanising, and set in place stereotypes that continue to do harm today. A Ngaanyatjarra man named Mr West explained the request:

> Put that film away. Put it away, for history. Hold it, but don't show it to people. Yes, they used it for the referendum, I understand that [but] they made it bad, because they didn't understand what they were doing. It's still the same now ... instead of encouraging them to stand on their feet, they put them down. Show the worst things.[70]

Grayden achieved something remarkable in 1957, using photography, print, and the emerging medium of television to create a viral media storm with historic impact. But it also helped set a template for representations of Aboriginal and Torres Strait Islander people in the media that have continued to disempower and stigmatise them across the decades. Grayden and Murdoch might have arrived at opposite conclusions, but in some respects their missions were alike: both went into the desert expecting to capture, whether in black and white ink or moving colour, a definitive truth of how Yarnangu lived. They were each in their own way misguided, flattening complexities that could not be captured in a single newspaper exposé or a short film.

For Pastor Doug Nicholls, the whole experience proved difficult to look back on: 'The thing became a political football,' he later told his biographer. 'It is wrong to make people a football.'

SOME YEARS LATER, Grayden explained why he had never followed through on his threat against Murdoch after his initial flurry of comments to the press. The first lawyer he had contacted, a rather gung-ho QC nicknamed 'Roaring Jack', encouraged Grayden to launch his suit.[71] But Grayden was already having second thoughts. 'Because [Murdoch] had a very prominent position in the eastern states—well, his relatives did—with *The Herald* newspaper, I decided to get a second opinion,' he recalled years later.[72] When a second lawyer advised strongly against legal action, Grayden focussed instead on his follow-up trip, a book, and the film to refute Murdoch's claims. But, of course, by 1957 neither Murdoch nor his relatives had a 'prominent position' at the Herald and Weekly Times. Ever since Sir Keith had died, Rupert had been battling it out against his father's old company, but in this instance at least, that old, enduring misconception that the Herald and Weekly Times was essentially an organ of the Murdoch press had got him out of trouble.

At the time, however, Murdoch was concerned enough by the mounting threats against him to send a letter to the editor of *The West Australian*. 'To set the record straight, I would like to state the reasons for my investigation,' he wrote on 12 February, at the height of the furore.[73] Within a few years, his choice of words would come back to haunt him; the Wilson case of 1955 and the Warburton Ranges controversy of 1957 showed how *The News*' appetite for headline-grabbing, socially conscious journalism could be fraught with danger, and could invite a very real risk of prosecution and jail for libel and contempt. Both were just a taste of what was to come for Rupert Murdoch, Rohan Rivett, and *The News*.

# CHAPTER TEN

# It depends what you call monopoly

'*Audi Vide Tace*' reads the bronze lettering above the four tall Grecian columns that front Adelaide's Grand Lodge of the Freemasons. The Latin dictum translates as 'Hear, See, Be silent', but in the first week of May 1958, Rupert Murdoch found himself doing an awful lot of talking. The North Terrace lodge loomed large over the city's east end, past the art gallery, the university, and the church where he and Patricia had been married two years earlier. A towering block of sand-coloured concrete, it was the kind of building that seemed designed to make visitors feel small and speechless; stepping through its heavy doors, the eyes couldn't help but be drawn from one piece of arcane iconography to another, as each footstep echoed off the checkerboard tiles and up into the vast ceiling overhead. Like its newspaper industry, the colony's chapter of Freemasons predated settlement, with its first members immortalised in street names across Colonel Light's grid. But when it came to members-only institutions with a shadowy influence over the rest of South Australia, by the 1950s it was little match for the Adelaide Club up the road.

In May 1958, Murdoch had come to the board room of the Grand

Lodge to take part in a peculiar rite of passage, a public inquisition, all in pursuit of joining the ranks of an exclusive new order: he wanted to become a television mogul.

'I think you were anxious to go to Brisbane and be heard so that any discussion to grant two licences in Brisbane might not create a precedent for Adelaide,' said Antony Larkins QC. 'Is that a fair summary of the reason for your going?'[1]

Larkins was a seasoned lawyer from Sydney with a penchant for courtroom drama. Long before he became a justice of the High Court of Australia, Michael Kirby often briefed Larkins while working as a clerk in the 1950s, and he remembers 'Larko' as an impressive, elegant man, with a surprising sense of humour and a hint of vanity. 'At the time I knew him, he wore a monocle, which was unique at the New South Wales bar,' Kirby recalled.[2] 'At particularly dramatic moments in a trial, he would release the monocle, and it would fall onto his black waistcoat.'

Larkins and his monocle had come to Adelaide on behalf of Television Corporation Limited, a shell company owned by Frank Packer's Australian Consolidated Press. As the Australian Broadcasting Control Board's (ABCB's) Adelaide hearings wore on, he seemed to enjoy making Murdoch embarrass himself on public record.

'That was not the reason for my going,' Murdoch replied, 'but that was the reason for my speaking there.'

'You claimed that falsehoods had been put forward?' Larkins said.

'I retracted that statement in cross-examination last week,' Murdoch said.

'It was a serious thing to say on oath, don't you think?'

'You pointed that out last week.'

'Would you agree that it indicates some impulsiveness on your part?'

'I think it does.'

Larkins kept pursuing Murdoch: 'Do you think that impulsiveness, combined with your comparative youth, and your fears for the future, are qualities that are to be looked for in an application of that kind?' In a room dominated by older men with greying hair and combovers, the 27-year-old Murdoch did seem like an outlier. And in a competitive three-way race, those points of difference could be used as ammunition to knock him and his new, largely hypothetical Southern Television Corporation, out of contention.

'I think a lot of us here suffer from impulsiveness,' Murdoch said.

'You agree, do you?' Larkins said. One only had to cast a quick look around the room to notice that, with perhaps the exception of Frank Packer, the crowd seemed to skew fusty and conservative.

'At times I think we are all liable to be a little impulsive,' Murdoch replied.

Since Bill Grayden's threat to haul him before parliament proved empty, this was the first time Murdoch had testified in front of an official hearing, and it certainly would not be his last. He would spend the coming hours and days attempting to strike a delicate balance of humility and confidence — even if some of his responses strained credulity. He had big plans for 1958, but with every embarrassing disclosure, and every heated exchange, it all seemed increasingly up in the air.

THE RISE OF television had been on Murdoch's radar for years, and as he looked to his future there seemed no greater prize than a slice of the broadcasting spectrum. In those uncertain weeks after his father's death in 1952, it was among the first things he discussed with Colin Bednall.[3] It remained a new and uncharted area for Australian policy-makers, and, after the Menzies government announced it would begin allocating commercial licences in June 1950, Bednall had spent two years lobbying for newspaper and radio operators to get a piece of the action.[4] When Menzies announced a royal commission into television, Bednall was invited to sit on it, and within two years he had escaped newspapers altogether to become an executive at Melbourne's first commercial television station, the Herald and Weekly Times-aligned GTV-9. As he wrote to Bednall from Oxford, Rupert brimmed with 'ideas and dreams and plans', and made sure to include television broadcasters in his brief tour of America before relocating to Adelaide.[5]

He wasn't the only one preparing for television's arrival in Adelaide. As the first Melbourne and Sydney stations started broadcasting in

1956, he received an invitation from Sir Lloyd Dumas, who had summoned all interested parties to meet at *The Advertiser*'s offices.[6] Dumas was about embark on a fact-finding trip to America, and offered to share his findings with no strings attached. But with the *Sunday Mail* agreement only a few months old, Murdoch was in no hurry to shackle himself to his father's old colleagues any further—especially when the potential rewards were so great. Dumas never got around to forwarding his report, but on 1 July 1957 wrote to News Limited chairman Sir Stanley Murray, formally inviting the company to co-sponsor an application for the first Adelaide licence.[7] Murdoch baulked at the offer; in Murdoch's reading, what *The Advertiser* board and Dumas framed as equal ownership was slightly weighted in the bigger firm's favour. He didn't want to be anyone's junior partner, and, as he would later tell the ABCB, he 'had unfortunate experiences of partnerships with Advertiser Newspapers Limited'.[8]

Three months went by before Murdoch deigned to respond, when he visited *The Advertiser* offices to tell Dumas in person that whatever News Limited's plans, they would be going it alone. He had just completed his own two-month tour of the United Kingdom and Canada, and after seeing how television was transforming the northern hemisphere and its newspapers, he was full of ideas.[9] But by the time he walked into Dumas's office it was a moot point. That very morning, the postmaster-general—a Country Party MP from Queensland named Charles Davidson—had announced that the federal government was open to the idea of allocating multiple licences in each city. Co-sponsoring a single application now risked clearing the field for another party, such as Frank Packer's Consolidated Press, to swoop in to claim the second station—a situation that neither Dumas nor Murdoch could stomach.

In April, when the ABCB's inquiry into Adelaide and Brisbane licences began in the chamber of Brisbane's Legislative Council, Murdoch sat in the public gallery as Packer made his pitch. While the postmaster-general had left the door open to granting two licences in Brisbane and Adelaide, it remained unclear which way the board would swing. Packer was banking on two licences being approved—in a three-way race for one licence, it seemed unlikely that a Sydney bid would trump two local applicants. Murdoch had planned to simply observe the Brisbane hearings, but upon hearing the other applicants' evidence, grew concerned that the two-licence model might take root; the Queensland capital was of similar size to Adelaide, and he worried that any decision there would set a precedent back home.[10] He was granted leave to make a short statement, but Larkins quickly swung into action, questioning Murdoch about his attempt to lay sole claim to the Adelaide market. Murdoch tried to duck Larkins' questioning, hoping to save his answers for the upcoming hearing in Adelaide, but the lawyer was relentless.

'I will tell you next week,' Murdoch said, but now even the chairman, Robert Osborne, was losing patience.[11]

'We need not fence unnecessarily,' Osborne interjected. 'Why go on like this?'

'You do not shrink from the fact that it is a monopoly, do you?' said Larkins a few minutes later.[12]

'In one sense it is a monopoly,' Murdoch replied. 'Not in the sense of the viewers. They can always turn to the ABC. They have an alternative.' Rather than encouraging better programming, he claimed, competition did the opposite. Murdoch's feelings about monopolies had clearly undergone some evolution since the attack on Dumas's 'bid for press monopoly' five years earlier. 'The situation is broadly the same in any form of mass communications,' he said. 'Take my own position in Adelaide where there is a monopoly evening paper. We would claim that the paper would be an infinitely better paper, from the public's point of view, than perhaps Sydney evening papers, where competition tends to lower standards. Indeed, some of Mr Packer's publications claim to improve as their competitors drop out.'

'What point do you seek to make by all that?' Larkins asked.

'That competition does not necessarily improve quality,' Murdoch replied. 'Rather, it *lowers* quality.'

'You think the press of each capital city would be a better press if it were controlled by monopoly? Is that your view?' he replied.

'No,' Murdoch said.

'Is not that what you are saying?' Larkins asked.

'It depends what you call monopoly,' Murdoch replied.

'That is what you are asserting, isn't it, that the press would be better without competition in each of the capital cities?'

'I am asserting that those papers which have a field to themselves or a market in enough of their particular type of paper do better than where there is a wild scramble for circulation.'

'You claim that you could make that a *better* paper if you could get rid of the opposition?'

'I claim it is a better paper because we have not got opposition.'

Larkins tugged the thread. Was competition a 'bad thing' only because it would force a publisher such as Murdoch to lower their standards? Murdoch took the bait.

'I would be forced to,' he said.

'Would that be your attitude as the operator of a commercial television licence?' Larkins replied.

'That I would lower standards?'

'If you had competition?'

'There would be a danger I would be forced to lower standards to chase the ratings.'

'You would not *hesitate* to do it,' Larkins asked.

Murdoch said he would fight against it all the way, but, when asked if it was a choice between losing money and lowering standards, he answered plainly: 'Wouldn't you?'


AS MURDOCH SEETHED and floundered in the face of Larkins' questioning, his performance at the inquiry began to recall his days as a teenage debater at Geelong Grammar a decade earlier—rambling, flustered, and defiant. It probably didn't help that one of the members of the board was none other than Dr James Darling, the imposing Englishman who had been his old headmaster at Geelong Grammar. All that was missing was the mortar board, gown, and pipe as Darling impressed upon his former pupil the gravity of the 'very great personal power and personal responsibility' he was seeking.[13] Darling knew Packer as well; his two sons, Clyde and Kerry, had passed through Geelong Grammar just a few years after Rupert. Ever the educator, he also questioned the wisdom of handing a television licence—a medium with once-in-a-blue-moon potential for inspiring and educating the public—to the sole discretion of one proprietor. 'If this is a great public responsibility more so than a competitive newspaper, and if it is regarded as an opportunity to educate the public, isn't it the kind of thing on which there should be representative and responsible people who will look at the responsibilities from that point of view, rather than the profit point of view?' Darling asked.[14]

At one point, Murdoch even seemed to slip into the old power dynamic of his school days, responding to one question with a deferential 'Yes, sir.'

By the third day of the Adelaide hearings, it seemed Murdoch had begun to grasp that the anti-competition line he had tried in Brisbane was having an unintended effect. He was trying to warn the board against a general race to the bottom, but in Larkins' hands these talking points became evidence of Murdoch's own inability to resist the lure of the gutter. Or, worse, a kind of threat.

'Are you afraid of being crippled in competition?' Larkins asked.[15]

'I am frightened of my *standards* being crippled,' Murdoch replied.

'You would not hesitate to let your standards go if you saw a danger of being crippled, would you?'

'I would hesitate. I would resist any reduction in standards as long as was conceivably possible.'

'I put it this way,' Larkins explained. 'You yourself feel honestly that you cannot be trusted to maintain standards if you are one of the two commercial licences?'

'We will always be subject to the limitations of the Control Board,' Murdoch replied.

'Would you agree with me that you cannot be trusted to maintain high standards?'.

'It depends how high.'

'Well, will you agree that you cannot be trusted to maintain the high standards of programming if you are but one of two licensees?'

'Yes,' Murdoch said. It was an unflattering admission, but just by repeating the question—and its refrain that Murdoch could not be trusted—Larkins seemed to be giving Packer his money's worth. He had, in a brief exchange the day before, established in the board's mind that Murdoch essentially was *The News*, and that any application it sponsored was inextricably tied to the young man before them.

Now Larkins worked to frame Murdoch in the worst possible light — that he was impulsive, inconsistent, inattentive, and prone to fudging the details, or simply making them up in pursuit of his personal ambition. And again and again, Murdoch continued to oblige. One minute he was backed into contradicting the evidence of one of his own executives. The next, he was pressed to confirm whether the News Limited board had formally approved raising the extra money — between £600,000 and £1 million over three years — that might be needed if two licences were approved. The implication was clear: the young Murdoch was playing fast and loose, with little oversight and hundreds of thousands of pounds at stake. And if his own board wasn't always in the loop, how could the inquiry trust any of his submissions?[16]

'I do not remember if there is any minute or not,' Murdoch said, as he agreed to track down a set of board minutes during the day's lunch hour.

'You know there isn't, don't you?' Larkins shot back. 'Do you really hope to find a minute?'

'I do not mind whether I do or not,' Murdoch replied, losing patience while explaining that he did not have a 'photographic memory'.

Larkins continued to chip away at the contents of Southern Television's application — a 'handsome document', he said facetiously. On paper, Murdoch's team had sought to stress their experience and preparation for the challenges of television, but now his focus was on playing up News Limited's independence and local credentials. These two themes didn't always add up, and Larkins seized upon the contradictions.

'You have had a close association with ATV [Amalgamated Television Services] and GTV-9 [General Television Corporation] in connection with this application?' he asked.[17]

'Not a close association,' Murdoch replied. He had spoken often with the Fairfax subsidiary ATV in Sydney and Bednall at GTV-9 in Melbourne, and in the last six months they had allowed him to inspect their premises and numbers—Murdoch even took his architects to see how the studios he planned to build on a block of land in North Adelaide could be modelled on ATV. But it was not, Murdoch said, a 'regular thing'.

Larkins pressed him on the denial. 'Then why did you say in your application that you and members of your staff had had the benefit of many trial-and-error experiments made in both Sydney and Melbourne as seen by the executives directly involved? Is that true?'

'No, we have just had general conversations from time to time,' Murdoch said.

Larkins invited Murdoch to re-read his own company's application. He had walked into another trap.

'It would be an exaggeration,' Murdoch said.

'An exaggeration on oath?' Larkins pounced.

'It is your exaggeration, not mine.'

'Have a look at page six. Look under the heading 'Inter-state research'. Look at the last three lines—those are the very words I have just put to you.'

The young publisher seemed to crack a smile at being caught out—a flash of the old 'Bullo Murdoch' seen by his Geelong Grammar classmates.

'You are amused, are you? Are you amused, Mr Murdoch?'

'It does not worry me very much. I withdraw what I said and I agree with this. I am sorry.'

Larkins pressed further. Was Murdoch withdrawing his answer contradicting the application, or his earlier support of it?

'I withdraw my answer, in that it was the *phraseology* of yours which I was objecting,' Murdoch said.

Larkins was incredulous—the 'phraseology' he had put to Murdoch was, almost verbatim, what his own company had submitted.

'No,' said Murdoch, 'you said, "month to month". I said "*every* month."'

'You will find that, following upon that, I read you the precise words that are there in that last sentence and I asked you if that was correct,' Larkins said. 'Do you not recall that?'

'Yes, I take your word for it.'

'And you had earlier told your counsel that what was contained here was true, had you not?'

'Yes. There is a conflict there, I grant you that.'

A particularly low point came later that afternoon, when Larkins asked Murdoch, yet again, whether he would entertain the original offer from Dumas should only one licence be granted.

'No, no, no, no,' Murdoch pushed back.[18]

'You do not sound very emphatic,' Larkins said sarcastically.

'I said "no" *four times*,' Murdoch said. 'I will say it again if you like.'

'Is that a complete answer?'

'It is the truth, the *whole truth*.'

By that point, of course, Larkins had conjured plenty of doubt for all those in attendance whether even Murdoch could judge how true or false his statements were.

BACK IN 1954, the royal commission's report had warned against the 'undesirable concentration of ownership' of any planned stations across the country, and suggested the licensing process be the venue for preventing levels of concentration that would be 'contrary to the public interest'.[19] On a brief stopover on his way back from Brisbane, Murdoch had given a hastily arranged television interview at Melbourne airport to GTV-9 in which he elaborated on his reasons for being in Queensland: he was also there to stop the spread of the Herald and Weekly Times' monopolistic growth. In Adelaide, Murdoch was more specific on the question of control—he believed it should be *locally* controlled. Now a Mr Pickering, counsel representing *The Advertiser*'s Television Broadcasters Limited, took over and picked up a point Larkins had raised earlier. Murdoch had told Larkins and the ABCB that the Melbourne *Herald* and *The Advertiser* were 'to a large extent one and the same thing', and now Pickering was calling him on it.

'You claim that yours is local and that ours is not, or not to the same extent,' Pickering asked. 'The other argument you say is control; what do you mean by difference in control between *The News* and *The Advertiser*? Well, let us be brutally frank about it, what exactly are you suggesting?'

'That *The Advertiser* is controlled by the Melbourne *Herald*,' Murdoch replied.

'You come down to this then, do you: you claim that the board should prefer your application to ours by reason of the fact that ours is controlled by the Melbourne *Herald*?' Pickering asked.

'I think that is the compelling reason, yes,' Murdoch replied.

'Well, let us just deal with the control of *The News* for the moment, which you claim is local. Cruden Investments has the power to control *The News*, has it not?'

'Yes.'

'And through *The News*, power to control Southern Television Corporation?'

Pickering then turned to the role of Harry Giddy, who remained on the board of both the Herald and Weekly Times and Cruden Investments.

'I may be repeating something that Mr Larkins said, but you object to him in that capacity as far as we are concerned, but you have no objection to him as far as News Limited is concerned?'

'He plays no other part in Cruden Investments other than as a director.'

'Assuming that the chairman of Cruden Investments and the Herald and Weekly Time plays no part in *The Advertiser*, would that cut away your objections?

'No,' Murdoch replied. 'Because they have the power to take part.' When Pickering asked why the same power didn't extend to News Limited policy, Murdoch claimed Giddy was morally bound by his father's will, and that unless he went 'around the bend', Giddy and the Cruden board were obliged to support him.

'I think the actual words are these, are they not,' Pickering replied: '"The support of my trustees, if they consider him worthy of that support". Do you recall those words as being an extract from the will?'

The implication was clear: nothing prevented Giddy from one day deciding that Rupert was no longer worthy and relieving him of control. After days of questioning, such a scenario didn't seem so far-fetched—Murdoch had so far come across as impulsive, careless with detail, and willing to take on extraordinary losses with little accountability. Later, Pickering even pointed out that Murdoch's death—however unlikely at the age of 27—would render News Limited once again a Victorian-controlled company under the Cruden arrangement. Alderman, for his part, downplayed this hypothetical prospect. 'There might be half a dozen children by then, too,' he said prophetically—Patricia Murdoch was, at that moment, pregnant with her and Rupert's one and only daughter, Prudence, who arrived a few months later as the only Adelaide-born Murdoch.

Throughout the inquiry, both Murdoch and *The Advertiser* invoked the memory of Sir Keith Murdoch to justify their case. Rupert knew *The Advertiser* and Dumas were beholden to the Melbourne *Herald*, he claimed, because his own father had set it up that way. Eventually, Osborne had to ask Dumas to 'clear up a matter of Australian newspaper history' and to offer a truncated account of *The Herald*'s role in Adelaide from the time Sir Keith's syndicate took over *The Register* and *The Advertiser*. There was a period, Dumas conceded, when the likes of Murdoch, Fink, and Baillieu could, from the *Herald* office, make big, unilateral decisions concerning Adelaide—like amalgamating its oldest paper, *The Register*, into the stronger *Advertiser*.

'But that is all gone,' Dumas said. 'All I can say is that in the whole of my experience no control has been exercised by the Melbourne *Herald* nor has there been any attempt at control.'

But Dumas's testimony wasn't always convincing, either; when asked about the recently knighted Sir John Williams' participation in *The Advertiser*'s board meetings—Williams was both managing director of the Herald and Weekly Times and a director of Advertiser Newspapers—Dumas insisted that there existed no real crossover between his role at *The Advertiser* and his responsibilities at the Herald and Weekly Times.

'How do you manage to tell the difference?' asked Alderman.

'By the inflection of his voice,' Dumas replied.

'Over some 400 miles of telephone line, you can tell by his voice, can you?' Alderman shot back. In his concluding remarks, he repeated the argument:

The fact that *The Herald* has not yet exercised any overwhelming control over *The Advertiser* directorate does not show that it is not there. It is always there ready to be used and like the policeman strolling along doing nothing Sir John Williams in Melbourne is doing nothing, but let the *Advertiser* board get out of hand, with £3 million of TV assets tied up between Melbourne, Brisbane and Adelaide, and we might find that the leisurely policeman would at once become a very active and vigorous person.[20]

The inquiry had been an unedifying experience for all parties, and the drawn-out cross-examination of both Murdoch and Dumas meant that the Adelaide sessions had spilled over into follow-up hearings in Melbourne the following week. The official records, unfortunately, make no mention of how often Larkins' monocle dropped for dramatic effect, but if the sheer abundance of 'gotcha' moments in the raw transcript is any indication, it spent much of the week in free-fall. Even Osborne seemed to despair as the questioning wore on. ('We have also come to the conclusion that it will be improbable that the hearing here will finish tomorrow, although we very much hoped it would be,' he said on the second-to-last day in Adelaide.)

But when it was finally all over, and the board delivered its report on 25 July, Murdoch's pro-monopoly argument seemed to have prevailed. It wasn't all Murdoch's doing, of course; the Film and Television Council had also delivered a submission warning of 'a sort of 'Gresham's Law' in which highly competitive television would see 'good and wholesome programmes' give way to 'cheap, low-standard' material. Dumas had made similar points, but wisely sought to differentiate a 'lowering of standards' from a 'reduction of services', lest he be cornered into making the same sort of admissions as Murdoch.

But the ABCB's findings were unambiguous: applications should be invited for *one* licence apiece in Brisbane and Adelaide, and, as far as practicable, the successful company should be 'substantially locally owned and not controlled in any way by any of the companies holding the licences for existing stations or significant shareholders in these companies'.[21] According to the report, the main issue that arose from the inquiry was whether groups who were 'already powerful in the fields of mass communications' be allowed to expand their interests, or whether it was in the public interest to prioritise independence and local ownership.

For Murdoch, this was a coup—based on these criteria, Southern Television's application was a shoo-in. The protracted debate over who was the more 'local' contender had muddied the water, but it was clear that *The Advertiser*'s links to *The Herald* should knock it out of contention. But weeks went by, and no word came from either the board or the federal government.

In August 1958, Arthur Calwell stood up in question time to ask why there had been no decision. 'If no decision has been made, is that due to the fact that the government wishes to hold the matter over until after the general election campaign is finished, or is it that the government wishes to avoid offending too many people by granting licences to the present group of newspaper companies or other groups which hold a monolithic monopoly?'[22]

'I do not quite know why the honourable member refers to a "monolithic monopoly", because monopoly, in its nature, ought to be monolithic,' retorted prime minister Robert Menzies.[23] 'Therefore, he is guilty of redundancy, I think. So far as I know, no report has been made. I have not seen one; and the matter has not engaged the attention of the government.'

This was not entirely true—the report had been completed and filed nearly a month earlier. When the government did finally consider the report on 10 September, it rejected its three key findings, with postmaster-general Davidson telling the House of Representatives that, despite the board's findings, the government had decided that *two* licences should be granted in each city. In a follow-up report on 26 September, the ABCB now recommended that both Southern Television Corporation and Television Broadcasters Limited gain licences.

A rumour soon spread that Menzies himself made the decision to overrule the board, after being quietly briefed by nameless *Advertiser* executives.[24] (It's certainly plausible—in April 1962, Dumas lobbied Menzies to delay a third television licence being granted in Adelaide. The third station didn't arrive for another three years.[25]) The opposition, meanwhile, was outraged that the 'power-mad' government had not only disagreed with the board's recommendations, but had effectively ignored them.

'The government is serving, not the interests of the community, but the interests of the monopolies in all fields,' Jim Cairns, the Labor member for Yarra, said in parliament.[26] 'One of the most effective of the monopolies, because of its power over public opinion, is the monopoly of television. If this procedure is allowed to go on much longer, control of public opinion in Australia will fall into very few hands; hands which do not represent the interests or the needs which should be of concern to the people … the Government is showing all the signs of political corruption and it will come to an end very soon.'

Once again, predictions of the Menzies government's imminent doom were overly optimistic, and by the time the 1958 federal election came and went, Murdoch had been delivered another formative lesson about power and influence in Australian politics. Now that South Australian television was no longer a one-horse race, it was imperative that Murdoch be the first across the finish line.

SYDNEY CAMPBELL WAS soundly sleeping in the early hours of 30 June 1959 when the smell of smoke roused him. It wasn't unusual at that time of year for a whiff of winter bonfires and farming burn-offs to drift down from the hills and across the city, but this felt much closer and more alarming. Looking out through his bedroom window, he saw that the building next door was shrouded in plumes of black and grey, while a dull, ominous glow seemed to radiate from within.[27] Before long, six fire trucks from the North Adelaide and city brigades had descended on Wellington Square, where Campbell waved them through the opened gates of his block of flats. The men made short work of the fire; under floodlights, they smashed through the building's brand-new plate-glass front door, cut all power, and doused the blaze from above, using a 35-metre extension ladder. It was all over in 20 minutes, but it was clear that the damage bill from the fire and water would easily number in the thousands of pounds. In one room, the heat was so intense that the ceiling had begun to sag and bow, while its mighty steel girders buckled — to one observer, they looked like burnt matches.[28]

The burning building on Tynte Street, North Adelaide, was the brand-new, state-of-the-art studio of Adelaide's first commercial television station, NWS-9. When it was announced in January 1959, it was projected to be the largest studio in the country, and Murdoch had spent £300,000 on land, construction costs, and equipment, and hired over 60 staff.[29] In a week's time, the transmitter would be powered up for the first full-power test broadcast — the culmination of years of planning, long, painful public hearings, and enormous publicity from broadcasters and electronics retailers alike. This wasn't even the first time the studio had combusted — another minor fire had caused a smaller damage bill back in January — but, mercifully, the fire only affected the second studio, while the most expensive equipment, £190,000 worth of state-of-the-art Pye cameras, telecine film scanners, and editing equipment, and a labyrinthine tangle of cables, monitors, and wires, were spared. The studios were so new that the insurance policy was still held by the construction company — they were due to officially hand it over to Southern Television Corporation the very next day. In the pages of *The News*, the paper that gave NWS-9 its callsign, the company defiantly announced that a full program would be broadcast the following night regardless.[30]

It made good on the promise, and after a month of tests, the station officially started broadcasting at midday on Saturday 5 September 1959, with its enormous, 150-metre-tall transmission tower at Mount Lofty beaming Fred Astaire as far as Port Augusta, 320 kilometres away. In the lead-up to the official launch, the pages of *The News* became filled with advertising from electronic retailers selling television sets in sizes, styles, and payment plans to suit every household. In one publicity stunt, a visiting Sir Edmund Hillary — 'the man who stood on top of the world!' — had climbed the tower and posed for *The News*' cameras.[31] In September, Southdown Press launched an Adelaide edition of *TV Week*, a weekly guide that Murdoch modelled on the highly profitable US magazine *TV Guide*, whose success he had glimpsed on his American research trips. The station had even invited Sir Thomas Playford to make his televised debut with a pre-recorded statement to be broadcast on the first night of official programming.[32] Given the state of News Limited's relationship with the Playford government in early September 1959—certain events on the second and third of September saw them plunge to an all-time low—it was a sign of television's revolutionary potential that the premier agreed at all.

NWS-9 also sought to recruit talent from the local community, with regular callouts published in *The News*. The initial programming even featured a performance by a young Malayan crooner named Kamahl, who Patricia Murdoch had introduced to Rupert after hearing him perform in a nightclub on Anzac Highway.[33] She remembered serving him as a schoolboy when she still worked at the Myer Emporium, and now Murdoch had plucked him offstage and put him on the screen. Television had arrived in Adelaide, and although it had done so in a more explosive fashion than anyone had predicted, not even fire could dampen the excitement.


MURDOCH'S TESTIMONY HADN'T finished in Adelaide. In late July 1958, he flew to Perth to front the ABCB once more, but he was in an awkward position. He had just spent hours selling his South Australian credentials and the importance of local ownership, but now had to convince the board that Western Television Services, his Western Press-aligned consortium, was worthy of a different state's television licence.

Osborne, having now sat through weeks of testimony, was sceptical. 'I think you were at some pains in Adelaide to demonstrate you were a citizen of South Australia,' he said, before asking why Murdoch was putting himself forward as a 'champion protecting the people of Western Australia from the domination of its television by a newspaper company'.[34]

Murdoch agreed that he was a 'patriotic South Australian', and downplayed his and News Limited's role in Western Television Services—he was merely a helpful investor, driven by a desire to prevent *The Sunday Times* from being placed at a disadvantage if its competitor gained a television licence.[35]

'You know my feelings already about monopoly,' Murdoch said. '... should WA Newspapers have a monopoly of television as well as the newspapers, it would put Western Press in a tight corner—I have always believed in a split-up if it was possible here'.[36]

The young man had made many statements over the past three months that had proved to be inconsistent, or inaccurate, even within moments of uttering them. Others, such as his self-serving thoughts on monopolies, and the veiled threat that competition would lead to lower standards, offered a curious glimpse of the proprietor he would later become.

But of all the assertions he made under oath in 1958, he saved his best—and most laughably hollow—for Perth: 'There is no attempt to build an empire or anything like that,' he said on the third day of the inquiry.[37] 'It would not interest me.'

## CHAPTER ELEVEN

# A matter of some delicacy

A LITTLE AFTER 2.00 am on a miserable, wet September night in 1958, two South Australian police officers caught a glimpse of something shiny and metallic in their high beams.[1] The pair had been trundling down a muddy back road, 60 kilometres on the wrong side of the South Australian–Victorian border, when suddenly through the rain and windscreen wipers they made out a car pulled over in the scrub near Lake Cullulleraine. The sedan was one reported stolen the day before, in a fruit-growing district over the South Australian border, and inside they found a sleeping 21-year-old Englishman.[2] He was dressed in civilian clothes, but the officers knew this must be the very person they and a flock of their colleagues across two states had been searching for: Senior Aircraftsman Michael Julian Brown from the Royal Air Force.

Later that morning, Brown appeared before a country courthouse back in South Australia to face the vehicle-theft charge, and despite being found with just a few shillings in his pocket, was somehow able to immediately make bail.[3] Whoever footed the bill might have had something to do with the two men who ushered him out of the courtroom, put him in a car, and drove all the way back to the airbase in northern Adelaide he had escaped from two days earlier. Within days, Brown was bundled onto a specially chartered Royal Australian Air Force plane and whisked back to south-east England under armed escort, where he faced three charges under the Air Force and Official Secrets Acts.

Despite triggering a manhunt that straddled state lines for almost a month, the Australian and British security services had managed to keep Brown's initial arrest, breakout, 400-kilometre cross-country drive, and eventual rendition back to Britain under wraps. This was made even more remarkable given that, in early September, the security services at the Department of Supply had received a request for comment from an afternoon newspaper in Adelaide called *The News*. The paper's long-time aviation reporter, Frank Shaw, had caught wind of the story on his rounds, and to the horror of authorities was planning to publish.

Shaw was a resourceful reporter, with slicked-back hair and a thick moustache, who carried with him a scratched and battered tobacco pipe—one nick for every month he had spent in a Nazi prison camp after being shot down during an RAF bombing mission in World War II.[4] With Adelaide now a key player in an arms and space race, Shaw had his hands full on the aviation beat—a month before the Brown case, he claimed to have flown to Maralinga and Woomera 'more times than he can remember'.[5] He didn't have all the details—luckily for the authorities, the paper had reached out before Brown's escape and flight across the border on 16 September—but what he had was enough to cause alarm at the highest levels of two governments.

A few weeks later, on 13 October, once the story finally hit the British press, Shaw recounted the scoop of the 'Woomera spy drama' and the 'alleged betrayal of secrets to Russia' in *The News*.[6] He told readers how ASIO had dispatched a team of investigators to Adelaide's northern suburbs after the young airman was arrested in bed, accused of smuggling carbon copies of classified documents from a secure area and showing them to 'foreign agents'. The man was held and questioned for two weeks before being sent back to England, where he faced serious charges over the troubling leak of 'secret Woomera information'.

Over the coming days, Shaw revealed fresh details as he learnt them, from the 'Big SA Probe on Spy Ring' that saw 'scores' of Brown's contacts canvassed for information, to the details of his arrest.[7] At the RAAF's Edinburgh airbase, Brown had worked as a clerk, where his official duties included re-typing confidential documents relating to missile projects within the secure Weapons Research Establishment—a repurposed World War II munitions factory in the suburb of Salisbury, 25 kilometres north of the city. Under questioning, Brown revealed that he had endeavoured to sell the copies, which related to a supersonic surface-to-air missile named the Bloodhound, to a pair of Ukrainians in Adelaide. (It later emerged that Brown told investigators that he supported the Soviet Union and was a member of the Young Communist League—claims he later recanted, along with the story about the Ukrainians.)[8]

When Shaw broke the story of Brown's escape and re-arrest at Lake Cullulleraine the next day, he also added a 'sensational twist': the 'interests and activities of a well-known Adelaide professional man' had been raked over by investigators, who believed he had acted as a go-between for Brown and the buyer.[9] Central to the investigation were the growing satellite suburbs of Gepps Cross, Elizabeth, and Salisbury, whose swelling populations of British migrants included hundreds of workers spread across the various military installations.[10] It was feared that communist agents might use seemingly innocuous organisations—such as church groups and welfare bodies—as 'fronts' to gather a patchwork of intelligence unwittingly leaked by employees. A decade into the Cold War, after years of ASIO operations in South Australia—the sparrows, the clandestine operations, the questioning of Labor MPs and university academics—it seemed that the closest thing to a real spy scandal had come not from Fabians or Aboriginal activists, but from within Britain's own ranks.

One intriguing subplot in Shaw's scoop was the story behind the story: at the top of his 13 October exposé, it was revealed that *The News* had suppressed its exclusive for five weeks 'at the personal request of the Prime Minister', who had invoked the national interest.[11] Alongside Shaw's report ran a small column in which federal supply minister Athol Townley praised *The News'* cooperation, while downplaying the severity of the breach. It was 'most unlikely' that a foreign power had gleaned anything truly important, Townley said, but 'as the matter was one of some delicacy', the government had asked *The News* to delay its reporting. 'That a great newspaper should set national interest above its own immediate interest in this way is a matter for congratulations.'[12]

In reality, the Commonwealth government was extremely worried about the Brown case and what it might mean for Australia's place in the Cold War. In a telegram to his British counterpart, Harold MacMillan, on 2 September, Menzies expressed his mystification that the RAF's vetting processes had allowed a young trainee, who he claimed had a 'poor personal history in England', to be given access to secret material.[13] For both prime ministers, the risk of sensitive material reaching enemy hands was secondary to the humiliation they would face if the public—and their American allies—heard about it. The United Kingdom and Australia were already on thin ice with the Americans after a string of embarrassments, from the defection of members of the Cambridge spy ring, to the 1948 breaches that led to the restructuring of Australia's security apparatus and the foundation of ASIO. The stakes were high: any further revelations risked the United States further limiting the all-important flow of classified intelligence and technology.

At Brown's court martial months later, it was revealed that his copying of classified material had been discovered almost by accident, when officers searched his kit after reports of other, less high-stakes thefts at the base.[14] When Brown escaped his British minders at Edinburgh airbase on 15 September by swapping out the padlock on his cell, Menzies was furious, sending a terse cable to MacMillan complaining that the British commanders in charge of the operation either underestimated the 'gravity of this matter' or were 'grossly incompetent'.[15]

Compounding Menzies' worries was the news of Shaw's story, which arrived shortly before Brown's dash across the South Australian–Victorian border. The government initially provided a response of 'no comment', but convinced *The News* to delay publication by a day pending further high-level discussions. By the time Menzies told MacMillan that an 'evening paper' was sniffing around the case, he was able to add that he had successfully killed the story—by meeting with the paper's editor and 'appealing to his patriotism'.[16]

For years, there remained an element of mystery regarding just how *The News* was enlisted to participate in Menzies' and MacMillan's cover-up. When the details of their highly strung telegram exchanges became public four decades later, a flurry of fresh speculation broke out as to which 'editor of the evening paper' Menzies had referred to.[17] Nan Rivett told a reporter that Rohan was no fan of Menzies, and despite his wartime patriotism was unlikely to have spiked the scoop merely to save the two prime ministers from embarrassment—the story did, after all, present enormous and far-reaching implications for South Australia's social, industrial, and political development. According to Rivett's personal papers, he wasn't even in the country between August and October 1958, having embarked on another round-the-world trip through America, Spain, Britain, and Thailand.[18]

From New York, Rupert Murdoch also issued a firm denial, claiming to have 'no memory' of ever having met Sir Robert Menzies—with the possible exception of any forgotten boyhood encounters as the son of an influential press lord.[19] But 14 years later, the publication of ASIO's official history shed new light on the Brown affair, drawing on previously unpublished and still-classified archival material. According to a 'Note for Record Purposes' dated 15 September 1958, Menzies did, in fact, meet with Murdoch in person, who agreed to hold the story while maintaining that a leak was inevitable once news of Brown's case hit the United Kingdom.[20] The date of this meeting was shortly after the Menzies government moved to overrule the Australian Broadcasting Control Board to allow for two television licences in Adelaide; the news that Murdoch's Southern Television Corporation and *The Advertiser*'s Television Broadcasters Limited would each receive a licence landed on the same day that Shaw's report was eventually published.

If the ASIO note is correct, the Brown episode marks an important flashpoint, not only for the roles of Britain and Australia in the Cold War, but for Murdoch's own evolution. As a schoolboy he had once savaged Menzies' government as a failure, but at the first opportunity, at a time when it could not be clearer how important having direct access to a prime minister could be for the growth of his media interests, Murdoch decided to grant a favour to a desperate Menzies—even if it meant burying an explosive, exclusive story This September 1958 compact would become the first of many secret and not-so-secret meetings with prime ministers over the decades, some of which Murdoch would later profess to having limited memory of.

Shaw's story was only delayed by five weeks, but Menzies' intervention showed that, when faced with a question of national security, the former Comrade Murdoch had made a choice to uphold the will of the government in its battle against communism. Unbeknownst to him, in just a few months' time there would another crime, another manhunt, and another sensational story that would see the fledgling Murdoch press accused of mounting a seditious attack on the most important institutions of the state.

# CHAPTER TWELVE

# A race with death

ON THE AFTERNOON of 24 July 1959, Rohan Rivett walked down the road from the News Limited offices to a dining room in the University of Adelaide Staff Club. This section of the single-storey sandstone building was typically reserved for graduates paying their alma mater a visit, but it had only recently been annexed by the club; a few years earlier, it was still known as the university's Anatomy Room, a place with a dark history that spoke to the foundations of the college, the city, and the state.[1] It was a history in which the leading men of South Australia's medical, scientific, and academic fraternity seized, violated, and trafficked the bodies of Aboriginal men and women around the world as if they were scientific curiosities. It was in rooms such as this that men of science and enlightenment created a legacy of death and secrecy that haunted Adelaide's grand North Terrace institutions.

Rivett turned up a little after midday to discuss another matter of life and death. Sitting across from him was a Catholic priest named Father Thomas Dixon, as tall as Rivett, with the strong body of a former rugby player and thinning white hair that matched the crisp dog collar wrapped around his neck. He wore thick-rimmed glasses, and spoke with a gentle but deep voice and a sense of purpose. The meeting had been set up by the two other men present: Ken Inglis, a 31-year-old history lecturer and onetime Fabian who moonlighted as Adelaide correspondent for the Sydney journal *Nation*, and the Reverend Frank Borland, a Presbyterian minister and warden of the university. But it was Dixon who did most of the talking—so much that he barely touched his lunch.[2] At any rate, the story he was telling was enough to put anyone off their food.

Rivett already knew some of it. It had all begun seven months earlier, on a tiny peninsula on Wirangu Country, 800 kilometres north-west of Adelaide. Between the port town of Thevenard, which sits on a small spit of land jutting out from the coastline, and its bigger neighbour, Ceduna, is a strip of sand, seaweed, and limestone cliffs arching westward to the Nullarbor plain and the Great Australian Bight. In towns such as these, the products of the vast golden wheat fields of the state's mid-north, as well as the gypsum and salt mines around Lake MacDonnell, were held in giant stacks and mounds before being bundled onto ships and sent away. The towns themselves became magnets for itinerant labourers, farmers coming in off the land, Greek migrants who fished whiting in the waters of the Bight, and travellers making their way up and down the west coast.

Almost halfway between Thevenard and Ceduna stood, for the time being, a small metal shack—a tumbledown sort of structure pieced together out of panels of galvanised iron. But the family who lived there, the Hattams, knew it wasn't going to be forever. They had only been in Ceduna for 18 months, and on the morning of 20 December 1958, Glen Hattam spent his Saturday digging foundations for the home he planned to build for his wife, Joy, and their two children, Peter, ten, and Mary, nine.[3] While their father toiled in the December sun, the Hattam children did what they usually did on a hot summer afternoon: they put on their swimming togs, and went to the beach.[4] At around 2.30 pm, Peter and the neighbours' kid, another boy named Peter, left the water for about half an hour, and when they returned, Mary was nowhere to be seen. It was only when his son reappeared at the shack for dinner, alone, that Glen Hattam thought anything was wrong. After a frantic search, he began to raise the alarm: his daughter was missing.

The message reached Ceduna police station a little after 9.00

pm, while many of the town's residents were inside the Memorial Hall watching a film — Alfred Hitchcock's *Dial M For Murder*.[5] The commanding officer, Sergeant Harold Walker, took the call, and immediately fetched a storm lantern and made for the seafront.[6] As he set out to begin the search, he paused only to order one of his subordinates, Constable Howard Herde, to arrest a young Aboriginal man he had encountered in a local cafe and suspected of consuming alcohol.[7] Ceduna was 25 miles from Koonibba, a community established by Lutherans at the turn of the century whose residents often ventured into town to find work, distraction, or some brief respite from the control of mission authorities. For some, that meant having a drink, which for Aboriginal men and women had been forbidden under South Australian law since 1839 — this fellow wasn't even the first man they'd locked up that evening.[8] To Herde, the man didn't seem to be drunk or to be behaving inappropriately, but as the urgency of Mary's disappearance sunk in, and the search party fanned out between Thevenard and Ceduna, he followed Walker's orders and took the man to the station.[9] He hadn't even bothered to enter his name, time of arrest, or details of the offence before locking him up and heading back out to join the search.

Herde wound up at the beach, where, a little after midnight, a volunteer called out to him. The man was standing by the opening of a small cave about halfway between the two towns, a three-foot-high cavity carved out of the limestone cliff-face by water and time.[10] As Herde shone his torch inside across the sand and stone floor, the men could make out a pair of red and white bathers, a white plastic sandal, and then, to their horror, the body of a girl around nine years of age.[11] It was an awful scene. There was blood everywhere — on the sand, on the cave walls, and on the girl herself. She appeared to have died from devastating head wounds, but it quickly became apparent that she had also been sexually assaulted.[12] It was such a harrowing sight that, when the case went to trial three months later, the counsel representing her accused murderer sought to prevent the jurors being shown photographs of the scene.[13] As he stood on the rocks waiting for a photographer and the local doctor to arrive, Herde thought he could make out half a dozen footprints in the sand.[14]

The Ceduna police now changed gears. They released the two men still locked up from the night before, and pivoted their search from a lost little girl to the perpetrator of a brutal murder.[15] The next morning, two detectives from the Criminal Investigation Branch in Adelaide—Detective Sergeant Paul Turner and Constable Richard Jones—flew in, while the state's newspapers buzzed with the shocking news and seized upon all kinds of leads. One man had been seen along the highway, suspiciously diving into the bushes whenever a car approached.[16] Another was reported hitchhiking to Western Australia in the early hours of Sunday morning. The search turned up a pair of discarded trousers further along the beach, but it seemed they had been there for some time. Police also tried to track down the owners of a blue older-model Holden seen parked above the beach in the afternoon.

The police enlisted the help of a 50-year-old Aboriginal man they knew by the nickname of Sonny Jim to inspect the footprints that Herde had noticed the night before. Sonny Jim was a tracker, and he told the officers that a man had walked barefoot directly between the cave and a rockpool just above the tideline, around 25 yards away.[17] He also claimed, with absolute certainty, that another child had accompanied Mary up to the cave's entrance.[18] Each lead seemed to go nowhere, until on Monday afternoon a call came through from a Detective Alexander Phin at Whyalla, another port town on the Adelaide side of the Eyre Peninsula. That morning, a travelling carnival had arrived in town—a rickety sort of operation called Funland, run by a lanky 35-year-old named Norman Gieseman and his wife, Edna. Along with a motley bunch of ride-along workers, they had recently travelled over to Western Australia from Burpengang in Queensland, down through to Norseman, and then across the Nullarbor. As Phin spoke to Gieseman to get the measure of his troupe of newcomers, the man mentioned one worker who had left the company after their last stop, a two-night run in Ceduna.

Rupert Max Stuart was a 26-year-old Arrernte man, born on a cattle station 16 kilometres east of Alice Springs. Since adolescence, he had travelled and worked around the country as a stockman, a petrol station attendant, and even a fighter with the travelling boxing troupe of infamous promoter Jimmy Sharman.[19] Stuart had one white grandparent, and so, depending on where in the country he travelled, he existed on the periphery between policies of protection and assimilation. Phin learned that Stuart had joined the Giesemans in Halls Creek, but they parted ways after Stuart had spent much of the Ceduna leg absent or under the influence. When Stuart arrived back at camp on Sunday morning, as they were due to pack up and begin the long drive to Whyalla, Gieseman told him he was done. As far as Gieseman knew, Stuart had found work back in Ceduna.

Phin immediately sent word to his counterparts in Ceduna, and on the evening of Monday 22 January, Walker led a party to the Australian Wheat Board, where casual labourers camped out in tents beside the wheat stacks. They found Stuart wandering in the dark, and, after some brief questioning, brought him back to the Ceduna police station. It wasn't the first time he'd seen the inside of a police station — as it turned out, he was the man Herde had locked up on the night of 20 December, as the rest of the town searched for Mary. When Armin Kleinig, the welfare officer from the Aboriginals Department of Ceduna, arrived back at the police station at around 1.30 am, it was all over. He had been summoned to the station earlier that day by Walker, who asked him to fetch a possible witness from Koonibba whose name had come up during police enquiries. It was a fruitless mission, and by the time Kleinig completed the 80-kilometre round trip and returned to the police station, he could see through the window that Stuart was sitting inside. He was seated at a table, having already been stripped naked, searched, and interrogated by half a dozen policemen — Kleinig could make out the two plainclothes officers from Adelaide, Turner and Jones, standing by, while a third sat at a typewriter. As Kleinig stood outside listening to the tap, tap, tap, of the typewriter, one of the constables said to him, 'Sorry to have sent you out there, Stuart has confessed.'[20]

Precisely what happened in the station that night would be the subject of three court hearings in Adelaide, an appeal to the High Court, a last-ditch bid to the Privy Council in London, a royal commission, seven dates with the hangman, and, eventually, a libel trial. But one thing was certain: the officers left the room with a typed confession that ran two pages long, explaining in detail how Mary Hattam had been raped and killed, signed with the only two words the chief suspect knew how to write: *Ropert Stuart*.

WHEN FATHER DIXON first met Stuart at Adelaide Gaol on 10 May 1959, he was already a condemned man less than two weeks from the gallows. He wore the prison-issue uniform of wrinkled, off-white trousers, black boots, and a grey flannel over-shirt, and if Dixon had paid closer attention to the newspapers that year, he might have already recognised the young man with tousled black hair and big forlorn eyes.[21] Stuart's face had been repeatedly captured by newspaper photographers and police mugshots since his arrest in December 1958, and whether his gaze inspired sympathy or anger tended to hinge on the viewer's conviction of his guilt or innocence.

*The News* was the first to print Stuart's photograph, taken while he was sitting beside Detective Jones in the back of a police car in Adelaide shortly after the confession was signed.[22] Despite the confession, when the trial reached the Criminal Court on 20 April, Stuart entered a plea of not guilty. He was represented pro bono by a lawyer named David O'Sullivan, a wiry Catholic who had made an unsuccessful run for the Senate as lead candidate for the Democratic Labor Party one month before Stuart's arrest. (It seemed Don Dunstan was right in predicting that the new party would never gain traction in South Australia). O'Sullivan and his associate, Helen Devaney, were assigned the case by the Law Society; at the time, South Australia made no provision for government-supported legal aid for defendants such as Stuart, who had no money or capacity to hire their own representation. Instead, the legal profession itself coordinated this work out of a sense of public duty, and shared around 1,000 briefs a year among its 374 members.[23]

In a sign of how seriously the government considered the trial, the prosecution would be led by none other than crown prosecutor Reginald Roderic Chamberlain, News Limited's onetime sparring partner who in recent years had saved his own in-court appearances for only the most high-profile cases. Chamberlain called upon the police officers who had been in the room with Stuart on the night of his confession, who told the court that Stuart had initially denied knowing anything about the girl. When they said they didn't believe him, he admitted that he had seen her, but spun a story about a white man driving a car, who forced him at gun point to carry her body down to the cave. The police didn't buy that, either, and finally, they said, he told them the story that appeared in his confession. He had supposedly spent the morning with one of his Funland colleagues, a 15-year-old named Allan Moir, drinking flagons of wine at the beach and in town, before catching a taxi to Thevenard. After finding some more wine, he had started to walk back along the beach, when he saw Mary Hattam:

> I was pretty full then. She was standing in a pool of water playing. I said to the little girl, 'there is some little birds over there'. I pointed towards the cave. She said, 'I will go and have a look'. She walked in the cave. No I am wrong I crawled in the cave first and she crawled after me. She said, 'Where's the birds', I said 'they are gone now'. I punched her on the side of the head. She went unconscious. I took her bathers off. Then I raped her. She was hard to root. I done her. Then I hit her with a stone. Before I raped her I took my clothes off. I was wearing a shirt and pants. I also took my boots off. I think I hit her six times with a stone. I left her. I think she was dead. I went and had a wash in the sea. I had no clothes on. I went back to near the cave where I had taken my clothes off and put them on.[24]

He continued on his way, returning to Funland for around two hours, and later headed back into Ceduna. The police knew the rest of the story—that was where Herde had arrested him as the search party got underway. The confession's narrative, in which Stuart meticulously avoided being covered in blood despite being 'pretty full', helped explain the lack of evidence tying the mess of the cave to his person. Before the end of the typed confession, he also added, for good measure, his motive: 'I killed her because I did not want her to tell what I done.' Finally, it concluded, 'I cannot read English. I have heard this statement read to me and it is true and correct in every detail'.[25]

From the moment they met, O'Sullivan had struggled to communicate with his client, who spoke Arrernte as his first language and seemed to have trouble with English. But Stuart had told him one important thing: he had only signed the confession after the police had attacked and threatened him. It was a bold claim, if not entirely unheard of, even in South Australia. But it was Stuart's word against the six policemen, and O'Sullivan was reticent about putting Stuart in the box. First, he had little confidence in Stuart's language skills when called to tell his story. But more pressingly, challenging the integrity of police witnesses would invite the prosecution to attack Stuart's own character, and to tell the jury about his criminal history, which included convictions for assault and alcohol offences. O'Sullivan tried a third option: an unsworn statement. Typically read from the dock, it carried less weight than one given on oath, but could not be challenged by cross-examination. But Stuart's illiteracy presented a problem: unlike most defendants, he couldn't read from a prepared statement, nor could O'Sullivan easily walk him through its contents in court. O'Sullivan proposed a novel compromise: someone else could read the written statement on his behalf.[26] Justice Sir Geoffrey Reed, who had returned to the South Australian bench after concluding his ASIO directorship in 1950, flatly rejected his request, and instead Stuart stood up on the second-to-last day of the trial and made a short statement:

> I cannot read or write. Never been to school. I didn't see the little girl. I didn't kill her. Police hit me, choked me, made me said those words. They say I kill her. That is what I want to say.[27]

He also added, with some prompting from O'Sullivan, that he wanted someone to read out the prepared statement for him. The police rejected the accusation of violence, insisting that the confession had been freely given and accurately transcribed. 'It was typed by [Detective Frank] Whitrod word for word as the defendant dictated it,' Turner said, denying that anyone had grabbed Stuart by the throat or threatened him.[28] Whitrod, who was the brother of ASIO officer Ray Whitrod, added that 'I typed down his actual words ... there was no violence or threat of violence on that occasion of him being questioned or during the making of the statement or prior to the making of the statement. Definitely not.'[29]

The jury had also heard other evidence, but much of it was flawed in one way or another. After the confession was signed in the early hours of 22 December, the police poured sand into the yard of the station and made Stuart walk across it. They asked Sonny Jim, and his 65-year-old uncle, Harry Scott, if the resulting tracks were the same as those on the beach, and after a curiously long, pregnant pause, both men agreed.[30] But, according to their testimony, they had already been told by the police that Stuart was guilty.[31]

Upon his arrest, the police had also noticed scratches and cuts on Stuart's knees and back, but they had declined to document them, ostensibly because they didn't think they would photograph well against the shade of his skin.[32] They hadn't measured, photographed, or taken casts of the beach footprints, either.[33] At the trial, Turner also presented a sample of hair he had collected from Stuart's head, which he had asked a doctor at the Institute of Medical and Veterinary Science to compare to a strand found in Mary Hattam's hand. This expert, however, was more cautious than the one who sent Colin Ross to his death back in 1921, and told Turner that the best he could do was confirm that both hairs were human.[34] The third piece of evidence came from a local boy who helped run his father's taxi service; he testified that he picked up Stuart and a younger man he assumed to be Stuart's brother at Ceduna after 2.00 pm, just before Mary Hattam was last seen, and dropped Stuart at Thevenard.[35]

In his closing remarks, Justice Reed told the jury that the Crown's case hinged on the confession. 'If you are not satisfied beyond reasonable doubt to accept the confession of the defendant, what is left in the case is not very strong,' he said.[36] 'Once you remove the confession, then what is left is something, but something which is not of a very strong nature to support a verdict of guilty of murder.'[37]

The defence's case, on the other hand, was largely based on the suggestion that the police had taken Stuart into custody, and, 'being fairly certain that this man might be guilty, proceed to get him to say so by the use of some violence and threats and consequently the confession which is obtained is one which is unreliable and one which you should not act upon'.[38] 'Apart from the answers of the defendant to the police and his signed statement,' Reed added, 'it would be a very dangerous procedure to draw the inference that he was guilty of murder'.[39] In short, there was 'really not a great deal in this case' beyond the confession.[40] At 2.20 pm on 24 April, the jury retired to consider their verdict. They returned just an hour and fifteen minutes later, and were unanimous: Stuart was guilty.

But O'Sullivan and Devaney weren't finished yet, and in May they took the case to the Court of Appeals. Appearing before Chief Justice Sir Mellis Napier, Justice Abbott, and Justice Mayo, O'Sullivan and Chamberlain argued over the circumstances of the confession and Justice Reed's rejection of Stuart's written, unsworn statement. Justice Abbott asked O'Sullivan if he really believed six police officers had perjured themselves at trial.

'We all know it is done,' said O'Sullivan.[41]

Abbott replied that while he had heard instances of one or two policeman coercing a suspect, he had never heard of a *group* of police officers accused of such conduct.

'From the stories you hear,' O'Sullivan insisted, 'it is done.'

At Abbott's request, O'Sullivan explained how he believed the confession had been written: 'By the police asking questions, getting answers, disregarding some, getting him back onto the track, more questions, more answers, stopping him as he rambled off on some other subject. They asked a lot of questions and after the assault he said "yes" to anything because he thought he was going to be killed.'[42]

Now the chief justice spoke up. 'That is utter rubbish,' Napier interjected.[43] The court's ruling was only slightly more equivocal; while there may have been some 'irregularity' in the original trial, the court saw no reason or miscarriage of justice to warrant disturbing the original conviction. Stuart was, once again, destined to hang on 22 May.

ALTHOUGH HE WAS currently tending to a parish in the inner-western suburbs of Adelaide, Father Dixon had spent his formative years as a missionary living among Aboriginal and Torres Strait Islander communities in remote areas. In 1942, shortly after taking the cloth, he was posted to Palm Island off the coast of Queensland, a place with its own complicated history—thousands of Indigenous peoples from across the state had been forcibly relocated to the island throughout the 20th century.[44] After seven years, he headed to the desert to help establish a mission at Santa Teresa, 80 kilometres south-east of Alice Springs.[45] It was at Santa Teresa that Dixon sought to learn the Arrernte language of the people he was charged with converting, but since leaving the Territory had had little cause to use it.

Then, in May 1959, Dixon heard from a neighbouring minister whose flock included inmates at Adelaide Gaol. Stuart had volunteered 'Catholic' as his religion, and this priest had been summoned to prepare the condemned man for death. Like O'Sullivan, the priest had struggled to get much out of the prisoner, but Stuart did mention that he had once lived at Alice Springs, and had heard of Father Dixon. Dixon could not recall Stuart when the priest arrived at his door, nor did he know much about the case. But he agreed to visit Stuart anyway, and on 10 May made his first trip to Adelaide Gaol.[46]

Sitting opposite one another, the two men spoke in a mix of English and Arrernte—nothing too complicated to begin with. After all, it had been two years since Dixon had spoken the language with anyone. At first, they didn't discuss Mary Hattam's death; Dixon's primary concern was preparing Stuart's soul for what awaited him on the scaffold on 22 May, and, with the help of an Arrernte dictionary published by a local linguist at the University of Adelaide, the pair eventually developed a rapport.[47] But try as he might, Dixon could never bring Stuart to admit his guilt, or to discuss what had happened that afternoon in Ceduna.

As Dixon prepared to baptise Stuart before his execution, he looked up the address of his lawyers, O'Sullivan and Devaney, to confirm the date.[48] Dixon was surprised to learn that, unlike in Queensland, where statements made by an Aboriginal defendant could not be admitted unless made in the presence of legal counsel or a welfare officer, Stuart's confession had been signed without representation, while Kleinig was on the road somewhere between Ceduna and Koonibba.[49] Dixon was also shocked that no interpreter had been present during questioning or the trial; and when O'Sullivan then showed Dixon a copy of the confession, the priest was floored. Compared to his own conversations with Stuart, in which he could hardly describe the afternoon's events, or speak at any great length in English, the confession's clarity and turn of phrase was surprising.

He told the lawyers that he would contact Professor Theodore G Strehlow, the linguist whose dictionaries he had consulted and whom he had met a handful of times at Santa Teresa, to look over the confession. Strehlow's father had been a Lutheran missionary at Hermannsburg on the lands of the Western Arrernte people, where he grew up surrounded by the language. As an adult, Strehlow combined his early learning with academic training as a linguist and classicist, and spent years in the field recording and studying Arrernte language and culture. He had even known Stuart as a boy, having employed his parents during the years he spent as a Commonwealth patrol officer and a deputy director of native affairs in the Northern Territory. Even so, Strehlow was initially reticent to be drawn in—when he first heard about the case, he had taken the involvement of Aboriginal trackers as a strong indication of guilt.[50] But, after learning of Justice Reed's remarks downplaying Sonny Jim and Harry Scott's evidence, he agreed to accompany Dixon to Adelaide Gaol on 18 May. After speaking at length with Stuart in Arrernte, then re-reading the confession at O'Sullivan and Devaney's office, Strehlow wrote an affidavit offering his expert opinion that much of the confession's phrasing was 'in complete opposition' to Northern Territory English.[51] In short, Stuart simply could not have spoken the words attributed to him.

With Strehlow's affidavit in tow, O'Sullivan and Devaney won Stuart another brief reprieve as they escalated their appeal to the High Court of Australia. Fronting the bench in Melbourne on 1 June, O'Sullivan cited the same Queensland law that Dixon was familiar with. 'Had this man been in his home state in the Northern Territory, and had already been in Queensland, of course he could not have been probably charged at all, or in these circumstances at least there would have been no evidence against him because both of those States would not have allowed evidence to be received in this way, to have been used against the accused,' he pleaded.[52]

'Those might be very desirable provisions,' Justice Windeyer of the High Court replied, 'but apparently you do not have them in South Australia.'

'Not in South Australia,' O'Sullivan conceded grimly.

He told the High Court that he would have sought an interpreter from the start had he imagined the unsworn statement would be blocked. The handful of words that Stuart did say at the trial, he said, came only after hours of coaching in the courthouse's holding cells—and even then, he required further prompting. 'But this is not indicative of his general knowledge of English, this is what he, like a parrot, could be taught to "say this, say that".'[53]

The following afternoon, Chamberlain urged the court to throw out the appeal and Strehlow's evidence. 'Whether Strehlow is aware of this or not, the fact is that his affidavit challenges the truthfulness and good faith of the five officers who gave evidence at the trial,' he said.[54]

The High Court initially reserved its decision, but, after several nerve-wracking weeks, finally ruled to uphold the original verdict on 19 June. A new date of execution was set for 7 July, but the opening line of the court's judgment, in which it admitted that 'certain features of this case have caused us some anxiety', gave Stuart's supporters some hope.[55]

As Stuart's new execution date loomed, Dixon found himself moving with a different crowd to his usual congregation. A week after the High Court verdict, he was the guest of honour at the Magill home of Dr Charles Duguid, where some 50 people met to hear about Stuart's situation.[56] There, among supporters of the anti-death-penalty movement the Howard League, he met Professor Norval Morris, the dean of law at the University of Adelaide. Along with Strehlow, the pair were granted an off-the-record meeting with attorney-general Colin Rowe, and when that went nowhere, they wrote to federal Labor leader Dr HV Evatt, a former High Court judge himself, to lobby Playford to commute the sentence.[57] A petition was started, as well as a legal fund to raise money for a Privy Council appeal in London. After his wife, Judy, attended the meeting at Duguid's house, Ken Inglis was drafted to write a four-page pamphlet entitled 'Why Not Hang Rupert Stuart?—Some questions about a murder', which was printed and circulated around the city.[58] Meanwhile, Don Dunstan, Murdoch and Rivett's old acquaintance, prepared to introduce a private members' Bill abolishing the death penalty to parliament.

The local papers had paid only passing attention to Stuart since the guilty verdict, but soon the campaign's growing momentum—and ensuing backlash—drew headlines. On 4 July, the secretary of the police union wrote a letter to *The News* insisting that 'the public should be reminded of the real facts'.[59] The letter claimed that, far from being unable to speak English, in an earlier trial in Darwin, Stuart had 'conducted his own defence' and had 'fluently cross-examined a number of witnesses in English'. The next day, O'Sullivan shot back, describing the statement as 'false in almost every detail', and pointed out that, far from being a 'disinterested opinion', the Police Association's president was none other than Detective Sergeant Paul Turner.[60] The Law Society's president, John Leo Travers QC, also weighed in, writing that he was 'appalled' to read a statement that seemed to 'surpass the bounds of ordinary decency, to say nothing of the question of contempt of court'.[61] All the while, Stuart's supporters gathered more signatures ('Petitioners Run a Race With Death', read *The News*' July 5 headline), and on 9 July, O'Sullivan airmailed a petition seeking leave to appeal to the Privy Council. Within a fortnight, both he and Chamberlain had flown to London to argue the case once more, this time before the highest court in the Commonwealth.

Despite all this commotion, Dixon had kept out of the spotlight—a 29 June report in *The News* made only passing reference to a 'churchman who asked to remain anonymous'.[62] Until, that is, on 20 July, when he spoke to Tom Farrell, a former copy boy and cadet at *The News* who had since become a senior reporter for *The Sydney Morning Herald*. Farrell had won praise years earlier for doggedly investigating and eventually demolishing the 1946 murder conviction of a sheep shearer named Fred McDermott, and when he read about Stuart in one of Inglis's *Nation* reports, booked a flight to Adelaide.[63] Farrell convinced Dixon that the most meaningful appeal for Stuart lay in the court of public opinion, and soon an interview with Dixon was published in *The Sydney Morning Herald* and broadcast on television (in the eastern states, at least—NWS-9 was still months away from launch). Dixon had previously received a tip from an old contact in the Queensland police force that Gieseman and the Funland crew had resurfaced up north, and used the interview to make a televised appeal for more information. Shortly after the broadcast, *The Brisbane Telegraph* contacted Dixon and encouraged him to make the trip to Queensland to track down the funfair.[64] But there was a problem; Dixon had wrongly assumed the paper would pay his way to Queensland. He would have to find the money some other way—and fast.

THIS, DIXON EXPLAINED at the university, was where the editor-in-chief of *The News* might come in. When the priest finally stopped talking, Rivett leaned in and asked, 'Are you an abolitionist?'[65] Rivett had been following the Howard League's work, and was wary of *The News* being drafted into a bigger, more contentious, campaign. He'd been burnt before—his brush with libel and contempt in 1955 had all started when some well-meaning lawyers tried to use *The News* as a vehicle for their own agenda. To Inglis, the contrast between the larger-than-life Rivett and the quietly spoken priest who soberly recounted this twisting, high stakes story could not have been greater. It wasn't lost on Rivett, either; he had tested the bounds of acceptability in Adelaide before, but here was a witness—a priest, no less—who seemed to be genuinely motivated by a sense of justice, not publicity or some grandstanding cause célèbre. After nearly three hours of discussion, Rivett was convinced of Dixon's integrity, and made a proposal: *The News* would bankroll the Queensland trip, on the condition that one of their reporters tag along. Any breakthroughs would first be cabled to O'Sullivan, who was due to land in London at any minute. But then *The News* would get the scoop exclusively.

Dixon left Adelaide the next day, and touched down in Cairns on 26 July, travelling under the fake name 'Jones', but easily identifiable to any local press—he hadn't even removed his collar. The local papers also noted that Dixon was travelling alongside a 'mystery man', revealed with some glee by *The News* as its own police roundsman, Jack Clark.[66] They made a strange pair, Clark wrote in his firs, but shared a 'zeal for justice'.[67] Having followed the case since the initial manhunt in Ceduna, Clark had confidence in the original police investigation, but became intrigued by the priest during the long drive through sugar cane and cattle country to the town of Atherton, in the tablelands beyond Cairns. At the local showgrounds, they found Norm and Edna Gieseman, and as Dixon sat in their caravan, he filled them in on Stuart's plight.

'I'm afraid I can't help you,' Norm Gieseman told Dixon, while Clark waited in the car outside.[68] Gieseman hadn't been following the case, and didn't realise that his conversation with the detective in Whyalla had helped lead police to his former employee. Dixon explained that Max was an outsider in Ceduna, and aside from the Giesemans there were few people in town who knew him or could account for his movements. 'Well, we did not see much of him; the only time we saw him was from two 'til four,' Norm replied.[69] Dixon was so shocked, he thought he might fall through his seat.[70] Had the man just placed Stuart at the funfair during the exact window of time he was suspected of committing the crime? Dixon stopped him from saying another word without additional witnesses, and returned to the car, where Clark could see that the priest was shaking with excitement and emotion. Later that day, the Giesemans, along with Betty Hopes, the young woman who had worked alongside Stuart at Ceduna, met up with Dixon and Clark at the Atherton Catholic Presbytery, where a justice of the peace who had travelled with them was waiting. On Clark's typewriter, the trio dictated and signed three affidavits all placing Stuart at Funland on the afternoon of 20 December.

Clark broke the story in the Wednesday edition of *The News*. 'PRIEST: STUART HAS PERFECT ALIBI', read the headline, accompanied by a front-page editorial with a call to 'DELAY THIS HANGING!'.[71] The editorial pointedly distanced itself from the Howard League, and professed no desire to keep the true perpetrator of the 'dastardly crime' alive, before revealing details of Rivett's meeting with the 'utterly sincere' Dixon the previous Friday.[72] '*The News* thought it was a poor thing that a man should hang in the South Australia of 1959 just because no one would put up a few hundred pounds to investigate the possibility of his being innocent,' it read. In light of these fresh claims, it was the 'bounden duty' of the Executive Council to delay his hanging until all matters are investigated.[73] As Devaney visited Adelaide Gaol to have Stuart sign a fresh petition to the Executive Council for his reprieve, a further 10,000 copies of the 'Why Not Hang Stuart?' pamphlet were printed and circulated around the city by Borland, Morris, and Inglis.[74]

The government had refused to be drawn on the case since Rowe's meeting with Dixon and the university men, but now the premier appeared backed into a corner. On the same day that Dixon's Queensland revelations came to light, word reached Adelaide that O'Sullivan's appeal to the Privy Council had been swiftly denied. He had received news via telegram of the new affidavits, but it made no difference — the Privy Council made its decision in minutes. The council would not intervene in the High Court's ruling, but it did suggest lobbying the Executive Council back in Adelaide to test the new evidence in some other venue.

On 30 July, Playford stood up in the House of Assembly after a morning of uncharacteristically heated debate. Labor opposition leader Mick O'Halloran had just moved a motion to suspend standing orders in the chamber, seconded by Dunstan, when the premier made a dramatic announcement: Stuart would receive another one-month reprieve, until the government could parse through these new claims.[75] To do so, Playford would deploy a time-honoured mechanism favoured by governments seeking to take the heat out of a controversial issue, while also washing their hands of the process: there would be a royal commission.

# CHAPTER THIRTEEN

# The gravest libel

DAVID BOWMAN FELT a chill as he made the half-mile walk from the Supreme Court building in Victoria Square to News Limited's offices on the afternoon of 21 August 1959.[1] It was a little after lunchtime, and as Bowman walked he saw that the kiosks along King William Street had already taken delivery of the first edition of *The News*, and with it, the posters that blasted the day's headlines in fresh red ink. Eight tumultuous years had passed since he had first watched Rohan Rivett blow into *The News* as a 21-year-old cadet. In 1954, Bowman had left Adelaide to make the pilgrimage to Fleet Street, but after only four months at *The Sunday Pictorial*, he abandoned the paper to join a sailing expedition. The crew planned to search for a treasure-laden shipwreck in the southern waters of New Zealand, but just two months after leaving England, their yacht sunk as well, having struck a coral reef off the Sudanese coast.[2] After making it ashore, Bowman spent three weeks in Sudan before hitchhiking across the continent, ending up in Durban two months later still sporting the same pair of shorts he'd been wearing when the boat sank. Eventually, he caught a ride to Melbourne on a passing Swedish ship, and by August 1955 he was back at *The News* looking a little more bronzed than when he'd left it.

He had since worked his way up to senior reporter, a safe pair of hands who could be trusted with the paper's most important stories. And there was no bigger story than the Stuart royal commission, where Bowman, Frank Shaw, and another *News* reporter named Noel Prisk had spent the morning working in 15-minute shifts, jotting every word down and then dashing to the telephone to relay their scribblings to a typist back at the office. The three of them had done their best that morning, but as his eyes scanned the placards and he took in his own newspaper's account of what he had just witnessed, Bowman grew increasingly anxious. 'SHAND QUITS—"YOU WON'T GIVE STUART FAIR GO"', read the five-inch-tall block letters. Then there was the front page itself: 'Mr Shand, QC, indicts Sir Mellis Napier—"THESE COMMISSIONERS CANNOT DO THE JOB"'.

It had been an eventful morning at the inquiry, which had already produced plenty of drama. Jack Shand QC, the high-profile silk who had flown over from Sydney to represent Stuart, had stood up before the commissioners, read out a short statement, and promptly walked out. Shand was a short-statured 62-year-old with a reputation for big wins, having appeared before several controversial royal commissions and murder trials over his career. In 1951, he had famously represented Fred McDermott in the inquiry that followed Tom Farrell's bombshell exposé in *The Sydney Morning Herald*. McDermott had walked free, and there was no question that Stuart's supporters hoped that Shand might bring the same luck to Adelaide.[3] But as the inquiry wore on, the lawyer seemed strained; his skin looked sallow, his blue eyes tired and bloodshot, and when he addressed the courtroom, his voice had grown so hoarse that Bowman and his colleagues struggled to decipher the words. What no one in the courtroom knew was that Shand was dying—he had advanced bowel cancer, and within a fortnight of walking out of the Supreme Court building, he would be in hospital undergoing surgery. Two months later, he would be dead.

Shand's decision to withdraw from the commission that morning with a short, pointed statement was certainly abrupt, but to Bowman it had seemed neither as blunt nor defiant as *The News*'s coverage suggested. Recounting the episode decades later, Bowman returned to North Terrace to find Rohan Rivett in a 'refulgent' mood, striding around the newsroom with a cigar in hand.[4] 'Isn't it great?' he asked the reporters present, but Bowman said nothing. *The News* had made no secret of the doubts it harboured about the royal commission's integrity ever since the premier had floated the idea in parliament on 30 July. Now it seemed that those concerns had been vindicated. All the same, Bowman was troubled: 'The posters seemed to go too far and the matters were too grave,' he later recalled.[5] But it was an opinion that he kept largely to himself for the next eight months, if not for the next 40 years. He did so with good reason: anything else might have landed his editor-in-chief, his fellow reporters, and perhaps even himself in custody.

IF SIR THOMAS Playford thought that announcing a royal commission might satisfy his critics, he was sorely mistaken. As soon as the details of the probe were revealed, more outraged commentary followed. First it was the terms, which followed four lines of inquiry, ranging from the new alibis that Father Dixon had tracked down to the question of why they hadn't been produced at trial. Then there was the commission's composition: two of the three judges that Playford had appointed, Justice Sir Geoffrey Reed and Chief Justice Sir Mellis Napier, had already heard Stuart's case, and would, it seemed, be reviewing their own work.

At first, Stuart's counsel threatened to boycott the inquiry entirely, while *The News* ran another front-page editorial telling readers 'There's Still a Long Way to Go'.[6] Playford's announcement was a welcome acknowledgment of public opinion, it read, but the fine print seemed to 'arouse the gravest doubts and fears'.[7] Further into the paper, cartoonist Norm Mitchell satirised the commissioners' appointments with a caricature of Playford in a hospital ward being advised by a conga line of identical doctors all bringing identical second opinions. The caption read: 'Blimey! Tom's not calling in the same docs again, is he?'[8] Pressed once again in the House of Assembly on 4 August, Playford insisted that 'every matter connected with this case [would be] sifted to the ground'.[9] But the third term of reference — why the alibi provided by the Giesemans hadn't been heard at trial—raised another problem. If O'Sullivan himself was to be called to answer for his own performance, he and Devaney would have to find someone else to represent Stuart at the commission. They aimed high, and by some miracle Shand accepted the brief and flew to Adelaide.[10]

At 9.45 am on Monday 17 August, a crowd of some 70 people huddled on the steps of the Supreme Court building, hoping to score one of the public gallery's 15 seats.[11] Having spent the weekend absorbing a mountain of transcripts and evidence from the five previous hearings, Shand opened with an appeal to widen the terms of reference to explicitly include the question of Stuart's confession. In the McDermott inquiry, it was Shand's cross-examination of a detective inspector that exposed serious flaws in the police investigation, and it seemed that he aimed to pull off a similar feat in Adelaide. 'In fairness to a man who is in the very shadow of death, depending on this inquiry, it should be made quite open that this confession should be inquired into,' he said.[12] Shand even flagged some explosive new evidence: he had learned that, on Friday, three new witnesses had approached the commission claiming to have heard one of Stuart's interrogators admit they 'bashed it out of the black bastard'.[13] The trio—a Port Lincoln man named Alan Wardrop, and his wife and daughter—weren't the only ones to come forward. On 11 August, Devaney's office took a call from a man who claimed to be a Ceduna local and who had been on the beach with his wife on 20 December.[14] He said that concerned mothers on the beach had warned off a youth who 'was making a nuisance of himself with children and young girls in the water', but declined to give his name and hung up. Devaney was out of the office at the time, and despite public appeals, the man never resurfaced.

Then there was the question of Allan Moir, the teenage Funland worker mentioned in Stuart's confession. Moir never appeared at the trial, but, according to police, it was his testimony at Whyalla that pointed Detective Phin to Stuart in the first place. In Queensland, Dixon and Clark had tracked down the boy shortly after they spoke to the Giesemans, and in a convent at Collinsville on 30 July they had him dictate and sign an affidavit outlining Stuart's movements on 20 December 1958. But his testimony proved more complicated than the

Giesemans' 'perfect alibi'. Moir claimed he went down to the beach with Stuart around 9.00 am, returned to the carnival alone an hour later, and next saw Stuart at the funfair around 1.30 pm. Around 4.00 pm, they went down to the beach for a drink, and continued drinking until sundown, when they went into town. But he also added, almost as an afterthought, a detail that Clark felt left the whole case 'clouded' with 'fantasy'.[15] 'There is one thing, and that is that when I was down the beach Max Stuart said to me, "There is blood on my chest."'[16] Moir could not see any blood, but also claimed Stuart said he had 'knocked off' a man named Lennie, and dumped the body at sea. Then, shortly before giving his statement to Dixon, Moir asked Clark, 'What happens if Stuart gets off? Do they look for another bloke?'[17]

At the commission, Shand wondered aloud why, if Moir was the one who had led Phin to suspect Stuart, the prosecution hadn't called him as a witness.[18] The authorities did little to dispel any air of official impropriety when Moir flew into Adelaide the day before the hearing began; Dixon, the Giesemans, and his older brother, Les, had all planned to meet him at the airport, but as soon as Allan stepped off the plane, he was seized by men who claimed to be from the sheriff's department. When Dixon protested, telling them that Stuart's solicitors had already arranged accommodation, he was brushed off as the men escorted Moir into a waiting car, forming a ring around him to stop any of the waiting journalists speaking to the boy. 'Push off or I'll book you,' one of the men told a newspaper photographer, as he trod on his foot and pushed him aside.[19]

Stuart's supporters were outraged by this intervention, and in a fiery exchange in parliament the premier claimed he had only just been informed of the move by Jim Brazel QC, News Limited's former counsel who had appeared during Rupert Murdoch's 1956 speeding incident, and then again in the libel settlement with the magistrate Derek Wilson.[20] In what was seen as a betrayal by many — Rivett called him 'Judas Iscariot' — Brazel had accepted the job of counsel assisting the royal commission, and it was he who had authorised the men who grabbed Moir. Brazel denied that Moir had been taken into custody, arguing at the commission that 'it would be wrong to allow a strange boy, so young to be wandering at large in a city of this size without protection and guidance from some responsible adult'.[21] Napier added, in the first of many broadsides towards the press, that 'we do sometimes read the newspapers and it would be easier for us if we were allowed to go about our business without being told what witnesses are going to say before they are called'.[22]

There were 15 witnesses slated to appear. First, it was the Giesemans and Stuart's fellow Funland workers, who repeated their earlier testimony that Stuart had been at the funfair in the afternoon, from around 1.45 pm to 4.00 pm—even confirming that they had adjusted their clocks when crossing the border into South Australia. When questioned by Chamberlain, Gieseman said all he had told Phin in Whyalla was that Moir and Stuart had been absent from the funfair on 20 December.[23]

Stuart's counsel weren't the only ones with new witnesses; as soon as the premier announced the inquiry, two officers from the Adelaide CIB travelled to Ceduna.[24] They spent six days scouring the area for new witnesses in a black sedan emblazoned with the South Australian Police insignia, and after interviewing dozens of people—many of them Aboriginal men and women who lived and worked in the area—the pair returned with a handful of fresh affidavits to cast doubt on Stuart's alibi.[25] As the first week of testimonies unfolded, one wharf labourer told the commission that Stuart arrived back at the funfair in a taxi at around 3.00 pm, but drove off again. He also claimed Stuart told him that he 'had a maiden down on the beach', and saw him returning from the direction of the cave around 4.00 pm. Two more said they were at the carnival during the Giesemans' alibi window, but did not see Stuart, while two barmaids at the Thevenard Hotel placed him on the pub's veranda around 2.30 pm. But this new testimony wasn't exactly watertight; of the two men who never saw Stuart at the funfair, one told the commission that police came back to him 'because the times were wrong', and the other admitted to Shand that he was short-sighted and would have trouble recognising anyone from several metres away. (He could not tell the time either.)[26]

But on Tuesday, it was Moir who took up most of Shand's attention. He quizzed the teenager on why he hadn't told police the full story he had since told reporters and Father Dixon. He asked why, if Stuart told him he had 'knocked off Lennie', he had brushed it off despite assuming that 'knocked off' meant 'killed'.[27] Shand asked him about the razor blades he told Phin were in Stuart's coat, which had appeared in some but not all of the police accounts of Stuart's questioning.[28] He also asked about Moir's history, and whether he'd told Phin about his expulsion from a Catholic school after being accused of touching girls' breasts. ('I had only one touched one girl but she complained to her father,' Moir protested.) Shand then asked about him having previously been in trouble with the police for stealing bags of biscuits, and being fined in court for stealing rope from a sports ground.

Phin had retired from the police force by the time he fronted the commission on Thursday 20 August, and Shand began by asking why he had immediately judged Moir a trustworthy witness — even telling him he had 'nothing to worry about' — when, for all Phin knew, he could have been the culprit.[29] Arriving on the heels of Moir's own cross-examination, in which Shand had successfully destroyed his credibility, it seemed Shand had found a strategy: by exposing the sloppiness of Phin's questioning of Moir, and his apparent lack of curiosity about the boy's own possible guilt, questions could be raised about what other leads had been dismissed prematurely. This might, in turn, help discredit other aspects of the investigation that had made the police and prosecution so sure of Stuart's guilt.

'I am asking you why you did not ask some questions of Moir, and you have given three possibilities,' Shand asked Phin after a lengthy exchange rehashing a detail from Moir's story that Phin had omitted from his own statement, and that he appeared to have conflated with other parts of the boy's account.[30]

'I have previously explained that I might have overlooked that,' Phin replied.

'Is that the one you say is the real explanation?' Shand shot back.

The chief justice interjected, telling Shand that Phin was not obliged to explain anything. 'It is for him to say whether he wishes to go any further or whether he wishes to leave his evidence where he is,' Napier said.

Shand seemed taken aback. 'If you want me to stop cross-examining, I will stop,' he told the chief justice.

'I have not the slightest intention of stopping you,' Napier replied, 'but as far as I am concerned, I have heard enough of this.'

'If you are going to take that attitude when cross-examination is going on, I think in this case cross-examination must be essentially severe,' Shand said.

'If you feel it is helping you to convince us, well and good,' Napier said.

'I feel it is *impossible* to convince Your Honour on this because Your Honour says you don't want to hear any more of it.'

Now Justice Reed spoke up: 'That is a rather startling remark to make,' he told Shand.

'It may be, but I make it and maintain it,' he replied.

Napier told Shand that it was his call to keep poring over relatively minor gaps in Phin's testimony, but 'everybody makes mistakes at times'. Shand replied that if Napier decided it was a simple mistake before he had completed his questioning, 'it is useless to cross-examine further and I sit down'.

That was his choice, Napier said, while adding that he was 'perfectly at liberty to continue and you can stay here as long as it suits you'. Shand paused, asked a few more small questions, then allowed Phin to withdraw. Now Brazel started speaking, telling the commissioners that he had in his possession the full statements of the Wardrop family backing Stuart's claims of police violence — the testimony that Shand had alluded to a week earlier. Shand had requested copies of the statement that morning, but before he handed them over, Brazel asked Shand whether he already had his own version of the Wardrops' story. (He did not.)

'I draw attention to the fact that there are two glaring inaccuracies uttered with great publicity contained in Mr Shand's statement last Monday morning,' Brazel said.[31] 'Mr Shand took it upon himself to make assertions of fact before Your Honours, which he now concedes were *not* gleaned from documents.'

Brazel claimed that when Shand made those comments, the Wardrops had yet to give their statements; therefore, what Shand had 'so confidently alleged' had no relationship to the family's actual testimony.

'We made a public statement, the statements are a little stronger than I indicated, and I admit it,' Shand replied, before requesting an adjournment. 'I would like to consider my position,' he said.

It was a tense end to the day's session, as the barely concealed animus between Shand, Napier, Brazel, and Chamberlain spilled out into the open. To one observer, those tensions ran deeper than the raw transcript tends to reveal. Charles Bright, a lawyer and future Supreme Court judge, had applied, alongside John Jefferson Bray QC, to represent O'Sullivan at the commission, who feared he might be made a scapegoat.[32] Napier shot down the request, but the pair continued to observe from two rows behind the counsel—a 'ringside' seat, as Bright later called it. Between 27 October 1959, the day after the hearings finally concluded, and 11 November, he wrote 20 pages of handwritten notes, which he then sealed in an envelope marked: 'These are notes on the Stuart Case. Not to be opened before 1985 and are then not to be used unless all persons concerned are dead'.

Inside, Bright committed to paper a set of often incisive observations about each of the royal commission's six key players: Shand, Napier and his fellow commissioners, Chamberlain, Brazel, and Bray. As a member of the legal fraternity and the Adelaide Club, Bright gave a candid insider's account of the gossip and behind-closed-door tensions that most outside observers could only have speculated about—and in the heated context of 1959, might have proved too incendiary to break ranks over at the time. ('What a note this is!' he wrote after a particularly scathing takedown, 'I am sorry, posterity, to have inflicted it upon you.') They found their way into the archives of the State Library of South Australia, where they were eventually unsealed in 2012.

Bright's account sought to remind future readers of the intense public interest in the case, stoked in the afternoons by *The News* and downplayed each morning by *The Advertiser*. On every day of the commission, the jury box teemed with reporters, while a pack of photographers jostled with the public queuing outside. He shed light on how the events of Shand's walkout represented a perfect storm of long-brewing grudges, crossed wires, and personality clashes. Napier had long dominated the bench of the Supreme Court, Bright wrote, and it wasn't unusual for him to interrupt counsel, even in mid-address. The habit, Bright wrote, was 'ingrained' but not 'malicious'—even if it was 'intensely irritating'. But as an outsider to the quirks and power dynamics of the South Australian courts, Shand seemed 'astonished'.

Bright was friendly with Napier, and even claimed credit for having convinced the chief justice to allow Shand to appear in the first place. But he felt Napier was 'impervious' to any argument in favour of Stuart, and that both Napier and Chamberlain's attitudes towards the Stuart case, and the interstate pressure that it had invited, were compounded by longstanding 'petty resentments'. The High Court, which lacked any South Australian members, had recently ordered a handful of retrials in the state, and its comments about 'certain features' of the Stuart case had left Napier so 'vexed' that when it sat in Adelaide in August 1959, he simply left town.

Brazel, on the other hand, seemed to be working hand-in-glove with Chamberlain. 'They sat together, frequently whispered together, often chuckled together and outside the Court commonly stayed together,' Bright wrote, which 'lent a lot of colour to the theory that the Judges were biased':

> It was common gossip among lawyers and court officials that Chamberlain and Brazel were both looking to be appointed judges and both lost no opportunity of ingratiating themselves with the existing judges. It was at times amusing to see Chamberlain get up and say something offensive about Stuart or his witnesses to be echoed by Brazel.

Bright liked Chamberlain, but conceded he could have a bitter, polarising presence; he could be 'smiling and apparently benign' in the comfortable surrounds of the Adelaide Club, but never shied from sharing his grievances, and was prone to rile people the wrong way. Having spent the best part of three decades with the Crown, he seemed to resent the legal profession as 'the enemy', while treating the police as his clients—a 'sad mistake', Bright thought. Chamberlain seemed to show a 'ferocity, a single-minded determination' to confirm Stuart's guilt and to absolve the police, and occasionally appeared to be 'white-faced and trembling with emotion'.

Bright thought the chief justice, too, felt torn between impartial justice and upholding the authority of the police force, whose conduct Bright felt could not be dismissed so easily. ('No police force is composed of angels and no one is going to believe that ours is incapable of doing wrong,' he added.) Reflecting upon the clash between Napier, Brazel, and Shand that afternoon, Bright wrote that many people took the view that Shand had brought about a stunt, deliberately designed to derail the commission. Bright disagreed: 'I believe that he honestly thought it was futile to go on.'

But the clash on the 20th was just the beginning. When the commission resumed at 10.10 the next morning, Shand drew the court's attention to the morning edition of *The Advertiser*, which misquoted him as saying, 'the statements are not quite as strong as I indicated'.[33] It implied that Shand's request to 'consider his position' stemmed from Brazel's suggestion he had over-egged the Wardrops' claims. 'Of course I did not do that,' Shand said. 'It was a question of my cross-examination that came up—that was why I asked for the adjournment,' he said, 'that is the "glaring inaccuracy"'. In light of the previous day's events, Shand said that he and the rest of Stuart's team wished to make a statement:

> My instructing solicitors and myself consider after yesterday that we are not being given, nor will be given, a thorough investigation in this matter. We consider that our continued association with this commission will in no way help Stuart and will in fact handicap him. We think the particulars have established that this commission is unable properly to consider the problems before it and we therefore withdraw.[34]

Bray and Charles Villeneuve Smith, who had acted as Shand's junior, had spent the evening trying to persuade him to go on, but he had made up his mind. Napier replied that any attempt to limit Shand's questioning of Phin stemmed simply from a matter of not wasting the commission's time. To Bright, Shand's husky and seemingly meandering style of questioning was slow but effective. But it was clear that Napier was unconvinced that Shand's attempt to push Phin on a seemingly minor point was worth holding up not only the commission, but the entire South Australian legal system, which had ground to a standstill while the three judges were tied up.

Shand was unmoved: 'I am not concerned to argue with Your Honour, beyond saying this, that cross-examination has more in it than is involved in Your Honour's statement. Time and time again it happens, what might be considered severe cross-examination brings out the truth in other respects, and, personally—in the cross-examination which no one suggested was unfair and which had some object—I have never in my career been stopped before.'[35] He stood up, walked out, and by midday was on the next plane out of Adelaide.

WHILE ONE OF his colleagues phoned the latest developments through to North Terrace, Bowman left the court room in search of Devaney or Shand, hoping one of them might give him a written copy of the statement that had been so difficult to make out in the room. He eventually tracked Devaney down at her office just before 3.00 pm, and raced back to squeak in a few minor changes to the late edition.[36] But the substance of the day's headlines remained, while a second poster, reading 'COMMISSION BREAKS UP — SHAND BLASTS NAPIER', seemed just as incendiary as the first one he'd seen upon leaving the courthouse.

The headlines made Bowman nervous, but they left the commissioners furious. Neither Brazel nor the chief justice mentioned *The News* directly when the commission briefly reconvened on 31 August, but their feelings towards the paper were unmistakeable. Stuart was now left without representation, while the chief justice and premier faced intense pressure in parliament and the national press.

First, Brazel and Napier attempted to clear the air—and attack both Shand and *The News*. 'Strenuous efforts have been made to confuse the public mind,' Brazel said, claiming that the chief justice's comments had been 'distorted' in various places to suggest that Shand had been prevented from doing his duty.[37] It was on 'this flimsy pretext' that Shand made his statement on the morning of 21 August. Shand

had accused the commission of a 'grave dereliction of duty', Brazel
said, but there 'was not a vestige of justification for this mischievous
suggestion'.[38] He also took aim at the reporting of Shand's walkout:
'A section of the press has seen fit to make these issues an excuse for
vituperative and indecent attacks upon members of this commission.'[39]

Napier added that the events of Thursday bore 'every appearance
of a deliberate act of sabotage of this enquiry', and thought that many
of the criticisms, which seemed directed at him personally, had been
a 'rude awakening'.[40] The chief justice had already been pushed to
the limit that week; his beloved wife had suffered a stroke on the day
Shand questioned Phin, and died shortly afterwards.[41] Now he was
dismayed to find his reputation of 18 years as chief justice was 'no
more than a pack of cards to be toppled', and he found it 'difficult to
believe that what has been published in a section of the press represents
the real opinion of the public of this state'.[42]

Since July, there had been mutterings about the nature of *The
News*'s arrangements with Father Dixon and Stuart's counsel, but now
Brazel and Napier seemed to accuse the paper of a conspiracy to derail
the commission and its pursuit of the truth. But as Bright's notes
reveal, it was not a one-way street:

> One feature relating to the chief and the other judges was
> distressing to me. Time after time there would be invective
> against *The News* uttered by Brazel in court. Later I would see the
> Chief and his brothers in the smoke room of the Adelaide Club
> laughing and apparently joking with Sir Lloyd Dumas, editor in
> chief of *The Advertiser*.[43]

The author Geoffrey Dutton also observed this 'daily comedy', as
the Dumas camp held court in the dining room while a handful of
News Limited men (chairman Sir Stanley Murray was a long-time
member) glared from afar.[44] Eight years after Rivett first raged at the
influence of Dumas and the Adelaide Club on the city, it seemed a line
had finally been drawn.

A few metres down the road, Playford was now under extraordinary
pressure as the case entered its tenth month. In all his years in office he

had never encountered this kind of antagonism from the opposition; with 22 unions joining the chorus against the commissioners, and the young MP Don Dunstan acting as a mouthpiece for Adelaide's more vocal progressives, Labor leader Mick O'Halloran finally showed some backbone. On 2 September, he moved a motion of no-confidence in the government, the first time in 21 years that the Playford had faced such a censure.[45]

When the premier stood up in the House of Assembly to stare down the uprising opposite, he had a prop with him. As he waved the 21 August edition of *The News* in front of the chamber, decrying the appearance of 'mob rule', he took Brazel and Napier's earlier condemnation one step further: 'The documents which I have here should be exhibited because a very important lesson could be learned,' he said, before reading out the headline, 'Mr Shand, QC, Indicts Sir Mellis Napier: "THESE COMMISSIONERS CANNOT DO THE JOB"'.[46] 'These words, or anything like them, were never spoken,' he said. 'They are the gravest libel action ever made against any judge in this state.'

'Why wasn't a libel action taken against them?' one Labor MP asked the premier.

'If the Government were to take action now it would be accused of trying to stifle public debate,' Playford shot back, before adding ominously: 'The government will consider action at the appropriate time to protect our judges, make no mistake.' It was a heavy threat. Rivett and *The News* had faced contempt charges before, and had paid the price for it, but Playford was threatening a different kind of action—something that hadn't been seen in South Australia in three decades. Rivett and Murdoch had been in Adelaide for just a few years, but those with longer memories knew what happened the last time a rabble-rousing young newspaper editor had pushed South Australia's establishment one step too far.

## CHAPTER FOURTEEN

# Wicked, malicious, seditious

IN THE FINAL days of September 1928, Adelaide looked like a city on a war footing. A bizarre scene was unfolding on North Terrace as a steady stream of men filed into the brand-new Adelaide Railway Station. On any given weekday, this grand, cavernous building was a hive of activity as crowds of commuters in woollen suits and wide-brimmed hats poured in and out like a brown-and-grey tide. But on this day they walked straight past the train carriages lined up in the station's bowels, headed for a set of corrugated-iron sheds out the back, and re-emerged gripping rifles and bayonets, with bright-red armbands fastened over the sleeves of their civilian clothes.[1] By midday, hundreds of these newly sworn 'special constables' had assembled into platoons and battalions, erected makeshift military camps on the riverbank, and piled into lorries and trucks fortified with coils of wire mesh that whisked them beyond the city limits.

Many of them ended up in Port Adelaide, 11 kilometres north of the city, where tensions were running high. The waters of the Yerta Bulti river were once home to swampy, mangrove forests teeming with life, but for fresh-off-the-boat settlers in the 19th century, the wetlands made for a sticky, mosquito-ridden landing they renamed 'Port Misery'. By the morning of 27 September 1928, those waters had been long since dredged and reshaped into a busy shipping district that on a normal Thursday morning would hum with the sound and sweat of thousands of labourers. Day after day, these 'wharfies' performed the backbreaking task of dragging a colony's worth of cargo on and off every ship that came ashore. But these were not normal times.

Earlier in the year, a contentious new federal wage ruling had brought chaos to the waterfront. Adelaide was flush with unemployed men desperate for work, and the new award stripped protections from maritime workers while eroding the Waterside Workers' Federation's control over who could work on the docks. On the morning of 27 September, thousands flocked to the waterfront as union officials tried to broker a compromise to stem the flow of lost work to non-union volunteers—scornfully nicknamed 'scabs' by the union men.

Among them was Ted Dickinson, a blonde, charismatic 27-year-old who had only been in Adelaide for a few months. Born in the northern English port city of Grimsby, Dickinson emigrated to Australia as a boy, and by his early twenties his radical politics and stirring turn of phrase had made him a popular fixture among open-air speakers' corners of Melbourne's Yarra Bank and the Domain in Sydney.[2] He arrived in Adelaide in early 1928 as a member of the Industrial Workers of the World, with a very specific purpose. Most of the local membership had been imprisoned, leaving its South Australian chapter rudderless at a critical moment. Part of Dickinson's mission was to restart *Direct Action*, a newsletter of the IWW that had sat idle since 1917, and to use it to re-establish the local branch and fire up the broader workers' movement. It wasn't the only labour-friendly publication circulating around Adelaide in the 1920s, but the city's mainstream press remained firmly on the side of big business and the state. The first issue of *Direct Action* under Dickinson's editorship, published in July, heaped scorn on its counterparts in the commercial press: 'The capitalist class own the press and are not interested in bringing about their own expropriation by printing class education,' it declared, giving special mention to one afternoon daily:

*The News* is merely the evening sheet generally found on butcher shop counters to be used as a sausage wrap. Other general uses are in outhouses or to kindle fires. Now you know why on Friday nights the newsboys on the Gresham corner bawl out 'THE NEWS' OR 'THE TRUTH'.[3]

In the face of press barons and their opaque corporate backers, *Direct Action* and its new editor planned to 'breathe the revolutionary air, express revolutionary thoughts and [be] a living vital healthy protest against a rotten system'.

BACK AT THE waterfront, things looked ready to explode. By mid-morning, between 4,000 and 5,000 union men had assembled in the middle of the port, vastly outnumbering the smattering of police on standby.[4] Many made their way to the Volunteer Labour Bureau, housed next door to the police station in a handsome, colonial-era building in the centre of town. But all attempts to register for work were rebuffed; the ship-owners not only planned to persevere with scab labour, they now refused to hire unionised workers until branches at *all* ports around the country recognised the new award. The crowd was seething, and as they streamed out of the bureau's redbrick archways some caught sight of a handful of ships docked at the nearby quay. But these weren't just any ships. Loading in or out of the Port, on a morning when the unionised workforce had been so spectacularly locked out, meant only one thing—these were scab ships. The crowd started moving towards the quay. On board one of the vessels, the *Port Gisborne*, an officer tried to hoist up his ship's gangway to avoid being boarded, but it was no use; the nimble-footed wharfies simply scrambled over and up the cargo nets festooned between the boardwalk and deck.[5]

Faced with this crush of angry workers, some volunteers simply raised their hands in defeat and filed ashore, while others panicked, diving into the harbour to escape their wrath. One witness on board the *Port Gisborne* likened the workers to ants swarming a bowl of sugar, as volunteers were man-handled off the boats and shepherded away.[6] According to a report in *The Advertiser* five men were later admitted to hospital with mostly minor wounds, with the exception of one middle-aged volunteer who refused to leave his post. He was later found by police, battered but alive, with puncture wounds on his buttocks and thighs inflicted by bale hooks used to haul cargo on and off the water.[7]

But it wasn't over yet. In the afternoon word spread that more ships laden with volunteers were due to arrive at Outer Harbor, and so a 2,000-strong crowd marched out from the port and down to the mouth of the river the river to continue their picket. But a few hours had made all the difference; the police finally seemed to regain some semblance of control, as a hundred mounted officers managed to corral the men into a corner, trapping the mob. A detective later claimed that at the front of the throng was none other than Ted Dickinson, who roused the crowd with the call: 'We are going on to the boats to pull off every scab'.[8] After a while the workers gradually dissipated, but the raw power seen at the waterfront sent a shockwave through South Australia's government and the private sector.

ALARMED BY THE scenes at the port, the state's Liberal and Country League premier, Richard Layton Butler, resolved to assemble a Citizens' Defence Brigade—a quasi-official squad of enforcers somewhere between a unit of Pinkerton guards and an over-eager neighbourhood watch group. While its volunteer ranks initially consisted of retired police officers and young men without military training, the brigade's numbers soon swelled into the thousands as pastoralists came in from the country, and city workers from the public service and private business were granted leave to pick up arms. The brigade would be led by Arthur Seaforth Blackburn, a celebrated former soldier and politician who had been awarded the Victoria Cross for bravery at Gallipoli, and subsequently served as a Nationalist Party member for Sturt between 1918 and 1921 (and who, some years later, would be tapped by *The Advertiser* to join the board of its new television company, Television Broadcasters Limited). Over the weekend, the special constables of this anti-worker militia were deployed to key locations along the waterfront, waiting for another showdown.[9]

Workers taunted 'Blackburn's Scab Protectors', who they claimed were little more than an 'army of pampered university students, college boys and prominent businessmen looking for trouble'.[10] But Butler's show of force seemed to make a difference. When work resumed at the waterfront on Monday, the only storm approaching was a literal one, as dust clouds and gales damaged jetties and roads up and down the coastline. As for the workers, a union decision to negotiate with their employers took the heat out of the week, if not quite diffusing it entirely. No one knew that the Great Depression was just around the corner, and that it would soon leave thousands upon thousands of men and their families destitute. For now, they had little choice but to accept this new status quo — after all, the combined forces of capital and state had them quite literally at gunpoint.

But the government wasn't content to simply avoid any further clashes with workers; it also wanted to send a message. On Monday, as if to drive the point home before any fresh resistance could take root, a new prosecution was announced. Just days after the police had claimed to see Dickinson whipping up the crowds at the docks, authorities received word that over the weekend a new and inflammatory edition of *Direct Action* had hit the streets, uncowed by the efforts of the Citizen's Defence Brigade. It took a further two months for the Crown to deliver on the threat: South Australia would be prosecuting Ted Dickinson for the crime of seditious libel.

With its origins in the 15th century, the charge was a rare one, part of the vast and often-unnoticed legal baggage that colonies such as South Australia had inherited automatically from English common law. Libel cases, of course, had been abundant since the early years of *The Register*; in Melbourne, even Sir Keith Murdoch's father, the Reverend Patrick Murdoch, had spent a night in custody for contempt of court, after refusing to pass on a letter that was to be used as evidence in a slander and libel trial. But seditious libel was a more serious lever, and as far as anyone on either side of the bench could recall, South Australia had never seen anyone prosecuted for such a crime.

Dickinson's trial began in December 1928, and in emotive language the prosecution accused the editor of being 'a wicked, malicious, seditious and ill-disposed person' who had scattered 'pernicious seeds of advice' over volatile soil.[11] The seeds in question were printed in the special 'Strike Edition' of *Direct Action*, which had featured a scathing reflection on the events of 27 September credited to Dickinson. The rank and file, it claimed, had been betrayed by trade union officials who had colluded with the bosses to accept the new award. The article concluded with an allusion to Marx ('We have nothing to lose but our chains and a world to gain'), and a blunt call to action: 'GET INTO IT'. But the prosecution largely ignored this first article, fixating instead on the one below it. Titled 'Open Letters from a Wob' (a slang term for a member of the Industrial Workers of the World, otherwise known as the Wobblies), it included an incendiary passage:

> There's a revolution looming up. We know not when it will be here, whether it will be bloodless or bloody. We hope it will be bloodless, but if a bloody revolution is forced on the workers it will be so forced by the master class. If that is what capitalism aims at, well, let us give what is asked with interest a thousand and one per cent added.[12]

The open letter was credited to another writer, but it was Dickinson who was named as publisher on the back page, as he had been in every issue since *Direct Action* was revived in May 1928. This was all that the prosecution needed to know. In court, Dickinson floated an unconvincing cover story, claiming that the first he had seen of the special 'Strike Edition' bearing his name was at Adelaide Gaol, when it was put to him as evidence.[13] Someone else, who he couldn't or wouldn't name, had written the copy under his by-line and assembled the offending issue in his absence.[14] It was a story that held little water; he had been *Direct Action*'s editor and driving force, and his whereabouts over the weekend had been no mystery—he was back at Botanic Park, giving another rousing speech that formed part of a secondary charge of inciting a riot.

It took two hours for the jury to reach their unanimous verdict: guilty, but with a plea for leniency given Dickinson's young age. Chief Justice George Murray ignored the jurors' request.[15] After all, 27 wasn't that young—the crown prosecutor opposite wasn't much older himself. The sentence would be nine months' imprisonment: three months for his role in the riot, and six for the seditious publication. To Murray's apparent dismay, hard labour was off the table, so he added a £50 fine: 'He would be as lenient as possible under the circumstances, but he would impose both imprisonment and fine, as imprisonment without hard labor was little or no punishment.' South Australia had never seen such an attack on the establishment, whether on the waterfront or the printed page, and Murray was intent on sending a message: 'The right of freedom of speech and the liberty of press did not permit the enunciation of doctrines of that sort.'[16]

*Direct Action* LIMPED on after Dickinson's trial, barely printing half a dozen editions before a final issue appeared in November 1930, almost a year after the last. But the hostilities between workers, government, and the press endured, peaking with the events of 9 January 1931—a day that came to be known as the 'Beef Riot'. When the Labor government of premier Lionel Hill decided to switch the meat quotient of all ration tickets from beef to mutton at the height of the Great Depression, around 1,000 men, women, and children marched from Port Adelaide, joined by another 1,000 unemployed men on the city's fringe. Singing revolutionary anthems and chanting 'We want beef', the crowd marched down North Terrace, past the Railway Station and Parliament House, and then turned inwards to Victoria Square.[17] They arrived at the Treasury building hoping to sheet their demands home to Hill, but the premier was nowhere to be seen. Instead, they found a small army of police mounted on horseback and motorcycles, with batons swinging. The protestors fought back, and after a bloody melee, 12 men were arrested—six of them Communist Party members—and 17 people admitted to hospital. 'Men dropped to the ground with blood streaming from head wounds,' read *The News*'s report that afternoon, 'and hats, coats and placards were strewn in disorder over the footpath..[18]

Hill was eventually expelled from the Labor Party for his support of austerity measures, but retained the premiership under a new coalition. *The Advertiser*'s unflinching support of Hill earned the ire of workers, and at Botanic Park he was condemned as a 'Newspaper Premier' by Labor activists, who called for a boycott of *The Advertiser* and any Labor leaders cowed by the 'capitalistic press'.[19]

> When 'The Advertiser' starts to praise a Labor man, that man is no longer Labor. I have seen Lionel Hill and Billy Hughes sell out to the vested interest newspapers. Thousands of you people will soon have to say with one voice that you will not read 'The Advertiser' and that you will withdraw your advertisements.[20]

Labor's loss of the 1933 state election, which returned Butler to office and elected a first-time MP named Thomas Playford, was blamed on 'the misrepresentation and suppression of the newspapers, both *The Advertiser* and *The News*', while the former's recent takeover by 'some big people in Melbourne' — Sir Keith Murdoch's syndicate — hadn't gone unnoticed, either.[21] Left-wing circles spread conspiracy theories that the paper had become 'the official organ of the Broken Hill Proprietary Group', virtually indistinguishable from the 'gutter press of Baillieu & Co'.[22] They weren't always wrong, however; in his memoir, Sir Lloyd Dumas admitted that Hill consulted him twice weekly, perhaps more than anyone else.[23] One afternoon at Botanic Park in 1932, a speaker wondered aloud 'if there is an *Advertiser* reporter about hiding behind the trees taking notes'.[24] Of course, there *was* an *Advertiser* man listening, who transcribed this statement and all the above ones in a series of private memos marked 'not for publication', sent directly to Dumas himself. 'As he spoke directly towards me,' the reporter wrote, 'I think he probably knew who I was.'

AFTER HIS RELEASE from prison, Dickinson eventually left Adelaide and Australia altogether, sailing back to England, where his campaigning spirit took another turn. In London, he co-founded the International Freedom League in protest at Sir Oswald Mosley's growing fascist movement in the United Kingdom. Then, in 1936, he walked into the King Street headquarters of the Communist Party in London, and signed up to join the fight in Spain, where General Franco's fascist forces were seeking to overthrow the democratically elected Republican government.[25] Issued with a one-way ticket, he was among the first of 66 Australian volunteers who joined the International Brigade supporting the People's Army.[26]

In February 1937, the river Jarama, east of Madrid, became the centre of the fighting, and Dickinson's machine gun unit was caught in the middle. On 13 February, they were routed by the fascists, and a handful of men were selected for execution. Dickinson was the third of his comrades to face the firing squad; with his back pressed up against an olive tree, he raised a fist in solidarity, looked at the survivors, and gave a final cry of 'Salud, boys, keep your chins up!' Moments later, a bullet cut his radical life short at the age of 33.

While sentencing the 27-year-old Dickinson back in 1928, Chief Justice Murray speculated that the accused was 'one of those who, while advocating certain things in private, elected to keep out of the trouble himself', but who was also 'prepared to make use of violence to effect his object'.[27] It seems Murray was both right and wrong about the young editor.

When a handful of his beret-clad South Australian comrades finally arrived home from Europe in 1939, they told the press waiting at Outer Harbor about Dickinson's defiant death among the olive groves of Spain, and shared a few more of his final words to his executioners. 'To hell with you!' Dickinson said. 'If we had 20,000 Australian bushmen here we'd sweep you into the sea.'[28] Perhaps somewhere in those defiant, doomed words lay the memory of that rousing morning in September 1928 when his comrades had run their foes into the Yerta Bulti river.

IN HIS BIOGRAPHY of Sir Thomas Playford, published in 1991, Stewart Cockburn recounts an apocryphal story of how, in 1959, the premier decided, like his predecessor Sir Richard Layton Butler 30 years earlier, to charge a newspaper editor with the obscure crime of seditious libel. Rifling through a thick tome of old statutes and common law charges in search of legal ammunition, Playford supposedly prodded one triumphant finger at the page and exclaimed, 'That's it. We'll have a go at him on this.'[29]

But Playford might also have taken a suggestion from another source, someone who was intimately aware of the ancient charge and its potential use against a hostile press, and who had been his closest advisor throughout the case against Rupert Max Stuart. In December 1928, it had been a 27-year-old lawyer, still in his first year as a crown prosecutor, who had spelled out the charges against Dickinson, his opening salvo dripping with contempt for the 'wicked, malicious, seditious and ill-disposed' outsider in the docks. The young prosecutor's name was Reginald Roderic Chamberlain, and three decades later, in his final remarks to the Stuart royal commission, he would close out his career for the Crown with an echo of the Dickinson trial: 'The lesson to be learned from the Commission is that attempted trial by newspaper is a dangerous and a malignant thing.'[30]

## CHAPTER FIFTEEN

# That poisonous material

'LOOK AT THE size of it, the *set-up*,' John Leo Travers QC thundered before the South Australian Criminal Court, the same building where Rupert Max Stuart had first been condemned to death a year earlier.[1] The court's attention was drawn to a familiar-looking poster, its paper a little yellowed over time, but the tall red letters—'SHAND QUITS—"YOU WON'T GIVE STUART FAIR GO"'—were as vivid as the day they were printed. As Travers paced the courtroom, the lawyer at times seemed like a strange, middle-aged parody of the newsboys who had first bellowed the poster's contents on street corners around Adelaide the previous August. It was 7 March 1960, six months after Playford had brandished *The News*'s headlines in front of parliament, and three months since detectives Calder and Giles had done the same to Rupert Murdoch and Rohan Rivett in the lawyer's office on Grenfell Street. For two-and-a-half hours, Travers pored over the posters, the headlines, and the events that created them; but, unlike the newsboys, Travers wasn't trying to sell a newspaper—he was there to prosecute one.

Travers's very presence in the courtroom was a source of outrage to the News Limited camp. In November, both Roderic Chamberlain and Jim Brazel had finally won their coveted Supreme Court appointments, and in their absence the government had tapped Travers to lead the Crown's case. Travers was one of the city's most prominent silks: the president of the Law Society, a former Playford government MP, and a sharp cross-examiner to boot. But Travers's brief wasn't just a sign that Playford was willing to throw every resource available at News Limited and its editor-in-chief. Travers had once been a vocal critic of the government's handling of the Stuart case, frequently quoted in *The News*'s columns — he had even offered to represent Stuart, with *The News*'s financial support, in the wake of Jack Shand's walkout. But, like Brazel before him, his allegiance had now flipped, and every heated word he threw at Rivett and *The News* carried an edge of betrayal for those who were now on the receiving end.

In this case, Travers told the panel of 12 jurors, much of the evidence was plain to read, all laid out in black and white and red. They would be shown proof of how 'that poisonous material' came about, of how Rohan Rivett, editor-in-chief of *The News*, had set aside the accurate reportage of his journalists and subeditors, which presumably 'was not false enough or scurrilous enough'.[2] This poison then poured out across the city and the state, posted prominently to catch the attention of not only those who bought the paper, but anyone who happened to pass within half a mile of the unmissable posters. 'The cunning mischief of it!' Travers said, as he accused Rivett of having a 'mind that was either unbalanced or seething with malice'.[3]

Then he tore into another article, a front-page editorial printed on 3 September 1959, the day after Playford lashed *The News* in parliament. Under the headline 'Let's get the record straight', the piece read like a peace offering, but only inflamed Travers further. 'What a magnificent gesture!' he spat sarcastically as he read it to the courtroom.[4] A degree of mystery still shrouded its authorship; a clear chain of witness testimony now implicated Rivett in all but one of the alleged libels published on the 'D-Day' of 21 August, but the origins of this postscript had become an important subplot. Whoever wrote it admitted that much of its 21 August coverage 'should never have seen the light of day'; but, rather than clear the air, the editorial seemed to double down on the most damaging claims.

'They are getting the record straight by telling the public,

"We were wrong in what we published, but you hang on to your opinions",' Travers said.[5] He lingered over its final line, and mocked the performance of Murdoch and Rivett when Inspector Calder and Detective Giles paid them a visit on those hot days in January. '"*The News* is quite prepared to defend itself at the proper time and in the proper place, as may be directed",' he quoted, before adding scornfully, 'You will be shown that when the police interviewed the heads of the company, they had lost some of their fighting spirit'.[6]

As the trial began, Rivett's counsel successfully applied for the courtroom to be cleared of witnesses, but there was one person who remained notably present: Rupert Murdoch. Rivett was there, too, spared the indignity of the dock, and allowed to sit behind his lawyers. Much had changed in the seven fiery years since Murdoch had arrived in Adelaide, but sitting in the courtroom that day, the two men were once again in it together. Whether they were partners in crime, however, would be a matter for the court.

THE QUESTION OF Rupert Max Stuart's fate, meanwhile, had reached a muted conclusion in the final weeks of 1959. After Shand's withdrawal, the royal commission sat in limbo for a month and a half, until the morning of 5 October, when, shortly before the hearings were set to resume, the premier called Chamberlain to his office. 'Joe,' Playford said, addressing Chamberlain by his nickname, 'we've got to commute the sentence on Stuart.'[7] Playford had faced enormous pressure throughout the trial, even from within his own family. But it was word from his federal counterparts, wary of the damage being done to Australia's international reputation, that forced his hand. In August, a full-page story in London's *News Chronicle* had declared that 'Rupert Max Stuart would be dead today ... but for a newspaper that did its job,' describing the commission as a 'farce' and Rivett as 'the Zola of South Australia', while legal and civil rights figures from Delhi to London had also weighed in throughout the hearings.[8] (*The News* proudly republished the *News Chronicle* story, then a week later ran it again as a house ad, proclaiming '4,000,000 Britons saw this'.)

Chamberlain relayed Playford's decision to the commission later that morning, provoking both relief and outrage across the state (with the premier himself receiving a death threat to his home phoneline that afternoon).[9] But this breakthrough, after no less than seven postponements and seven new execution dates, also cleared the way for Stuart himself to finally appear. Napier had previously said that unless Stuart addressed the royal commission, its findings would be a 'foregone conclusion', but while his date at the gallows loomed, it had seemed like a lose-lose proposition. After Chamberlain's latest update, Stuart's new counsel—a prominent Victorian QC named John Starke—eventually agreed that his client would front the inquiry on 13 October 1959. Rupert Murdoch attended the hearing that day, passing Father Dixon on the steps of the court building—they had met only once before, when Rivett brought the priest to meet the publisher shortly after the commission was announced. ('Well, Father, how is he going to do?' Murdoch asked the priest.)[10]

When Stuart entered the box, dressed in a lightly coloured suit and tie, with a lean look about him, Starke led him to recount his movements on his brief, fateful trip to Ceduna. They went over the day of Mary Hattam's disappearance, his interrogation by police, and his previous entanglements with the law in Alice Springs and at Cloncurry. To Starke, he disclosed for the first time that during his visit to Thevenard on the Friday, he had paid a young woman for 'naughties' behind the hotel.[11] He had not disclosed this to O'Sullivan, he said, for fear it might make him seem guilty.

When Chamberlain took over, he sought to demolish this new claim—even to the point of compelling the girl in question to undergo an invasive doctor's examination to determine her sexual history. Chamberlain's laborious cross-examination also prompted Stuart to corroborate part of the police's account of the interrogation, in which he had initially lied about being forced at gunpoint by a white man. That part, he said, was true—he had told the lie out of fear. Chamberlain's strategy, of undermining Dixon, O'Sullivan, and Strehlow's claims about Stuart's language troubles, while also portraying him as a habitual liar, now became clear.

It's true that while Stuart gave mostly monosyllabic answers throughout Starke and Chamberlain's questioning, he occasionally spoke in comfortable sentences. He was not, it seemed, quite as helpless as Strehlow and Dixon had claimed—or at least, Napier reflected, no worse than an uneducated white man. Chamberlain later boasted that he had never faced an easier task, but according to one contemporary report, even he grew frustrated at times, exclaiming 'I give up!' after Stuart gave a series of confused and conflicting answers.[12] As he questioned Stuart, Chamberlain even tried to introduce the testimony of three jail warders who claimed to have heard Stuart all but admit culpability after his initial sentencing. (Starke objected successfully to this attempt.)

After Stuart's testimony concluded, the commissioners recalled his interrogators, who gave at times contradictory accounts of the interrogation. Starke also quizzed Detective Sergeant Turner on his own recent history.

'Prisoners have asserted that you have assaulted them, leaving out Stuart?' Starke asked.[13]

'I cannot recall any specific one,' said Turner. 'I think it has happened though.'

Starke reminded him of a case several years earlier of a man named Martin, also accused of a sexual offence, who had claimed that Turner and another officer brutally assaulted him in custody. A doctor had been called to corroborate seeing bruises and a black eye on the man, and the case was thrown out.

'Mr Turner, do you say you did not assault that man?' Starke asked.

'No,' Turner replied.

'You agree he was acquitted, do you not?'

'Yes.'

When the royal commission's report was finally tabled to parliament on 3 December, 11 months after Mary Hattam went missing, few were surprised by its findings. With regard to Stuart's English, the commissioners agreed with Chamberlain: 'although uneducated, he is—by any standard—intelligent and quick-witted', even as the evidence he gave was deemed 'untrustworthy'.[14] They found the 'perfect' alibi Dixon had coaxed from the Giesemans to be 'far from convincing', and seized upon what they claimed were 'dangerous' differences in the accounts given by the Giesemans and their employees, and dismissed the Wardrops' claims that Whitrod had been heard to admit the police 'did our blocks and really belted [Stuart]'.[15] They did, however, wave away the discrepancies between the accounts of the police witnesses and the officers themselves, finding that there was 'nothing sinister' in their differing stories or their investigation. The commissioners concluded, ultimately, that there was 'no valid reason for apprehending any miscarriage of justice'.[16]

For those convinced of Stuart's guilt and intent on seeing him executed, it was an overdue vindication. For his supporters and those who had rallied behind him out of opposition to capital punishment, they had saved a man's life. Stuart, meanwhile, was eventually sent to Yatala Labour Prison to serve out a life sentence.

BY TIME IT reached the Criminal Court, the case against Rohan Rivett and News Limited had already become a sensation of its own—the '"Poison Pen" Charges' and 'Silent Men' made headlines around the country as Travers, the Crown, and Playford's Executive Council used every means at their disposal to break through *The News*'s wall of silence.[17] When the preliminary hearing began on Monday 25 January 1960, the first two witnesses arrived at the Police Court flanking the defendant. On Rivett's left was Murray Willoughby James, *The News*'s 47-year-old chief of staff, and the shorter of the three with waves of wiry, light-brown curls carefully tamed into place for the occasion. On the right walked Kenneth Spencer May, a News Limited lifer who had been *The News*'s political reporter until the previous September, when Murdoch made him his personal assistant and all-round fixer. With sharp eyes, thinning hair, and a pencil moustache, May fixed a photographer from a rival newspaper with a disdainful stare as the trio were snapped outside the courthouse.

The room was packed as Chamberlain's successor, the new crown solicitor, Joseph Kearnan QC, began with a basic question: 'Are you a journalist, Mr James?' James replied much as Rivett and Murdoch had in January, declining to answer on the grounds of self-incrimination.[18] The presiding magistrate, Reginald J Coombe, interjected: did James honestly believe that something as basic as his job title might prove ruinous? Kearnan then asked James to confirm whether he had, just moments earlier, replied 'journalist' when asked his occupation by the court clerk.

'Yes,' James said.

'Did you think *that* might tend to incriminate you?' Kearnan asked.

'No.'

'Then why do you decline to answer my question as to your occupation?'

He declined, once again on the grounds that it might incriminate him. Kearnan pressed on, but James stuck to the line, repeating it over and over as the prosecutor grew just as frustrated as Inspector Calder had back in January.

'You have learnt that as a phrase to use to answer any question put to you?' Kearnan asked, before another string of denials from James.[19]

'These answers show a completely *mala fide* approach by the witness,' Travers interjected, comparing James to a trained parrot.[20] Coombe stepped in again, and told James that he was not the sole arbiter of what might or might not incriminate him. When James declined to comment once more, the judge did what might once have been unthinkable: he ordered that James be detained until the court rose at the end of the day. As James was taken into custody just after 3.00 pm, May took his place in the witness box, and continued to bat away Kearnan's questions—even after a warning from Coombe. He was ordered into custody, too, but this time News Limited's counsel, Harry Alderman QC, stepped in, and after a five-minute adjournment, May returned with a change of heart.

'Yes sir, I am now the personal assistant to the managing director,' May said, and once he started talking, he didn't stop.[21] He told them how he had been associated with News Limited for 30 years, and walked the court through its hierarchy, from managing director Rupert Murdoch at the top, then Rohan Rivett, then assistant editor James Wilson, and downwards to over a dozen subeditors. He detailed the mechanics of the newsroom as it performed the daily task of turning an endless churn of cable news and scraps of inbound copy from on-the-ground reporters into each day's *News*. He described how the paper's four editions fanned out through a decentralised network; first, the company's fleet of vans sped bundles of papers to hundreds of drop points, where they were picked up and taken to the nearest shops, newspaper kiosks, and newsboys. And tucked into the top of many of those bundles were large posters.

'The purpose of them is to advertise the highlight or selling point of that particular edition of *The News*,' May explained.[22] 'A poster is one of the things we rely upon to help sell the paper. Apart from the poster or any particular cry of a newsvendor, no one knows what's in the paper until they buy it … therefore the poster is a vital part of our advertising method to inform the public of anything startling in *The News*.'

This was an important point for both the prosecution and the defence; half the charges levelled at Rivett and News Limited were based on these posters, and it was essential that Travers and Kearnan establish who authorised them. May said the task of drafting and approving them would fall to one of three or four people at the top of the editorial pyramid, but neither Murdoch nor Rivett had told him who authorised the posters in question. 'Mr Murdoch could desire or require to be consulted on matters of editorial policy and he is at times,' May told the court.[23] 'Mr Murdoch is on the ground floor of the building and Mr Rivett is on the first floor,' he said, adding that the men conferred on a semi-regular basis. 'They can confer often but not that frequently, but they do confer frequently.'

When the trial resumed the next day, the Crown's questioning fell to the 3 September editorial, which May admitted had occupied a 'reasonably rare' position in the front of the paper.[24] The task of writing each day's editorial, he said, usually fell to one of five people, from Rivett as editor-in-chief to a senior reporter such as David Bowman. 'To my knowledge Mr KR Murdoch has written some leaders—the editor-in-chief would be aware of who wrote a particular leader for a particular day,' May said.[25] It was possible, he added, that Rivett was away when the September editorial may have been written or dictated by the managing director.

'I think that each journalist develops a style in their reporting—in some cases I could pick up a piece of prose and without knowing who wrote it I could say "So and so wrote that,"' May said. 'I can see the style of the managing director in portions of this editorial.' He read aloud its central point, the one that so bluntly, and perhaps rashly, admitted fault:

> Well, the Premier is right and we were wrong. Mr Shand did not use these words, and the headline should never have been published and we regret that it was. Also, Mr Shand did not single out Sir Mellis Napier in his attack, and a poster which read 'Shand Blasts Napier' should not have seen the light of day and again we regret that it did.

James was then recalled, having been released from his 75-minute stint in custody when the court adjourned the previous afternoon. Like May, James could only speculate about the editorial's authorship, but he confirmed it must have been approved by Murdoch or Rivett. 'That is a direct admission that certain things which were published should never have been published or that is the interpretation,' he said.[26] 'For a newspaper to make such a statement would be a matter of very considerable importance to its editor-in-chief and managing director.' To drive the point home, Kearnan asked again if those words could *only* have been written by or with the express authority of either Rivett or Murdoch. 'It would be most unusual for it to have been written without the direction of either,' James replied. 'If anyone published that without the authority of the managing director or editor-in-chief, then I would expect a drastic action — that has not happened to anyone.'

Rivett was the named defendant, but now Murdoch was directly implicated; if he had written or authorised the 3 September editorial, he had not only failed to stop the government launching its prosecution, but had practically handed the Crown its case. So far, the Crown had used the threat of imprisonment to force its first two witnesses to reveal incriminating evidence about both their bosses, but there were more revelations — and unprecedented courtroom tactics — still to come.

AT 11.00 AM on Thursday 28 January, Travers called news editor Norman Sewell to the witness box. He pressed Sewell for more details about Rivett's movements on 21 August; but, like his colleagues, the editor gave little away, claiming privilege over a dozen times. Then Travers did something unexpected. Perhaps recognising that threatening to lock up journalist after journalist might not be the best look in a case that threatened to become a proxy battle for press freedom, he reached into his pocket, pulled out a piece of paper, and handed it to Sewell.

'Would you mind reading the document?' Travers asked. Sewell's eyes scanned the letter. 'Have you read it through?' the lawyer asked.[27]

'Yes,' replied Sewell. The document was a free pardon granted by the Executive Council, a get-out-of-jail card that made it untenable for Sewell to stay silent — any fear of self-incrimination was now eliminated. After a five-minute discussion with his counsel, Sewell began to talk, and after days of hearing about the minutiae of newspaper production, and endless, repetitive denials, Travers and Kearnan were finally getting to the nub of it all.

'Looking at Exhibit A ["SHAND QUITS — "YOU WON'T GIVE STUART FAIR GO'"], do you know whether Mr Rivett wrote that exhibit?' Travers asked.

'He drafted it, I wrote it out at his dictation,' Sewell replied.[28] He couldn't say whether Rivett wrote 'Shand Blasts Napier' himself, but the editor-in-chief certainly approved it. As for the 22 August edition headlined 'Mr Shand, QC, indicts Sir Mellis Napier "THESE COMMISSIONERS CANNOT DO THE JOB"', Rivett dictated them to Sewell, too. Sewell explained that he gave the editor his own suggestion, 'Shand QC Walks Out of Enquiry — Stuart Shock', but after a moment's consideration, Rivett decided it wasn't right, and with minimal discussion dictated the headline that went to print.

'Did he say anything like, "We want to make it hotter", or anything like that?' Travers asked, reaching for some proof of malice or negligence.[29]

'No,' Sewell replied, 'this was a hurried conference.'

By the end of the five-day hearing, Travers and Kearnan had combed through every part of the editorial process — from the morning conference where Bowman, Shaw, and Prisk were sent to cover the commission, to the courtroom, where they strained to transcribe Shand's 'muffled' and 'husky' voice. They had even dug out the small slips of paper upon which *The News*'s expert typists had accurately dictated the reporters' notes over the phone every 15 minutes. Thanks to Sewell, they had narrowed down the moment of creation for all but two of the headlines to the subs' table, and they had Rivett's fingerprints all over them. But would it be enough to convict?

The Crown also called upon Ewan Waterman and Sir Stanley Murray, both members of the News Limited board of directors, to tease out more unflattering testimony. Waterman claimed that he and four other board members were 'disquieted, confused, and most unhappy about what had been published', and confirmed that Murdoch and Rivett operated with little direct oversight from the board.[30] 'On any matter of importance, the editor-in-chief and managing director arrive at a decision and then carry it out,' Waterman said.

At 10.15 on Friday morning, Travers finally called the managing director himself, Rupert Murdoch, who also gave his occupation as 'journalist' to the court reporter. The last time he had fronted this kind of public questioning, he had spoken freely, and had dug himself plenty of holes along the way. But the stakes in 1960 were different from those in 1958 — missing out on a television licence was one thing, but the very real threat of prison was another.

'Were you carrying out the duties of managing director in August and September of 1959?' Travers asked.[31]

'I decline to answer,' Murdoch replied, echoing the trail of subordinates that had come before him.

'On what grounds?'

'On the grounds that it might tend to incriminate me.'

Travers asked a further 40 questions: whether Murdoch knew who drafted any of the posters and headlines in question; whether he agreed that they 'distorted' the meaning of Shand's exit; and whether he'd taken any steps to 'disassociate' himself from the offending material or to reprimand those responsible. But he was unyielding, holding the line, no matter what Travers threw at him.

'Is there anything at all you want to say to the court in the way of explanation or justification or excuse as to the contents of the Exhibits A to B?' Travers asked.

'I have nothing to say,' Murdoch replied.

Travers had no further questions, and Alderman advised that Rivett and News Limited reserved their defence. The charges were confirmed: the case would proceed to trial.

BY THE TIME Travers was making his opening salvo at the Criminal Court in March 1960, Rivett had hired his own lawyer in John Jefferson Bray QC, reprising his brief appearance at the royal commission with Bright. A poet and aesthete, with greying hair and a peppery moustache, Bray was another anti-establishment son of another venerable old Adelaide family—his grandfather had served as premier shortly before 'Honest' Tom Playford in the 1880s. The company line of silence that Rivett had dutifully followed since the detectives arrived at his office in January had crumbled; the combination of Sewell's pardon and the broader threat of custody had opened the floodgates; and the mounting evidence seemed to flow straight to Rivett. Ken Inglis had continued to observe the Police Court hearing as he prepared to write a book on the Stuart case, and he wrote to the editor of *Nation* that it was 'all very depressing':

> Every lawyer in town seems to think Alderman's handling of the defence this week was bewildering, and damaging to Rivett. Much of Travers' and Kearnan's cross-examination of witnesses subpoena'd from *The News*, the lawyers say, could have been objected to successfully, but Alderman said not a word.[32]

It seemed that Alderman had written off the preliminary hearing as a mere formality, and was reluctant to show the defence's hand before it went to trial. 'But every lawyer whose opinion I've heard (and they all quote others similar) thinks that the effect of this curious inactivity is to reduce the chances of acquittal later,' Inglis wrote. With Bray as his lawyer, Rivett would now be mounting his own defence independent of News Limited's.

Sir Herbert Mayo presided over the court case, a choice of appointment that surprised no one—all the other Supreme Court judges had either been members of the royal commission panel, or, as in the case of the newly appointed judges Chamberlain and Brazel, had been sitting on the other side of the bench. *Truth*'s gossip round-up joked that the jurors must have realised what they were in for when they clocked the piles of legal tomes brought in by each legal team—a stack of 17 books was heaped around the defence counsel, while the prosecution seemed practically fortified behind 40.[33]

When Travers finally finished his two-and-a-half hour opening remarks, he summoned May back to the witness box, as Kearnan once again asked him to outline how the offending posters fitted into *The News*'s distribution model.

'One way of arousing people's interest is to have what I may call a scare headline—something that hits them between the eyes?' Kearnan asked.[34]

'I would say a *bold* headline,' May replied.

'What you would call a sensational headline?'

'It could be.'

May then explained that the decision about which headlines to run across the paper and its posters usually rested with two people: Rivett and Sewell. Pressed by Kearnan, he conceded that, in special circumstances, Murdoch might also be included—but 'it would be a departure from normal'.[35]

On the second day of the trial, Kearnan took on the contentious question of quotation marks. The prosecution claimed that 'These Commissioners Cannot Do the Job' and 'You Won't Give Stuart Fair Go' were lies, and that Shand never spoke those precise words. The defence, and the parade of journalists who would testify over the trial, pointed out that such paraphrasing was a commonplace practice in newspapers. It was one of many arguments about the finer points of newspaper convention aired throughout the trial, with Bray also arguing that headlines, whether on posters or on front pages, could not be read in isolation from the contents of the paper.

'I would be making a mistake if I told the jury they could consider it on its own apart from the paper?' Justice Mayo asked.[36]

'My submission is that the poster would be so connected that it would be wrong to treat it alone as defamatory,' Bray replied.

'In other words, the poster means, "Read this, but don't take any notice of it 'til you read the paper?"' the judge asked.

'Yes,' Bray confirmed.

As the questioning of May continued, he became the first of several witnesses to testify to the busy nature of the newsroom. 'The editor-in-chief would have an extremely busy time during the morning, very high pressure during the morning,' May explained.[37] 'It would be fair to say, until the paper goes to press, I suppose an outsider might think it would be a scene of orderly chaos.' It was an important point for Rivett's case. In Bray's legal notes, he listed five lines of defence, with the final point reading: 'It may be desirable to paint a picture to the jury of the urgency and speed prevailing when an edition is going to press ... much of this may be obtained in cross-examination of May who will probably be called by the prosecution'.[38] Bray and Alderman had to tread a fine line, and to convince the jury that any sensationalism present in the headlines reflected the explosive nature of Shand's walkout, which *The News* had reported quickly and dispassionately—there simply wasn't time to contrive a campaign of wilfully seditious misinformation.

'This story of what happened on 21 August as it came in from the typiste, would that be regarded as an exceptional story?' Alderman put to May.[39]

'Oh yes,' May said. 'A story like that, I would expect the editor-in-chief to be in close contact with the managing director Mr Murdoch if he were there.'

Kearnan probed further, asking May to elaborate on his suspicion that Murdoch himself had penned the 3 September editorial. 'It is a fact, isn't it, that journalists achieve a style of writing which becomes their own?' Kearnan asked.[40]

'The best of them do,' said May. 'Mr Murdoch has been a journalist all his business life. I am reasonably familiar with Mr Murdoch's style—someone once described style as being the man himself ... looking at it, I haven't any doubt that Mr Rupert Murdoch wrote all or most of that editorial.'

It was only on the fifth day, when Travers called James Wilson, the associate editor of *The News*, that fresh information began to flow. Sporting thick-rimmed glasses and a brushy moustache, Wilson had become an indispensable part of *The News* in the years since Rivett had successfully poached him from the Melbourne *Herald*. After May's informal literary analysis, Wilson was able to finally state unequivocally that it was Murdoch who had sought to 'get the record straight'.

'He writes editorials most infrequently,' Wilson explained, telling the court that, while around seven people were usually responsible for writing editorials, he couldn't recall another occasion where the managing director had stepped in.[41] On 3 September, however, Murdoch not only wrote the editorial, but directed staff to put it on the front page. ('You could call it quite a rare thing to put on the front page,' Wilson added.) Wilson told the story of how on 3 September, at around 9.00 am, he was summoned to Murdoch's office on the ground floor, where he found the managing director sitting behind a typewriter.

'I sat alongside Mr Murdoch as he typed the editorial, and he handed it to me as he typed small sheet after small sheet,' he said.[42] He talked as he typed, a small word or query here and there, but there was no great discussion, nor an invitation for Wilson to review or edit the piece in any way. 'I do remember when he called me down and told me he wanted it published, and he did mention the words that the premier had used — some extravagant language about *The News*,' Wilson said.

It seemed that Murdoch had been sufficiently worried on the morning of 3 September to take it upon himself to fire back at the premier while Rivett was out of town. The experienced journalists around him, who might have argued, as they had just done in court, that many aspects of Playford's complaint were readily defensible newspaper practices, either stayed silent or were ignored. But Murdoch did it anyway, even using similar language to the last time he had found himself in damage control, when he wrote to *The West Australian* on 12 February 1957 'to set the record straight' after being threatened with contempt of parliament by Bill Grayden.[43] Despite the forthright tone of the editorial, one fact was now clear: left to his own devices, and in the face of unprecedented pressure from the establishment, the Boy Publisher had blinked first, and had handed their enemies an ill-worded admission of guilt.

But one question of authorship remained: the headline dubbed Exhibit B, 'COMMISSION BREAKS UP — SHAND BLASTS NAPIER'. 'I don't know who drafted that poster,' Sewell said when called back to the box.[44] On a typical day, the second poster would be discussed and drafted at the midday news conference, taking into account any breaking news. But on 21 August, at around 12.30 pm, Rivett came over to Sewell's corner of the subs' room and handed him a draft handwritten in pencil. Rivett told Sewell to send it 'down to the poster man', but Sewell never saw Rivett put pencil to paper.

While the Police Court had heard an almost uninterrupted stream of testimony implicating Rivett in the posters, with little pushback from Alderman, Bray had also resolved to ask each of Rivett's colleagues what they thought of their editor-in-chief. May told the court that the paper 'has gone from strength to strength and is a much stronger paper today' since Rivett took over. 'To my knowledge everything that comes before him is treated promptly and competently from editorials and leaders to the main news items of the day,' he said, adding, 'accuracy is his motto, yes'.[45]

James said he had been in nearly constant, daily touch with Rivett for eight years, and found him a 'most conscientious editor and a completely responsible personality'. He could have a 'terrific drive', and be 'intensely enthusiastic', but had never 'seeth[ed] with malice', or shown signs of 'an unbalanced mind', as Travers has claimed.[46] 'Such epithets as applied to Mr Rivett are incredible and completely without any form of foundation.' All of which served to prime the jury for Rivett's own appearance at the trial's climax.

ON 17 MARCH 1960, the eighth day of the hearing, a weary-looking Rivett entered the witness box. It had been a long three months, compounded by the stress of the trial, the all-too-familiar prospect of imprisonment, and being kept away from his work at *The News*. Then there was the added indignity of feeling like even more of a pariah than usual; for all the praise that he and *The News* had received for their principled stance in the Stuart case, it soon became clear, once the charges were announced, how many of the acquaintances that the Rivetts had charmed over their eight years in Adelaide were little more than 'fair-weather friends'.[47] Many had stopped acknowledging them on the street, and even Rohan's 14-year friendship with his old *Herald* colleague Stewart Cockburn had fallen apart over the case. Cockburn was now a prominent reporter for *The Advertiser*, and in September they had a huge row; Rivett accused his old friend of losing any 'shred of integrity', while Cockburn thought *The News*'s handling of the royal commission was 'unfair and rotten and unprofessional and calculated to lower the prestige of all newspapers and newspapermen'.[48]

For the duration of the preliminary hearing and now the trial, Rivett had barely said a word. He had simply sat in silence as his workplace, his colleagues, and his very state of mind were picked over by Travers and Kearnan. He had been tempted to use his turn in the witness box to finally take a stand, to use his platform to strike a blow for press freedom and to call out Playford's repressive tactics. One draft of his statement even included a rallying cry that a newspaper's job was to report 'facts', not 'tranquilisers':

> To play down, suppress or minimise the significance of a Queen's Counsel walking out on a Royal Commission on the grounds Shand gave would have been gross dereliction of duty by any newspaper with a sense of responsibility towards its community. The facts as others saw them hurt some people. But what purpose is there in having so-called freedom of speech if facts or comments that hurt some members of a community are to be suppressed from them?[49]

But before the jury had heard from the defence's three witnesses, Justice Mayo told the jury that he was striking out the three charges of seditious libel.[50] The grandstanding declarations of Rivett's draft might have been a fitting rebuke to the Crown's most serious and disproportionate accusations, but with six charges still looming, it seems that staying out of jail became more important than martyrdom. When

Rivett stood up in the courtroom to deliver an unsworn statement, just as Stuart had done all those months ago, there was no trace of those stirring words—just a sober, 1,700-word statement of fact.

'Your Honour and gentlemen of the jury,' Rivett said, 'I am 43, married, and have three children.'[51] He walked the courtroom through his personal history: starting work as a journalist months before enlisting in the AIF, his captivity under the Japanese, and his eventual return to work for Sir Keith Murdoch after the war. He told the court that when Father Dixon's story of an alibi for Stuart had first reached him, he 'formed no definite opinion except that it should be investigated'. 'The community would be shocked if there remained any doubt about the conviction of a man who was to be hanged within a few days,' he said, and explained how he briefly travelled to Queensland in August to pursue a lead. 'We felt it was the duty of a responsible newspaper to urge that every aspect of the case be sifted, so that all should be satisfied that justice had been done and appeared to be done.' When the royal commission began, he said, *The News* gave it fair and extensive coverage 'so that our readers would have a complete picture'.

Then he approached 'D-Day'. 'Reading carefully what had happened on Thursday afternoon, August 20, it was quite clear that the reason why Mr Shand wanted time to consider his position in the case was because he thought he was not getting and would not get a fair go,' he said. 'To me the morning of August 21 was ordinary, but there was keen interest in developments,' he said. 'I do not suggest that I did not have time for the Shand story, but I certainly had no time for the subtleties which I think have been attributed to me, and I was certainly never angry nor malicious. Why should I be?'

Based on the reports that arrived over the telephone, combined with those from the previous afternoon, he argued there was no conclusion that he—or indeed anyone—could make other than that Shand had accused the chairman of unfairness, and that he might as well withdraw rather than continue to participate. 'If such an accusation by a QC to a royal commission is not a blast or severe criticism, which is common usage, I do not know what is,' he said. It seemed clear that the commission had adjourned indefinitely—or 'broken up' — in the wake of Shand's withdrawal, and that Shand's statements were aimed particularly at Sir Mellis Napier.

> I believe that the 60 words of Shand's statement, particularly the words, 'This commission is unable properly to consider the problems before it', were fairly and accurately summarised in the heading 'These Commissioners Cannot Do the Job'. I believe that the words 'You Won't Give Stuart Fair Go' fairly and accurately summarise Shand's words as reported in the state edition of *The News*, read in the light of the previous day's events ... we used the quotes in accordance with almost invariable practice in headlines to make it clear that the statement was not ours.

Rivett claimed that he never personally doubted the 'integrity of knowledge of the law' of the three commissioners. Then he said something that clarified the one lingering question over the whole trial: who wrote the two remaining headlines?

> I was in constant touch with Mr Rupert Murdoch, the managing director. It is with his authority, and, indeed, at his request, that I state what follows. We discussed the report of Shand's walkout immediately before my conference with Mr Sewell and Mr Wilson at about 10.30. Mr Murdoch knew of the first poster before it went out. He suggested the headline 'These Commissioners Cannot Do The Job'. Later, because on further consideration he thought the first poster too long, he gave me the wording for the second poster 'Commission Breaks Up — Shand Blasts Napier'. He offered no other criticism of the first poster. Nonetheless, I accept responsibility as an editor should. I am mentioning my conversations with Mr Murdoch only to indicate that no individual feelings of mine were involved and that I had no motive or intention other than a desire to give a fair and accurate report of the proceedings.

As for Travers's claim that he had lost his 'fighting spirit' when confronted by detectives, he maintained that it was only on the company's advice that he kept his silence. 'Left to myself, I would have been happy to answer his questions,' he said. He concluded with an affirmation of loyalty usually reserved for those accused of Cold War defection or wartime treason:

> I am a loyal citizen of South Australia and I respect the administration of justice in this State. I had no intention of defaming anyone. I did not knowingly publish anything false, and I don't think anything I published was false. I only intended in the posters and headings to give a fair and accurate summary and index of what happened at the Royal Commission and I think that's what I did. I am not guilty of the charges laid against me.

KEARNAN SUMMED UP the prosecution's case on 18 March, the ninth day of the trial. He told the jury how the rather anti-climactic reality of Shand's decision to withdraw had frustrated *The News*'s continuing campaign. 'What was expected to be highly explosive material was a bit of a damp squib,' he said, and in lieu of the 'drama and sensation' he was expecting, Rivett had authorised headlines without a 'scintilla' of truth.[52] By doing so, *The News* levelled charges at the commissioners that Shand had never done—suggesting they were dishonest, impartial, and, perhaps most damning of all to Australian sensibilities, they hadn't given the defence a 'fair go'.

The fact that Murdoch and Rivett had collaborated to 'contrive libels', Kearnan said, did not excuse Rivett from his responsibility as editor to stop libellous material from reaching his newspaper's readers. Kearnan also noted that even if Murdoch had written some of the headlines, the managing director had seemed 'ashamed and frightened' for himself when he penned the 3 September editorial that disavowed his 'own brainchild'.

In response, Bray argued that the 'guts' of the case lay in what Shand meant on 20 and 21 August 1959, and how fairly *The News* relayed those sentiments.[53] Shand may well have misinterpreted Napier's words when his interrogation of former detective Phin was interrupted, but it was no fault of *The News* for fairly and accurately reporting his disgruntled response and walkout. Bray even suggested that in conjuring up the rare charge of seditious libel, the government was as guilty of sensationalising the events of August 1959 as it claimed *The News* was.

'Why sedition?' Bray asked. 'Is not it magnifying the thing enormously to build it up like that?'[54] Responding to Kearnan's remarks, he said that Rivett's new claim that Murdoch had contributed the second poster headline was not an attempt to share the blame or downplay the notion that Rivett alone was pursuing some private vendetta. Rivett himself had claimed full responsibility for all of it. But none of it was defamatory, he said, and certainly not seditious—it was simply a report of what happened in the royal commission that day, however distasteful those events were.

As he concluded his remarks, Bray again claimed that the words of the premier in parliament on 2 September had themselves been grossly exaggerated, and set the tone for an often-hysterical prosecution. Out of Playford's own wounded pride, the Crown had been sent 'vainly on the scent of an imaginative conspiracy', and in attempting to build their case had put the very practices of 20th-century newspaper journalism on trial.

Mayo spent an hour and a half summing up the case, and at 2.45 pm the jury retired to deliberate. There were only 11 of them left—one juror had fallen ill on the third day, and had been forced to withdraw. The survivors returned after another hour and a half to clarify one small point: were they to view the poster 'Shand Quits—You Won't Give Stuart Fair Go' in isolation?[55] Mayo responded that it was up to them to decide the words' meaning. They spent four hours deliberating, and asked for an additional 50 minutes' consideration, before they returned at 7.35 pm. The verdict was in: they had decided to acquit Rivett and News Limited on eight of the nine charges.

Three of those charges were a moot point—Justice Mayo had already directed the jury there was no case to answer for seditious libel. To be cleared of four additional charges was an undeniable relief, but it wasn't over just yet. The jurors remained split over the headline they had sought to clarify earlier in the afternoon. It was not a seditious libel, and they agreed it was not a defamatory libel 'with knowledge of falsity'; but on the third charge, of simple defamatory libel, they remained divided. Rivett was released on bail, but for weeks, while the case remained *sub judice*, the premier refused to confirm or deny whether the Crown would drop the charge or mount a new prosecution.

For 75 long days, the final charge continued to hang over *The News* and Rivett, until 6 June 1960, when the Crown asked Justice Ross in the Criminal Court to enter a *nolle prosequi* (a decision not to prosecute) over the two remaining libel counts against Rivett and News Limited. Two days later, *The News* ran a chastened editorial soberly headlined 'An Aftermath'. The column's author reaffirmed the paper's confidence in the Supreme Court and its judges, and claimed that, in retrospect, certain statements had been 'misunderstood'.[56] The paper never intended to suggest that Stuart or his counsel were not being given 'a fair go' at the commission: 'It is with satisfaction now that, after the dust of the conflict has settled, we can reaffirm what we have always believed, that the members of the Supreme Court of this State are men in whom we and the public do and can have the utmost confidence.' Like the 3 September editorial, Rivett had nothing to do with the piece.

The case against Rohan Rivett and News Limited had destroyed friendships, shaken the notion of press freedom in South Australia, and made it clear that while Rivett had become the public face of *The News*'s handling of the Stuart case, the paper's most controversial acts bore the fingerprints of both its editor and managing director, Rupert Murdoch. And, despite extraordinary pressure from the Crown, its journalists had shown great loyalty to their editor and *The News*'s reportage of the royal commission. But there was another, bigger shock around the corner, which would turn North Terrace upside down.

# CHAPTER SIXTEEN

# Wonderful evening
# of combat

A LITTLE AFTER nine o'clock on the evening of 7 June 1960, a car pulled up outside 3 Queen Street, Chippendale, in Sydney. The warehouse belonged to Anglican Press, a small company that printed a mixed bag of religious and secular publications, ranging from *The Anglican* newspaper to *Nation*, the journal that had published Ken Inglis's commentary on the Stuart case. It was a small player in Sydney's long-running newspaper wars, with its ownership shared by a variety of Anglican parishes around the country. That all changed when a small gang of men spilled out of the car—among them, two young men with lumbering frames and similarly pugnacious faces. Twenty-six-year-old Clyde and 23-year-old Kerry were the sons of the now-knighted Sir Frank Packer, and they had arrived on Queen Street on a mission for their father. A lawyer who came with them announced that their party had authority to take possession of the building, with documents to back it up. When they were rebuffed at the door by another lawyer, waving his own piece of paper that voided the Packers' claim, Clyde was heard to mutter something about breaking in as they walked off.[1]

226

It wasn't an idle threat. Before long, they had slipped into the building through a back entrance, yanked the phonelines from the telephone switchboard, and begun barricading the windows.[2] Thomas Willis, the general manager of Anglican Press, found the Packers in his office—Kerry carrying an 18-inch torch, and one of their associates brandishing what Willis later described as a 'jemmy'.[3] Clyde gave Willis an ultimatum to leave the building by 11.00 pm, and when the hour arrived, the brothers took off their jackets and grabbed him. He tried to resist, bracing his foot on the door frame, but they prised him loose, marched him down to the front door, and threw him out onto the footpath. As they did, the flash of a camera bulb lit up the scene, an image of which was splashed across the next morning's front page of a Sydney tabloid called *The Daily Mirror*. There, in black and white, was Clyde Packer 'forcibly ejecting' the man, above the bold headline 'Knight's Sons in City Brawl'.[4] *The Daily Mirror* had, just weeks earlier, gained a new proprietor, who had spent months gradually, surreptitiously making inroads into the Sydney newspaper market. A fortnight later, a courtroom would hear that the Packers' bid to acquire Anglican Press had been trumped at the eleventh hour by a newly formed company whose board included two Anglican bishops, and, inexplicably, the new, 29-year-old owner of Mirror Newspapers: Keith Rupert Murdoch.

WHILE ROHAN RIVETT and the rest of News Limited were at the eye of the storm in Adelaide, beset by a libel trial and the very real threat of imprisonment, Rupert Murdoch was beginning to look further afield. In a way, his hand had been forced; the previous October, as the royal commission reached its crescendo, he had launched his most audacious gambit yet: a bid to take over nothing less than *The Advertiser* itself. The offer, valued at £14 million, would see the companies merge—albeit with Advertiser Newspapers' shareholders only granted voting rights 'on special occasions'. The fact that this was a 'bid for press monopoly' nearly identical to the one that Sir Lloyd Dumas had so outrageously presented to his mother in 1953 did not seem lost on him. Hoping to pre-empt any critics who might throw his words back at him, Murdoch

proposed to safeguard *The Advertiser*'s independence by the creation of
an editorial trust, modelled on *The Times* and *The Observer* in Britain;
a letter from Sir Stanley Murray suggested that the trust could include
public figures such as the chancellor or vice-chancellor of the university,
the chief justice, and business and union leaders.[5]

In Adelaide, there was no bigger or more public swing for Murdoch
to take. But it was an almost immediate miss; the offer was made on
21 October 1959, a Wednesday, and three days later, Dumas publicly
rejected it on page 10 of the Saturday *Advertiser*.[6] The bid, Dumas
wrote, was 'not, on examination, so attractive as it might superficially
appear', and had been shot down 'as a matter of public spirit'.[7] He
rubbished the merits of News Limited's growth forecast compared to
*The Advertiser*'s own prospects. ('When the two pictures are viewed side
by side, it is not surprising that our Board should be unimpressed.')
There was also the obvious fact that a takeover of *The Advertiser* would
hand Murdoch a stake in the Herald and Weekly Times, given each
company was the other's major shareholder — ostensibly to ward off a
raid just like this one. Most pointedly, he scoffed at the notion of an
'irrevocable' trust.

After all, this wasn't the first time that Dumas had watched
a Murdoch make a play for *The Advertiser* — hadn't Rupert's father
made similar assurances to Sir John Langdon Bonython back in 1929,
even while grooming Dumas himself to edge Bonython out as soon
as the deal was finalised? The notion that the trust might include the
chancellor and chief justice was equally laughable — both posts were
occupied by none other than Sir Mellis Napier, who was still seething
after *The News*'s coverage of the Stuart inquiry. 'We believe that our
shareholders — and the South Australian community generally — have
a real pride in *The Advertiser* and would never agree to its being
modelled on *The News*,' Dumas said, before repeating the same point
he had made in 1953, and then at the television inquiry in 1958:

A controlling interest in News Limited is owned by Cruden
Investments Pty Limited, a Victorian company. A representative
of that company, therefore, would have complete individual
control over *The Advertiser* as he has today over *The News*.

It was clear which 'individual' he was referring to. According to one former *Advertiser* copy boy, Murdoch had been seen pacing in the lane beside its Waymouth Street headquarters as the board made its decision on the Friday: 'Sir Lloyd Dumas came out and virtually ignored him and walked off.'[8]

In *The News* that afternoon, Murdoch tried to save face, insisting that the offer remained open, and maintaining that his family company's Victorian registration was a technicality.[9] 'Its largest shareholder is a South Australian,' he added, but he wouldn't remain a South Australian for long. Whether or not Murdoch ever seriously thought that *The Advertiser* would entertain his offer, it was certainly a show of confidence that no one in the Australian newspaper business could ignore. A man who could muster this kind of bid with a straight face couldn't be dismissed so easily, and with his options in Adelaide now limited, he looked east. He had outgrown the city, and now had the means and momentum to leave it behind.

SYDNEY WAS THE one market that his father had never managed to crack, run by an infamously tough set of paper barons who viewed outsiders with suspicion. Between the Fairfaxes, the Packers, and the ageing Ezra Norton, each of the big players zealously guarded their turf — even with their fists, if it came to it. But if Murdoch played his cards right, he could finally regain the kind of east-coast foothold he had lost with the family's Queensland Newspapers shares in 1953. Between visits to the Police Court in late January and the Criminal Court in March, Murdoch had landed a deal to take over an obscure Sydney show called Cumberland Newspapers. The company's main trade was far from prestigious — just a chain of 27 free 'throwaway' papers of varying quality that circulated around the suburbs of Sydney from Hurstville to Katoomba in the Blue Mountains. A shrewd entrepreneur named Earl White had assembled this suburban fiefdom piece by piece over 30 years, buying up ailing smaller papers and old, unwanted printing presses and linotype machines from the big metropolitan dailies. By 1960, he had taken full advantage of the growing population that was pouring out into Sydney's suburban sprawl to create a rather efficient operation with a combined circulation of 400,000. But at 60 years of age he had decided to cash out, and eventually agreed to a £1 million deal fronted by a well-connected Sydney businessman named John Glass. It was only after the deal was completed that Glass was revealed as having acted as a proxy—the true bidder was Rupert Murdoch all along.[10]

Rupert also managed to land *The Daily Mirror*, another evening paper that was by Sydney standards a rather downmarket publication. It had been bought by Fairfax two years earlier from Norton, which took on its old competitor chiefly as a means of keeping the Herald and Weekly Times at bay. But the paper was proving a deadweight, and Fairfax's chief officer, Rupert Henderson, needed capital to invest in television. For decades, Fairfax had repelled Sir Keith Murdoch and his successors on Flinders Street, but now it seemed that palming *The Daily Mirror* off to his son might not be the worst idea—the cost of taking on the struggling paper might even act as a handbrake on the young publisher's ambitions.

It was John Glass again who helped smooth the deal; he was well known for hosting exclusive lunches for Sydney's movers and shakers at the Carlton Hotel, where he heard Henderson complain about *The Daily Mirror*'s woes.[11] Glass promptly passed this intel on to Murdoch, and made the case to Henderson that the son of Sir Keith was the only good option. After years of being foiled by the Adelaide Club, it seemed that Murdoch was getting the hang of behind-closed-door dealings. Murdoch paid £600,000 up front for the group, with a further £1.3 million to be paid over the next three years.[12] But for Murdoch, it was a coup—Adelaide had shown him how an afternoon newspaper could be turned into a high-circulation profit-maker, and he had proven in Perth that he didn't necessarily need the guidance of older men installed by his father to do it. In a full-page ad published in *The Daily Mirror* two weeks after its acquisition, Rupert Murdoch made a personal appeal to readers that foreshadowed a 'gradual change in the paper's editorial policy' while promising 'a lack of bias' in his 'new, objective, yet more stimulating and provocative newspaper'.[13]

But Murdoch's encroachment into Sydney hadn't gone unnoticed. Sir Frank Packer and his sons had also been eyeing the suburbs, and before Henderson decided to sell *The Daily Mirror*, they had formed a truce with Fairfax to use the *Mirror's* facilities to print their own giveaway papers. When those presses fell into Murdoch's hands, the Packers suddenly found themselves in need of a city printer. Anglican Press was managed by an eccentric character named Francis James, a high-flying RAF pilot turned Sydney gadfly often seen bashing out copy in the back of his battle-scarred 1928 Rolls Royce. But the company had been running at a steady loss, and by May 1960 had gone into receivership.

James knew that the Packers were sniffing around Anglican Press, which now owned the only unaligned newspaper printing plant in the whole of the city. On the morning of 6 June, James presented the receivers with a bid from Australian Church Press Limited, a new company of which Rupert Murdoch was a director. The receiver told James he already had a cheque for £42,000 from the Packers' Consolidated Press, and that he felt bound to accept it.[14] But James hit back, presenting a letter signed by the Australian Church Press board committing to beat any other offer by £500. The negotiations continued into the night, and James later told a courtroom that he saw the shadow of a man crouched ominously outside his window. When he finally ushered the receivers out of the office, he saw Clyde Packer standing outside.[15] The next day, James took drastic action: Anglican Press would dump its receivers, withdrawing their authority to accept any bid and rendering the Packers' cheque useless. James was having dinner the next evening, cautiously confident that he had outflanked the Packers, when he received a call: Clyde and Kerry Packer and a group of thugs had taken possession of Queen Street, and had turfed out its workers.

According to James's account, he then called Murdoch, who in turn enlisted a man with a colourful reputation and the right connections for dealing with this kind of problem. Frank Browne had been a boxer, a racing correspondent, a failed political candidate, and, if the rumours were true, a decorated volunteer soldier during the Spanish Civil War.[16] In 1955, he had spent three months in custody for breaching parliamentary privilege rules, and was called an 'arrogant rat' by Arthur Calwell. By 1960, however, Browne was dabbling as a sports reporter for *The Daily Mirror*, where he crossed paths with its new owner, Rupert Murdoch. A little after midnight, James and Browne met on the steps of Sydney's Town Hall, joined by a gang of four enormous men whom Browne had recruited from a shady corner of the city. Murdoch was there, too, counting out dozens of £10 notes, which he placed in James's hand before they headed to Chippendale without him.[17]

A 28-year-old named Douglas Golding had been working for James at Anglican Press on the night of the siege, and joined Browne's posse as they regrouped on Queen Street. James knew the building well, and while the Packers had presumably blocked off the back entrance they had come in through, he knew there was a small back window they might have missed. 'My job was to create a rumpus at the front while Frank Browne broke in through the toilet at the back,' Golding recalled years later.[18] 'I'm in the front and Willis is in the back, swinging the 6 x 4 against the door to try and break it down, but unfortunately Kerry stuck his head out to see what was going on, and copped it in the eye—so one of the *Mirror* photos was Kerry bleeding.'[19]

By 2.00 am, James, Browne, and their gang had cast out the Packers and retaken the building. Inside, they found that a steel safe had been broken into and emptied of the company's ledger, receipts, and cash book.[20] In the next day's *Daily Mirror*, readers were told that the Packer's newspaper turf war amounted to a violent affront to Christian morality—with no reference to its new proprietor's involvement. Anglican Press's 76-year-old chairman, the Adelaide-born Bishop of Armidale, told the paper that even he would happily take a cricket bat to the Packers 'in good conscience'.[21]

Sydney newspaper battles, it seemed, had an altogether different flavour from those in South Australia, but Murdoch proved a cunning combatant. He had retaken the building and its all-important printing press, and *The Daily Mirror* had delivered a humiliating shot across the bows for the Packers and the rest of the city. The legal battle dragged on for weeks, but the Packers' play for Anglican Press was dead in the water.[22] 'The order was later annulled by a higher court,' said Golding of the Packers' bid. 'That was the sort of inglorious end of the wonderful evening of combat.' Years later, he would meet Kerry Packer again, this time as he sold a small Canberra paper of his own to Australian Consolidated Press. 'I didn't think to remind him,' Golding said. Murdoch had well and truly arrived in Sydney; and, as in Adelaide, he was an outsider unafraid of upsetting the old order.

Back in Adelaide on the day after the Queen Street brawl, the news finally arrived that the last charge against Rivett and News Limited would be dropped. For a moment, it seemed that Rivett might join Murdoch in Sydney, now that his name had been cleared. A 15-year-old copy boy named Les Hinton, whom Rivett had hired months earlier, fresh off the boat from Britain, recalled the editor-in-chief triumphantly telling him about *The Daily Mirror* takeover. This day would be forever remembered, Rivett told the boy, as the day that Rupert Murdoch moved beyond Adelaide to create 'a great Australian newspaper company'.[23]

But Rivett's optimism was misplaced. Before the showdown on Queen Street, Ken Inglis happened to be in Sydney during the week that Murdoch landed the Mirror Newspapers deal, and saw Murdoch bounding up the stairs of the George Street office of *Nation*.[24] Panting at the top of the stairs, Murdoch had eagerly shared the news and immediately tried to lure *Nation*'s founder and editor, Tom Fitzgerald, to join him. Fitzgerald said no — he would spend the next decade turning down job offers from Murdoch before eventually caving, in 1970. But one thing was clear: whatever Murdoch's plans were for Sydney, they didn't seem to include Rohan Rivett in the editor's chair.

## CHAPTER SEVENTEEN

# Body without a soul

'I SHOULDN'T HAVE opened these,' whispered Betty Gillen as she walked into the editor-in-chief's office, a bundle of letters in her hands and tears welling in her eyes. 'It's going to be a terrible shock to you.'[1] It took a lot to startle metropolitan newspaper editors or their secretaries, and even though Gillen had only been Rohan Rivett's secretary for a matter of months, sifting through his morning post tended to unleash a rather full spectrum of human emotion from one envelope to the next. On this brisk Thursday morning, however, her usual routine had brought on the mortifying feeling of having walked in on a very private conversation that, once overheard, threatened to turn the world upside down. Between sobs, she placed the letters on his desk and slipped out of the room, carefully shutting the door behind her. Rivett looked up from his typewriter and leafed through the papers, stopping at a letter dated 5 July 1960, two days earlier. It was from Sydney, with the letterhead of the newly acquired Mirror Newspapers at the top of the page, just above the underlined words *Personal & Confidential*.[2]

It had been one month since the Crown had finally dropped the last libel charge, and after two-and-a-half months of limbo, both he and Rupert Murdoch, whom he'd named at trial as co-author of the offending material, seemed to be out of the woods. Rivett didn't just feel free; he felt energised, inspired, even a little defiant. He had spent the morning tapping away at an editorial eulogising Aneurin Bevan, the Welsh Labour politician whose death the day before had made him take stock. To Rivett, Bevan was one of history's great rebels, whose 'corrosive, devastating speeches' gave voice to the 'bitter frustrations of two million forgotten men', and threatened to upturn the old order.[3] 'Some of them went to Spain to fight alongside Spanish minors and factory workers against Franco with his Moorish mercenaries and his Nazi dive-bombers and Fascist tanks from Hitler and Mussolini,' he wrote. 'Some of them died there, dreaming of a transformed Britain, of a Britain with a social conscience of which word-spinner Nye had drawn them a blueprint'.

After all those weeks of forced silence, it felt good to be writing again. And, if it reminded readers of events a little closer to home, then all the better. Rivett had long been impressed by Bevan, and there was a time when he wasn't alone; during his first year as editor at *The News*, he had christened Bevan the 'man of the moment'. That piece, of course, was based on a letter written by a 21-year-old Rupert Murdoch in the days before Sir Keith died. Setting the obituary aside, he picked up this latest letter from Rupert, which barely filled a single page.

> For some days I have been trying to write this letter, but it seems best to be brief and to the point. After much long and tortuous consideration, I have come to the unhappy conclusion that you will have to step down from the Editor-in-Chief's Chair.
>
> Doubtless you would not agree with my reasons, which are many, so it is better not to go into them at this stage.[4]

A few more sentences followed, giving Rivett the option of continuing as a 'star writer' or resigning with 18 months' salary as severance, then Rupert's signature. There was another page tucked inside the envelope, written in a hand that Rivett knew all too well:

> I feel I must add a personal note on this business. I must say that I have never loathed writing any letter more. In coming to

this decision to 'close your innings' as editor of *The News* I have not lost sight of all your achievements and our long personal friendship makes the whole thing impossibly hard. But here it is![5]

Rivett placed the letter down on the desk. He called Gillen back in, and, in a reassuring voice, asked her to keep its contents to herself and to carry on as usual for the time being. It had been nine years, almost to the day, since Sir Keith had set this whole business in motion, half-dressed at Claridge's Hotel, and Rivett reacted the same way he did that night: he picked up the phone and called Nan. It was a shock, of course, but it wasn't as if the thought of life without *The News* hadn't crossed their minds; 16 months earlier, he had said to Nan that there were days when it all ran so smoothly that he barely had anything to do. 'It is always better when I am away,' he told her.[6]

After hanging up the phone, he turned back to his typewriter. Rupert probably expected him to jump straight on the telephone, or perhaps even the next flight to Sydney, to force an explanation or change of heart. But he wasn't going to do that. He kept writing, perhaps thinking back to his time as a student before the war, when he volunteered in a Welsh mining camp: 'Yesterday, on a summer afternoon, Aneurin Bevan, the boy from the pits, whose voice and deeds helped to shake down the last edifices of an old social order, went forth to join the other mighty revolutionaries who have done so much for Britain through the ages.'[7] He tapped out the final full stop with a sense of satisfaction that seemed surreal, given everything that was unfolding around him. Whatever came next, he was, all things considered, quite pleased with how the article had turned out.

He attended the midday conference, following the same routine that Travers and Kearnan had laid bare for the court back in March. He handed over the typewritten tribute, and told them to put it on the front page, but otherwise gave his colleagues little indication that everything was about to change. By the afternoon, it seemed the silence had gotten to Murdoch; someone in Sydney had phoned Ken May and *The News*'s production manager, telling them about the letter and asking what on earth Rivett was doing. In Rivett's office, the three of them mulled over what to do. Murdoch's letter had suggested that he hand over to James Wilson until Ron Boland arrived to serve as acting editor-in-chief, but Wilson was at home, bedridden by nervous heart trouble. The pair left Rivett in his office, more than a little bewildered by what had happened and what would come next—surely Rivett or Murdoch would pick simply up the phone? But they didn't, and when Rivett left the building at 6.00 pm, he still hadn't heard another word from Rupert.

The next day, Rivett wrote a letter to Sir Stanley Murray to update him on the situation and to ask his advice about his status as director. Murdoch might have had the power to unilaterally dismiss an editor-in-chief, but sacking a member of the board required an extraordinary general meeting and a shareholder majority. Murray told him to sit firm and to keep attending board meetings, the first of which was scheduled for that day. Murdoch dialled into the meeting via May, who offered to put Rivett on the phone. But Murdoch refused, unwilling to talk to Rivett while others were present. Instead, he sent a telegram that came through just after 4.00 pm. He had expected to hear from Rivett the previous night, it read, but would talk things over the following week. Meanwhile, to 'avoid any staff trouble', he suggested that Rivett hand over to Murray James instead of Wilson.[8]

Rivett called James up to his office and told him to cancel his plans to take the next few days off: he was now acting editor-in-chief. Leaving him to handle the Friday edition, he called Gillen back into his office, and together they began the long task of cleaning out his office, sorting through eight years of accumulated detritus—the scrapbooks of newspaper clippings, thick files of correspondence, and pages of typewritten drafts. They decided what to burn, what to leave for James and Boland, and what to take home with him for posterity. When he left the office that afternoon, he was, for the first time in years, no longer editor-in-chief of a newspaper.

IN THE DAYS that followed Murdoch's letter, Rivett claimed to be at a loss as to the 'many problems' it had vaguely alluded to. Only a few months earlier, the pair's relationship seemed as close as ever. On 23 April 1960, just after Murdoch had landed the Cumberland deal,

Rivett sent him a buoyant letter. Jokingly addressing Murdoch as 'dear old man', he gleefully relayed a rumour that Menzies himself had told his cabinet that he 'hoped Tom [Playford] won't be such a bloody fool as to go back for his hat' in pressing the final libel charge.[9] 'Tom will keep,' Rivett wrote, suggesting that they tread lightly for the next few months: 'just keep our ammunition dry and wait the time'.

So what happened? For years, the precise reason behind the split has been a point of contention; had the stress of the Stuart case and libel trial finally torn them apart? Had Rivett grown 'unhinged' by the threat of prison?[10] Had *The News* pushed too far, and alienated its readers under Rivett's leadership? Or, as some *News* staffers speculated, was Murdoch simply tired of sharing power and the spotlight with an editor who shone brighter? One recurring theory is that the Crown's abandonment of the final libel charge came out of some deal quietly brokered between Playford and Murdoch. The trade-off, the story goes, was the conciliatory editorial of 8 June and an undertaking to tone down *The News*'s scrutiny of the Playford government.[11]

One curious episode that supports this idea emerged in 1972, when a Walkley-winning reporter for the Murdoch-owned *Sunday Australian* interviewed Rupert Max Stuart, now serving out his sentence at Yatala Labour Prison north of Adelaide. But when the journalist sought a comment from Sir Tom Playford, he was told by the now-retired premier to call Ken May. May subsequently killed the story.[12] In later years, May vowed never to discuss the Stuart case, the Murdoch family, or Rivett with the many biographers and television producers who came to his door seeking answers.[13]

Murdoch has never been drawn on whether any deal was struck with Playford, but by the 1990s he claimed that Rivett's 'bold and intensely controversial policies' had polarised much of *The News*'s readership.[14] He told one biographer that Rivett had launched a fresh attack on the government, despite Murdoch's wish to 'cool it for a while' after the final charge was dropped.[15] But looking at the last month of *The News* under Rivett's editorship, there is only one editorial that seems to fit that bill; published on 15 June, it reflected on a recent debate in the British parliament to call for ministerial renewal in South Australia. 'In the past quarter-century this State has been ruled largely by one party and one man,' it read, before asking whether the 'lethargy that characterises so many governments be swept away and their functions vitalised by new minds at the top?'[16] But it also went out of its way to qualify its critique; it was not an attack on Playford himself, who had proved to be 'an outstanding leader, as the state's present prosperity testifies', but of his frontbench more generally. Murdoch claimed it was a front-page story that denounced Playford 'more angrily than before', but it matched neither description.[17]

But their final weeks of correspondence also hint at another source of tension, born not of politics, justice, or temperament, but cold commercial reality. They had clashed over money before; in December 1957, the arrival from England of a new, state-of-the-art £150,000 Scott-Vickers press prompted Murdoch to run advertising on the back page of *The News*.[18] He needed the cash, but there was a problem: it meant bumping the sports pages from their prized position. When the sports-mad Rivett returned from a conference in India, he was aghast—it seemed like Murdoch had waited until he was overseas to force through the change.[19] He tendered his resignation but was convinced to reconsider. To an observer such as David Bowman, this was just one of many concessions the editor-in-chief made in the face of a 'steady encroachment' from the 'brash, opinionated, ambitious' Murdoch, which few at the time could truly appreciate.[20] With Rivett's capitulation, it was clear that something had changed between the two men—a long-brewing power shift on its way to an inevitable conclusion.

Sometime between April and June 1960, that distance grew starker than ever, and on 24 June the pair had a particularly heated argument. Its cause was financial, and perhaps a little ideological; for years, Rivett had represented News Limited at negotiations with the Australian Journalists Association (AJA), and the editor-in-chief had enjoyed such good relations that after his dismissal, union members at *The News* lamented the loss of the 'best friend AJA members ever had'.[21] But for a newspaper proprietor with expansion on his mind and a growing pile of debt to service, that friendship ran counter to his own interests, particularly set against the fraught state of industrial relations that closed out the decade.

It had been a decade of closures, mergers, and redundancies, from the Herald and Weekly Times' buyout of its Melbourne morning rival, *The Sun*, in August 1953 to the closure of *The Argus* in 1957.[22] In April 1954, relations between proprietors and unionised journalists had grown so vexed that the parties were forced into arbitration for the first time since 1917.[23] When then-conciliation commissioner Arthur Seaforth Blackburn's new award raised wages for higher-grade journalists, many employers, including *The News*, responded by downgrading previously promoted staff.[24] Throughout the 1950s, News Limited had felt wage costs keenly; the 1956 chairman's address bemoaned the 'sharply increased expenditure' facing the industry caused by the 'seeming perpetual increases' in two new industrial awards.[25] The same point was made in 1959, as new awards for journalists, printers, and other workers increased the company's wages bill by 10 per cent.[26] These tensions were felt all around the country; but in Sydney, Murdoch had waded into the site of some of Australian journalism's most bitterly fought disputes.[27]

As Murdoch made his play for Sydney, he grew frustrated by costs that seemed to be quietly blowing out across the company. He needed every cent to repay his latest borrowings, and perhaps someone the union considered its 'best friend' was the last thing that News Limited needed at the bargaining table—even if it meant sidelining a long-time ally. In a 13 April memo to Rivett, Murdoch said he was 'disturbed' to discover that for six months the editorial department's weekly wages bill had climbed by £300.[28] Then, on 24 June, the day of the argument, he sent a memo informing Rivett that May would represent the company instead of him at an upcoming conference with the AJA in Melbourne. While the memo authorised the payment of a new set of wage rises, Murdoch insisted that if any further demands arose at the conference in Melbourne, 'these men will get none of it'.[29] A pointed exchange followed, recounted in a fiery letter sent by Rivett on 29 June just days before Murdoch pulled the pin:

> Once upon a time—not many years ago—I would have been so incensed at some of your volleys and counter-volleys of our 'little discussion' of Friday morning that I probably would have said or

done several foolish things. However, as I don't believe that you actually think I am 'financially irresponsible' any more than you always believe many of my more sweeping generalisations, as far as I'm concerned the matter's over.[30]

Rivett disagreed with Murdoch's 'no concessions at any price' attitude; in a lengthy plan, headlined 'the Murdoch papers and the future', he explained that many of the country's journalists and photographers regarded News Limited with a respect and cautious optimism that was never extended to men such as Henderson and Packer. He was keenly aware of the baggage that existed between unions and proprietors in Sydney, and implored Murdoch not to squander such a clean slate so lightly—even if it cost him in the short term:

> I believe we would be blowing off our noses to save a couple of fingernails if we for the sake of a few hundred pounds a week *at this moment* pursue a policy of 'give nothing'. Firstly in the long run it will cost us a damn sight more financially. Secondly, in dealing with the best journalists—young and old—as your father repeatedly wrote and preached to me, there are things much more important than money. Goodwill and respect are the two main things. Journalists will do anything for a proprietor, an editor, a chief-of-staff or chief sub who is willing to do himself, what he asks them to do.
>
> It is vital for News Limited, and above all, for Mirror Newspapers, that Rupert Murdoch not be identified in any shape or form with the policies that have made Henderson execrated by all the responsible officials of the AJA in all states.

There was a time when appealing to the memory of Sir Keith might have swayed his son's thinking, but those days were long gone. So, it seemed, was the schoolboy whom Rivett had met all those years ago: the one who had argued that the abolition of trade unions would 'result in the complete and utter end of the British way of life';[31] the one whose clumsy but impassioned support for left-wing politics prompted mockery from his classmates and consternation from his father. Sir Keith needn't have worried. Economic necessity had finally superseded Rupert's youthful radicalism, and although the party allegiance of his papers would oscillate over the coming decades, depending on the prevailing political winds, leapfrogging from Whitlam to Fraser in Australia, and from Thatcherism to New Labour in the UK, he could rarely be accused of being left-wing or pro-union.

Some years later, Keith Dunstan recounted the contents of a note that Rivett sent him early in his Adelaide tenure. As two of Sir Keith's bright young men navigating a world without their late mentor, the pair had swapped observations about his heir, then a 'young radical just out of Oxford'. The 'metamorphosis of the young left winger, in the space of just four weeks, to a right wing, hungry, self-seeking conservative was the most remarkable thing [Rivett] ever witnessed … He didn't realise that a grub could turn into a moth so quickly,' Dunstan recalled.[32]

ON MONDAY AFTERNOON, once *The News* had been put to bed, Rivett called together the editorial staff and several dozen executives for a floor-wide meeting. These 'fireside chats' weren't unusual; every month or two for the past eight years, Rivett had gathered them all to discuss the paper's direction, propose new initiatives, or give departing staff a proper send-off. These weren't always welcome — not everyone cared for 'Big Red' and his grandstanding speeches against the power of 'the establishment'.[33] Even Rivett's admirers admitted that he wasn't always the easiest person to work for, and there were plenty of fights on the newsroom floor over the years. But, as they gathered around, they all gave their full attention.

'We have seen people married, and farewelled people, said goodbye to people going overseas,' he told them.[34] 'It is different today only in this: that I have come here to say goodbye to you because *I* am finishing. In fact, I finished, as far as being editor-in-chief is concerned, late on Friday afternoon.'

It was a bombshell, but Rivett held his composure and did his best to reassure his shocked staff. He told them he felt no regret; eight years, seven months, and six days was an awfully long run for any editor, and a record for *The News* that surpassed even JE Davidson's tenure in the 1920s. In the days that followed, many of those present could hardly believe the 'guts' the now ex-editor showed as he spoke. For the last time, he regaled his staff with the story of Claridge's Hotel, of flying across with Sir Keith in December 1951 and feeling wholly out of his depth. He knew no one, he said, but was given the kind of help that 'makes it impossible to destroy any institution', and no one in the room could ever know how much that meant to him. He cast their minds back to the Sunday battle, 'when everybody was in, boots and all, seven days a week—it was the greatest, bloodiest, and most wonderful battle ever, and for once Goliath was slain'.

As his staff looked on in stunned silence, he repeated what he'd said to Nan all those months ago: 'a very intelligent 14-year-old child could edit *The News* with reasonable success because there are so many good men around to help him—providing, naturally, he was prepared to listen to good advice'. He quoted the words of failed US presidential candidate Adlai Stevenson II, who said, 'It hurts too much to laugh, and I am too old to cry', when interviewed after losing to Eisenhower by 7 million votes in a landslide in 1952. 'That's about the situation,' Rivett added.

Of the thick stack of letters Rivett received in the days that followed—envelopes stuffed with expressions of shock, outrage, and solidarity—some of the most frank and poignant came from Murdoch's own family. The first of these came from Rupert's younger sister, Anne, who was 'most unhappy' to hear the news, but knew nothing of its circumstances beyond a 'rift' between the men.[35] A week later, Rupert's great uncle, Professor Walter Murdoch, wrote that he was 'greatly perturbed' by the 'wild rumours' he was hearing from Perth.[36] When Rivett told him the full story, it left him 'mad (in the American sense)'.[37] As the 'white-haired patriarch of the clan', he planned to demand Rupert explain the stories he'd heard—'all of them ugly'—and hoped his nephew still valued his opinion enough to provide answers. Finally, after many weeks, a letter from Lady Elisabeth arrived. Rivett had called her soon after the events of 7 July, but she had wanted to see Rupert first to hear about 'the sad situation' firsthand.[38] She told Rivett how fond she was of him, how grateful she was for the loyalty he had showed to Sir Keith, and what comfort it had brought her over the years to know he was by Rupert's side in Adelaide. But, she added, the break had seemed inevitable, given their 'rather unique and such different temperaments'.[39]

It would take months to fully extricate the Rivett family from News Limited; they lived in a company-owned house, Rohan drove a company car, and he remained on the board of directors. Eventually, with the help of Norman Young—who, by 1960, had joined the NWS-9 board, only to then quit on principle when Rupert bypassed it entirely to sign an expensive programming deal in America—a generous settlement was made in exchange for his resignation.

But, on the afternoon of Wednesday 13 July, once he and Betty Gillen had cleared out the shelves, the desk, the filing cabinets, and he'd shaken the last hand and exchanged the last goodbyes, Rohan Rivett made his final exit from the North Terrace office just before 4.00 pm. Rupert had sent his letter over a week before, but he still hadn't picked up the phone, and as days passed, Rivett still heard nothing. 'This seemed to me and to everyone who has expressed an opinion on it a strange course of action,' Rivett wrote to Murray shortly afterwards. Within a year, the Rivett family, like the Murdochs, would leave Adelaide for good.

Looking back, years later, Rivett tended to agree with Elisabeth Murdoch: the letter had been a shock, but not a surprise. When Rupert had landed in Adelaide in 1953, he was already showing 'tremendous ambition and drive', but even if he could have asserted himself more fully, there was little sense in sidelining an editor who had turned the paper into a profitable asset for the family. However, by 1959 they had differed on enough fronts that the end of the road seemed in sight. 'I wasn't prepared to change policies or toe the line, whereas, like all proprietors, Rupert Murdoch, who was the young successor and proprietor after Sir Keith, began to talk at that time about other factors which must affect all proprietors, people with wide interests and even wider ambitions for expansion,' he said.[40] Rivett had, from December 1953 to July 1960, enjoyed an 'almost total control' that was nearly unparalleled in 20th-century newspapers in Australia. But from Lord Northcliffe to Sir Keith Murdoch, to his son, Rupert, any aspiring press lord worth his salt knew that control—complete, one-man control—was the most essential commodity in the newspaper business. Looking back, it was a wonder that their power-sharing double act had lasted so long.

For those that remained at News Limited, it felt like the end of an epoch. 'It was shattering,' reflected David Bowman years later. 'Constantinople had fallen, Christendom lay open to the unbelievers.'[41] One staffer said at the time that *The News* seemed 'suddenly like a big, healthy body without a soul'.[42] For another employee, North Terrace became 'just another damned newspaper office'.[43]

# CHAPTER EIGHTEEN

# No *News* is good news

ONE NIGHT IN 1987, John Scales found himself looking out at the twinkling lights of the Los Angeles skyline from the balcony of a lavish Hollywood Hills mansion. The 49-year-old was a long way from home, having been flown out from Australia for a party with 100 newspaper editors and executives from around the world. It had been a memorable evening; a small orchestra played all through the night, and at dinner, each place-setting featured a miniature stack of famous mastheads from New York to London, all impaled on a personalised brass toothpick. All those newspapers, just like the one Scales worked for, were now owned by the same global media corporation.

Scales had been working in newspapers since he was a teenage copy boy at *The Advertiser* in 1956; by fate, coincidence, or virtue of living in a small city, Scales had ink in his blood—his great, great, great, great grandfather was Robert Thomas, the publisher whose attempts to print a second edition of South Australia's first newspaper had met such difficulty in 1837.[1] One hundred and fifty years later, Thomas's descendant had worked his way up to cadet, then reporter, then editor, where in 1987 he found himself, quite by surprise, a part of the News Limited stable. It now had a new name, News Corporation, and stretched far beyond Western Australia and Sydney, with outposts in virtually every English-speaking market in the world.

It was in this new capacity that he had been invited to Misty Mountain, a crescent-shaped, Mediterranean-style mansion perched high up in the Hollywood Hills. It was a breathtaking address that came infused with a certain old-Hollywood glamour, the kind of history and status that any new arrival would love to buy into. It was a wild kind of place, built during Prohibition for the producer who made *Ben-Hur*, where visitors ranging from Katharine Hepburn to Joan Didion had to be wary of snakes, mountain lions, or, in the case of one neighbour, the murderous disciples of Charles Manson. One former owner loved to recount the story of when Orson Welles, at the height of his *Citizen Kane* fame, visited the house with his then-girlfriend, Mexican film star Dolores del Rio.[2] The pair were no strangers to media moguls or their secluded mansions, whether it was Randolph Heart's coastal castle *La Cuesta Encantada* or Charles Foster Kane's *Xanadu*, but to Welles, the house reminded him of Berchstagen — Hitler's eyrie. It was, it seemed, taken as a high compliment.

Most of those old tycoons had died out by 1986, the year that Rupert Murdoch purchased Misty Mountain from the estate of its former owner for $7 million.[3] He had just entered the American movie business himself, and the property was a fitting west-coast nest for a man who had come to represent a new kind of media baron for a new age marked by globalisation, corporate synergy, and technological disruption.

Much had changed since Murdoch's Adelaide youth, and the next day Scales and his group would move on to Aspen, Colorado, where the guest of honour would be former president Richard Nixon, whose post-Watergate reputation was in the process of being rehabilitated by some of Murdoch's American outlets. ('It was an indication, I suppose, to all his editors as to how right-wing Murdoch was,' Scaled later said.)

But back at Misty Mountain, as Scales looked out over the balustrade at the shimmering panorama of city lights and smog, a familiar Australian accent perked up behind him. 'What do you think, John?' the voice asked. Since buying the place, Murdoch had come to relish the way its views left guests awestruck — whether they were his employees, a rival whose business he was hoping to acquire, or an official he was hoping to charm.[4]

'Yes, Mr Murdoch,' Scales replied, before adding, 'it reminds me of Windy Point.' With its rows of parked cars and blinking taillights overlooking the Adelaide skyline, Windy Point had been a popular spot for generations of South Australians seeking to smoke, laugh, drink, or get lucky. It was a place that anyone who had spent their twenties in Adelaide, let alone one who enjoyed driving fast cars along winding roads, knew all too well. Murdoch gave out a patronising, pained sort of groan, and turned around and walked away. 'He didn't want to be reminded of Adelaide, I think,' Scales reflected decades later.

SINCE THE MURDOCH family had left Adelaide for Sydney in 1960, Rupert had stretched himself around the globe. From Canberra, he launched *The Australian*, the country's first national, daily broadsheet and his biggest gamble yet. It lost money at first, struggling to translate the literate, left-wing readership it initially courted into revenue. But it eventually established itself as the lynchpin of the Murdoch stable, a title that gave it something more important than short-term profits: influence and power. A 1967 television interview with the Australian Broadcasting Commission captured Murdoch in a buoyant mood, where he admitted to 'enjoy[ing] the feeling of power'.[5] But it was press diversity, he added, that kept it in check: 'I think the important thing is that there be plenty of newspapers with plenty of different people controlling them ... this is the freedom of the press that is needed,' he told the reporter while making a cup of tea in a humble-looking kitchenette. '[Not] just for one publisher to speak as he pleases, and try and bully the community.'[6]

In 1967, he hired John Menadue, an Adelaide expat who had once served as secretary of Clyde Cameron's Fabian Society while studying at the University of Adelaide. He had since risen to become private secretary to the deputy opposition leader, Gough Whitlam, before Murdoch recruited him to become general manager of *The Australian*. There, he had a front-row seat as the former Boy Publisher, whose progressive campaigns at *The News* Menadue had once followed with excitement, pursued ever greater political and economic power. Over the seven years he worked with Murdoch, he saw a pattern that had been established in Adelaide recur in each new territory. *The News* of the 1950s, with its progressive, worldly, campaigning stance under Rivett, may have followed a different political compass to subsequent publications, but it set the template for what came next. His exile in Adelaide had made Murdoch an outsider and an opportunist, with a keen sense for identifying under-served audiences—whether they were frustrated progressives of Adelaide, or older American conservatives with cable news subscriptions—and giving them what they wanted.

'He saw himself as an outsider,' Menadue explained. 'And in each of the markets he went to, he was treated as an outsider, first in Adelaide, then Sydney. I think Rupert had an ideological open mind, at least in those days, but he would have also seen it as a media opportunity—that was the way he approached new markets,' Menadue recalled. 'Usually down-market compared to the established papers, *The Sydney Morning Herald* or the Melbourne *Herald*, and, I suppose, going into London. You go into a media environment in which there's an opening at the bottom, a smaller market, a minority market, and you build from there.'[7]

But he wouldn't remain an outsider for long; throughout Menadue's tenure, he watched as Murdoch finally seemed to win the kind of acceptance his father and Dumas had, when his papers threw their support behind Menadue's old boss, Labor leader Gough Whitlam, in the 1972 federal election. Menadue also saw what happened when that acceptance proved short-lived, when *The Australian* turned on the Whitlam government to become one of its most vocal critics and partisan antagonists in the lead-up to the 1975 constitutional crisis and Whitlam's dismissal by governor-general John Kerr. In the eyes of the Australian left, Rupert Murdoch had gone from the 'hope for the side' to a villain on a par with his father a generation earlier.

He turned his sights to his father's old stomping ground of Fleet Street, where, in 1968, he managed to take over *The News of the World*, a 125-year-old Sunday paper with a long and colourful history of page-turning sensationalism. He had convinced the Carr family, which had owned it since the 19th century, to sell him a stake, in part by leveraging their disdain for another contender, Czechoslovakian-born politician Robert Maxwell. Once he had a foot in the door, he soon squeezed out the Carrs to seize absolute control. He then took over a daily labour paper, *The Sun*, and refashioned it to compete with the dominant mass-circulation sheet *The Daily Mirror*. The rebranded, red-topped *Sun* became a brassy tabloid appealing to a younger, broader, more liberated readership who appreciated the liberal doses of gossip, sex, and scandal that would have made the old Perth *Mirror* blush. Murdoch soon became a dominant force in British newspapers — even if respectable British society sneered at the 'Dirty Digger' (an unflattering nickname, which stuck, coined by the British satirical magazine *Private Eye*).

In 1976, he took on New York, snapping up the failing *New York Post*, another afternoon newspaper once known for its liberal-leaning readership. His arrival was viewed with trepidation; in January 1977, he famously appeared on the cover of *Time* as King Kong straddling the skyscrapers of New York, beneath the headline 'Aussie Press Lord Terrifies Gotham'. He rolled out the same model as *The Sun*, and in a city teeming with juicy tabloid-ready stories — 1976 alone included a chaotic city-wide blackout, a string of bombings, a mayoral election, and the unsolved murders of the publicity-courting 'Son of Sam' serial killer — Murdoch had plenty to work with. The editors at esteemed mastheads such as *The New York Times* might have decried his 'mean, ugly journalism', but by that point it didn't matter.[8] He still wrote headlines; in a November 1977 interview with *More: the media magazine*, he was asked about a recent *New York Post* story covering the release of a woman convicted of killing her children. Murdoch himself took credit for the clumsily worded headline ('Alice Crimmins — 5–20 Years'), which had sought to sow outrage over the justice system's leniency, but simply confused readers, who thought she had been sentenced again. ('It was meant to be ironic,' he told the journalist.)[9]

As his empire continued to grow, the question of his home country lingered in the background, a novel point of difference from the rest of the American press. It came up in that same interview, as he sought to assure New York readers that he was not quite the monster his critics claimed. Now the needle on his oscillating views on monopoly had once again swung towards moderation, citing Australia as an example of his own self-restraint: 'There are basically three groups in Australia, and that's too few already,' he said. 'If I were to grow bigger and take over one of the other groups — or be taken over — that would be against the public interest.'[10]

THE *More* INTERVIEW came back to haunt him two years later, when he returned to Australia to make another play for his father's old empire. On 20 November 1979, three decades after his first pass at *The Advertiser*, he announced a new A$143 million bid for the Herald and Weekly Times. 'It has always been my ambition, sub-consciously,' he told his own reporters during a doorstop interview in Melbourne.[11] The next day, a puff piece circulated through his papers framing their owner as a 'newspaper groupie', as he claimed a place among the great newspapermen of history. 'Every big newspaper organisation has been built initially by one man — Thompson, Beaverbrook, my own father,' he told the journalist. 'It's the nature of the business.'[12] His mother also made a statement from Cruden Farm. After 25 years in the 'wilderness', Rupert's *Herald* homecoming had 'always been at the back of [her] mind', and she was overjoyed to see 'one of my dreams coming true'.[13]

She would have to wait a little longer. That morning, the Herald and Weekly Times board called a special conference in Melbourne. Sir John Williams had retired from the group in 1972 after 49 years, and its current chairman, Sir Keith MacPherson, made no secret of his attitude towards a Murdoch takeover, dismissing the offer as 'bargain basement'.[14] He also declared that the company's profits were up, and that it would be making a one-for-two free share issue — a textbook move not unlike the one Sir Lloyd Dumas had made in 1959. MacPherson wasn't the only one against the merger; Murdoch later claimed he intended to sell off *The Advertiser* and a handful of other titles to head off the concerns of regulators; but, even with some pruning, News Limited would still emerge as a leviathan without equal in Australia.

In an extraordinary intervention, Murdoch's bid was foiled by none other than John Fairfax Limited, publishers of *The Sydney Morning Herald*, who swung in to save its long-time Melbourne rivals. Rupert Henderson, the man who had palmed off the failing *Daily Mirror* to Murdoch in 1960 earlier, had retired, but the new board harboured no illusions about the threat that Murdoch posed. Murdoch and Sir Kenneth May—still on the board of directors, with a knighthood in tow—personally visited the Sydney Fairfax offices on the afternoon of 20 November. But there was nothing they could do; the next day, Fairfax began buying up parcels of Herald shares, and within 24 hours it was all over. Murdoch withdrew, leaving Fairfax with a 14.9 per cent stake in the Herald and Weekly Times at a cost of $50 million—any higher stake would have drawn attention from regulators.

On 22 November 1979, *The Herald* published a front-page editorial that read like a homage to *The Mail*'s 1953 'Bid For Press Monopoly'—this time, with the roles reversed. Titled 'Murdoch and its Monopolies', it cited Murdoch's words from the *More* interview, and noted its agreement.[15] In a coordinated set of public statements from the chairmen of The Herald and Weekly Times, Fairfax, and Queensland Newspapers, these strange bedfellows echoed the importance of *The Herald*'s continued independence. 'At a time when, around the world, there are many threats to the ability of a free press to present a wide diversity of views, it was alarming to think that this freedom might be under threat in Australia—not from without, but from within the press,' said John Fairfax.[16] MacPherson, meanwhile, spoke of his 'great respect' for the standards and integrity of Fairfax, and said 'there is no other media organisation which would be more welcome'.[17] It was a pointed comment that left Murdoch, once again, on the outside.

Murdoch tried to save face, insisting that taking back *The Herald* was never the 'obsession' that people assumed.[18] A few days later, his mother backtracked; while she was excited by the prospect of the Murdoch name returning to Flinders Street, she said the family never saw the Herald and Weekly Times as Rupert's birthright, claiming Sir Keith 'was very against nepotism—that was why he was building up the Adelaide *News* with his own money as a starter working base for

Rupert' (a curious definition of 'nepotism' by any stretch).[19] While he had lost the main prize, Murdoch did salvage one small victory: by reselling the $21 million worth of Herald and Weekly Time shares it had already bought, News Limited had even made a tidy $3.27 million profit, thanks to the temporary spike in the share price caused by its own buying spree.[20]

*The News* of 27 November saw the Murdoch papers revert to a familiar anti-monopolist stance, noting with alarm that '2 Media Giants Now Control 18 Major Papers' and adding, bitterly, that smaller shareholders had 'missed the boat' and could 'kiss goodbye' to the possibility of cashing in on his offer.[21] When the Fairfax board met the following Monday to debrief, it was agreed that, while their intervention was worthwhile, it was unlikely to deter him forever. 'We have scotched the snake,' said Sir David Griffin, a former Sydney lord mayor turned Fairfax board member, 'not killed it'.[22]

The *More* feature wasn't the only interview that Murdoch gave as he swept through America in the 1970s. In October 1978, he spoke candidly to a reporter for *The New Yorker* who was documenting the cloak-and-dagger power plays of New York's media class during a protracted union dispute.[23] The magazine's portrait of Murdoch at 46 years of age looked and sounded an awful lot like the Boy Publisher in Adelaide—a little slimmer perhaps, but still 'charg[ing] around the *Post* in his shirtsleeves, with all the insouciance of a copy boy'.[24] After breaking a tentative alliance with *The New York Times* and *Daily News* to strike his own deal with the unions, making the *Post* the only major daily being printed during the lucrative pre-Christmas advertising blitz, he made a telling comment to the reporter: 'Monopoly is a terrible thing—till you have it.'[25] Of all his contradictory statements about monopoly that he made over the years, this might have been the closest one to the truth.

WHILE MURDOCH WAS busy slaying giants or trying to become them, *The News* carried on. But something had indelibly changed since Rivett and its publisher had left Adelaide; one commentator noted upon its 50th anniversary that the paper had become a shadow of its former self, 'a dedicated money-mill' with staff, equipment, and ideas all hamstrung by economies.[26] Under the more cautious and conservative editorship of Ron Boland, the crusades of the Rivett era were long past, and by the time *The News* took up a social cause, it had already become accepted.[27]

Having spent the late 1950s antagonising a long-serving state Liberal government, by the late 1970s *The News* had become an enemy of Labor nationally. The defeat of the Whitlam government was still an open wound when, in 1979, Des Corcoran, the successor to Don Dunstan, who had just retired after a decade as premier, was unexpectedly swept from office. After the electoral washout, the Labor Party condemned *The News*'s 'distortion, slanting and omission, classic weapons of newspaper owners who have a score to settle or a sense of power to exercise', made worse by the paper's 'monopoly' of the afternoon.[28]

In the final week of November 1979, Rupert Murdoch's first newspaper also became the target of his first major boycott, when Labor and the United Trades and Labour Council declared a five-day campaign. The boycott was publicised with pamphlets encouraging readers to 'show Mr Murdoch he can't run South Australia', bumper stickers proclaiming, 'NO NEWS IS GOOD NEWS', and A3 posters that parodied the signature red-and-black placards that had landed Rivett and the company in hot water all those years ago. 'What we suggest is simple,' the campaign declared, 'FIVE DAYS WITHOUT MURDOCH'S NEWS—TO TEACH HIM A LESSON'.[29] A complaint was also made to the Press Council of Australia, which agreed that *The News* had been 'intensely partisan' during the campaign, and 'did not disguise the fact that its object throughout the campaign was to present the case against the government'.[30]

The paper's politics might have shifted since the Rivett era, but some old rivalries persisted. Working the crime and politics rounds for *The Advertiser* in the 1970s, Mike O'Reilly couldn't help but be impressed by the dogged determination of his rivals, always pushing the envelope to try to scoop *The Advertiser* in time for the afternoon edition with whatever resources they could muster. '*The News* was just so hungry, and so time-compressed,' he recalled. 'Just absolutely scurrilous, they were there to go fast, go hard, and get those headlines—whereas *The Advertiser* tended to be a little bit more temperate.'[31] When O'Reilly crossed the town himself a few years later, he began to see why: the paper was being run incredibly leanly, and every reporter had to prove their worth. 'It was very hard, very fast, tremendously exciting, but it was a bit crucifying as well,' O'Reilly said.

By the mid-1980s, *The News*'s North Terrace operation had earned the nickname 'The Dinosaur', the last of Murdoch's Australian papers that still ran on hot metal, even as newspapers around the world embraced computerised typesetting and printing that was upending the old ways of making news. It became a running joke that one of the typewriters was once used by Murdoch himself, while the odometers of company cars boasted comically high mileage. 'I was working on 60-year-old typewriters during the day—the copy boys and girls would pin the paper together with carbon paper, and reuse and reuse it until you could hardly bloody see it,' O'Reilly said. 'They would put new engines into old cars until they were claptraps, but saving money, because Rupert wanted money out of *The News* to do other things with.'

The sunny picture that Murdoch had given to the Australian Broadcasting Control Board back in 1958, that monopolies could lead to a reinvestment of profits and a raising of standards once the need to constantly compete had passed, hadn't quite panned out. The truth was that, since he'd first eyed *The Sunday Times* in Perth, Murdoch was in a state of constant growth, and the profits in one city were funnelled away to fuel the latest expansion and to service the corporation's mountain of debt. In the company's 1986 annual report, it even admitted that its antiquated systems were the main reason for *The News*'s 'disappointing' performance.[32]

But if *The News* was treated like a neglected older child, it still played an important role. O'Reilly would often be tasked with looking after a string of young, aspiring journalists fresh off the plane—'wet-behind-the-ears Pommy kids'—whose well-connected relatives had asked a favour of Murdoch.[33] 'Rupert would say, "If they're serious, they're going to Adelaide, they're going to start where I started,"' O'Reilly said. 'That percolated right through the organisation—they were sent out across the world.' When Murdoch bought a new paper and wanted to reset its culture, just as he'd done at *The Sunday Times* in 1956, he often imported people who had cut their teeth in Adelaide—an 'Adelaide mafia', led by the likes of Ken May, Frank Shaw, and, later, Les Hinton, the English copy boy turned executive whom Rivett hired in 1959. Uprooted and dispersed around the world, this meant that the overriding loyalties of each new generation of Murdoch men weren't to their city, or their colleagues, but to the man who had given them their break and raised them up. Working at *The News* let you walk into any newspaper office from London to New York, but the 'royal treatment' that awaited also came with a side of suspicion and fear: 'They're all going "Jesus, an Adelaide guy's here? Who's going to lose their job, what's going to happen?"' O'Reilly said.

Rupert himself remained a rare sight on North Terrace, appearing once or twice a year around the time of the company's annual general meeting, when the global organisation briefly turned its gaze back to Adelaide. 'It was a big thing, but you never knew when Rupert was going to turn up,' O'Reilly explained. Until one day, someone noticed a painter giving the stairwell a fresh coat of whitewash—the tell-tale sign that Murdoch's arrival was imminent. Once the painting began, the pressure was on: they'd need to hit record circulation numbers by the time Rupert Murdoch started bounding up the steps.

THE DISAPPOINTMENT OF 1979 had done nothing to curb Murdoch's ambitions, and in December 1986 his focus returned once more to Australia. It had already been a triumphant year, with News Corporation posting a record worldwide turnover of US\$3,823 million and an after-tax profit of \$96 million.[34] A year prior, he had become a proper Hollywood mogul with the acquisition of 20th Century Fox, a company that traced its origins back to the silent film era, when his father was still an eager young Northcliffe disciple in London. The deal made a lot of sense; Murdoch had been negotiating with studios since his first television agreement with Paramount in 1958; and with a growing suite of television interests around the world, he had been eyeing his own movie studio for a while. Fox held a deep library of old classics, ranging from *The Sound of Music* to George Lucas's blockbuster space opera, *Star Wars*, but a series of expensive flops across film and television had made it vulnerable. In March, News Corporation was able to snag a 50 per cent stake for US$250 million, and six months later bought out its previous owner for another US$375 million.[35] He now had full control over a brand name, Fox, that would eventually become as synonymous with the Murdoch family name as News.

Even as the company's reach grew larger, Murdoch would continue to make the same point in his chief executive's statement, year in, year out: 'Despite the worldwide trend toward monopoly ownership, we have no monopolies.'[36] No matter what the market or medium, to Murdoch the company still had to compete for every reader and advertiser, taking nothing for granted. This, he said, was why the company had developed a 'highly competitive' management style that could 'plan boldly and move quickly'.[37] In short: it could move as fast as one man's decision-making.

Things had also changed back in Melbourne; in 1982, another power struggle at Flinders Street had seen MacPherson finally retire, and by 1986 *The Herald*'s circulation had fallen by half since its 1969 peak. The new regime could see where the numbers were heading, and were more open to offers. On 3 December 1986, Murdoch went public with a fresh A$1,800 million bid, offering $12 cash per share—well above the going $8.40 rate—or a stock swap. At a jubilant press conference the next morning, it all seemed like a done deal; he confidently told reporters it was a 'great thrill' and 'an emotional moment', while his mother watched on from the press pack beaming with pride.[38] That afternoon, *The News* ran a photograph of Murdoch reverentially placing his hand next to a plaque of his father's face in the foyer of Flinders Street, and another photo of him having a celebratory drink with the current Herald and Weekly Times chief executive. Even Bob Hawke, the current Labor prime minister, seemed to approve; in Adelaide, he told reporters that Murdoch had met with him to personally outline the 'very interesting' offer. Hawke saved his strongest words for Murdoch's competitors at Fairfax, who he had 'total and unqualified contempt for'.[39] There was a lot of water under the bridge between the ALP and News Limited, but at this moment in the mid-1980s, clearly both men recognised their own self-interest.

Of course, it was never going to be that easy. The press conference was just the start of a bitter two-month-long battle, as old rivals and new ones sought to spoil Murdoch's biggest victory yet. First, there was Rhodesia-born telecommunications magnate Robert Holmes à Court, whose earlier bid for the Herald and Weekly Times in 1981 had been rebuffed by MacPherson almost as forcefully as Murdoch's 1979 run. Holmes à Court unveiled a $2,000 million counter-offer on Christmas eve, and a week later Fairfax re-entered the game with a $910 million bid for Queensland Press—which would also give them a 24 per cent stake in the Herald and Weekly Times.

Murdoch was furious at Fairfax's latest intervention, and cancelled a flight back to America—he was due to launch a new national Fox television network—to resume crisis talks with his Australian executives.[40] On 9 January, he hit back, raising Holmes à Court's offer by $230 million, and declaring he was 'playing to win' in the face of Holmes à Court's 'legal ploys'.[41] Holmes à Court had launched a legal challenge based on Murdoch's recently acquired US citizenship, taken up in 1985 to circumvent American foreign ownership laws. The move incensed Murdoch, who maintained that he had been an Australian '40 or 50 times longer' than Holmes à Court, who had only gained Australian citizenship the year before.[42]

After six weeks of brinkmanship, Murdoch picked up the phone from New York on 15 January. It was 2.00 am where he was, and the two men gradually reached a compromise: Holmes à Court would withdraw in exchange for News Corporation selling him its Melbourne television station and *The West Australian* newspaper.[43] Five days later, a special board meeting of Advertiser Newspapers confirmed the decision to sell its 11.8 per cent stake in the Herald and Weekly Times, taking a convertible note option that made it a 'silent investor' in News Corporation.[44] Murdoch had also stitched up a deal to buy Queensland Press's 24 per cent interest, when at the eleventh hour, Fairfax re-entered the fray with a $16 share offer.[45]

As questions began to arise once again over Murdoch's citizenship, News Limited's board issued a stunning statement: it claimed that Murdoch was no longer a director, held 'no office in the company', and had 'no authority to speak on behalf of or to bind News Limited'.[46] Just as Murdoch had sought to distance himself from his Perth television licence bid in 1958, it was a roundly unconvincing claim— Murdoch himself told reporters that same day that 'I have got 42 per cent of the shares'.[47] In the end, the Fairfax bid failed to gain traction—it was too little, too late. The snake had returned, just as Sir David Griffin predicted in 1979, and this time he'd consumed his prey.

SCALES WAS IN Melbourne in early 1987, seconded to Flinders Street to coordinate national coverage across the Herald and Weekly Times' stable. Sir John Williams was long dead, as was Sir Lloyd Dumas, and few if any remained who could even remember the days when the building was known as the Colin Ross memorial. One day in February, in the middle of Fairfax's last-ditch effort to spoil Murdoch's takeover, a distinctive voice could be heard on mahogany row. 'You beaut! We've won!' it crowed, as a terrified hush fell over the same reporters' room where, 40 years earlier, Sir Keith Murdoch had introduced Rohan Rivett and Stewart Cockburn to his teenage son.[48] 'Everyone was dreading that Murdoch had taken over,' Scales recalled. 'Murdoch had always been the enemy; he had a reputation for ruthlessness, and tabloid journalism.'

As it turned out, it was a different victory that Murdoch was celebrating that day—he had just won a long and bitter industrial dispute in London, in which he had sacked *en masse* the entire printing staff of his biggest British papers. For many years, publishers such as Murdoch had been embroiled in costly rolling disputes with the unions that ran their printing departments. But now technology existed that would make those workers and their unions obsolete, and for months Murdoch had been secretly developing a new state-of-the-art headquarters in Wapping, a riverside suburb of London well away from the historic publishing heartland of Fleet Street. When the unions next downed tools, he called their bluff with the backing of the Thatcher government, dismissing all 6,000 workers on 24 January 1986 and setting the new Wapping presses rolling. Clearly, the Rupert Murdoch who had left Adelaide in 1960 had continued along the trajectory that had caused his split with Rohan Rivett, leading to its natural, union-crushing conclusion. It was in February 1987, while the Herald and Weekly Times deal was still up in the air, that Murdoch received the news that the strikers who had picketed Wapping for over a year had finally given up.

When the deal did go through, Scales assumed that, as a lifelong *Advertiser* man, his number was up. Instead, he found himself the newest member of the Adelaide mafia. It was his long-time colleague Don Riddell, *The Advertiser*'s current editor-in-chief, who became the latest in a long line of editors to clash with Murdoch. Whether they jumped or were pushed, Rivett and Riddell now bookended a deep gallery of turfed Murdoch editors from *The Australian*'s Adrian Deamer to Harold Evans at *The Times*—Murdoch had bought Lord Northcliffe's old paper and its sister paper, *The Sunday Times*, in 1981, with familiar but hollow promises of editorial independence.

Riddell was dismayed that the Herald board had all but rolled over and welcomed Murdoch into Flinders Street and Waymouth Street, recalling years later that 'they were just frightened of the ghost outside the door'.[49] 'I admired his chutzpah, his dash, but I loathed his journalism—I wish he was on the side of the angels, because the bloke's a genius,' Riddell recalled. There are several versions of the story, some in which Riddell storms into Murdoch's office; others, where Murdoch storms into his. According to Riddell, none of these are true, but the pair did have an argument, in which Murdoch accused him of being a 'creature of "the Establishment" and the Adelaide Club'. Riddell was puzzled; *The Advertiser* had changed since Murdoch had left Adelaide, and while reporters like Stewart Cockburn might have disagreed with Rivett during the Stuart case, they were nonetheless spurred on by its example as a campaigning newspaper. 'Since I'd spent 10, 12 years fighting the Adelaide Club, I thought there's no future for me here,' Riddell said. 'I couldn't go onwards and upwards in News Corporation, because I was not a "News" man.'

Eventually, Scales ended up back in Adelaide, the last person to have progressed from copy boy to editor-in-chief in *The Advertiser*'s history. Murdoch might once have been the enemy, but Scales grew to like the man, who, as a 56-year-old mogul, could still be awkward one minute, and assertive the next. 'He was always rather diffident as a social person when he was just mixing with people,' Scales said, 'but sitting down at the table, he'd take control.'[50] After all these years, he wasn't afraid of rewriting his editor's material, either, as Scales found out in in the days before the July 1987 federal election, when he sent off his editorial backing a change in government for Murdoch's approval. 'Mine came back with a diagonal line right across it, with Murdoch's handwriting saying, "Sit on the fence",' Scales said. 'He quite deliberately didn't want to be seen to be supporting one party, for whatever reason, so I had mine rewritten.'

IT HAD TAKEN nearly half a century, but Rupert Murdoch had finally eclipsed his father, as well as all other Australian newspapermen who had come before him. But his 1987 takeover of Flinders Street required a sacrifice: *The News*. In addition to its trade-off with Holmes à Court, News Corporation was ultimately forced to offload a bundle of its print and broadcast interests to appease the Trade Practices Commission. A Lismore-based company called Northern Star Holdings, backed by the Westfield investment group, agreed to take over its Queensland radio interests for $17.5 million, and in February 1987 *The News* was tacked onto the deal.[51] But it was only a short-term arrangement; Northern Star's real interests lay in television, and on 7 August it announced a deal to expand its Channel 10 network by buying the Adelaide, Perth, and Canberra stations that Murdoch had sold earlier to a Perth businessman named Kerry Stokes. A footnote to the announcement was the fact that *The News* would have to be sold again, this time in a management-led buyout fronted by its 46-year-old managing editor, Roger Holden, and its general manager, Reg Cordina. It was an ignominious exit for a masthead that had once been the company's bedrock; in the scramble to claim control of the Herald and Weekly Times, and then a television network, *The News* had been reduced to mere leftovers.

'It's every journalist's dream,' Holden said hopefully, before adding that it would be the 'challenge of my lifetime'.[52] In an editorial published the next day, *The News* welcomed its new era, and declared that it would be independent and unrepentantly South Australian ('Our only bias is bias towards South Australia,' it read).[53] But the fine print of the deal, initially shrouded in secrecy, raised eyebrows—after all, how could Holden and Cordina summon the $14.7 million needed to pay off Northern Star?[54] It later emerged that a deal had been struck between Northern Star, News Corporation, and Citibank, the financiers of Holden's consortium. The $14.7 million loan had been guaranteed by News Corporation, who also, thanks to a pre-existing deal with Northern Star, would continue to print *The News* for the next five years and offset any financial losses (a necessary sweetener for Northern Star to agree to take over a struggling newspaper in the first place). An identical deal had been struck in Queensland, where management had taken over Brisbane's *Daily Sun* and *Sunday Sun*. (The Herald and Weekly Times deal had seen Murdoch finally retake *The Courier-Mail*, the Brisbane paper that his mother had given up in 1953.)

The notionally independent *News* didn't just have a close fiscal relationship to its old owners, but a physical one as well; when News Limited moved into the refurbished *Advertiser* building on King William Street, *The News* came too. The papers shared the same premises, printing facilities, and distribution, and drew from the same network of News Corporation bureaus—and in 1988, Cordina had even crossed over to become operations manager of *The Advertiser*. Observing these 'incestuous' connections, one local academic in 1988 questioned whether South Australia had become a de facto monopoly, with *The News* a 'covert colony of the Murdoch empire'.[55]

One of the deal's most vocal critics was none other than David Bowman, now a seasoned, snowy-haired veteran and former editor of *The Canberra Times* and *The Sydney Morning Herald*. In the 1980s, he turned freelance media critic, and observed from afar the 'hardening of [Murdoch's] political and social arteries', his old boss's tendency to build 'not by five-year plans but by seizing the moment', to tactically 'diminish himself and overstate the opposition', and to 'blur the debate by joining the press with television and the rest of the media'.[56] By the end of the decade, Bowman was writing a media column for *The Adelaide Review*, a free arts and culture journal, and in a string of pointed articles between 1988 and 1992, he tracked the progress of 'Mr Murdoch's orphans'.[57]

'The Trade Practices Commission let Rupert Murdoch get away with murder in Adelaide in the ownership upheavals of 1987,' he wrote in January 1990, 'with the result that in terms of competition the city is now worse off than any other State capital except Hobart'.[58] By October 1991, as *The News's* old deal with its former parent neared its end, he wrote optimistically that '*The News* will have emerged clearly from the shadow of News Ltd and any outside perception of possible influence on *The News*, presumably by the Trade Practices Commission, will be put to rest.'[59]

But if ownership of *The News* had been a dream for Holden, it proved to be an impossible one. On 26 March 1992, Holden gathered the staff at North Terrace for another fireside meeting, just as Rivett had done so many times before. But this time, no one was shocked as Holden confirmed what he and his staff had long seen in each other's eyes. 'We've lived with the dread in our heart for too long to pretend,' he said.[60] In the five years since *The News* had been cut loose, its circulation had been in freefall, and by 1992 it could barely muster 90,000 copies a day. A vicious cycle had set in, as its falling circulation eroded advertising sales, which in turn produced smaller, less appealing papers. 'Back in the heyday of newspapers in the 70s, big headlines and dramatic presentation worked,' Holden later reflected.[61] 'When they stopped working, newspapers failed to change and folded. We tried to change ... and folded, too.'

There were external factors; in 1991, the collapse of the government-owned State Bank had plunged South Australia into a recession and claimed the scalp of Labor premier John Bannon. A last-ditch effort was made in the final six months to relaunch the paper, with a swathe of job cuts to keep the ship afloat, but it was too late. By March 1992, the paper was down 8,000 advertising columns and on the cusp of losing millions, when Holden received legal advice forcing him to cease trading on 21 March. *The News* might have enjoyed a cosy relationship with its former company, but in the days that followed, Holden hit out at News Corporation, claiming that *The News's* efforts to reposition itself had been undermined by its former company's 'indifference to its printing obligations' during the transition to new printing facilities, which left *The News* hitting the streets one to three hours late nearly every day in the critical period of its relaunch.[62] For an afternoon paper reliant on street sales, it was the kind of disruption that could prove fatal.

In his final address to staff, Holden lamented how years of gossip and speculation about *The News*'s imminent demise had become a self-fulfilling prophecy, turning away advertisers and readers. Chief among them was the most influential man in Australian media, who had begun to promote the '24-hour newspaper' as the way of the future. 'What chance had we from the moment that Rupert Murdoch told the nation afternoon newspapers were dead?' Holden said ruefully. By the following Monday, *The Advertiser* had already launched an extra midday edition to soak up what little readership and advertising was left. Having been put out to pasture, and then given a public death sentence by its former Boy Publisher, it was almost as if *The News* had never existed. And, for the second time in its history Adelaide had become a one-paper town—a Murdoch town.

# A useful altruistic and full life

ON A BRIGHT, brisk morning in the winter of 2022, I drove out into Melbourne's eastern suburbs, winding through leafy streets and wide verges before pulling up in front of a redbrick cottage. I was greeted by a four-legged ball of energy and sooty fur, clambering and yelping at the screen door. 'Down, Clancy!' came a voice from inside the house, followed by its owner, Rhyll Rivett. I had been corresponding with Rohan and Nan Rivett's daughter for the best part of a decade, since I first started looking into *The News* as a university student, but we had never met in person. We talked for hours over cups of black coffee, about her parents, her childhood, and their decade in Adelaide.

She filled in some of the gaps that the archive never quite captures, and I shared with her things I had learnt that children aren't always privy to. As I ruffled Clancy's curls under the table, Rhyll told me about the house in Wattle Park, and the visits to her father's work on North Terrace, where she marvelled at the funny old men in overalls and the enormous presses they operated. Then, those strange and tense weeks in 1960 when her parents were away in court all day, and the shattering upheaval when they left Adelaide the following year. We

talked about her mother, Nan, and the strength she showed holding
it all together while Rohan was running around meeting deadlines,
living and breathing *The News* with every waking moment.

Rhyll handed me a framed photograph of Rohan sitting in his
office in North Terrace, taken near the end of his time at *The News*.
It's a fly-on-the-wall shot of an editor in his natural habitat, a lit cigar
between his fingers as he flicks through the open newspaper in front
of him. I'd seen the photo before, grainy and pixelated on some corner
of the internet, but here I could make out new details. The spines
on his overflowing bookshelf were now legible: a handbook called
*The Reporter's Trade*, Hugh Cudlipp's *Publish and Be Damned*, and a
book titled *Defense of Freedom*, written by the embattled editors of *La
Prensa*, an Argentinian newspaper seized by the government in 1951.
Pinned on the wall to the left is a photograph of Rivett shaking hands
with a smiling Sir Thomas Playford. But Rohan's head doesn't look
right, and I realise it's a crude cut-and-paste job, probably made as a
joke by *The News*'s art department.

She also brought out another photograph, brown and scuffed
from years of sun exposure, of her father and Rupert Murdoch. It was
taken at the old Adelaide airport sometime in 1955, and captures the
pair in the middle of an animated, slightly windswept conversation. A
typewritten label on the back compares them to 'two spivs at the races',
Rivett frozen in mid-speech, hands in pockets, while Murdoch listens
intently, hands on hips, with a rolled-up broadsheet bulging out of his
suit pocket. It was taken just past the mid-point of their relationship,
and they've already been through so much: almost a decade had passed
since Sir Keith had brought the teenage Rupert into Flinders Street,
then the Oxford years, the job offer at Claridge's Hotel, the death of
Sir Keith, the contempt trial and Roderic Chamberlain, and the war
with Sir Lloyd Dumas and *The Sunday Advertiser* that was still raging.
And there was so much ahead of them, too — Rupert and Patricia's
wedding, Bill Grayden, Father Thomas Dixon, and Rupert Max Stuart.

They're standing so close, faces barely a foot apart, but had the
paths of these two men, and the company they ran together, already
begun to fork? As Rupert listened to Rohan over the airport noise, had
he already begun to resent his old friend's authority? Had the course

that Rivett had set, where News Limited's pages would be used in passionate pursuit of freedom, justice, and equality, already begun to diverge from Murdoch's future, where power, profit, and growth were irretrievably entwined? Was it already clear that *The News* of the 1950s would be a fleeting aberration in the history of Australian metropolitan dailies, while Murdoch stood to not only inherit the legacies of press barons past, but eclipse them all?

The Rivetts left Adelaide not long after the final settlement with News Limited was signed. The libel trial had made Rohan something of folk hero in journalism circles, and in 1961 he took a post as director of the International Press Institute in Switzerland, uprooting the family once more to the other side of the world.[1] Returning from this self-imposed exile in 1963, they settled in a house on Wattle Valley Road, Camberwell, a few minutes away from where I visited Rhyll.[2] Rivett continued to write and report at an often exhaustive pace across print, radio, and television—one article from 1964 speculated that 'Rivett could be our Ed Murrow'.[3] At one point he even dreamed of turning publisher himself, pitching a new magazine titled *The Australian Adult* catering to a literary-minded audience turned off by the 'smuttier revelations' that were now commonplace in newspapers.[4] The magazine never panned out, but he remained busy, too busy perhaps, serving as president of the Melbourne Press Club, giving lectures, freelancing for various papers, and publishing a biography of his late father in 1972.

He remained in regular contact with Father Tom Dixon, who left the priesthood in 1969, got married, and spent the rest of his life working to prove Stuart's innocence. Ken Inglis's account of the trial and royal commission, *The Stuart Case*, was published in 1961, but Dixon was disappointed that the book stopped short of exoneration. Chamberlain, meanwhile, was intent on proving Stuart's guilt. Forced to retire from the Supreme Court bench after his 70th birthday, the now-knighted Sir Roderic joined the South Australian Parole Board, which had rejected Stuart's applications for parole. Chamberlain then made headlines when he reportedly told a pair of cadets from the Melbourne *Herald* that he 'would have pulled the lever myself', and called Stuart an 'animal'.[5] Chamberlain claimed his comments were never intended for publication, but after pressure from Don Dunstan—now premier of South Australia—he recused himself.

In 1973, Chamberlain published his own account of the case, *The Stuart Affair*, which mounted a bitter defence of the police, the judiciary, and his own convictions. Despite Chamberlain's efforts, Stuart was eventually paroled, and after a few false starts ended up in Santa Teresa, Father Dixon's former community. He lived a long and full life back on Arrernte Country; he became a father, a respected Elder and lawman, and chairman of the Central Lands Council. He even met Queen Elizabeth II in March 2000, 40 years after her Privy Council had knocked back his appeal.[6]

Over the years, Stuart participated in a handful of interviews and film projects revisiting the case, and in 2002 spoke to Ken Inglis for the first time—Inglis was working on a new edition of *The Stuart Case*, timed to coincide with the release of a film adaptation called *Black and White*. While researching the case, the filmmakers spoke to former Detective Sergeant Paul Turner, now retired and dying of emphysema, who admitted that Stuart's confession had been coerced, more or less as O'Sullivan had described in the Appeals Court (and dismissed as 'rubbish' by Sir Mellis Napier).[7] But Turner remained untroubled, convinced as ever of Stuart's guilt, even if the conviction had been based on a fiction. In recent years, the hair-comparison evidence he tried to raise at trial has been unequivocally debunked as junk science—the posthumous exoneration of Colin Ross is one of many examples. Meanwhile, in Ceduna, the gates to the local cemetery bear the wrought-iron letters 'M' and 'H', a tribute to Mary Hattam, the young girl whose death was long overshadowed by the flawed investigation and global controversy that came after it.

Despite calls for an official pardon in the years since the royal commission, and after the film's release, Stuart rarely talked about the case to the media or his family in his final years. 'He only wanted to live his life out without judgement,' his niece told me in 2022.[8] 'He lost a part of his life in jail, and didn't want to be reminded everyday of what he went through.' He died in 2014, having lived into his eighties.

From time to time, Rivett would be asked for a comment when Stuart or Murdoch re-entered the news cycle, but he mostly kept his cards to his chest. Around the time of Stuart's first parole, he told one journalist that telling the full story was a defamation risk, and it was better to say nothing than to print an incomplete version.[9] Then, in late 1973, a newspaper reported that he'd been spotted at lunch with an executive from Gold Star, a Melbourne publisher of pulp paperbacks, who had apparently agreed to release Rivett's account of the case. The book, which promised to 'shake Adelaide's establishment', never materialised.[10] 'I'm not sure what he was writing half the time,' Rhyll told me.

By 1977, Rohan's ginger hair had thinned and greyed, his lanky frame slightly more filled out than when he arrived in Adelaide in 1951. 'I don't think it was the happiest time of his life; he'd diversified in what he was doing, but I don't think it was all as satisfying as it had been,' Rhyll recalled. In August, his doctor told him to slow down; the years of overworking had begun to catch up with him, and, as he told one friend soon after, it had only just sunk in that at 60 he could no longer maintain the pace of a 25-year-old.[11]

The night of 4 October 1977 marked the 25th anniversary of Sir Keith Murdoch's sudden death at Cruden Farm, and the following evening Rohan and Nan settled in to watch television in the den at Wattle Valley Road. Rhyll was there, too, having recently moved back home after a spell in South America. It was a little after 8.30, and the ABC was screening a teleplay about Philby, Burgess, and MacLean, members of the Cambridge spy ring who caused one of the greatest espionage scandals of the Cold War. The Rivetts watched with interest; the program's timeline overlapped neatly with their time in London, Sir Keith's final years, and then the months of subterfuge and machinations that followed his death.

At one point, Nan ducked to the bathroom, and Rohan got up to make his nightly cup of hot cocoa before settling back in front of the television with his mug steaming. Then, all of a sudden, he called out for Nan. Rhyll saw the colour draining out of her father's face, and, with the spy saga still playing in the background, leapt up to get her mother. By the time they returned, it was all over—Rohan had suffered a coronary occlusion. 'Something just exploded inside him,' Rhyll told me. 'He died in a couple of minutes.'[12]

A LOT HAD changed since I had first started talking to Rhyll, and I had learned some bracing lessons about the media of my own. After graduation, I found a dream job at a long-running Adelaide street press, one I had devoured as a teenager. It had recently killed off its print edition, and was attempting to adapt to the new and uncertain world of online media, with its collapsing revenues and unpredictable social media algorithms. The afternoon newspaper was long dead, but there was a funny sort of lineage between the world of clickbait headlines I navigated and the bright-red posters and headlines that *The News* once lived by. Then, in June 2016, it was abruptly shuttered by the rarely seen Spanish media tycoon who owned it. He had bought it years earlier as part of a long-term strategy of one day taking on Murdoch and *The Advertiser*, but as I opened my redundancy letter, it seemed things weren't panning out how either of us had hoped.

As this already small pond began to shrink a little further, I was offered a few weeks of freelance work copy-editing a restaurant guide for *The Advertiser*. Although I entered Keith Murdoch House with my eyes open, even this most inoffensive corner of the Murdoch empire could be a strange place at times. One day, while I sat at one of the empty workstations, the televisions around the office played a feed of the farcical presidential debate between Hillary Clinton and Donald Trump—another mogul's son turned billionaire outsider with a knack for populist rhetoric. Rupert Murdoch had initially dismissed Trump's candidacy, but as a ratings-friendly Republican nominee, he was now being backed in hard by Fox News, just as Murdoch's British papers had stoked the insular populism of the Brexit movement in a shock referendum a few months earlier.

One afternoon, the lights and computers in the office flickered on and off—an enormous storm had caused a state-wide blackout, and I watched in real time as the crisis was embraced as a cause célèbre among pro-coal, anti-renewable-energy pundits. Even prime minister Malcolm Turnbull, once an advocate for climate action, launched an opportunistic attack on the Labor state government, mindful perhaps of the way that News Corporation papers had helped his predecessor stoke fears of a 'carbon tax' to turf the previous Labor prime minister out of office. ('Kick This Mob Out!' read the front page of *The Daily Telegraph* in August 2013.) Weeks after the magazine was sent off to the printers and I handed in my swipe card, I accepted an invitation to attend the launch party on the terrace of Keith Murdoch House. As the speeches began, and the emcee made their joke, I was reminded again that this was a Murdoch town, a Murdoch country, and perhaps even a Murdoch world.

But it also felt like an empire in decline. Like my previous workplace, Keith Murdoch House could have the uncanny feeling of a place where more people used to work. In the years that followed my brief spell at Waymouth Street, I started receiving LinkedIn requests from the people I had briefly worked with — never a good sign. When I inexplicably agreed to return to my previous employer to work on *The Adelaide Review* in 2018 — Bowman's old paper had been the Spaniard's first Adelaide acquisition in the late 1990s — its columns began to feature a growing cohort of ex-*Advertiser* writers I had met during those weeks in 2016.

When the global pandemic hit in 2020, I was not surprised to find that the economic upheaval had shaken our Spanish owner's commitment to South Australia's free press. I drafted another closure announcement, opened another redundancy letter, and, a few weeks later, exited a floor that was now completely empty. Keith Murdoch House also had its share of empty floors; the local bureau of *The Australian* had been whittled down to one columnist, and in 2021 it was announced that two of its floors would be rented out to the South Australian government.[13] *The Advertiser* and the government might have enjoyed cosy relations in the era of Bonython and Dumas, but they rarely shared the same address.

The rest of the Australian media landscape is almost unrecognisable from the one Sir Keith Murdoch knew. Beyond his son's conquest of the Herald and Weekly Times, all the big dynasties of the 20th century have sold out and moved on, the last trace of the Packer and Fairfax names scrubbed from their former mastheads. In 2016, the Nine

Entertainment television network entered into a landmark merger
with Fairfax that made concerns over concentration and cross-media
ownership from the 1950s and 1980s seem quaint by comparison.
The deal, made possible by the Turnbull government's scrapping of
ownership laws in 2017, left Australia's commercial media landscape
dominated by three monoliths controlling the majority of print,
online, and broadcast media—even as that pool continued to shrink
after decades of closures and cuts. Facing the British Leveson Inquiry
in April 2012, Murdoch himself admitted that the paper and ink that
defined his father's world, and built his own, would one day die: 'The
day will come when we'll just have to say, "It's not working, we can't
afford all the trucks, we can't afford all the huge presses, and so on."'[14]

As that day approaches, the Murdoch empire is more focussed on
the news business than ever. For years, speculation over succession
plans centred on his two sons, Lachlan and James, both men now
closer in age to Sir Keith at the time of his death than their father
was when he assumed control of News Limited. The Murdoch family
trust, in which Rupert wields a controlling vote, retains around 39
per cent of voting stock, but his unique grip on the company, born
of his extraordinary success, has allowed him to install his children in
executive positions in a way his father never could at the Herald and
Weekly Times.[15]

But absolute control, even when kept within the family, is a
tricky thing. For years, Murdoch's reluctance to anoint a successor
and relinquish control left his children, like Sir Keith's bright young
men, jostling for favour and dominance. For a time it seemed that the
empire might be cleaved in two, after the phone-hacking scandal that
engulfed its British tabloids in 2011 forced the company to separate its
film and television interests from the publicly disgraced news division.
The two companies, News Corporation and the newly spun-off
Twenty-First Century Fox, would answer to two heirs-in-waiting, with
James serving as chief executive of Fox and Lachlan as co-chairman of
both companies alongside their father—who remained, as always, at
the top of the pyramid.

By 2017, however, the fragile power-sharing arrangement had
broken down, and after decades of being the great consumer of old-

media dynasties, dividing and conquering old proprietors and family trusts to create his own mega-corporation, Murdoch found himself embracing the only other opportunity left: breaking up and selling out. A US$71 billion deal with Disney sold off the Hollywood arm, saw James bow out entirely, and left Lachlan to preside over the remains—which included the lucrative and controversial Fox News network.

'I think this is returning to our roots,' Rupert told Sky News in December 2017, but it remains to be seen just what the future looks like for a company reared on endless, voracious growth and the leadership of one man.[16] In August 2022, the company posted a buoyant $US760 million profit driven by digital growth, but cut 15 Australian jobs the following week.[17] A long, quiet atrophy appears to have taken root in its 'traditional home', as the family's Australian newspapers grow thinner, and more journalists are shed each year. What goes on at Keith Murdoch House today is a faint echo of the industry that Rupert inherited—the army of workers, the deafening roar, the countless hours of labour that went into a single edition.

Sir Keith Murdoch wished for his son a 'useful altruistic and full life in newspapers and broadcasting', and he has, at the very least, led a full one. As his company swallowed up and remade the giants of Fleet Street and New York in his image, Murdoch became not only the inheritor of Sir Keith's dreams, but perhaps the last great press baron in a lineage that stretched back through his father, Lord Northcliffe and beyond. Rupert Murdoch did not invent these legacies, but by aggregating and amplifying them on a global scale, in a modernising world, he has achieved more influence, and invited more of the same familiar criticisms, than perhaps any of his predecessors.

Set against this extraordinary rise over a lifetime, those years in Adelaide have often been relegated to a fleeting footnote. But would things have panned out differently if his father had lived a little longer? If Lady Elisabeth had managed to hold on to the Queensland papers and Rupert had never moved to Adelaide? Without the spark of indignation, and the siege mentality born of feeling cheated out of his inheritance, would he have fought back as hard, and set himself on a path of endless expansion? If he hadn't been forced to start with the second-best paper in Australia's fourth-best city, would he have become that incendiary blend of outsider and insider — unafraid of challenging orthodoxies and good taste, but still equipped with all the tools and privileges of a press lord's heir? Or the hungry opportunist comfortable with embracing the unwanted scraps of a new market just to get a foothold?

It was in Adelaide, a city seemingly predisposed to press monopolies on a cyclical basis, that he gained a vivid lesson about the limits of outsider-hood, while competitors such as Dumas reaped the benefits of political influence. Rupert might have been happy to enter a market at the bottom, but for the rest of his life he made sure he never stayed there for long — as the substance of his political values became secondary to the influence or opportunities they brought him. In 1998, a 26-year-old Lachlan told the *Financial Times* that after four years working in his father's company, he had come to believe its culture was defined by Adelaide and *The News* in the 1950s: 'It was a paper going broke, in an incredibly competitive environment, that had to fight its guts out to survive.'[18] But, perhaps most importantly, Adelaide is where Rupert Murdoch first asserted absolute control over News Limited. It belonged to him, not to his mother, the board, or the other shareholders, and certainly not any editor who mistook a long leash for free rein. Even if that editor was one of his oldest friends.


WHEN I ENDED up at Rhyll Rivett's door in 2022, I didn't come empty handed; I was there to share with her something I had found among her father's papers at the National Library of Australia months earlier. Within those three dozen folio boxes were the years of correspondence, diaries, and clippings that Rohan and Betty Gillen cleared out of his office on North Terrace in July 1960, along with photographs and postcards from his life before the war, unpublished short stories, letters from his final years, and the original doctored photo of Rohan and Playford's fake handshake. But I had gone to Canberra in search of one item in particular: at some point in the 1970s, Rohan Rivett began writing a book, a novel drawing on his last year in Adelaide, from the royal commission to his own trial and his break with Rupert Murdoch.

I had only seen one mention of it before, a fleeting reference by Ken Inglis 20 years earlier, and when I first raised it with Rhyll, she had no idea of its existence.

Late on my second day in Canberra, as Lake Burley-Griffin grew cold and dark through the library window, I untied a white ribbon holding together a thick cardboard folder. Inside it were 200 typewritten pages, thin as Bible paper, that told a familiar story about an afternoon newspaper grappling with the establishment in a 'sleepy, ultra-solemn Australian city, respectable to the point of primness, conservative to the point of torpor'.[19] The manuscript, entitled *Chronicle*, is not a subtle book, and the fictionalisation is often so light as to be non-existent. Its afternoon newspaper is called *The Chronicle*, its familiar-sounding editor-in-chief is named Donald Dare, the young publisher is Armand Russell, and a list of pseudonymous supporting characters on its front page took all of ten minutes to decode: Sir Thomas Playford is Tim Buttforth; Don Dunstan is Art Hunken; Roderic Chamberlain is Archibald Starkface; Rupert Max Stuart is Les Darby; and Norman Young, the executive who led Patricia Booker down the aisle and later negotiated Rivett's severance, is named Horton Baines. That it was never published by Gold Star or anyone else is perhaps not surprising; the novel centres upon the libel trial of Dare and *The Chronicle*, but also weaves through a variety of pulpy subplots, ranging from an unmarried journalist who falls pregnant, to a middle-aged sports reporter who has a fling with a younger colleague. If those characters are as grounded in truth as the trial at its core, it may have opened a whole new set of problems for the author and his former co-workers.

As I read through it, I could see that the primary storyline contained at least half-a-dozen scenes in which Rivett's fiction mirrors real-life transcripts and sources, almost to the letter. But there are also small, intriguing details that are impossible to corroborate. When the police arrive to interview Dare in the middle of a heatwave, he asks his secretary to make them wait outside his office while he quietly lights a cigar to compose himself. During the libel trial, he is plagued by a series of ominous 3.00 am phone calls—a 'nerve war' of harassment and 'filthy tricks'.[20] In one passage, a *Chronicle* staffer reflects on how

Russell had a reputation for saving money: 'In moments of financial pressure or some monetary downturn in the weekly books he had been known to go round the office soon after it emptied before five o'clock personally switching off every burning light'.[21]

The most interesting of all are a series of private conversations between Dare and Russell in the lead-up to the trial and the editor's fateful sacking. These exchanges, read with every caveat that they are intended as fiction, fill in the gaps of those final months in 1960. When they meet one day in June in the Russell family home on East Terrace, Armand is bursting with the latest news from his empire's latest front, where he had hired or fired nearly 20 workers as he shook up his new Sydney paper, *The Reflector*:

> There was a compulsive strain behind the acquisitiveness that had been there even when he first came back from Oxford. It seemed that each new takeover or fusion or additional use of plant was merely a stepping stone for another leap forward. Tremendous energy was thrust for 12 or 14 hours a day into seeing the new property—whether a suburban giveaway, a small country station, or a major daily—was in the black. Then targets were set for the executives responsible for that particular sector. Meanwhile the restless, rushing mind was reaching out in conversations, or with other proprietors or friends of proprietors, for new possibilities elsewhere.[22]

It also makes explicit the tensions behind the pair's break-up, whether it is Russell's use of *The Chronicle*'s staff to populate his new acquisitions with loyal workers—'casually taking three *Chronicle* personnel from Accounts, Advertising and the Machine Room to plug gaps in his Sydney structure'—to his newfound reluctance to provoke the state's premier.[23] *The Chronicle* might have been enjoying a record year, but the publisher insists that they cannot afford to waste money on lawyers' fees or fines with his battle in Sydney underway. The editor is less than pleased to learn that his paper is now 'just the milch cow to fatten Sydney':

Armand got up and threw his arms up in disgust. 'Look, Donald, things have changed. I want you to get our priorities straight. This is an all-in brawl in Sydney. I can't afford to be attacked at the home base where our monies are coming from.'

Donald suddenly wondered for the first time if between the police court hearing and the present trial in the Supreme Court, if the company's lawyer had made some deal with Starkface which kept Armand as an individual not only out of the indictment but also out of the witness box.

But he was so disturbed to find his friend back-tracking on years of occasionally impetuous and occasionally inspired opposition to the conservative view that Buttforth was an all-wise and benevolent dictator, that he decided enough had been said for tonight.[24]

When Dare is sacked by letter soon after, in the middle of writing an obituary of Aneurin Bevan, his wife and friends lash the publisher as a 'young bastard'. But Dare is more circumspect; earlier in the novel, he had reflected, in an echo of Lord Northcliffe's telegram about control all those years ago, that, 'We who don't own newspapers, don't even own many shares, must always remain essentially freelance mercenaries whose sword is up for sale to those who've inherited papers or chains from dad or grandpa or uncle George.'[25] He was grateful for the opportunity given to him by Armand's late father, and pleasantly surprised that his mentor's son had kept him on as long as he had.

In the manuscript's epilogue, written half a century ago, he takes stock of the 'Armand Russell' empire and its future. In writing this book, I have collected and pored over dozens of biographies of Rupert Murdoch, each attempting to make sense of the man and predict his next move. Books published before my first birthday feature words such as 'decline' or 'apotheosis' in their title, only for Murdoch to plough on through 30 more years of scandals, takeovers, marriages, divorces, children, market crashes, industry-wide upheavals, and succession gossip. But perhaps some truth can be gleaned from this manuscript that predates almost all of them, written by the one man who lived through Murdoch's formative years in newspapers more intimately, and more intensely, than any other person:

> Armand now has a newspaper, television, and radio empire in three continents. Although still in his early forties he has aged sharply. Friends say he is too tense to enjoy it all. They suspect his never-stated ambition is still to regain the Australian papers his father controlled and to add them to his own. Horton Baines was reconciled to Armand and among his many other chairmanships accepted that of the Australian section of Armand's empire as Armand lives now mainly in America. But Horton never advises friends to buy shares in Armand's enterprises. As he says, 'If Armand steps off a kerb without looking, or catches the wrong jet, the shares will go through the floor overnight.'[26]

# Acknowledgements

THE RESEARCH AND writing of this book took place on the lands of the Kaurna, Gadigal, and Ngunnawal peoples. To explore the history of this continent is to reckon with deep and complex legacies, and I've done my best to tread lightly and with respect. Thank you to staff at the Ngaanyatjarra Council, Central Land Council, and Central Australian Aboriginal Congress for help along the way.

In writing this book I've drawn from published and unpublished material held in public and private collections around Australia. For permissions and encouragement, I must thank Susan Morgan and the Bednall family, Margaret Bowman, Tim Bright and the Bright family, Rinker Buck, Jennifer Cockburn, Jill Sykes and the Dumas family, Jack Dunstan and the Dunstan family, Samela Harris, Louis Inglis and the Inglis family, Michael S Parer and Alella Books, Piers Plumridge, Dimity Torbett, and Rhyll Rivett.

I gratefully acknowledge the National Library of Australia, State Library of South Australia, State Library of New South Wales, Barr Smith Library at the University of Adelaide, Australian Institute of Aboriginal and Torres Strait Islander Studies, State Library of Western Australia, Geelong Grammar, and Oxfordshire History Centre for their assistance and the use of material in their collections. Special thanks to front-of-house and collections staff who have been helpful and accommodating in the face of lockdowns and myriad other challenges, in particular Eva Bernroider, Sophie Church, Jay Dominick, Anthony Laube, and Chris Read.

This book was completed without the participation of the Rupert Murdoch or his family, but I thank Mathew Charles and his colleagues at News Corporation Australia for their help and fair-spiritedness.

My work on this book was supported by a literature grant from Arts South Australia, which proved transformative. I am also grateful to the History Council of South Australia for awarding the Wakefield Essay Prize to a very early fragment of this work, initially completed as an honours thesis under the supervision of Paul Sendziuk at the University of Adelaide.

Thank you to the many people I've crossed paths with who generously shared their research, memories, contacts, enthusiasm, and hospitality: Jeanine Baker, Amanda Blair, Michael Bollen, Keith Conlon, Douglas Golding, Tom Griffiths, Jon Halpin, Peter Harries, Michael Kirby, Helen Leake, Bob and Jean Macaulay, Teresa McCarthy, Pamela McGrath, John Menadue, Robert Moles, Patrick Mullins, Mike O'Reilly, Don Riddell, John Scales, Tory Shepherd, Seumas Spark, Clare and Shirley Summerskill, Daniel Thomas, Richard Walsh, and David Washington. Thank you also to Bronwyn Haseldine, Bronwyn Stuart, and the Stuart family.

Thank you to Henry Rosenbloom and all at Scribe for their faith in this project.

My immense gratitude and appreciation to friends and colleagues who have provided material and moral support while writing this book: Jessica Alice, Gemma Beale, Sophie Byrne, John Carty, Stephanie Convery, David Knight, Alyx Gorman, Steph Harmon, Royce Kurmelovs, Kylie Maslen, Saskia Scott, and Sebastian Tonkin.

Thank you to my Marsh and Duff families for years of love and encouragement, particularly my parents, Janis and Simon, my late grandfather William, Kate, Christo, Stephen and Michael, Peter and Jenny, and all the little ones.

And, most importantly, to my partner, Sia Duff, for everything.

# Bibliography

**Articles**

Ray Broomhill, 'Dickinson, Edward Alexander (1903–1937)', *Australian Dictionary of Biography*, National Centre of Biography, 1981

Rinker Buck, 'Can The Post Survive Rupert Murdoch?', *MORE*, November 1977

Jean Chalaby, 'Northcliffe: proprietor as journalist', in Peter Catteral, Colin Seymour-Ure and Adrian Smith (ed), *Northcliffe's Legacy: aspects of the British popular press, 1896–1996*, pp. 29–33

Kevin Duggan, 'Chamberlain, Sir Reginald Roderic St Clair (1901–1990)', *Australian Dictionary of Biography*, National Centre of Biography, 2007

'Rupert Murdoch has potential', *Esquire*, 11 September 2008 [https://www.esquire.com/news-politics/a4971/rupert-murdoch-1008]

David Fickling, 'News Corp Falls Between Adelaide and Delaware', *The Guardian*, 3 September 2004 [https://www.theguardian.com/media/2004/sep/03/newscorporation.rupertmurdoch

Wilma Hannah, 'Fink, Theodore (1855–1942)', *Australian Dictionary of Biography*, National Centre of Biography, 1981

Roger Holden, 'Why The News Was Forced to Close', *Ad News*, 24 April 1992

Gilbert Ralph, 'The Broken Hill—Collins House Connection: Mining

Personalities', *Journal of Australasian Mining History*, Vol. 2, September 2004

AH Raskin, 'The Negotiation—Changes in the Balance of Power', *The New Yorker*, 22 January, p. 50

AH Raskin, 'The Negotiation—Intrigue at the Summit', *The New Yorker*, 29 January 1979

Ruth Ryon, 'Rupert Murdoch to Restore Stein House', *Los Angeles Times*, 21 September 1986 [https://www.latimes.com/archives/la-xpm-1986-09-21-re-8848-story.html]

William Shawcross, 'Murdoch's New Life', *Vanity Fair*, October 1999 [archive.vanityfair.com/article/1999/10/murdochs-new-life]

Gavin Souter, 'Browne, Francis Courtney (Frank) (1915–1981)', *Australian Dictionary of Biography*, National Centre of Biography, 2007

Dimity Torbett, 'The King of Fleet Street', *Times on Sunday*, 7 June 1987, p. 26

David Washington, 'Memories of the Murdoch world', *Offset*, November 1985, p. 5

David Washington, 'News Corp Becomes a Landlord to State Govt Department', InDaily, 16 August 2021 [https://indaily.com.au/news/2021/08/16/news-corp-becomes-a-landlord-to-state-govt-department/

Evan Whitton, 'Rupert Murdoch: Our Part in His Evil Upfall', *tasmaniantimes.com*, 14 June 2016, accessed 11 August 2022 https://tasmaniantimes.com/2016/06/rupert-murdoch-our-part-in-his-evil-upfall/

## Newspapers and periodicals

*Barrier Miner*
*Cherwell*
*Chronicle*
*Direct Action*
*Financial Times*
*Fudge*
*House News*
*If Revived*
*Labor Call*

*Mary's Own Paper*
*Nation*
*Nation Review*
*National Times*
*News Chronicle*
*Offset*
*On Dit*
*Port Pirie Recorder*
*Smith's Weekly*
*South Australian Gazette and Colonial Register*
*Southern Australian*
*Sydney Morning Herald*
*The Adelaide Review*
*The Advertiser*
*The Age*
*The Corian*
*The Daily Mirror* (Sydney)
*The Digger*
*The Examiner*
*The Guardian*
*The Herald*
*The Journalist*
*The Mail*
*The Mirror*
*The News*
*The Register*
*The Register News-Pictorial*
*The Sun*
*The Sunday Times*
*The Tasmanian*
*The Telegraph*
*The West Australian*
*Tribune*
*Truth*
*West Coast Recorder*
*Western Mail*

## Archival Papers

*National Library of Australia*
Papers of Colin Blore Bednall, NLA, MS 5546
Papers of Rohan Rivett, NLA, MS 8049
Papers of Keith Arthur Murdoch, NLA, MS 2823
Papers of Sir Alfred Charles William Harmsworth, NLA, M1641
Papers of Sir Lloyd Dumas, NLA, MS 4849

*State Library of South Australia*
Papers Relating to Libel Case Against News Limited and Rohan Deakin
    Rivett, SLSA PRG 1098/31
Papers Relating to Rupert Max Stuart, SLSA, PRG 1098/30/1
Papers of Harry Plumridge, SLSA PRG 1757
Papers of Kenneth Stanley Inglis, SLSA, PRG 194
Legal Notes of Sir Charles Bright, SLSA, D 6452(L)

*State Library of New South Wales*
Papers of George Munster, SLNSW, MLMSS 7627
Fairfax Media Limited Business Archive, 1795–2006, Mitchell Library,
    SLNSW and Courtesy Fairfax Media Ltd, MLMSS 9894/Box
    431—File 55
Fairfax Media Limited Business Archive, 1795–2006, SLNSW, MLMSS
    9894/Box 410

*Australian Institute of Aboriginal and Torres Strait Islander Studies*
Papers of Father Dixon and the Stuart Case 1958–1987, AIATSIS, MS 3764

*Barr Smith Library at University of Adelaide*
Papers of Stewart Cockburn, Barr Smith Library at the University of
    Adelaide, MSS 0091

## Broadcasts
Australian Broadcasting Commission, *Five Australians: the rise of the
    media mogul Rupert Murdoch*, 25 July 1967, [https://www.abc.net.
    au/education/five-australians-the-rise-of-the-media-mogul-rupert-
    murdoch-196/13759198]

Rupert Murdoch, Sky News, 15 December 2017 [https://fb.watch/
    ftCCTY4SEx/]

## Reports

News Limited, Annual Report, June 1932
News Limited, Chairman's Address, Annual General Meeting, 30 September
    1954
News Limited, Chairman's Address, Annual General Meeting, 30 September
    1955
News Limited, Directors' Report and Balance Sheet, 30 June 1955
News Limited, Directors' Report and Balance Sheet, 30 June 1955
News Limited, Chairman's Address, Annual General Meeting, 26 October
    1956
News Limited, Chairman's Address, Annual General Meeting, 30 October
    1959
News Limited, Annual Report and Balance Sheet, 30 September 1960
News Corporation Limited, Chief Executive's Review, Annual Report, 1981
News Corporation Limited, Chief Executive's Report, Annual Report, 1986
News Corporation Limited, Annual Report, 1986
News Corporation, Annual Report, 2020 [https://newscorp.com/wp-
    content/uploads/2020/10/news-corp-2020-annual-report.pdf]
News Corporation, Fiscal 2022 Full Year and Fourth Quarter Key Financial
    Highlights, August 2022 [https://newscorp.com/wp-content/
    uploads/2022/08/Q4-FY2022-Earnings_FINAL_8-Aug-2022-12PM.
    pdf]
Report of the Royal Commission on Television, 1954, NLA
Australian Broadcasting Control Board, Report and Recommendations to
    the Postmaster-General on Applications for Commercial Television
    Licences for the Brisbane and Adelaide Areas, September 1958
Law Society of South Australia, Annual Report, 1959, SLSA, 340 L415 b

## Books

Paul Barry, *The Rise and Rise of Kerry Packer Uncut*, Bantam, Sydney, 2008
David Bowman, *The Captive Press*, Penguin, Ringwood, 1988
Asa Briggs, *Special Relationships: people and places*, Frontline Books, London,
    2012

Ray Broomhill, *Unemployed Workers*, University of Queensland Press, St
    Lucia, 1978

Arthur Calwell, *Be Just and Fear Not*, Rigby, Adelaide, 1978

Clyde Cameron, *Confessions of Clyde Cameron*, ABC Enterprises, Crows
    Nest, 1990

Sir Roderic Chamberlain, *The Stuart Affair*, Rigby, Adelaide, 1973

Neil Chenoweth, *Virtual Murdoch: reality wars on the information highway*,
    Secker & Warburg, London, 2001

Mavis Thorpe Clark, *Pastor Doug*, Rigby, Adelaide, 1972

Stewart Cockburn, *Playford: benevolent despot*, Axiom, Kent Town, 1991

Hugh Cudlipp, *Walking on Water*, Bodley Head, London, 1976

Christopher Day, *Kamahl: an impossible dream*, Random House, Sydney,
    1995

Phillip Deery, *Spies and Sparrows*, Melbourne University Publishing,
    Carlton, 2022

Father Thomas Dixon, *The Wizard of Alice: Father Dixon and the Stuart
    Case*, Alella Books, Morwell, 1987

Sir Lloyd Dumas, *The Story of a Full Life*, Sun Books, Melbourne, 1969

Don Dunstan, *Felicia: the political memoirs of Don Dunstan*, Macmillan,
    South Melbourne, 1981

Keith Dunstan, *No Brains At All*, Penguin, Ringwood, 1990

Geoffrey Dutton, *Out In The Open*, University of Queensland Press, St
    Lucia, 1995

John Faulkner and Stuart Macintyre (ed), *True Believers: the story of the
    federal parliamentary Labor Party*, Allen & Unwin, Crows Nest, 2001

William Grayden, *Adam and Atoms*, Frank Daniels, Perth, 1957

Harry J Greenwall, *Northcliffe: Napoleon of Fleet Street*, Wingate, London,
    1957

Sir Ian Hamilton, *Gallipoli Diary Vol II*, Edward Arnold, London, 1920

John Hetherington, *Australians: nine profiles*, FW Chesire, Melbourne, 1960

David Horner, *The Spy Catchers: the official history of ASIO 1949–1963*,
    Allen & Unwin, Crows Nest, 2014

Amirah Inglis, *Australians in the Spanish Civil War*, Allen & Unwin, Sydney,
    1987

Ken Inglis, *The Stuart Case*, Melbourne University Press, Parkville, 1961,
    and Black Inc, Melbourne, 2002 editions

Thomas Kiernan, *Citizen Murdoch*, Dodd, Mead, New York, 1986

Michael Leapman, *Barefaced Cheek: the apotheosis of Rupert Murdoch*, Hodder and Stoughton, London, 1983

Joan Lindsay, *Time Without Clocks*, FW Chesire, Melbourne, 1962

Clem Lloyd, *Profession: Journalist*, Hale & Iremonger, Sydney,1985

Andrew Male, *Other Times: the life and work of Max Fatchen*, Wakefield Press, Kent Town, 1997

Leonard Marquis, *South Australian Newspapers: a selection of material from the extensive research notes gathered for a proposed history of the press in South Australia*, Ronald Parsons, Lobethal, 1998

John Monks, *Elisabeth Murdoch: two lives*, Macmillan, Chippendale, 1994

Keith Murdoch, 'Gallipoli Letter', Allen & Unwin, Crows Nest, 2010

Jean Prest, *Sir John Langdon Bonython: newspaper proprietor, politician, and philanthropist*, Australian Scholarly Publishing, North Melbourne, 2011

Simon Regan, *Murdoch: a business biography*, Angus and Robertson, London, 1977

Rohan Rivett, *Behind Bamboo*, Angus and Robertson, London, 1956

Tom Roberts, *Before Rupert: Keith Murdoch and the Birth of a Dynasty*, University of Queensland Press, St Lucia, 2015

William Shawcross, *Murdoch: ringmaster of the information circus*, Pan Books, London, 1993

Geoff Sparrow (ed.), *Crusade For Journalism: official history of the Australian Journalists' Association*, Australian Journalists' Association, Melbourne, 1960

Jean Stein, *West of Eden: an American place*, Random House, New York, 2016

Jerome Tuccille, *Rupert Murdoch*, DI Fine, New York, 1989

Denis Warner, *Not Always on Horseback*, Allen & Unwin, St Leonards, 1997

Denis Warner, *Wake Me If There's Trouble*, Penguin, Ringwood, 1995

Sir Norman Young, *Figuratively Speaking: the reminiscences, experiences and observations of Sir Norman Young*, N Young, North Adelaide, 1991

Sally Young, *Paper Emperors: the rise of Australia's newspaper empires*, NewSouth Publishing, Sydney, 2019

RM Younger, *Keith Murdoch: founder of an empire*, HarperCollins, Pymble, 2003

Desmond Zwar, *In Search of Keith Murdoch*, Macmillan, South Melbourne, 1980

## Thesis

Peter Harries, 2005, *From local 'live' production houses to relay stations: a history of commercial television in Perth, Western Australia 1958-1990*, PhD thesis, 2005

Pamela McGrath, 2010, *Hard Looking: a historical ethnography of photographic encounters with Aboriginal families in the Ngaanyatjarra Lands*, PhD thesis, 2010

## Pamphlets

Charles Duguid, 'The Rocket Range, Aborigines and War', 1947, SLSA PRG 387/1/8/3/2

Rennie Simmons, Aborigines Advancement League, 'Analysis of Mr Rupert Murdoch's Article on the West Australian Natives Published in *The News*, Adelaide, 1 February 1957', 1957

Australian Labor Party (South Australian Branch) and United Trades and Labour Council of South Australia, *Don't Buy The News* Campaign Pamphlet, November 1979, private collection

News Limited, *The Inside Story of Adelaide's Night Life*, 1955, SLSA, 079.42

## Transcripts

Australian Broadcasting Control Board, Transcript of Proceedings, Inquiry Into Applications Received for Licences for Commercial Television Stations in the Adelaide and Brisbane Area, 1958

Australian Broadcasting Control Board, Transcript of Evidence, Public Hearing into Applications for a Television Licence in Perth, July 1958

Rupert Murdoch, Oral Statement to the Leveson Inquiry, 26 April 2012

## Oral histories and interviews

Donn Casey, interviewed by Dimity Torbett, private collection

Stewart Cockburn, interviewed by John Farquharson, NLA Oral History, 2002, [https://nla.gov.au/nla.cat-vn1510788]

Max Fatchen, interviewed by Peter Donovan, 2004, JD Somerville Oral History Collection, SLSA, OH705

Tom Fitzgerald, interviewed by Ken Inglis, NLA Oral History, 1988, [https://nla.gov.au/nla.obj-198877459]

William Grayden, interviewed by Ronda Jamieson, State Library of Western Australia Oral History Collection, OH2344

John Grigg, interviewed by Dimity Torbett, 1984, private collection

Ken Kelly, interviewed by Dimity Torbett, private collection Cecil King, interviewed by Dimity Torbett, private collection

George E McCadden interviewed by Ian Hamilton, NLA Oral History, 1984 [http://nla.gov.au/nla.obj-195654535]

Dame Elisabeth Murdoch, interviewed by John Farquharson, NLA Oral History, 1995 [http://nla.gov.au/nla.obj-217242522]

John Pitcairn, interviewed by Dimity Torbett, private collection

Harry Plumridge, interviewed by Des Colquhoun, 29 July 1969, Papers of Harry Plumridge, SLSA PRG 1757

Rohan Rivett, interviewed by Hazel De Berg, NLA Oral History [http://nla.gov.au/nla.obj-220869210]

Michael Weimgall, interviewed by Dimity Torbett, private collection

Frederick Whitehead, interviewed by Dimity Torbett, 1984, private collection

## Author's interviews and correspondence

Michael Kirby, author's correspondence, 2022

Douglas Golding, author's interview, 2022

John Menadue, author's interview, 2022

Mike O'Reilly, author's interview, 2022

Don Riddell, author's interview, 2022

Rhyll Rivett, author's interview, 2022

John Scales, author's interview, 2022

Shirley Summerskill, author's interview, 2022

# Notes

THE FOLLOWING ABBREVIATIONS have been used:
National Library of Australia: NLA
State Library of New South Wales: SLNSW
State Library of South Australia: SLSA

COLLECTIONS OF PAPERS cited in these notes are held in the following repositories:
Papers of Rohan Rivett, NLA, MS 80492
Papers of Keith Arthur Murdoch, NLA, MS 2823
Papers of Sir Alfred Charles William Harmsworth, NLA, M1641
Papers of George Munster, SLNSW, MLMSS 7627
Papers of Sir Lloyd Dumas, NLA, MS 4849
Papers of Colin Blore Bednall, NLA, MS 5546
Papers of Harry Plumridge, SLSA, PRG 1757/6/7
Papers Relating to Rupert Max Stuart, SLSA, PRG 1098/30/1
The Queen v News Ltd and Rohan Deakin Rivett, Papers relating to libel case against News Limited and Rohan Deakin Rivett, PRG 1098/3

## Prologue

1   David Fickling, 'News Corp Falls Between Adelaide and Delaware',
    *The Guardian*, 3 September 2004 [https://www.theguardian.com/
    media/2004/sep/03/newscorporation.rupertmurdoch]
2   William Shawcross, 'Murdoch's New Life', *Vanity Fair*, October 1999
    [archive.vanityfair.com/article/1999/10/murdochs-new-life]
3   'Rupert Murdoch has potential', *Esquire*, 11 September 2008 [https://
    www.esquire.com/news-politics/a4971/rupert-murdoch-1008]
4   'Gaol Means Nothing to a 71-year-old Cat Burglar', *The News*, 20
    November 1953, p. 1 [http://nla.gov.au/nla.news-article131239082]
5   'Outstanding Courage', *The News*, 20 November 1952, p. 15 [http://nla.
    gov.au/nla.news-article131190401]
6   'Change Brings Drop of 40 Degrees', *The News*, 4 January 1960, p. 1
7   Dialogue reconstructed from police transcript, 4 January 1960, Papers
    Relating to Libel Case Against News Limited and Rohan Deakin Rivett,
    SLSA PRG 1098/31
8   'Night Was Hottest for 8 Years', *The News*, 15 January 1960, p. 1; 'What
    They Did to Beat the Heat', *The News*, 15 January 1960, p. 3
9   Dialogue reconstructed from police transcript, 15 January 1960, Papers
    Relating to Libel Case Against News Limited and Rohan Deakin Rivett,
    SLSA PRG 1098/31

## Chapter One: Absolute control

1   'Sir Keith Murdoch', *Smith's Weekly*, 3 February 1940, p. 2; John
    Hetherington, *Australians: nine profiles*, 1960, p. 82
2   Murdoch to Bednall, 28 December 1947, Papers of Colin Blore Bednall
3   Dame Elisabeth Murdoch, interviewed by John Farquharson, NLA Oral
    History collection, 1995 [http://nla.gov.au/nla.obj-217242522]
4   Murdoch to Rivett, 31 October 1950, Papers of Rohan Rivett
5   Murdoch to McKay, 30 April 1937, Papers of Keith Arthur Murdoch
6   Murdoch to McKay, 20 October 1950, Papers of Keith Arthur Murdoch
7   Murdoch to Northcliffe, 25 June 1922, Papers of Sir Alfred Charles
    William Harmsworth
8   Murdoch to Northcliffe, 15 December 1920, Papers of Sir Alfred Charles
    William Harmsworth
9   Murdoch to Northcliffe, 25 June 1922, Papers of Sir Alfred Charles
    William Harmsworth
10  Desmond Zwar, *In Search of Keith Murdoch*, 1980, p. 57
11  Wilma Hannah, 'Fink, Theodore (1855–1942)', *Australian Dictionary of
    Biography*, 1981

12    Colin Bednall, *A Temporarily Undesirable Person* unpublished manuscript, Papers of Colin Blore Bednall, p. 209

13    Ibid, p. 225

14    Keith Dunstan, *No Brains At All*, 1990, p. 249

15    Ibid

16    Cecil King, interviewed by Dimity Torbett, private collection

17    Will of Sir Keith Murdoch, 21 January 1948, Papers of George Munster

18    John Pitcairn, interviewed by Dimity Torbett, private collection

19    Keith Murdoch to Patrick Murdoch, 1909, Papers of Keith Arthur Murdoch

20    Ibid

21    Keith Murdoch, 'Gallipoli Letter', 1915

22    Sir Ian Hamilton, *Gallipoli Diary*, vol. II, 1920, p. 241

23    Ibid, pp. 240, 259

24    Murdoch

25    Jean Chalaby, 'Northcliffe: proprietor as journalist', in Peter Catteral, Colin Seymour-Ure and Adrian Smith (ed), *Northcliffe's Legacy: aspects of the British popular press, 1896–1996*, pp. 29–33

26    RM Younger, *Keith Murdoch: founder of an empire*, 2003, p. 45

27    Northcliffe to Murdoch, 30 September 1915, Papers of Sir Alfred Charles William Harmsworth

28    Murdoch to Northcliffe, 1 October 1915, Papers of Sir Alfred Charles William Harmsworth

29    Murdoch to Northcliffe, 13 October 1915, Papers of Sir Alfred Charles William Harmsworth

30    Northcliffe to Murdoch, 19 October 1915, Papers of Sir Alfred Charles William Harmsworth

31    Murdoch to Northcliffe, 10 June 1918, Papers of Sir Alfred Charles William Harmsworth

32    Denison to Murdoch, 3 April 1918, Papers of Keith Arthur Murdoch

33    Murdoch to Denison, 20 January 1921, Papers of Keith Arthur Murdoch

34    Murdoch to Northcliffe, 4 March 1920, Papers of Sir Alfred Charles William Harmsworth

35    Dimity Torbett, 'The King of Fleet Street', *Times on Sunday*, 7 June 1987, p. 26

36    Harry J Greenwall, *Northcliffe: Napoleon of Fleet Street*, 1957, p. 13

37    Murdoch to Denison, 20 January 1921, Papers of Keith Arthur Murdoch

38    Murdoch to Northcliffe, 15 December 1920, Papers of Sir Alfred Charles William Harmsworth

39  Northcliffe to Murdoch, 18 April 1921, Papers of Sir Alfred Charles William Harmsworth

40  Murdoch to Northcliffe, 24 March 1922, Papers of Sir Alfred Charles William Harmsworth

41  Lord Northcliffe, draft address, 1922, Papers of Keith Arthur Murdoch

42  Ibid.

43  Northcliffe to Murdoch, xx January 1922, Papers of Sir Alfred Charles William Harmsworth

44  Murdoch to Northcliffe, 12 March 1922, Papers of Sir Alfred Charles William Harmsworth

45  'Gun Alley Murder', *The Register*, 16 March 1922, p. 7 [http://nla.gov.au/nla.news-article63582780]

46  Murdoch to Northcliffe, 12 March 1922, Papers of Sir Alfred Charles William Harmsworth

47  Arthur Calwell, *Be Just and Fear Not*, 1978, p. 90

48  Murdoch to Northcliffe, 12 March 1922, Papers of Sir Alfred Charles William Harmsworth

49  Murdoch to Northcliffe, 24 March 1922, Papers of Sir Alfred Charles William Harmsworth

50  Northcliffe to Murdoch, 10 December 1921, Papers of Sir Alfred Charles William Harmsworth

51  Murdoch to Northcliffe, 1 January 1922, Papers of Sir Alfred Charles William Harmsworth

52  Murdoch to Northcliffe, 25 June 1922, Papers of Sir Alfred Charles William Harmsworth

53  Murdoch to Northcliffe, 30 December 1921, Papers of Sir Alfred Charles William Harmsworth

54  Ibid

55  Murdoch to Northcliffe, 12 March 1922, Papers of Sir Alfred Charles William Harmsworth

56  Ibid

57  Murdoch to Northcliffe, 7 December 1921, Papers of Sir Alfred Charles William Harmsworth

58  Murdoch to Northcliffe, 12 March 1922, Papers of Sir Alfred Charles William Harmsworth

59  'Keith Murdoch was Boss of Premiers' Conference', *Smith's Weekly*, 30 April 1932, p. 3 [http://nla.gov.au/nla.news-article234572483]

60  Dame Elisabeth Murdoch, interviewed by John Farquharson, NLA Oral History, 1995 [http://nla.gov.au/nla.obj-217242522]

61    Bednall, p. 299
62    Ibid
63    Murdoch to Dumas, 15 May 1949, Papers of Sir Lloyd Dumas
64    Murdoch to Bednall, 8 August 1950, Papers of Colin Blore Bednall

## Chapter Two: Comrade Murdoch

1     Stewart Cockburn, interviewed by John Farquharson, NLA Oral History,
      2002 [https://nla.gov.au/nla.cat-vn1510788]
2     Ibid
3     Dunstan, pp. 122–3
4     Don Riddell, author's interview, 2022
5     Rohan Rivett, *Behind Bamboo*, 1956, p. 254
6     Stewart Cockburn, interviewed by John Farquharson, NLA Oral History,
      2002 [https://nla.gov.au/nla.cat-vn1510788]
7     Ibid
8     Ibid
9     *The Corian*, August 1948, p. 90
10    *The Corian*, May 1948, p. 22
11    'Mr Lyons to Lead New Federal Party', *The Herald*, 12 March 1931, p. 1
      [http://nla.gov.au/nla.news-page 26384543]
12    Ibid
13    Anne Kantor, in John Monks, *Elisabeth Murdoch: two lives*, 1994, p. 323
14    Joan Lindsay, *Time Without Clocks*, 1962, pp. 214–15
15    Ibid
16    Dame Elisabeth Murdoch, interviewed by John Farquharson, NLA Oral
      History, 1995 [http://nla.gov.au/nla.obj-217242522]
17    Monks, p. 311
18    Lindsay, pp. 214–215
19    Simon Regan, *Murdoch: a business biography*, 1977, p. 34
20    William Shawcross, *Murdoch: ringmaster of the information circus*, 1993,
      pp. 56–8; Regan, p. 39
21    Shawcross, p. 58; Regan, pp. 37–9
22    Daniel Thomas, author's interview, 2022; Regan, p. 40; Shawcross, p. 59
23    Thomas
24    Donn Casey, interviewed by Dimity Torbett, private collection
25    *The Corian*, May 1948, p. 22
26    Shawcross, p. 91; Regan, p. 35
27    Shawcross, p. 59
28    *The Corian*, May 1948, pp. 21–3

29   *The Corian*, August 1948, p. 94

30   Ibid, p. 95

31   *The Corian*, May 1948, p. 23

32   Ibid, p. 22

33   *The Corian*, December 1948, p. 159

34   Ibid, pp. 13, 56

35   *If Revived*, November 1949, pp. 19–22

36   Ibid

37   *The Corian*, May 1948, p. 22

## Chapter Three: Bright young men

1   Rohan Rivett, interviewed by Hazel De Berg, NLA Oral History [http:// nla.gov.au/nla.obj-220869210]

2   Rohan Rivett, Draft Farewell Speech, July 1960, Papers of Rohan Rivett

3   'Fall In Profit of News Ltd', *The Age*, 15 September 1950, p. 6 [http://nla. gov.au/nla.news-article205375788]

4   Murdoch to Christiansen, 11 October 1951, Papers of Rohan Rivett

5   Murdoch to Rivett, 10 September 1949, Papers of Rohan Rivett

6   Murdoch to Rivett, 19 April 1949, Papers of Rohan Rivett

7   Ibid.

8   Dunstan to Rhyll Rivett, 29 January 1996, Papers of Rohan Rivett

9   Bowman to Rhyll Rivett, 7 December 1996, Papers of Rohan Rivett

10   Bednall, p. 215

11   Ibid, p. 208

12   Dunstan, p. 146

13   Neil Chenoweth, *Virtual Murdoch: reality wars on the information highway*, 2001, p. 24

14   Murdoch to Rivett, 10 September 1949, Papers of Rohan Rivett

15   Ibid

16   Murdoch to Rivett, 31 October 1950, Papers of Rohan Rivett

17   Murdoch to Rivett, 12 February 1951, Papers of Rohan Rivett

18   Ibid

19   Rohan Rivett, Draft Farewell Speech, July 1960, Papers of Rohan Rivett

20   Bednall to Murdoch, 12 October 1949, Papers of Colin Blore Bednall

21   Bednall to Murdoch, 19 March 1951, Papers of Colin Blore Bednall

22   Bednall, p. 208

23   Michael Weimgall, interviewed by Dimity Torbett, private collection

24   'Australians at Worcester', *Cherwell*, 28 April 1953

25   Murdoch to Rivett, 12 February 1950, Papers of Rohan Rivett

26    Rivett to Murdoch, undated (February 1950), Papers of Rohan Rivett

27    Rivett to Murdoch, 13 October 1950, Papers of Rohan Rivett

28    Rivett to Murdoch, 9 December 1950, Papers of Rohan Rivett

29    Rivett to Murdoch, February 1951, Papers of Rohan Rivett

30    Rivett to Murdoch, 14 October 1952, Papers of Rohan Rivett

31    Ibid

32    Rivett to Murdoch, 11 April 1951, Papers of Rohan Rivett

33    Ibid

34    Ibid

35    Rivett to Murdoch, February 1951, Papers of Rohan Rivett

36    Ibid

37    John Grigg, interviewed by Dimity Torbett, 1984, private collection

38    Frederick Whitehead, interviewed by Dimity Torbett, 1984, private collection

39    Ken Kelly, interviewed by Dimity Torbett, private collection

40    Rivett to Murdoch, 9 December 1950, Papers of Rohan Rivett

41    Rivett to Murdoch, 14 October 1951, Papers of Rohan Rivett

42    Rivett to Murdoch, 11 April 1951, Papers of Rohan Rivett

43    Rupert Murdoch to Rivett, July 1951, Papers of Rohan Rivett

44    Murdoch to Rivett, 30 July 1951, Papers of Rohan Rivett

45    Murdoch to Rivett, 12 February 1951, Papers of Rohan Rivett

46    Rivett to Murdoch, 14 October 1951, Papers of Rohan Rivett

47    Murdoch to Rivett, 21 October 1951, Papers of Rohan Rivett

48    Murdoch to Rivett, 26 October 1951, Papers of Rohan Rivett

49    Hugh Cudlipp, *Walking on Water*, 1976, p. 203

50    Murdoch to Chifley, 22 May 1949, in John Faulkner and Stuart Macintyre (ed), *True Believers: the story of the federal parliamentary Labor Party*, 2001, pp. 200–01

51    Rupert Murdoch to Rivett, 16 November 1952, Papers of Rohan Rivett

52    Faulkner and Macintyre, p. 201

53    Shawcross, p. 66

54    Asa Briggs, *Special Relationships: people and places*, 2012, p. 188

55    Rivett to Murdoch, 6 August 1951, Papers of Rohan Rivett

56    Shawcross, pp. 71–2, Shirley Summerskill, author's interview, 2022

57    Murdoch to Rivett, 7 July 1952, Papers of Rohan Rivett

58    Rivett to Murdoch, 31 October 1951, Papers of Rohan Rivett

59    Rivett to Murdoch, 4 January 1952, Papers of Rohan Rivett

60    Rivett to Rupert Murdoch, 13 January 1953; 25 September 1952, Papers of Rohan Rivett

61  Rupert Murdoch to Rivett, July 1951, Papers of Rohan Rivett

62  Ibid

63  Rupert Murdoch to Rivett, 27 July 1951, Papers of Rohan Rivett

64  Ibid

65  Ibid

66  Nancy Rivett, interviewed by George Munster, 1981, Papers of George Munster

67  Keith Murdoch to Rivett, 29 August 1951, Papers of Rohan Rivett

68  Bowman to Rhyll Rivett, 7 December 1996, Papers of Rohan Rivett

69  Ibid

70  Ibid

71  Ibid

72  Murdoch to Rivett, 29 August 1951, Papers of Rohan Rivett

73  Murdoch to Rivett, 26 May 1952, Papers of Rohan Rivett

74  Rohan Rivett, Draft Farewell Speech, July 1960, Papers of Rohan Rivett

75  Murdoch to Rivett, 15 April 1952, Papers of Rohan Rivett

76  Rivett to Murdoch, 21 May 1952, Papers of Rohan Rivett

77  Ibid .

78  Rivett to Murdoch, 4 January 1952, Papers of Rohan Rivett

79  Rivett to Murdoch, 13 December 1951, Papers of Rohan Rivett

80  Murdoch to Rivett, 8 January 1952, Papers of Rohan Rivett

81  Rivett to Murdoch, 23 July 1952, Papers of Rohan Rivett

82  Bowman to Rhyll Rivett, 7 December 1996, Papers of Rohan Rivett

83  *House News*, December 1957, p. 1

84  *House News*, March 1954, p. 20

85  *House News*, July 1954, p. 10

86  Rohan Rivett, *Nation Review*, 12 July 1974

87  Ibid

88  Rivett to Murdoch, 2 February 1952, Papers of Rohan Rivett

89  Rivett to Murdoch, 28 July 1952, Papers of Rohan Rivett

90  Rivett to Murdoch, 10 January 1951, Papers of Rohan Rivett

91  'Murder on Cricket Field', *The News*, 13 February 1952, p. 1 [http://nla.gov.au/nla.news-article130821972]

92  Rivett to Murdoch, 15 February 1952, Papers of Rohan Rivett

93  Ibid

94  Ibid

95  'In 3 Months, 5,000 Up—and Climbing', *The News*, 23 July 1952, p. 1, [http://nla.gov.au/nla.news-article130810898]; Rivett to Murdoch, 17 July 1952, Papers of Rohan Rivett

96    Rivett to Murdoch, 12 September 1952, Papers of Rohan Rivett

97    Max Fatchen, interviewed by Peter Donovan, 2004, JD Somerville Oral History Collection, SLSA, OH705

98    Rivett to Murdoch, 31 March 1952, Papers of Rohan Rivett

99    Rivett to Murdoch, undated (March 1952), Papers of Rohan Rivett

100   Ibid

101   Rivett to Murdoch, 24 January 1952, Papers of Rohan Rivett

102   Clyde Cameron, *Confessions of Clyde Cameron*, 1990, p. 59

103   Stewart Cockburn, *Playford: benevolent despot*, 1991, p. 218

104   Ibid, p. 143

105   John Scales, author's interview, 2022

106   Rivett to Murdoch, 28 August 1952, Papers of Rohan Rivett

107   Murdoch to Rivett, 18 July 1952, Papers of Rohan Rivett

## Chapter Four: A pernicious and corrupting monopoly

1     'The Colonial Register', *South Australian Gazette and Colonial Register*, 18 June 1836, p. 1 [http://nla.gov.au/nla.news-article73811312]

2     Leonard Marquis, *South Australian Newspapers: a selection of material from the extensive research notes gathered for a proposed history of the press in South Australia*, 1998, p. 3

3     Ibid

4     Wakefield to Jeffcott, 9 October 1837, in Marquis, p. i

5     *The Tasmanian*, 14 May 1839, p. 2 [http://nla.gov.au/nla.news-article233096327]; Royal Australian Historical Society, *Journal and proceedings*, 1918, pp. 134, 137 [http://nla.gov.au/nla.obj-596748076]

6     'Supreme Court', *South Australian Gazette and Colonial Register*, 19 May 1838, p. 3 [http://nla.gov.au/nla.news-article31749934]

7     'Opinions of the Press', *South Australian Gazette and Colonial Register*, 3 February 1838, p. 4 [http://nla.gov.au/nla.news-article31749784]

8     'Prospects of the Southern Australian', *Southern Australian*, 2 June 1838, p. 1 [http://nla.gov.au/nla.news-article71684556]

9     Jean Prest, *Sir John Langdon Bonython: newspaper proprietor, politician, and philanthropist*, 2011, p. 24

10    Prest, p. 25; Sir Lloyd Dumas, *The Story of a Full Life*, 1969, p. 32

11    'Notable Figures of the Australian and NZ Press', *West Coast Recorder*, 27 February 1930, p. 1 [http://nla.gov.au/nla.news-article262072823]

12    'Newspaper Enterprise', *Port Pirie Recorder*, 22 July 1922, p. 2 [http://nla.gov.au/nla.news-article102721559]

13    Ibid

14 'Consulting Industrialist to Mining Companies', *Barrier Miner*, 18 March 1919, p. 2 [http://nla.gov.au/nla.news-article4547680]

15 Gilbert Ralph, 'The Broken Hill—Collins House Connection: Mining Personalities', *Journal of Australasian Mining History*, Vol. 2, September 2004

16 Sally Young, *Paper Emperors: the rise of Australia's newspaper empires*, 2019, pp. 221–32

17 'Judge Who Faced the Facts,' *Smith's Weekly*, 18 October 1924, p. 13 [http://nla.gov.au/nla.news-article234428338]

18 'Pirie Smelters Threatened', *The News*, 14 July 1924, p. 1 [http://nla.gov.au/nla.news-article129805963]

19 'Judge Who Faced the Facts,' *Smith's Weekly*, 18 October 1924, p. 13 [http://nla.gov.au/nla.news-article234428338]

20 Murdoch to Dumas, 27 June 1929, Papers of Keith Arthur Murdoch

21 Harry Plumridge, interviewed by Des Colquhoun, 29 July 1969, Papers of Harry Plumridge, PRG 1757

22 Dumas, p. 22

23 Dumas, p. 38

24 Murdoch to Dumas, 27 June 1929, Papers of Keith Arthur Murdoch

25 Murdoch to Dumas, 17 July 1929, Papers of Keith Arthur Murdoch

26 Dumas to Murdoch, 29 May 1929, Papers of Keith Arthur Murdoch

27 Murdoch to Dumas, 17 July 1929, Papers of Keith Arthur Murdoch

28 Young, p. 209

29 News Limited, Annual Report, June 1932

30 'Last Register Today', *The Register News-Pictorial*, 20 February 1931, p. 3 [http://nla.gov.au/nla.news-article54173635]

31 Ibid

32 Robert Gouger et al, 'To Their Brother Colonists', *South Australian Gazette and Colonial Register*, 12 August 1837, p. 5 http://nla.gov.au/nla.news-article31749677

## Chapter Five: Palace revolution

1 Rohan Rivett, 1970, private collection

2 Denis Warner, *Wake Me If There's Trouble*, 1995, p. 126

3 Ibid, pp. 126–7

4 Denis Warner, *Not Always on Horseback*, p. 136

5 Murdoch to Demello, 8 June 1952, Papers of Keith Arthur Murdoch, NLA, MS 2823

6 Ibid

7    Murdoch to Rivett, 26 May 1952, Papers of Rohan Rivett

8    Murdoch to Demello, 8 June 1952, Papers of Keith Arthur Murdoch

9    Ibid

10    Desmond Zwar, *In Search of Keith Murdoch*, 1980, p. 108

11    Younger, pp. 332–3

12    Murdoch to Dumas, 10 July 1952, Papers of Sir Lloyd Dumas

13    Ibid

14    Ibid

15    Ibid

16    Ibid

17    Ibid

18    Ibid

19    Ibid

20    Younger, p. 345

21    Younger, pp. 334–5

22    Dumas to Murdoch, 9 June 1952, Papers of Sir Lloyd Dumas

23    Rivett to Murdoch, 23 May 1952, Papers of Rohan Rivett

24    Ibid

25    Rivett to Murdoch, 20 May 1952, Papers of Rohan Rivett

26    Murdoch to Rivett, 12 February 1952, Papers of Rohan Rivett

27    Ibid

28    Rivett to Murdoch, 29 August 1952, Papers of Rohan Rivett

29    Murdoch to Rivett, 8 September 1952, Papers of Rohan Rivett

30    Murdoch to Rivett, 25 June 1952, Papers of Rohan Rivett

31    Murdoch to Dumas, 10 July 1952, Papers of Sir Lloyd Dumas

32    Rivett to Rupert Murdoch, 25 September 1952, Papers of Rohan Rivett

33    Ibid

34    Ibid

35    Ibid

36    Rohan Rivett, Draft Farewell Speech, July 1960, Papers of Rohan Rivett

37    Rivett to Rupert Murdoch, 25 September 1952, Papers of Rohan Rivett

38    Ibid

39    'British Labour lunges to the left', *The News*, 2 October 1952, p. 15; Murdoch to Chifley, 7 November 1950

40    Rivett to Keith Murdoch, 2 October 1952, Papers of Rohan Rivett

41    Dunstan, p. 149

42    Calwell, pp. 89–90

43    'Murdoch Press Flayed', *Labor Call*, 10 April 1941, p. 1 [http://nla.gov.au/nla.news-article249645226]

44  Bednall, p. 237

45  Ibid

46  Younger, pp. 339–40

47  Calwell, p. 92

48  Ibid

49  Ibid

50  Bednall, p. 237

51  Bednall, p. 238

52  Dame Elisabeth Murdoch, interviewed by John Farquharson, NLA Oral
    History, 1995 [http://nla.gov.au/nla.obj-217242522]

53  Murdoch to Demello, 3 June 1952, Papers of Keith Arthur Murdoch

54  Ibid

55  Dame Elisabeth Murdoch, interviewed by John Farquharson, NLA Oral
    History, 1995 [http://nla.gov.au/nla.obj-217242522]

56  Ibid


## Chapter Six: Cunning old bastards

1   'Toorak Wedding', *The Sydney Morning Herald*, 11 May 1949, p. 7
    [http://nla.gov.au/nla.news-article18114612]

2   Rivett to Rupert Murdoch, 8 October 1952, Papers of Rohan Rivett

3   Dame Elisabeth Murdoch, interviewed by John Farquharson, NLA Oral
    History, 1995 [http://nla.gov.au/nla.obj-217242522]

4   'Murdoch funeral', *The Sun*, 7 October 1952, p. 5 [http://nla.gov.au/
    nla.news-article230996860]; 'Impressive Funeral of Sir K Murdoch',
    *The Advertiser*, 8 October 1952, p. 2 [http://nla.gov.au/nla.news-
    article47427644]

5   Rivett to Murdoch, 8 October 1952, Papers of Rohan Rivett

6   'Flowers at Church', *The Herald*, 7 October 1952, p. 5 [http://nla.gov.au/
    nla.news-article245298763]

7   Chenoweth, pp. 24–5

8   Younger, p. 348

9   'Funeral of Sir. Keith Murdoch', *The Age*, 7 October 1952, p. 2 [http://
    nla.gov.au/nla.news-article205412510] ; 'Late Sir Keith Murdoch, *The
    Journalist*, November 1952, p. 1 [http://nla.gov.au/nla.obj-2336190398]

10  Ibid

11  'Murdoch Home Sold: £35,000, *The Herald*, 24 February 1953, p. 3
    [http://nla.gov.au/nla.news-article249194559]

12  'Auction of Big Art Collection', *The Advertiser*, 18 February 1953, p. 3
    [http://nla.gov.au/nla.news-article48289808]

13   Murdoch to Rivett, 1 July 1953, Papers of Rohan Rivett

14   Rivett to Bridges, 28 July 1953, Papers of Rohan Rivett, NLA, MS80492

15   'New Week-end Paper for Adelaide', *The Advertiser*, 29 August 1953, p. 1

16   'The Express to Suspend Publication', *The Advertiser*, 30 March 1951, p. 2
     [http://nla.gov.au/nla.news-page3191288]

17   'An aim', *The News*, 8 October 1952, p. 1 [http://nla.gov.au/nla.news-
     article130863247]

18   Murdoch to Rivett, 6 April 1953; Murdoch to Rivett, 20 July 1953,
     Papers of Rohan Rivett

19   John Monks, p. 186

20   Murdoch to Rivett, 2 January 1953, Papers of Rohan Rivett

21   Rivett to Murdoch, 10 November 1952, Papers of Rohan Rivett

22   Ibid

23   Ibid

24   Rivett to Murdoch, 13 March 1953, Papers of Rohan Rivett

25   Rivett to Murdoch, 16 April 1953, Papers of Rohan Rivett

26   Bednall, p. 239

27   Murdoch to Dumas, 9 November 1950, Papers of Keith Arthur Murdoch

28   Bednall to Rupert Murdoch, 25 November 1952, Papers of Colin Blore
     Bednall

29   Murdoch to Rivett, 13 February 1953, Papers of Rohan Rivett

30   Bednall to Giddy, 3 November 1952, Papers of Colin Blore Bednall

31   Murdoch to Rivett, 2 January 1953; Murdoch to Rivett, 4 December
     1952, Papers of Rohan Rivett

32   Murdoch to Rivett, 2 January 1953, Papers of Rohan Rivett

33   Rivett to Murdoch, 13 January 1953, Papers of Rohan Rivett

34   Bednall, p. 242

35   Ibid

36   Ibid

37   John Monks, pp. 95–6

38   Bednall, p. 242

39   Ibid

40   Ibid

41   Murdoch to Bednall, 26 September 1945, Papers of Colin Blore Bednall

42   Bednall, p. 244

43   Ibid

44   Murdoch to Rivett, 20 July 1953, Papers of Rohan Rivett

45   Murdoch to Rivett, 1 July 1953, Papers of Rohan Rivett

46   Rivett to Sir Keith Murdoch, 16 September 1952, Papers of Rohan Rivett

47 Rivett to Rupert Murdoch, 10 November 1952, Papers of Rohan Rivett

48 *Mary's Own Paper*, August 1953, pp. 11–12, SLSA, 050 M c

49 Ibid

## Chapter Seven: The weekend battle

1 'The Newspapers of South Australia', *The Mail*, 21 November 1953, p. 1 [http://nla.gov.au/nla.news-article58877696]

2 Ibid

3 Ibid

4 Ibid

5 'The Newspapers of South Australia', *The Advertiser*, 24 November 1953, p. 2 [http://nla.gov.au/nla.news-article48923949]

6 Rupert Murdoch to Rivett, 8 April 1953, Papers of Rohan Rivett

7 Dumas to Plumridge, 7 July 1953, Papers of Harry Plumridge, PRG 1757/9/15

8 Ibid

9 Dumas to McFarling, 6 July 1953, Papers of Harry Plumridge, PRG 1757.9/18

10 Rivett to Murdoch, 19 June 1953, Papers of Rohan Rivett

11 Rivett to Murdoch, 27 June 1953, Papers of Rohan Rivett

12 Ibid

13 Murdoch to Rivett, 1 July 1953, Papers of Rohan Rivett

14 Murdoch to Rivett, 20 July 1953; Murdoch to Rivett, 17 May 1953, Papers of Rohan Rivett

15 Rivett to Murdoch, 19 June 1953, Papers of Rohan Rivett

16 Rivett to Murdoch, 3 March 1953, Papers of Rohan Rivett

17 Ibid

18 Plumridge to Dumas, 17 June 1953, Papers of Harry Plumridge, PRG 1757/9/19

19 Rivett to Bridges, 28 July 1953, Papers of Rohan Rivett

20 Plumridge to Dumas, Papers of Harry Plumridge, PRG 1757/9/9

21 'Your New Mail', *The Mail*, 8 August 1953, p. 1

22 'Your Family Paper', *The Mail*, 12 September 1953, p. 1; 'It's Easy To Read In Lift-Out Form', *The Mail*, 15 August 1953, p. 1

23 News Limited, *The Inside Story of Adelaide's Night Life*, 1955, SLSA, 079.42, p. 10

24 Rivett to Cockburn, 13 August 1953, Papers of Stewart Cockburn, Barr Smith Library at the University of Adelaide

25 Rivett to Murdoch, 17 August 1953, Papers of Rohan Rivett

26   Ibid

27   Murdoch to Rivett, 12 June 1953, Papers of Rohan Rivett

28   Murdoch to Rivett, 17 May 1953, Papers of Rohan Rivett

29   Murdoch to Rivett, 20 July 1953, Papers of Rohan Rivett

30   Murdoch to Rivett, 1 July 1953, Papers of Rohan Rivett

31   Murdoch to Rivett, 21 August 1953, Papers of Rohan Rivett

32   Ibid

33   'Kinsey Book in SA by Christmas', *The Mail*, 29 August 1953, p. 18

34   Murdoch to Rivett, 1 July 1953, Papers of Rohan Rivett

35   Murdoch to Rivett, 19 October 1953, Papers of Rohan Rivett

36   Ibid

37   Max Fatchen, interviewed by Peter Donovan, 2004, JD Somerville Oral
     History Collection, SLSA, OH705

38   Ibid

39   Ibid

40   Shawcross, p. 86

41   'Let Value Be Your Best Adviser … Buy The Sunday Advertiser',
     *The Advertiser*, 24 October 1953, p. 6. [http://nla.gov.au/nla.news-
     page3970970]

42   'The Sunday Advertiser', *Chronicle*, 5 November 1953, p. 4 [http://
     nla.gov.au/nla.news-article93991746]; and 'The Sunday Advertiser
     Praised', *Chronicle*, 12 November 1953, p. 4 [http://nla.gov.au/nla.news-
     article93989969]

43   'Mr Boland Overseas Studying Production', *House News*, July 1954, p. 4

44   'The E-in-C Says All Editors Have the Same Problems', *House News*, July
     1954, p. 4

45   'The Office Gets a Facelift', *House News*, July 1954, p. 2

46   Plumridge to Dumas, 17 June 1953, Papers of Harry Plumridge, PRG
     1757/9/19; Andrew Male, *Other Times: the life and work of Max Fatchen*,
     1997, p. 102

47   Max Fatchen, interviewed by Peter Donovan, 2004, JD Somerville Oral
     History Collection, SLSA, OH705

48   Ibid

49   Ibid

50   Ibid

51   Male, pp. 114–15.

52   'Big Sunday Paper Deal', *Fudge*, 1 October 1954, p. 1, SLSA, 079.94231
     F952 d

53   Ibid

54 'New Sunday Magazine', *The Mail*, 4 June 1955, p.1; George Munster, *A Paper Prince*, 1987, p. 41

55 'Mail or Sunday Advertiser?', *Mary's Own Paper*, November 1953, SLSA, pp. 5–6.

56 Nancy Cato, 'The Weekly Press, *Mary's Own Paper*, August 1955, pp. 9–10

57 *Mary's Own Paper*, November 1953, SLSA, p. 5

58 'Sunday Papers To Merge', *The Advertiser*, 19 December 1955, p.1.

59 Memo between Advertiser Newspapers and News Limited, 9 December 1955, Papers of Harry Plumridge, PRG 1757/6/7

60 Ibid

61 Dumas to Plumridge, 19 December 1955, Papers of Harry Plumridge, PRG 1757/6/7

62 Hill to Plumridge, 5 August 1953, Papers of Harry Plumridge, PRG 1757/9/26

## Chapter Eight: Boy publisher

1 'Topical Taps', *Truth*, 3 March 1956, p. 6

2 'Outpaced Police at 70 MPH', *The Advertiser*, 24 April 1956, p. 18

3 'Speed Cribbing is Senseless', *The News*, 5 November 1955, p. 22

4 Sir Norman Young, *Figuratively Speaking: the reminiscences, experiences and observations of Sir Norman Young*, 1991, p. 143

5 *House News*, March 1954, p. 3

6 Young, p. 143; *Mary's Own Paper*, May 1956, SLSA, p. 2

7 Young, pp. 143–5

8 Young, p. 146

9 Rhyll Rivett, author's interview, 2022

10 Ibid

11 Nancy and Rohan Rivett, *Holiday for a Housewife* unpublished manuscript; Rohan Rivett, Overseas 1938–68, Papers of Rohan Rivett, NLA

12 *House News*, May 1957, p. 1

13 Rhyll Rivett, author's interview, 2022

14 Ibid

15 Shawcross, p. 91; Regan, p. 89

16 News Limited, Chairman's Address, Annual General Meeting, 30 September 1955, p. 2

17 'News Ltd. Purchases WA Paper Interests', *Barrier Miner*, 27 October 1954, p. 1 [http://nla.gov.au/nla.news-article49970468]

18    Thomas Kiernan, *Citizen Murdoch*, 1986, p. 51

19    'Newspaper Deal', *The Age*, 28 October 1954, p. 6 [http://nla.gov.au/nla.
      news-article210669222]

20    'Western Press changes', *The Sunday Times*, 19 December 1954, p. 1
      [http://nla.gov.au/nla.news-article59699301]

21    Regan, p. 53

22    *The Mirror*, 11 August 1956, p. 1

23    Cameron, p. 154

24    Ibid, p. 155

25    Cameron to Munster, 1 March 1983, Papers of George Munster

26    John Menadue, author's interview, 2022

27    Cockburn, p. 218

28    Ibid

29    Cameron to Munster, 1 March 1983, Papers of George Munster

30    David Horner, *The Spy Catchers: the official history of ASIO 1949–1963*,
      2014, pp. 308–09

31    John Healey, 'Adelaide Woman Among the Reds—Intrigues Here in SA',
      *The Sunday Mail*, 16 December 1961, p. 28

32    Cameron to Munster, 1 March 1983, Papers of George Munster

33    Horner, p. 231

34    *Murdoch to Rivett, 10 November 1951*, Papers of Rohan Rivett

35    Connell, p. 155

36    Don Dunstan, *Felicia: the political memoirs of Don Dunstan*, 1981, p. 41.

37    Ibid, p. 42

38    Ibid, p. 61

39    Ibid

40    Ibid

41    Ibid

42    Rivett to Murdoch, 25 September 1952, Papers of Rohan Rivett

43    News Limited, Chairman's Address, Annual General Meeting, 30
      September 1954

44    'Big Issue for News Ltd', *The News*, 10 December 1954, p. 12 [http://nla.
      gov.au/nla.news-article131219114]

45    News Limited, Directors' Report and Balance Sheet, 30 June 1955, p. 6

46    'News Ltd. to Make New Share Issue', *The Mail*, 9 January 1954, p. 55

47    News Limited, Directors' Report and Balance Sheet, 30 June 1955, p. 6;
      News Limited, Annual Report And Balance Sheet, 30 September 1960,
      p.9.

48    'Capital Changes by News Limited', *The News*, 6 June 1960, p. 13

49 Ibid
50 Jerome Tuccille, *Rupert Murdoch*, 1989, p. 12
51 Shawcross, p. 91
52 Saunders to Rhyll Rivett, 14 July 1997, Papers of Rohan Rivett
53 Ibid
54 David Washington, 'Memories of the Murdoch world', *Offset*, November 1985, p. 5
55 *The Age*, 8 February 1956, p. 8
56 Washington
57 Mary Armitage, 'About People', *The Advertiser*, 3 March 1956, p. 21
58 Young, p. 147
59 Ibid
60 Armitage
61 Ibid

## Chapter Nine: The quality of mercy

1 'Move to Call Writer Before House', *The News*, 5 February 1957, p. 1
2 'MP's Threat Welcomed', *The Advertiser*, 6 February 1957, p. 17
3 'MHRs to Try Whole Steak!', *The Advertiser*, 30 October 1950, p. 3 [http://nla.gov.au/nla.news-article45665823]
4 'Federal Members will Eat Whale Tomorrow', *The Daily News*, 31 October 1950, p. 3 [http://nla.gov.au/nla.news-article82925413]
5 'Expedition's Jeeps Found Burning', *The West Australian*, 6 August 1953, p. 4 [http://nla.gov.au/nla.news-article49224897]; 'The Grayden Expedition', *Western Mail*, 10 September 1953, p. 6 [http://nla.gov.au/nla.news-article39359362]
6 Ibid
7 Pamela McGrath, *Hard Looking: a historical ethnography of photographic encounters with Aboriginal families in the Ngaanyatjarra Lands*, PhD thesis, 2010, p. 142
8 'Grayden Offers Plan for Tribe at Warburton', *The West Australian*, 17 October 1953, p. 8 [http://nla.gov.au/nla.news-article52934954]
9 'Grayden Insists on Clothing Natives', *The West Australian*, 24 October 1953, p. 10 [http://nla.gov.au/nla.news-article52936550]
10 Charles Duguid, 'The Rocket Range, Aborigines and War', 1947, SLSA PRG 387/1/8/3/2, p. 15
11 McGrath, p. 100
12 'National Shame', *The News*, 15 January 1957, p. 14
13 'Inequality of Man', *The News*, 21 January 1957, p. 12

14   '£50,000 Needed for Aborigines', *The News*, 14 January 1957, p. 5

15   'The News Fact-Finding Expedition Flies In', *The News*, 30 January 1957, p. 8.

16   'MP's Threat Welcomed', *The Advertiser*, 6 February 1957 p. 17

17   Shawcross, pp. 178–9

18   Rupert Murdoch, 'Aborigines Are Not Sick, Starving— "Scare" Report', *The News*, 1 February 1957, p. 3

19   Ibid

20   Ibid

21   'Good News, But Sad Tidings', *The News*, 1 February 1957, p. 29.

22   Ibid.

23   Ibid.

24   Regan, p. 56

25   Ibid

26   Ibid

27   'Report 'is a Relief", *The News*, 2 February 1957

28   Ibid

29   'Story Is Misleading Says MLA', *The West Australian*, 4 February 1957

30   William Grayden, *Adam and Atoms*, 1957, p. 79

31   'Report's Critic May Face House', *The West Australian*, 5 February 1957, p. 6; 'Welfare of WA Natives', *The Advertiser*, 5 February 1957, p. 6

32   'Report's Critic May Face House', *The West Australian*, 5 February 1957

33   'News Report Challenged', *The News*, 4 February 1956, p. 3

34   Ibid

35   'MP's Threat Welcomed', *The Advertiser*, 6 Feb 1957 p. 17

36   Ibid

37   Welfare of WA Natives', *The Advertiser*, Monday 11 Feb, 1957, p. 9

38   'Woman Gaoled for Theft', *The Advertiser*, 8 July 1955, p. 7

39   'Contempt Action', *The News*, 10 August 1955, p. 4

40   'Woman Gaoled for Theft', *The Advertiser*, 8 July 1955, p. 7

41   'Court Reserves Judgement on Contempt Claim', *The Herald*, 10 August 1955, p. 17

42   'Magistrate Criticised: Strong Protest on Gaoling of Woman, 22', *The News*, 8 July 1955

43   Ibid

44   Ibid

45   'The Quality of Mercy', *The News*, 8 July 1955, p. 18

46   'Writ issued by Magistrate', *The News*, 22 July 1955; 'To Seek Contempt Order', *Chronicle*, 28 July 1955

47    Kevin Duggan, 'Chamberlain, Sir Reginald Roderic St Clair (1901–1990)', *Australian Dictionary of Biography*, 2007

48    'Court Reserves Judgement on Contempt Claim', *The Herald*, 10 August 1955, p. 16

49    Ibid

50    Ibid

51    Ibid.

52    'Gaoling of Editor Demanded', *Daily Mirror*, 10 August 1955

53    Ibid

54    *The News*, 10 August 1955, p. 4

55    Ibid

56    'Paper Fined for Contempt,' *The Herald*, 26 August 1955

57    'Withdrawal on SM', *The News*, 13 November 1956

58    Ibid

59    'New Report on Natives', *The News*, 7 March 1957, p. 9

60    McGrath, p. 151

61    McGrath, p. 158

62    Mavis Thorpe Clark, *Pastor Doug*, 1972, Clark, p. 180

63    'Film Gives Murdoch the Lie on WA Aborigines', *Tribune*, 3 April 1957, p. 3 [http://nla.gov.au/nla.news-article236326287]

64    McGrath, p. 164

65    Rennie Simmons, Aborigines Advancement League, 'Analysis of Mr Rupert Murdoch's Article on the West Australian Natives Published in *The News*, Adelaide, 1 February 1957, p. 4

66    Ibid, p. 3

67    Ibid, pp. 3–4

68    McLarty Patrol Report No 1 1956/57, cited in McGrath, p. 149

69    McGrath, p. 172

70    West 2006, cited in McGrath, p. 176

71    William Grayden, interviewed by Ronda Jamieson, State Library of Western Australia Oral History Collection, OH2344

72    Ibid

73    'Murdoch: I Had No Alternative', *The West Australian*, 12 February 1957

## Chapter Ten: It depends what you call monoply

1    Dialogue constructed from Australian Broadcasting Control Board, Transcript of Proceedings, Inquiry Into Applications Received for Licences for Commercial Television Stations in the Adelaide and Brisbane Area, 1958, Fairfax Media Limited Business Archive, 1795–2006, SLNSW, MLMSS 9894/Box 343

2    Michael Kirby, author's correspondence, 2022
3    Murdoch to Bednall, 4 December 1952, Papers of Colin Blore Bednall
4    Ibid
5    Murdoch to Rivett, 17 May 1953, Papers of Rohan Rivett
6    Adelaide transcript, Australian Broadcasting Control Board, 8 May 1958, p. 177
7    Ibid, p. 180
8    Ibid, p. 205
9    'Publisher returns', *House News*, September 1957, Papers of Rohan Rivett
10   Australian Broadcasting Control Board, Brisbane transcript, 29 April 1958, p. 85
11   Ibid
12   Ibid, p. 92–3
13   'Dr. Darling, Leader with Vigor', *The Age*, 29 June 1961; Australian Broadcasting Control Board, 8 May 1958, p. 205
14   Australian Broadcasting Control Board, Adelaide transcript, 8 May 1958, p. 205
15   Ibid, p. 136
16   Ibid, pp. 152–3
17   Ibid, pp. 159–60
18   Ibid, p. 176
19   Report of the Royal Commission on Television, 1954, NLA, p. 103
20   Australian Broadcasting Control Board, Adelaide transcript, p. 434
21   Australian Broadcasting Control Board, Report and Recommendations to the Postmaster-General on Applications for Commercial Television Licences for the Brisbane and Adelaide Areas, September 1958, p. 31
22   Commonwealth of Australia, House of Representatives, *Parliamentary Debates*, 20 August 1958
23   Ibid
24   K Inglis, 'Aerial Warfare in SA', *Nation*, 25 April 1959, p. 5
25   Dumas to Menzies, 17 April 1962; Dumas to Menzies, 21 May 1962; Menzies to Dumas, 22 May 1962, Fairfax Media Limited Business Archive, 1795–2006, SLNSW, MLMSS 9894/Box 410
26   Commonwealth of Australia, House of Representatives, *Parliamentary Debates*, 18 September 1958
27   'Blaze at TV Studios does £10,000 Damage', *The News*, 30 June 1959, p. 1
28   Ibid
29   *House News*, January 1959, p. 1
30   'Blaze at TV Studios does £10,000 Damage', p. 1

31  'Climbs to Great Heights Again!', *The News*, 18 June 1959

32  'Premier faces NWS-9 camera', *The News*, September 1959

33  Christopher Day, *Kamahl: an impossible dream*, 1995, p. 45

34  Australian Broadcasting Control Board, Transcript of Evidence, Public Hearing into Applications for a Television Licence in Perth, July 1958, p. 129

35  Ibid, p. 129

36  Ibid

37  Ibid, p. 100

## Chapter Eleven: A matter of some delicacy

1   'Spy Case', *The News*, 15 October 1958, p. 2

2   'RAF Spy Suspect Escaped', *The Sydney Morning Herald*, 17 October 1958, p. 1

3   'Spy Case', *The News*, 15 October 1958, p. 2

4   'Talk of the Town', *The Barrier Miner*, 29 September 1949, p. 3 [http://nla.gov.au/nla.news-article48602031]

5   'It's in the Air', *House News*, August 1958, p. 2

6   'Woomera Spy Arrested', The News, 13 October 1958, p. 1

7   'Big SA Probe on Spy Ring', *The News*, 14 October 1958, p. 1

8   Horner, p. 481

9   Frank Shaw, 'City Man Sought Spy Contact', *The News*, 15 October 1948, p. 1

10  'Red Agents in SA Seek Secrets', *The News*, 16 October 1958, p. 1

11  Frank Shaw, 'Woomera Spy Arrested', *The News*, 13 October 1958, p. 1

12  John Bennetts, 'Minister Commends The News', *The News*, 13 October 1958, p. 1

13  Penelope Debelle, 'Who Agreed to an "Appeal to Patriotism"?', *The Age*, 22 January 2000, p. 4

14  Phillip Deery, *Spies and Sparrows*, 2022, p. 145

15  Ibid, p. 138

16  Penelope Debelle, 'Who Agreed to an "Appeal to Patriotism"?', *The Age*, 22 January 2000, p. 4

17  Deery, p. 137

18  Rohan Rivett, Papers of Rohan Rivett

19  Penelope Debelle, 'Murdoch Denies Stifling Spy Story', *The Age*, 24 January 2000, p. 4

20  Horner, p. 482

## Chapter Twelve: A race with death

1    Father Thomas Dixon, *The Wizard of Alice: Father Dixon and the Stuart Case*, 1987, p. 36

2    Ibid

3    Glen Hattam, Reg v Stuart, Evidence Transcript, 20 April 1959, Papers Relating to Rupert Max Stuart, pp. 1–2

4    Peter Hattam, Reg v Stuart, Evidence Transcript, 20 April 1959, Papers Relating to Rupert Max Stuart, pp. 2–3

5    Ken Inglis, *The Stuart Case*, 1961, p. 2

6    Harold Lindsay Walker, Reg v Stuart, Evidence Transcript, 22 April 1959, Papers Relating to Rupert Max Stuart, p. 90

7    Ibid; Howard Lloyd Herde, Reg v Stuart, Evidence Transcript, 21 April 1959, Papers Relating to Rupert Max Stuart, p. 52

8    *South Australian Gazette and Colonial Register*, 23 February 1939, p. 1 [http://nla.gov.au/nla.news-page 2052623]

9    Herde, Reg v Stuart, Evidence Transcript, Howard Lloyd Herde, Reg v Stuart, Evidence Transcript, 21 April 1959, Papers Relating to Rupert Max Stuart, pp. 38–9

10   Howard Lloyd Herde, Reg v Stuart, Evidence Transcript, 21 April 1959, Papers Relating to Rupert Max Stuart, pp. 35–6

11   Ibid, pp. 36–7

12   Ibid, pp. 35–6

13   Inglis, p. 21

14   Ibid, pp. 36–7

15   Ibid. p. 39

16   'Man Reported Diving for Cover', *The News*, 22 December 1958, p. 1

17   Richard Jones, Reg v Stuart, Evidence Transcript, 21 April 1959, Papers Relating to Rupert Max Stuart, p. 48

18   'Man Reported Diving for Cover', *The News*, 22 December 1958, p. 1

19   Rupert Max Stuart, Stuart royal commission, Transcript, Papers Relating to Rupert Max Stuart, p. 218

20   Rupert Adolph Kleinig, Affidavit, 31 July 1959, Papers of Father Dixon and the Stuart Case 1958–1987, AIATSIS, MS 3764

21   Dixon, p. 9

22   'Charged with Ceduna Killing', *The News*, 24 December 1959, p. 3

23   Law Society of South Australia, President's Report of the Council and Financial Statement, 28 September 1959, SLSA, 340 L415 b

24   Police v Stuart, Exhibit 'P', Papers Relating to Rupert Max Stuart, pp. 107 A-B

25   Ibid

26 David O'Sullivan, Reg v Stuart, Transcript of Notes Taken During Argument in Absence of Jury, 22–23 April 1959, Papers Relating to Rupert Max Stuart, pp. 99–105

27 Reg v Stuart, Defendant's Unsworn Statement from the Dock, 23 April 1959, Papers Relating to Rupert Max Stuart, p. 106

28 Paul Turner, Reg v Stuart, Evidence Transcript, 22 April 1959, Papers Relating to Rupert Max Stuart, p. 101

29 Whitrod, Reg v Stuart, Evidence Transcript, 22 April 1959, Papers Relating to Rupert Max Stuart, p. 103

30 Sonny Jim, Reg v Stuart, Evidence Transcript, 21 April 1959, Papers Relating to Rupert Max Stuart; pp. 26–7; Harry Scott, Reg v Stuart, Evidence Transcript, 21 April 1959, Papers Relating to Rupert Max Stuart, pp. 33–4

31 Ibid

32 William John Lowe, Reg v Stuart, Evidence Transcript, 22 April 1959, Papers Relating to Rupert Max Stuart, p. 95

33 Herde, Reg v Stuart, Evidence Transcript, 21 April 1959, Papers Relating to Rupert Max Stuart, p. 37

34 Richard Jones, Reg v Stuart, Evidence Transcript, 22 April 1959, Papers Relating to Rupert Max Stuart, pp. 65, 73

35 Denis Roger Blackham, Reg v Stuart, Evidence Transcript, 20 April 1959, Papers Relating to Rupert Max Stuart, p. 18

36 J Reed, Reg v Stuart, Evidence Transcript, 24 April 1959, Papers Relating to Rupert Max Stuart, p. 113

37 Ibid

38 Ibid, p. 117

39 Ibid. p. 140

40 Ibid. p. 139

41 Reg v Stuart, Transcript of Proceedings, 6 May 1959, Papers of Kenneth Stanley Inglis, SLSA, PRG 194, p. 24

42 Ibid, p. 39

43 Ibid; Donald Dunstan, Hansard, House of Assembly, 2 September 1959, p. 661

44 Dixon, pp. 1–3

45 Ibid

46 Dixon, pp. 9–10

47 Ibid, p. 10, 13

48 Ibid, p. 15

49 Ibid

50  Theodore G Strehlow, Comment on the Stuart Case royal commission of 1959, 2 March 1972, Papers of Father Dixon and the Stuart Case 1958–1987, AIATSIS, MS 3764

51  Inglis, p. 56

52  Stuart v Queen, Transcript of Proceedings, 1–2 June 1959, Papers of Kenneth Stanley Inglis, SLSA, PRG 194, pp. 20–1.

53  Ibid, p. 42

54  Ibid

55  High Court judgment, Stuart v Queen, Papers Relating to Rupert Max Stuart, p. 158

56  Dixon, pp. 23–5; Inglis, pp. 51–2

57  Inglis, pp. 26–7

58  Ibid, pp. 77–8

59  Ibid, p. 59

60  Ibid

61  Ibid, p. 60

62  'Plea to Reprieve Aboriginal', *The News*, 29 June 1959

63  Dixon, pp. 34–5; Inglis, pp. 64–7

64  Dixon, p. 35

65  Ibid

66  '"Mystery Man" Flies in with Priest', *The News*, 27 July 1959, p. 1

67  'Priest Flies North to Quiz Man', *The News*, 27 July 1959, p. 1

68  Father Thomas Dixon, Stuart royal commission, Transcript, Papers Relating to Rupert Max Stuart, p. 544

69  Ibid, p. 543

70  Dixon, p. 38

71  'Priest: "Stuart Has Perfect Alibi"', *The News*, 29 July 1959, p. 1

72  'Delay This Hanging!', *The News*, 29 July 1959, p. 1

73  Ibid

74  '10,000 Stuart Pamphlets to be Circulated', *The News*, 29 July 1959

75  '3-Judge Inquiry on Stuart', *The News*, 30 July 1959, p. 1

## Chapter Thirteen: The gravest libel

1  Bowman to Rhyll Rivett, 7 December 1996, Papers of Rohan Rivett

2  'Bowman Survives Lions', *House News*, August 1955, p. 2

3  'Funeral for Mr Shand, QC, to be Held Tomorrow', *The Sydney Morning Herald*, 20 October 1959, p. 5

4  Bowman to Rhyll Rivett, 7 December 1996

5  Ibid

6 'There's Still a Long Way to Go', *The News*, 31 July 1959, p. 1

7 Ibid

8 Norm Mitchell, *The News*, 31 July 1959

9 Hansard, House of Assembly, 4 August 1979 p. 279; 'We Couldn't Ask for More', *The Sun*, 5 August 1959, p. 3

10 'Noted Sydney QC will Defend Stuart', *The News*, 5 August 1959, p. 1

11 'Early Crowds at Stuart Inquiry', *The News*, 17 August 1959, p. 6

12 Jack Shand, Stuart royal commission, Transcript, Papers Relating to Rupert Max Stuart, p. 27

13 Ibid

14 'Mystery Man Rang Council', *The News*, 11 August 1959, p. 3

15 'Moir Supplies Stuart Declaration', *The News*, 31 July 1959, p. 3

16 Ibid

17 Ibid.

18 '3 Alleged 'Confession was Bashed Out of Stuart', *The News* 17 August 1959, p. 1

19 'Stuart Witness Whisked Away', *The Sun*, 17 August 1959, p. 4

20 Hansard, House of Assembly, 27 August 1959, p. 623

21 Jim Brazel, Stuart royal commission, Transcript, Papers Relating to Rupert Max Stuart, p. 34; 'QC 'Took Full Responsiblity for Alan Moir', *The News*, 19 August 1959, p. 1

22 Sir Mellis Napier, Stuart royal commission, Transcript, Papers Relating to Rupert Max Stuart, p. 35

23 '3 Alleged 'Confession was Bashed Out of Stuart', *The News*, 17 August 1959, p. 1

24 'Sydney QC for Stuart', *The Telegraph*, 6 August 1959

25 'Police Quiz Many Around Ceduna', *The News*, 4 August 1959, p. 1

26 '"Change Statement" Police Said', *The News*, 19 August, 1959, p. 1

27 'Moir in box: story of 'knocking off' Lennie', *The News*, 18 August 1959, p. 1

28 Alan Moir, Stuart royal commission, Transcript, Papers Relating to Rupert Max Stuart, p. 173

29 Alexander Phin, Stuart royal commission, Transcript, Papers Relating to Rupert Max Stuart, pp. 359–60

30 Rupert Max Stuart, Stuart royal commission, Transcript, Papers Relating to Rupert Max Stuart, p. 370–1

31 Rupert Max Stuart, Stuart royal commission, Transcript, Papers Relating to Rupert Max Stuart, pp. 372–4

32 Sir Charles Hart Bright, Legal Notes of Sir Charles Bright, SLSA, D 6452(L)

33 Jack Shand, Stuart royal commission, Transcript, Papers Relating to Rupert Max Stuart, pp. 374–6

34 Ibid

35 Ibid, p. 376

36 The Queen v News Ltd and Rohan Deakin Rivett, Transcript of Evidence, 28 January 1960, Papers relating to libel case against News Limited and Rohan Deakin Rivett, p. 85

37 Stuart royal commission, Transcript, Papers Relating to Rupert Max Stuart, p. 383

38 Ibid, p. 386

39 Ibid, p. 387

40 Ibid, p. 389

41 Inglis, p. 62

42 Ibid

43 Bright, pp. 6–7

44 Geoffrey Dutton, *Out In The Open*, 1995, p. 226

45 'O'Halloran Says: 'Grave Disquiet on Stuart', *The News*, 2 September 1959, p. 1

46 Hansard, House of Assembly, 2 September 1959, p. 272

## Chapter Fourteen: Wicked, malicious, seditious

1 'Crisis Expected on Monday', *The Advertiser*, 29 September 1928, p. 13 [http://nla.gov.au/nla.news-article29302282]

2 Ray Broomhill, 'Dickinson, Edward Alexander (1903–1937)', *Australian Dictionary of Biography*, 1981

3 'Editorial', *Direct Action*, 13 May 1928, p. 2 [ http://nla.gov.au/nla.news-page11928932 ]

4 'Volunteers Driven Off Ships', *The Advertiser*, 28 September 1928, p. 13 [ http://nla.gov.au/nla.news-article29302235]

5 Ibid

6 'Waterside Riot', *The Examiner*, 2 October 1928, p. 8 [ http://nla.gov.au/ nla.news-article51503781]

7 'Volunteers Driven Off Ships', *The Advertiser*, 28 September 1928, p. 13 [ http://nla.gov.au/nla.news-article29302235]

8 'Dickinson Guilty', *The Register*, 6 December 1928, p. 11 [http://nla.gov. au/nla.news-page4575757]

9	'Crisis Expected on Monday', *The Advertiser*, 29 September 1928, p. 13 [ http://nla.gov.au/nla.news-article29302282]

10	'A Glaring Contrast', *Direct Action*, 10 October 1928, p. 2 [http://nla.gov. au/nla.news-article111350420]

11	'Dickinson Case', *The Register*, 5 December 1928, p. 13, [http://nla.gov. au/nla.news-article53601942]

12	'Strike Edition', *Direct Action*, 3 October 1928, p. 1 [http://nla.gov.au/ nla.news-article111349429]

13	'Alleged Seditious Libel', *The Advertiser*, 5 December 1928, p. 20 [http:// nla.gov.au/nla.news-article73730084]

14	'Dickinson Case', *The Register*, 5 December 1928, p. 13, [http://nla.gov. au/nla.news-article53601942]

15	'Outer Harbor Riot', *The Advertiser*, 8 December 1928, p. 16, [http://nla. gov.au/nla.news-article35308880]

16	'Riot and Seditious Libel', *The Advertiser*, 18 December 1958, p. 10 [http://nla.gov.au/nla.news-article73731092]

17	Ray Broomhill, *Unemployed Workers*, 1978, pp. 176–7

18	'Riot in Adelaide Streets After Unemployed Parade', *The News*, 9 January 1931, p. 1 http://nla.gov.au/nla.news-article128995582

19	Memo to Dumas, 17 April 1932, Papers of Sir Lloyd Dumas

20	Memo to Dumas, 9 April 1932, Papers of Sir Lloyd Dumas

21	Memo to Dumas, 5 March 1931, Papers of Sir Lloyd Dumas

22	Memo to Dumas, 20 March 1931, Papers of Sir Lloyd Dumas

23	Dumas, p. 54

24	Memo to Dumas, 20 February 1932, Papers of Sir Lloyd Dumas

25	Amirah Inglis, *Australians in the Spanish Civil War*, 1987, p. 128

26	Ibid, p. 121

27	'Riot and Libel', *The Register*, 13 December 1958, p. 13 [http://nla.gov. au/nla.news-article53603295]

28	'How Adelaide Man Died in Spain', *The Mail*, 11 February 1939, p. 2 [http://nla.gov.au/nla.news-article55912832]

29	Cockburn, p. 309

30	Inglis, p. 256

## Chapter Fifteen: That poisonous material

1	The Queen v News Ltd and Rohan Deakin Rivett, Transcript of Evidence, p. 17

2	Ibid, pp. 19, 28

3	Ibid, p. 19

4     Ibid, p. 25

5     Ibid, p. 28

6     Ibid, p. 24

7     Sir Roderic Chamberlain, *The Stuart Affair*, 1973, p. 185

8     James Cameron, 'Rupert Max Stuart Would Be Dead Today... but for a newspaper that did its job', *News Chronicle*, 7 August 1959; *The News*, 12 August 1959, p. 3

9     'Aborigine Reprieved—Threat to Kill Premier', *The Guardian*, 6 October 1959

10    Dixon, p. 138

11    Stuart royal commission, Transcript, Papers Relating to Rupert Max Stuart, p. 728

12    Chamberlain, p. 201; Inglis, p. 223

13    Stuart royal commission, Transcript, Papers Relating to Rupert Max Stuart, p. 861a

14    Report of the Royal Commission in Regard to Rupert Max Stuart, 3 December 1959, pp. 16, 22

15    Ibid, p. 18; 'Stuart was Belted', *The News*, 5 September 1959, p. 7

16    Report of the Royal Commission in Regard to Rupert Max Stuart, 3 December 1959, p. 31

17    '"Poison Pen" Charges', *Truth*, 30 January 1960, p. 1

18    The Queen v News Ltd and Rohan Deakin Rivett, Transcript of Evidence, 25 January 1960, pp. 1–2

19    Ibid, p. 3

20    'Libel Case Hearing', *The Advertiser*, 26 January 1960, p. 6

21    The Queen v News Ltd and Rohan Deakin Rivett, Transcript of Evidence, 25 January 1960, p. 8

22    The Queen v News Ltd and Rohan Deakin Rivett, Transcript of Evidence, 25–29 January 1960, pp. 9–10

23    Ibid, p. 13

24    The Queen v News Ltd and Rohan Deakin Rivett, Transcript of Evidence, 26 January 1960, p. 18

25    Ibid, pp. 18–19

26    Ibid, p. 27

27    Ibid, pp. 94–6

28    Ibid, p. 95

29    Ibid, p. 98

30    Ibid, p. 43

31    Ibid, pp. 115–19

32    Inglis to Fitzgerald, 1960, Papers of Kenneth Stanley Inglis, SLSA, PRG 194

33    'Topical Taps', *Truth*, 19 March 1960, p. 8

34    The Queen v News Ltd and Rohan Deakin Rivett, Transcript of Evidence, 7–17 March 1960, pp. 11–12

35    Ibid, p. 15

36    The Queen v News Ltd and Rohan Deakin Rivett, Transcript of Evidence, 7–17 March 1960, p. G

37    Ibid, p. 10

38    JJ Bray, Defence Notes, Papers Relating to Rupert Max Stuart

39    The Queen v News Ltd and Rohan Deakin Rivett, Transcript of Evidence, 7–17 March 1960, p. 20

40    Ibid, p. 22

41    Ibid, p. 67

42    Ibid, p. 87

43    'Murdoch: I Had No Alternative', *West Australian*, 12 February 1957, p. 4

44    The Queen v News Ltd and Rohan Deakin Rivett, Transcript of Evidence, 7–17 March 1960, p. 79

45    Ibid, p. 27

46    Ibid, p. 48

47    Rohan Rivett, interviewed by Hazel De Berg, NLA Oral History [http://nla.gov.au/nla.obj-220869210]

48    Cockburn to Rivett, 10 September 1959, Papers of Rohan Rivett

49    Rohan Rivett, Draft Statement, 1960, Papers of Rohan Rivett, p. 4

50    'Editor Reads Statement from Hearing', *The Advertiser*, 18 March 1960, p. 7

51    Rohan Rivett, Witness Statement, Papers Relating to Libel Case Against News Limited and Rohan Deakin Rivett, SLSA PRG 1098/31, p. 1

52    'Libel Case Enters Ninth Day', *The Advertiser*, 19 March 1960, p. 1

53    Ibid

54    'Verdict in Libel Case', *The Advertiser*, 22 March 1960, p. 6

55    'Libel Case Verdict', *The Advertiser*, 22 March 1960, p. 1

56    'An Aftermath', *The News*, 8 June 1960, p. 1

## Chapter Sixteen: Wonderful evening of combat

1     'Herald Law Court Reports', *The Sydney Morning Herald*, 10 June 1960, p. 15

2     Paul Barry, 'Clash of the Titans: the night Rupert and Kerry went to war', *The Age*, 1 August 1993, p. 35; Ibid

3   'Church Printery Suit in Court', *The Daily Mirror*, 9 June 1960, p. 3

4   'Knight's Sons in City Brawl', *The Daily Mirror*, 8 June 1960, p. 1

5   '£14 million paper bid', *The News*, 24 October 1959

6   'Rejection of Take-Over Bid for The Advertiser', *The Advertiser*, 24 October 1959

7   Ibid

8   John Scales, author's interview, 2022

9   '£14 Million Paper Bid', *The News*, 24 October 1959

10  'The Earldom of Giveaways', *Nation*, 12 March 1960, p. 12

11  George E McCadden interviewed by Ian Hamilton, NLA Oral History, 1984 [http://nla.gov.au/nla.obj-195654535]

12  Shawcross, p. 104

13  'I Promise Sydney a Great Newspaper', *The Daily Mirror*, 10 June 1960, p. 8

14  'Herald Law Court Reports', *The Sydney Morning Herald*, 10 June 1960, p. 15

15  Ibid

16  Gavin Souter, 'Browne, Francis Courtney (Frank) (1915–1981)', *Australian Dictionary of Biography*, 2007

17  Paul Barry, *The Rise and Rise of Kerry Packer Uncut*, 2008, pp. 127–9

18  Dr Douglas Golding, author's interview, 2022

19  Ibid

20  'Herald Law Court Reports', *The Sydney Morning Herald*, 10 June 1960, p. 15

21  'Attempt to Take Over Printery', *The Daily Mirror*, 8 June 1960, p. 3

22  'Move for Injunction', *The Sydney Morning Herald*, 16 June 1960, p. 13

23  Les Hinton, *The Bootle Boy*, 2019, p. 85

24  Tom Fitzgerald, interviewed by Ken Inglis, NLA Oral History, 1988, [https://nla.gov.au/nla.obj-198877459]

## Chapter Seventeen: Body without a soul

1   Rivett to Murray, 17 July 1960, Papers of Rohan Rivett

2   Murdoch to Rivett, 5 July 1960, Papers of Rohan Rivett

3   'Nye Bevan joins the great rebels', *The News*, 7 July 1960, p. 1

4   Murdoch to Rivett, 5 July 1960, Papers of Rohan Rivett

5   Ibid

6   Rohan Rivett, Draft Farewell Speech, July 1960, Papers of Rohan Rivett

7   Rohan Rivett, 'Nye Bevan Joins the Great Rebels', *The News*, 7 July 1960, p. 1

8     Murdoch to Rivett, 8 July 1960, Papers of Rohan Rivett

9     Rivett to Murdoch, 23 April 1960, Papers of Rohan Rivett

10    Simon Regan, *Rupert Murdoch: a business biography*, 1976, p. 57

11    Kiernan, pp. 59–60; Young, p. 151

12    Evan Whitton, 'Rupert Murdoch: Our Part in His Evil Upfall',
      *tasmaniantimes.com*, 14 June 2016, accessed 11 August 2022 https://
      tasmaniantimes.com/2016/06/rupert-murdoch-our-part-in-his-evil-
      upfall/

13    May to Rhyll Rivett, 12 January 1996, Papers of Rohan Rivett

14    Murdoch to Rhyll Rivett, 1996, Papers of Rohan Rivett

15    Ibid; Shawcross, p. 101

16    'Hanging on for Too Long', *The News*, 15 June 1960, p. 1

17    Shawcross, p. 101

18    *House News*, December 1960; *House News*, September 1957, Rivett
      papers, NLA; Papers of George Munster

19    Nancy Rivett, interviewed by George Munster, 1981, Papers of George
      Munster

20    Bowman to Rhyll Rivett, 7 December 1996, Papers of Rohan Rivett

21    AJA members to Rivett, 14 July 1960, Papers of Rohan Rivett; Henderson
      to Rivett, 24 July 1960, Papers of Rohan Rivett

22    Clem Lloyd, *Profession: Journalist*, 1985, p. 250

23    Ibid, p. 251

24    Ibid, p. 253

25    News Limited, Chairman's Address, Annual General Meeting, 26 October
      1956, p. 3

26    News Limited, Chairman's Address, Annual General Meeting, 30 October
      1959, p. 2

27    Geoff Sparrow (ed.), *Crusade For Journalism: official history of the
      Australian Journalists' Association*, 1960, p. 124

28    Murdoch to Rivett, 13 April 1960, Papers of Rohan Rivett

29    Murdoch to Rivett, 24 June 1960, Papers of Rohan Rivett

30    Rivett to Murdoch, 29 June 1960, Papers of Rohan Rivett

31    *The Corian*, December 1947, p. 169

32    Dunstan to Rhyll Rivett, 26 January 1996, Papers of Rohan Rivett

33    Miles to Rhyll Rivett, 19 April 1996, Papers of Rohan Rivett

34    Rohan Rivett, Draft Farewell Speech, July 1960, Papers of Rohan Rivett

35    Kantor to Rivett, 11 July 1960, Papers of Rohan Rivett

36    Sir Walter Murdoch to Rivett, 26 July 1960, Papers of Rohan Rivett

37    Sir Walter Murdoch to Rivett, 3 August 1960, Papers of Rohan Rivett

38    Lady Elisabeth Murdoch to Rivett, Papers of Rohan Rivett

39    Ibid

40    Rohan Rivett, interviewed by Hazel De Berg, NLA Oral History [http://nla.gov.au/nla.obj-220869210]

41    Bowman to Rhyll Rivett, 7 December 1996, Papers of Rohan Rivett

42    Harrison to Rivett, 12 July 1960, Papers of Rohan Rivett

43    Wright to Rivett, 1960, Papers of Rohan Rivett

## Chapter Eighteen: No News is good news

1     John Scales, author's interview, 2022

2     Jean Stein, *West of Eden: an American place*, 2016, p. 264

3     Ruth Ryon, 'Rupert Murdoch to Restore Stein House', *Los Angeles Times*, 21 September 1986 [https://www.latimes.com/archives/la-xpm-1986-09-21-re-8848-story.html]

4     John Scales, author's interview, 2022

5     Australian Broadcasting Commission, *Five Australians: the rise of the media mogul Rupert Murdoch*, 25 July 1967, [https://www.abc.net.au/education/five-australians-the-rise-of-the-media-mogul-rupert-murdoch-196/13759198]

6     Ibid

7     John Menadue, author's interview, 2022

8     AH Raskin, 'The Negotiation—Intrigue at the Summit', *The New Yorker*, 29 January 1979, p. 81

9     Rinker Buck, 'Can The Post Survive Rupert Murdoch?', *MORE*, November 1977, p. 16

10    Ibid, p. 22

11    'It's a 'Personal Ambition', *The News*, 20 November 1979, p. 1

12    'A Love Affair with Newspapers', *The News*, 21 November 1979, p. 6

13    'A Dream is Coming True', *The News*, 21 November 1979, p. 6

14    'Herald Counter-Attack on News Bid', *The News*, 21 November 1979, p. 3

15    'The Melbourne Herald Quotes Murdoch', *The Sydney Morning Herald*, 23 November 1979, p. 2

16    John Fairfax, Statement by the Chairman, John Fairfax Limited, November 1979, Fairfax Media Limited Business Archive, 1795–2006, Mitchell Library, SLNSW and Courtesy Fairfax Media Ltd, MLMSS 9894/Box 431—File 55

17    KD Macpherson, Statement by the Chairman, Herald and Weekly Times, November 1979, Fairfax Media Limited Business Archive, 1795–2006,

Mitchell Library, SLNSW and Courtesy Fairfax Media Ltd, MLMSS 9894/Box 431—File 55

18  'Murdoch Tells of Bid's Failure', *The Sydney Morning Herald*, 23 November 1979, p. 2

19  Freda Irving, 'Why Rupert Started from Scratch', *The Sun-Herald*, 25 November 1979

20  'Murdoch Hints revival of Australian Media Bid, *The New York Times*, 23 November 1979, p. 81

21  '2 Media Giants Now Control 18 Major Papers', *The News*, 27 November 1979, p. 47

22  John Fairfax Limited, Minutes of the Meeting of the Board of Directors, 26 November 1979, Fairfax Media Limited Business Archive, 1795–2006, Mitchell Library, SLNSW and Courtesy Fairfax Media Ltd, MLMSS 9894/Box 431—File 55

23  AH Raskin, 'The Negotiation—Intrigue at the Summit', *The New Yorker*, 29 January 1979, p. 59

24  AH Raskin, 'The Negotiation—Changes in the Balance of Power', *The New Yorke*r, 22 January, p. 50

25  Ibid, p. 70

26  CM Evan, 'Well, There Are Worse Papers', *Nation Review*, 20 July 1973

27  Ibid

28  Australian Labor Party (South Australian Branch) and United Trades and Labour Council of South Australia, *Don't Buy The News* Campaign Pamphlet, November 1979, private collection

29  Ibid

30  Australian Labor Party (South Australian Branch), Media Release re: Campaign Against The News, November 1979, private collection

31  Mike O'Reilly, author's interview, 2022

32  News Corporation Limited Annual Report, 1986, p. 9

33  Mike O'Reilly, author's interview, 2022

34  Chief Executive's Report, News Corporation Limited Annual Report, 1986, p. 4

35  'Movie-maker Murdoch Set to Take on the Networks', *The Sydney Morning Herald*, 16 October 1985, p. 13

36  Chief Executive's Review, News Corporation Limited Annual Report 1981, p. 2

37  News Corporation Annual Report 1981, p. 3

38  'The Great Media Shakeout: I'm Thrilled—Murdoch', *The News*, 4 December 1986, p. 1

39   'Takeover Gets Hawke Approval', *The News*, 4 December 1986 p. 2

40   *The News*, 5 January 1987, p. 3

41   Bryan Frith, '"Bell Using 'Legal Ploys" Says Murdoch', *The News*, 12 January 1986

42   'Murdoch Hits à Court action', *The News*, 13 January 1987

43   'News Seals Herald deal', *The News*, 16 January 1987, p. 1

44   Sean Whelan, 'Advertiser Accepts News Offer', 20 January 1986, p. 1

45   'Fairfax Offer Stuns Share Markets', *The News*, 21 January 1987, p. 1

46   Rosemary Mullally, 'News Ltd Flash: Mr Murdoch Not Our Man', *The Age*, 23 January 1987, p. 1

47   Ibid

48   John Scales, author's interview, 2022

49   Don Riddell, author's interview, 2022

50   John Scales, author's interview, 2022

51   'News Deal to Sell Broadcast Interests', *The News*, 29 January 1987, p. 33

52   'Carrying on Our Proud Tradition', *The News*, 7 August 1987, p. 2

53   'Proudly South Australian', *The News*, 10 August 1987, p. 12

54   David Bowman, 'More Unanswered Questions', *The Adelaide Review*, May 1992, pp. 6–7

55   Kate Kennings, 'TPC's Probe into *The News* Raises Questions', *On Dit*, 27 June 1988, p. 5

56   David Bowman, *The Captive Press*, 1988, pp. 97, 104

57   David Bowman, 'Disentangling', *The Adelaide Review*, April 1990, p. 3

58   David Bowman, 'Moist and Limp, *The Adelaide Review*, January 1990, p. 4

59   David Bowman, 'Welcome Changes', *The Adelaide Review*, October 1991, pp. 6–7

60   'Beaten by Impossible Odds', *The News*, 27 March 1992, p. 2

61   Roger Holden, 'Why The News Was Forced to Close', *Ad News*, 24 April 1992

62   Ibid

**Epilogue**

1   'Press Chief at 6,000', *The Mirror*, 20 June 1961, Papers of Rohan Rivett

2   Rivett to Wilson, 4 July 1964, Papers of Rohan Rivett

3   'Rivett Could Be Our Ed Murrow', *Listener*, 7 March 1964, Papers of Rohan Rivett

4   Rivett to Wilson, 4 July 1964, Papers of Rohan Rivett

5   *The Herald*, 18 April 1973, cited Dixon, *The Wizard of Alice*, p. 394

6    Inglis, *The Stuart Case* [updated edition], 2002, p. 383

7    Helen Leake, author's interview, 2022

8    Brownyn Haseldine, author's interview, 2022

9    Bruce Muirden, 'Stuart's Story', *The Digger*, October 1973

10   'Max Stuart Book', *National Times*, 12 November 1973

11   Rivett to Donald, 3 August 1977, Papers of Rohan Rivett

12   Rhyll Rivett, author's interview, 2022

13   David Washington, 'News Corp Becomes a Landlord to State Govt
     Department', InDaily, 16 August 2021 [https://indaily.com.au/
     news/2021/08/16/news-corp-becomes-a-landlord-to-state-govt-
     department/

14   Rupert Murdoch, Oral Statement to the Leveson Inquiry, 26 April 2012

15   News Corp Annual Report, 2020 [https://newscorp.com/wp-content/
     uploads/2020/10/news-corp-2020-annual-report.pdf]

16   Rupert Murdoch, Sky News, 15 December 2017 [https://fb.watch/
     ftCCTY4SEx/]

17   News Corporation, Fiscal 2022 Full Year and Fourth Quarter Key
     Financial Highlights, August 2022 [https://newscorp.com/wp-content/
     uploads/2022/08/Q4-FY2022-Earnings_FINAL_8-Aug-2022-12PM.
     pdf]

18   John Gapper, 'A chip off the old block' , *Financial Times*, 5 October 1996,
     p. 15

19   Rohan Rivett, *Chronicle* unpublished manuscript, Papers of Rohan Rivett

20   Ibid, p. 159

21   Ibid, p. 51

22   Ibid, p. 154

23   Ibid, p. 153

24   Ibid, p. 157

25   Ibid, p. 205

26   Ibid, p. 242

# Index